The True Mystery
of The Mystical Presence

A Vindication of the Reformed or
Calvinistic Doctrine of the Holy Eucharist

original by

John Williamson Nevin

Edited & expanded by

Phillip A. Ross

Pilgrim Platform
Marietta, Ohio

Copyright ©2011 Phillip A. Ross
All rights reserved.

ISBN: 978-0-9839046-0-1
Edition: 3.2023

Published by

Pilgrim Platform
149 E. Spring St., Marietta
Ohio, 45750
www.pilgrim-platform.org

First published by J.B Lippencott & Co. in 1846

Printed in the United States of America

For
St. Paul's Evangelical Church
Marietta, Ohio
Pastor Thomas R. Hendershot

May the God of hope fill you with all joy and peace in believing, so that by the power of the Holy Spirit you may abound in hope.
–Romans 15:13

Books by Phillip A. Ross

The Work At Zion—A Reckoning, Two-volume set, 772 pages, 1996.

Practically Christian—Applying James Today, 135 pages, 2006.

The Wisdom of Jesus Christ in the Book of Proverbs, 414 pages, 2006.

Marking God's Word—Understanding Jesus, 324 pages, 2006.

Acts of Faith—Kingdom Advancement, 326 pages, 2007.

Informal Christianity—Refining Christ's Church, 136 pages, 2007.

Engagement—Establishing Relationship in Christ, 104 pages, 1996, 2008.

It's About Time! — The Time Is Now, 40 pages. 2008.

The Big Ten—A Study of the Ten Commandments, 105 pages, 2001, 2008.

Arsy Varsy—Reclaiming The Gospel in First Corinthians, 406 pages, 2008.

Varsy Arsy—Proclaiming The Gospel in Second Corinthians, 356 pages, 2009.

Colossians—Christos Singularis, 278 pages, 2010.

Rock Mountain Creed—The Sermon on the Mount, 310 pages, 2011.

The True Mystery of the Mystical Presence, 355 pages, 2011.

Peter's Vision of Christ's Purpose in First Peter, 340 pages, 2011.

Peter's Vision of The End in Second Peter, 184 pages, 2012.

The Religious History of Nineteenth Century Marietta, Thomas Jefferson Summers, 124 pages, 1903, 2012 (editor).

Conflict of Ages—The Great Debate of the Moral Relations of God and Man, Edward Beecher, 489 pages, 1853, 2012 (editor).

Concord Of Ages—The Individual And Organic Harmony Of God And Man, Edward Beecher, D. D., 524 pages, 1860, 2013 (editor).

Ephesians—Recovering the Vision of a Sustainable Church in Christ, 417 pages, 2013.

Galatians: Backstory/Christory, 315 pages, 2015.

Poet Tree—Root, Branch & Sap, 72 pages, 2013.

Inside Out Woman—Collected Poetry, Doris M. Ross, 195 pages, 2014 (editor).

God's Great Plan for the World, 306 pages, 2019.

John's Miracles—Seeing Beyond Our Expectations, 180 pages, 2019.

TABLE OF CONTENTS

Introduction..i
Nevin's Preface...1
Preliminary Essay..5
   1. Object and Nature of the Inquiry...5
   2. Historical Forms of Christianity—Parallel in the General Progress of
      Modern Reflection on its Nature...7
   3. Conception of Christianity as Doctrine..12
   4. Conception of Christianity as Moral Law....................................18
   5. The Religion of Redemption..19
   6. Christ's Personhood is Eternal Life..24
   7. Hegel and the Modern Speculation..26
   8. Constitution of Christianity as the Union of God and Humanity
      Through Christ...30
   9. Contrast with Heathenism and Judaism.....................................33
   10. The Absolute Religion in Which All Others Culminate—The
      Religion that is Jesus Christ Himself...38
   11. The True Center of the Christian System From Which All its Parts
      Gain Their Right Portion and Light..41
   12. Recapitulation—Mysticism and Reformation...........................49

THE MYSTICAL PRESENCE...59
Chapter 1:The Reformed Or Calvinistic Doctrine Of The Lord's Supper. 61
   Section 1: Statement Of The Doctrine...65
   Section II: Historical Evidence..79
      Early Helvetic Church..81
      Calvin...84
      Farel and Beza—Colloquy of Worms..93
      Beza and Peter Martyr—Conference at Poissy...........................95
      The Gallic Confession..98
      Old Scotch Confession..98
      Belgic Confession..99

Second Helvetic Confession..101

The Heidelberg Catechism..103

Ursinus, the Author of the Catechism..111

Hospinian..115

The Synod of Dort...116

Westminster Confession..117

Church of England..119

Hooker and Owen...120

Chapter II..127

The Modern Puritan Theory...127

Section I.: Historical Exhibition...127

Section II; Systems Contrasted..145

Section III: Faith Of The Early Church.....................................161

Section IV: Rationalism And The Sects......................................175

Chapter III: An Attempt To Place The Doctrine In Its Proper Scientific

Form...197

Section I: Preliminary Positions..198

Section II: The Mystical Union...212

Section III: The Lord's Supper...238

Section IV: False Theories Exposed..252

Chapter IV: The Biblical Argument..275

Section I: The Incarnation...275

Section II: The New Creation...284

Section III: The Second Adam..291

Section IV: Christianity A Life...296

Section V: The Mystical Union..311

Section VI: John 6:51-58..339

Section VII: The Sacrament Of The Lord's Supper...................351

Appendix I: The Contemplative Shape of Calvin's Eucharistic Thought. 372

Appendix II: John Calvin Tracts & Letters—The Supper Of Our Lord....391

Appendix III: The Six Senses of Man..407

INTRODUCTION

You have in your hands an unusual book—well worth your time and effort. I say this, not because it is my book, but because it isn't. It is a work of plagiarism of sorts, but don't be dismayed. This issue is not copyright infringement of the original 1846 book now in public domain. Rather, I have built upon this old foundation by blending voices. According to Augustine, Christians are supposed to copy the Word of God, to think God's thoughts after Him. Paul insists that Christians imitate him (1 Cor. 4:16, 11:1; 1 Thess. 1:6), 2:7-11; Luke 6:36; Matt. 5:48). We are to take God's Word, and the work of the great biblical writers and theologians, and make them our own. God is not after originality or novelty, but the faithful reproduction of His thoughts and ideas. This is what I have tried to do. Of course, Nevin was not God, nor am I denying that the bulk of the work belongs to him. Indeed, I stand in awe and have profound respect for his work.

So, it might be helpful to think of this as a contemporary edition of Nevin's book, *The Mystical Presence—A Vindication of the Reformed or Calvinistic Doctrine of the Holy Eucharist* (J.B. Lippencort & Co., 1846), wherein I serve as coauthor and commentator. This is not simply a reissue of an old book. Rather, it's a sort of dynamic equivalence approach to editing in order to make it more available to contemporary people. I have simply tried to take Nevin's work and make it my own, in the sense of comprehending its significance and application. In doing so, I have taken broad license to edit, interpret, clarify, and expand what I think Nevin was saying. My efforts will surely annoy Nevin purists, academics, and Type A intellectuals who are more concerned with form than content.

Why have I approached *The Mystical Presence* in this way? Actually, it is not that I sat down and planned this approach. It just took on a life of its own. I understand what Nevin said and it has so resonated with me that it dominated me for several months. His book, like no other I have ever read, has brought together various strands of my own life and pursuits in such a way that has astonished me and filled me with joy for having found such a kindred spirit. It is like he is already where I have been trying to get to. I have been working over the past forty years to get where he already was more than a century and a half ago. I'm humbled.

Nevin was the American voice of the German Reformed Church. Having studied under Charles Hodge at Princeton, he accepted a position to lead their only American seminary. It is wonderfully curious that German immigrants would put an American in such a position, but that's what they did. Nevin then called Philip Schaff, a Swiss born, German educated, Christian historian to join him in this effort. They then made a huge splash in the American Christian theological scene, after which Schaff went to Union Seminary to support the cause of liberal Christianity. And Nevin slipped into obscurity and an early retirement. It is often thought that Nevin also fed the liberal Christian stream in America, but that's not what happened. Nevin simply held his theological ground and the world passed him by.

But there has of late been a resurgence of interest in Nevin and Mercersburg Theology. It seems that Nevin is at the center of what is still a little known controversy that has erupted among the conservative Reformed churches (Orthodox Presbyterian Church (OPC), the Presbyterian Church in America (PCA), the United Reformed Churches in North America (URCNA), and the Reformed Presbyterian Church in the United States (RPCUS), and what has become the Communion Of Reformed Evangelical Churches (CREC), and a few others). Other Christians and denominations outside of these circles will likely be completely unaware of these issues.

That controversy is known as the Federal Vision.[1] The Federal Vision is often confused with the "New Perspective on Paul," another current controversy. The two issues are not the same and must not be conflated. It surfaced in 2002 at a conference entitled "The Federal

---

1   http://en.wikipedia.org/wiki/Federal_Vision; http://www.federal-vision.com/; http://www.opc.org/nh.html?article_id=478; etc. Much has changed regarding the Federal Vision since the original edition of this book.

Vision: An Examination of Reformed Covenantalism," which means that it's new. So the determination of exactly what the Federal Vision actually is and its impact on Christianity today is still in discussion. My concerns here are not for or against the current expressions of the Federal Vision, but for Nevin's contribution to American theology. Nevin will demonstrate that this concern is not new at all, but goes back to the original teachings of the Reformation. It was hotly disputed then, and still is today.

These things connect to my life because I was raised and ordained in the United Church of Christ (UCC), the heir of the German Reformed Church in America. And what is even more astonishing to me is that having grown up in, graduated from a UCC seminary and served UCC churches for fifteen years, I had never been exposed to Nevin in any meaningful way. In hindsight, this is all the more significant because it appears that Nevin's ideas provided the original impetus for the founding of the UCC and its initial ecumenical focus. It was Nevin's ecumenical vision of Christianity, supported by Philip Schaff, that provided the central stake for the UCC ecumenical efforts.

And yet, Nevin's name is not associated with the UCC in any significant way, probably because the UCC never actually did anything with Nevin's work. They likely got the idea that something important was afoot with Nevin, and got distracted by the excitement of what he was saying and how it blew open the future of Christianity in what was perceived to be a new way, and the UCC went their own way to do their own new thing. Unfortunately, what began as an effort to unite Christianity, the founding of the UCC in 1957, has actually resulted in bringing the most divisive issues into the church that have nothing to do with Nevin. Too bad! Had they run with Nevin, things would have been quite different. Anyway, Nevin connects me with my own Christian roots, which is important to me because I left the UCC more than fifteen years ago for a variety of reasons that are not germane here.

During my undergraduate years of wandering, I studied, both formally in school and informally on my own, philosophy, Eastern religions, mysticism, and New Religious Movements. My studies in mysticism led me to many mystics, Eastern and Western, and to Meister Eckhart, whom I adored for a while. I adored him because I thought that I understood what Eckhart was talking about. He was trying to bridge the subjective/objective bifurcation in consciousness in order to provide a greater human integration with God. Eckhart is important because he is one of the preeminent Christian mystics, and because Nevin's work corrects Eckhart's error—and that is no small feat! Eckhart continues to have a small and loyal following. So, I pray that Nevin's correction will be clear in the text. It's brilliant!

Nevin was also unapologetically Reformed. You might think it not unusual for a person who grew up in and was trained in the UCC to be Reformed, since the UCC claims to be an heir of the Reformation, as well. If so, you may not know that not all Reformed are Reformed in the same sense that "not all who are descended from Israel belong to Israel" (Romans 9:6). While Congregationalism began as the most consistent of the Calvinistic Reformed denominations, by 1865 it had mostly lost its Reformed distinctives, though there has always been a small cadre who have held on, who have tried to hold on to Reformed Congregationalism.

I belong to that cohort, though I didn't realize that I was Reformed until I read *Calvin's Commentaries* after a decade of church difficulties as a UCC pastor. These difficulties helped me better understand how far the church has fallen from being "a city set on a hill" (Matthew 5:9) in the new land of America. In the 1600s and early 1700s ninety-five percent of American churches were Reformed.[2] Today, those numbers are completely reversed. Today, there are two versions of Reformed—liberal and conservative. And Nevin faults them both for falling away from the original teachings of the Reformation in a number of ways. No doubt, this played a major role in Nevin's unpopularity among his contemporaries. He had a serious theological dispute with his teacher, Charles Hodge, where Nevin won the argument but Hodge won the day.[3] Popular opinion would not tolerate Nevin's biblical and historical fastidiousness. Of course, those who were not Reformed had little in common with Nevin to begin with. Others in the liberal wing of the Reformed churches liked his ecumenism, but not his biblical and historical integrity. And those of the conservative wing of the Reformed churches took umbrage at his accusation that they, too, had fallen from Reformation teachings. Up with such an accusation they would not put.

2 *The Churching of America, 1776-2005: Winners and Losers in Our Religious Economy*, Roger Finke & Rodney Stark, Rutgers University Press, 2005.
3 http://library.lts.org/mercersburg/MercersburgPrimarySources.pdf

Nevin didn't have much respect for Lutheran theology, either. His criticism of consubstantiation put Lutherans in the same category as the Roman Catholics and their transubstantiation. Both, Nevin argued, made the same error, but in different ways. Both mistake Christ's presence in the Eucharist with the physicality of the elements, which blurs the distinctions between spiritual and material by bridging the differences with various ideas of superstition and magic. Transubstantiation takes the hard position of saying that one substance actually becomes another, where consubstantiation takes a muted or blended view by saying that the spiritual substance is locally and materially near the material bread and wine. Nevin rejected both.

There is speculation that Nevin seriously thought about converting to Roman Catholicism because of his emphasis on the ancient church and the importance of liturgy. But it is hard for me to understand how anyone who has seriously read *The Mystical Presence* could entertain such a thought. Nevin's criticism of transubstantiation is so clear that he could not possibly convert without losing his own integrity. And besides, the Catholics simply would not have him. I'm not aware that Roman Catholicism has ever dealt with Nevin's criticism of transubstantiation or his doctrine of the mystical presence—nor is it likely that they would be able to, in my opinion. He got an obscure short shrift in the New Catholic Encyclopedia, 2007.

While *The Mystical Presence* is probably Nevin's most important book, it is also his worst. The edition I worked from is a facsimile of the original 1846 edition by J.P. Lippencott & Co. Why is this edition so bad? Because it seems as if the original editor read and edited the first few chapters, but stopped editing for various reasons. It is not simply that Nevin's English is antiquated by today's standards, or that he loves to wax philosophically and mystically eloquent—which he does, but that in too many places the language is too loose and inadequate.

So much so that I was compelled to improve it as best I can simply to understand it. Much mystical writing suffers from excessive fogginess, but Nevin's perspective is too clear for such excesses, at least my understanding of Nevin's perspective is. Short of completing my first reading of the book, I decided to edit the text in order to understand it better myself and bring greater clarity to some of his arguments. At least, that is my intention.

At first, I tried to maintain Nevin's voice, but as I progressed I found myself enthusiastically adding explanations and references to clarify and expand his thoughts simply because I knew exactly what he was saying. He was articulating the same kind of perspective that I have been writing about over the past twenty years. Or at the very least, his perspective and mine are in substantial harmony. Nevin's context and clarity so encouraged me that my own voice simply replaces his at various points. I pray that this will not trouble you, but will enhance your understanding of Nevin's perspective—and mine.

My concern has not been to produce a scholarly or intellectual work that accurately preserves Nevin's words or arguments, but to produce a work that honors and makes his arguments better available to people today. Indeed, Nevin is not an easy read. His language is labored and archaic, as was much of the literature of his age. And his ideas are absolutely grandiose by today's standards, but if you can catch on to what he says you will understand the necessity for his largess.

You may have noticed that old books often have long titles, subtitles, and tables of contents. In this case it seems that Nevin was working from an outline, and that outline was used as the table of contents. However, the headings of the table of contents are not found in the text. So, I have integrated them to provide both the outline and the text together in order to both break up the text and improve the readability. In addition, I have added three appendixes to further bolster the arguments. One is an early draft of a thesis by Michael J. Pahls, whom I thank for permission to use it. One is a selection from John Calvin's *Tracts & Letters on The Supper Of Our Lord*. Here Calvin makes his position clear. And the third is an essay of mine on the human senses called *The Eight Senses of Man*. It is an odd inclusion because it is not theological. Rather, it provides a glimpse into a different understanding of mysticism, suggesting that there are more human senses than ordinarily perceived. It suggests that there are subtleties of human experience that are still largely unknown

Nevin's work was very contemporary when it was first published, so he referred to various articles, people, and books as if they were common knowledge, too many without references. To acclimate himself to his seminary position and his new denomination, he immersed himself in contemporary (1850s) German theology, philosophy, and literature. Consequently, I have added many footnotes to identify the various people and references in the text. In addition, his own footnotes and text are strewn with Latin, Greek, and Hebrew—to the point of distraction for today's readers. So, I have endeavored to locate and translate these references so that contemporary readers today can focus on his arguments and not get distracted by the languages. My efforts in this regard are spotty, incomplete, and undoubtedly inaccurate in some cases. Again, I readily admit that I am not doing scholarship, and that scholarship is not my contribution here. Nonetheless, I pray that my efforts will be useful for the forwarding of Nevin's work and the Spirit's vision for the future of Christianity in the twenty-first century.

September 2011, Marietta, Ohio

I have read much more about Nevin and the Mercersburg theology since the first publication of this book. And it has not changed my mind. However, my previous understanding of Nevin and Schaff has proven to be shallow. I am now the pastor of the church to which this book was dedicated, and have been reading much about the history of the German Reformed church in America. That history is quite interesting and little known to the wider churches.

I have endeavored in this edition to use the *English Standard Version* for Scripture quotes in the hope of making the text more readable to contemporary people.

The most significant book that I have read to date is, *The Institutes of the Christian Religion* (2 volumes) by Emmanuel V. Gerhart, Funk & Wagnals, New York, 1891, 1896) Gerhart was a student of Nevin.

He served as president of Heidelberg College in 1851, then became professor of theology in the Theological Seminary of Tiffin, Ohio, when he was called to the presidency of Franklin and Marshall College in 1855, where he was the Professor of Mental and Moral Philosophy. In 1868, he was appointed professor of Systematic Theology at Mercersburg Theological Seminary, today called Lancaster Theological Seminary in Lancaster, Pennsylvania. He would continue there as president and professor for the rest of his life. Gerhart was also the editor of the Mercerbsburg Review journal for several years.

Gerhart's intention was to develop a theology that would provide for the continuing Reformation of the church. His work never got the critical evaluation that it deserves. It seems to have been widely ignored and is out of print. So, I intend to republish it, God willing.

Phillip A. Ross,
March 2023, Marietta, Ohio

NEVIN'S PREFACE

The following work has grown directly out of some controversy which has had place, during the past year, in the German Reformed Church, on the subject to which it relates. This stands related to it, however, only as an external occasion, and has not been permitted to come into view, in any way, in the work itself. It is not felt that any apology is needed for the publication. This is found in the importance of its subject, which must be left of course to speak for itself.

As the Eucharist forms the very heart of the whole of Christian worship, so it is clear that the entire question of the church, which all are compelled to acknowledge, the great life-problem of the age, centers ultimately in the sacramental question as its inmost heart and core. Our view of the Lord's Supper must ever condition and rule in the end our view of Christ's person and the conception we form of the church. It must influence at the same time, very materially, our whole system of theology, as well as all our ideas of ecclesiastical history.

Is it true that the modern Protestant church in this country has, in large part at least, fallen away from the sacramental doctrine of the sixteenth century? All must at least allow, that there is some room for asking the question. If so, it is equally plain that it is a question which is entitled to a serious answer. For in the nature of the case, such a falling away, if it exist at all, must be connected with a still more general removal from the original platform of the church. The Eucharistic doctrine of the sixteenth century was interwoven with the whole church system of the time. To give it up, then, would involve a renunciation in principle, if not in profession, of this whole system in its radical, distinctive constitution.

If it can be shown that no material change has taken place, were this system to be given up, it should be immediately done. Or if the change should be allowed, and vindicated as a legitimate advance of the original Protestant faith, we must be open to such a change. This study will let us know where we are and what we actually believe regarding this central question, as we examine the theological standpoint of our Catechisms and Confessions of Faith.

The relationship between the Eucharist and the idea of the true church, will easily be observed by every well-informed and reflecting person. If the fact of the incarnation is the principle and source of a new supernatural order of life for humanity itself, then the church is not based on an abstraction. Then the church must involve a true, living, divine-human constitution that exists in the world. Such a church will be organic in its nature—not a device or contrivance ingeniously fitted to serve certain purposes beyond itself, but the necessary, essential form of Christianity, in whose presence alone it is possible to intelligently conceive of piety in its individual manifestations.

The life of the individual Christian can be real and healthy only as it is born from the life of the church, and carried by the church to the end. We are Christians individually, by partaking in the general life-revelation of Christ, which is already at hand organically in the church, the living and life-giving body of Jesus Christ. Because it is real and organic, Christianity must also be historical. No greater wrong can be done to the church than to call in question its true historical character. To do so is to turn it into a phantasm, and to overthrow the objective basis on which its foundations eternally rest.

It must too be historical in its form and constitution because the reality of Christianity demands the presence of the actual life of Christ, flowing in unbroken dynamic continuity from the beginning as the medium of all particular union with Christ from age to age. Then, again, the historical church must be visible, not merely ideal but actual. The actual church may indeed fall immeasurably short of the idea it represents. The visible church may be imperfect, corrupt, false to its own conception and calling, but still be an actual, continuously visible church in the world. This must be so if Christianity is to have either truth or reality in the form of a new creation. A purely invisible, other worldly church is a *contradictio in adjecto* (a contradiction in terms) because the very idea of a church implies the actual manifestation of religious life as something social and common to believers.

The idea that the externalization of the Christian life is merely accidental to the constitution of this life itself is exceedingly derogatory to the church, and injurious in its bearings on religion and society. An outward, visible church is the necessary form of the new creation in Christ Jesus, by its very nature. And it must continue to be so throughout both time and eternity alike. Outward, visible social worship is to be regarded as something essential to piety itself. A religion without externals, must always be a false fantasy. The simple expression of religious feeling is needed for the perfection of the feeling itself because the spirit is objectively real. The Holy Spirit Himself is a constituent element of the very life of Christianity.

As a real, human, historical constitution in the world, the visible and invisible parts of the church cannot be divorced without peril to everything that is most precious in the Christian faith. We have no right to set the invisible in opposition to the visible, the spiritual in opposition to the corporeal. The incarnation of the Son of God is the principle form and the true measure and test of all sound Christianity. To be real, the divinity of Jesus Christ must ever externalize its inward, invisible life. All thinking, feeling, every spiritual state, must manifest bodily in order to be fully real. This is the proper, deep sense of all liturgy in religion.

This necessity is universal. The more intensely spiritual any state may be, the more irresistibly will it express itself to make itself complete, in an external form. Put away the idea, then, that the visible church is incidental to its true constitution, that is is a cunningly framed device for advancing some interest or another. To think of the church, and of Christian worship, simply as a means to something else is to dishonor religion itself in the most serious manner.

If the present work may serve to fix attention on the momentous point with which it is concerned, and contribute even indirectly to a clearer understanding of Christian truth, I shall feel that it has not been written in vain. May God accept it, and crown it with his blessing.

J. W. N.
Mercersburg, April, 1846.

PRELIMINARY ESSAY

In the January edition of the *Theologische Studien und Kriliken*, 1845, there is an admirable article, from the pen of Dr. C. Ullmann,[1] Professor in Heidelberg, on "The Distinctive Character Of Christianity," well worth careful study by all who have an interest in the present condition of the church. It has occurred to me that I cannot do better in the way of introducing the present work, than to furnish here a full abstract, or rather a free compressed translation of its valuable contents.

1. OBJECT AND NATURE OF THE INQUIRY

Christianity has always been substantially the same. The way it has understood itself, however, has varied with the unfolding progress of its history. At the beginning it was the fresh life of childhood, without reflection. The first efforts toward a Christian theology were gradually produced during the first centuries through apologetic controversies and their various errors. After the fourth century the entire intellectual strength of the church appeared to be devoted to settling and establishing particular doctrines, but still however only in their individual forms. The Scholastic period of the Middle Ages took up those individual doctrines and worked to reduce them to an overall general

---

1 The distinguished author of the work *Reformatoren vor der Reformation* (found in *History of the Christian Church*, by Philip Schaff. Volume VII. *Modern Christianity: The German Reformation*); for full historical knowledge, comprehensive views, clear, calm reflection, and masterly power of representation, one of the finest living writers certainly of Germany. The article here noticed has been published also as a separate pamphlet, and seems to have attracted more than usual attention. A new work, I may add, is recently announced from the same writer under the interesting title, *The Church of the Future*, in which no doubt the same views are more fully exhibited.

theological system. Throughout this process of theological development, however, the distinctive constitution of Christianity as a whole,
as compared with other forms of religion, barely came into view.

Even the Reformers of the sixteenth century, thoroughly imbued
as they were with its living spirit, were too fully occupied with the
work of setting it free from church oppression to bestow much reflection on this point. The question has been reserved for the modern
Period, which has felt a certain urgency for philosophical and historical
cultivation to give it much attention. During the last fifty years (1800-
1850) numerous attempts have been made to determine the characteristic nature and genius of Christianity, always reflecting their own
particular theological assumptions. In this way, Storr made the primary
distinction to be the supernatural, the miraculous, the positive, as
found in Christian religion. Herder[2] saw in it the character of universal
humanity; Chateaubriand,[3] its sublime and captivating beauty. But we
owe the Christological struggles of the modern era to define more
clearly the true nature of Christianity, and its central constitution.

The theological position of the present time may be considered
especially favorable, for a proper appreciation of the truth in the case of
the important inquiry here brought into view. Previously, it was too
common to proceed to prove some particular conception of Christianity, whether Primitive, Catholic, Protestant, etc. A denomination
would make some single historical issue, often arbitrarily chosen by
the pleasure of the inquirer, to be a matter of necessity and to stand for
the whole. This caused certain elements of the system to represent the
whole, whether its divinity for instance, or its humanity, its doctrinal,
or its ethical, or perhaps its aesthetic character.

Now however, as the result of our historical maturity, we stand on
higher ground. We are able to take a comprehensive survey of Chris-

---

2   Johann Gottfried von Herder (1744 -1803) was a German philosopher, theologian,
    poet, and literary critic. He is associated with the periods of Enlightenment. He
    turned away from the light of the eighteenth century. Seeking to reconcile his
    thought with this earlier age, Herder sought to harmonize his conception of senti-
    ment with reason, whereby all knowledge is implicit in the soul; the most elemen-
    tary stage is sensuous and intuitive perception which by development can become
    self-conscious and rational. To Herder, this development is the harmonizing of
    primitive and derivative truth, of experience and intelligence, feeling and reason.
3   François-René, vicomte de Chateaubriand (1768-1848) was a French writer, politi-
    cian, diplomat and historian. He is considered the founder of Romanticism in
    French literature.

tianity as an organic whole and evaluate all the aspects—its origin and development down to the present time. As a result, it is much easier to see the true life center of the whole, and to recognize its beating heart, which continues to perpetually animate both the whole and in its several parts.

When we speak of the distinctive character of Christianity, it implies the idea of something universal as well as particular in its composition. As universal it is *religion*; as particular it is the *Christian religion*. But these two constructs, in the case of Christianity, are inseparably bound together.[4] We cannot abstract from Christianity its particular unique character, and leave the idea of universal religion behind. Christianity must necessarily actually exist in its unique form, or it is nothing, a mere abstraction that is devoid of all reality.

Christianity is not first and foremost a religion, with something added to it to make it Christianity. Rather, as religion itself—not merely a specific kind or category of religion but the phenomena of human religion—it is at the same time in its most central identity, this particular form of religion, exclusively complete and whole in and of itself. Yet it is distinct in all its parts from every other religion, by the living Spirit which pervades the whole. Thus, it is individual and universal at the same time. It claims to be the absolute truth itself, not simply *a* religion, as one among many, but the one, universal, all perfect religion of humanity in its widest, fullest and most complete sense. What is both universal and individual in Christianity flow together, and cannot be considered to be different things.

2. HISTORICAL FORMS OF CHRISTIANITY—PARALLEL IN THE GENERAL PROGRESS OF MODERN REFLECTION ON ITS NATURE

The Modern period has brought to the fore a conscious reflection about the nature of Christianity. This consideration has its own history, which reveals the progressive unfolding of a uniquely universal perspective. This perspective provides both correspondence and contrast with previous perspectives that have provided an understanding of Christianity from its inception. The defining spirit of Christianity

---

4   They are not two unique constructs, but one bound together in trinitarian unity. For more on trinitarian unity see *Arsy Varsy—Reclaiming the Gospel in First Corinthians* (2008), *Varsy Arsy, Proclaiming the Gospel in Second Corinthians* (2009), *Colossians—Christos Singularis* (2010) by Phillip A. Ross, Pilgrim Platform, Marietta, Ohio.

has grown and changed over time, much like a person who has changed with age yet has not become something different than previously known, but has simply become more of what he has always been. This process of mature inquiry has been more rapid in the modern period because of its many efforts to determine the essential and real character of Christianity as a whole, rather than trying to prove a particular version or denominational expression of Christianity.

This effort began with the examination of the character of the new life, purportedly generated in the lives of Christians. This new life is found with complete harmony and perfection in the person of its founder—Jesus Christ. This new life is exhibited more inadequately in the stories and records of apostles and the apostolic churches. However, the mere existence of this new life was not sufficient to our understanding. It is necessary for Christians to come to a free and complete apprehension of what it involves. Such an effort requires the separation and reintegration of the various elements that previously brought confusion, conflict, and sectarian one-sidedness. The only way to do this is to grow beyond our own childishness, and from the simplicity of the childhood of Christianity itself, to the consciousness of a greater spiritual maturity. We must understand the long course of development revealed to us through the history of Christianity as an integrated whole.

In the process, the different constituent elements or forces included in Christianity must be ordered in the light of the whole and not simply given the position or importance they have claimed for themselves. Some things are more important than others, and some have been defined by the general character of the historical age in which they found expression. Thus, for every period of history there are particular elements of Christianity that have taken preeminence. By considering the whole of Christianity we are able to order the various parts in the light of the whole and see them, not as separate manifestations, but symmetrically united as a perfect whole that belongs to the one glorious life of Jesus Christ.

This process naturally began with the examination of doctrine in an attempt to resolve the various conflicting doctrines into a harmonious doctrinal whole. This dogma-producing period extended from the fourth century to the sixth. This effort was dominated by Greek philosophy through the emphasis on the special vocation of those engaged in philosophical analysis. With the collapse of the Roman

Empire, and the rise of a new life among the western nations, Christianity changed its focus. Moving from being the concern of intellectuals and the higher classes, Christianity became the foundation for manners, morals, culture, and the social order that regulated the life of the general population.

Accordingly, the main interest at this point in its development became moral authority. Particularly in the hands of the Roman Church it became a system of law, a teaching institution for social control and civil government. In this regard, however, it encouraged the opportunity to make the historical contrast between law and gospel, a distinction that particularly effected the German spirit.[5]

This new development included in its very core a passion for evangelical freedom from the abuses of social control and domination by the forces of both state and church. Gradually this movement asserted its ecclesiastical independence. With the Reformation, Christianity grew from being a social minority to a majority and reclaimed its proper foundation by emphasizing the Five Solas.[6] Here it reclaimed the importance of personal redemption, the justification of the sinner before God, and the principle of freedom for the consciousness of the justified person himself in all his relations.

Along with these three leading ideas of Christianity, 1) as doctrine, 2) as a system of law, and 3) as a source of redemption and spiritual freedom, we find a fourth idea unfolding from an early period with steadily increasing strength. It is the idea that makes religion generally to consist in the idea of the union of man with God. And this is particularly prominent with Christianity, particularly among the Christian mystics. In this regard, Christianity is regarded as the perfect religion because it fully unites the divine and human in the life of Jesus Christ.

This idea, which originates in remote antiquity, comes to the fore more decidedly in the mysticism of the middle ages. And appears now (1850s) to be completely revealed in the philosophical and theological speculation of the modern time.[7] From the beginning this scholarly

---

5   A reference to the fact that the Reformation began with Martin Luther in Germany.

6   *Sola scriptura* (by Scripture alone), *Sola fide* (by faith alone), *Sola gratia* (by grace alone), *Solus Christus* or *Solo Christo* (Christ alone or through Christ alone), *Soli Deo gloria* (glory to God alone).

7   A reference to the burst of Modern religious interest and scholarship, much of it coming out of Germany, and to Nevin's burgeoning relationship with Philip Schaff,

speculation can be grouped into two opposite categories: one is pantheistic in that it recognizes God in everything, and the other is
monotheistic, recognizing a uniquely individual God. Of the two,
pantheism has become more popular today, but in the final analysis
monotheism must be regarded as the only legitimate way to conceptu-
alize the God of the Bible, and is expected one day to prevail
universally.[8]

And these are the foundational religious categories (the universal
and the individual) by which Christianity itself has been differently
conceived in the varying historical circumstances. These two conceptions of Christianity manifest as different forms of church life. The
interest in doctrine is found in the Orthodox Church or the church of
Christian antiquity, which holds to the early expressions of Christianity dominated by Greek thought. As an institution of discipline,
Christianity found its essential character in the Roman Church, with
its claim of universal authority, giving itself the title *Catholic*, the
church of the Middle Ages. Claiming the idea of redemption and freedom, the German Church came to the forefront, calling itself
Evangelical, the church of the Reformation.

The final church, in which all these stages of development are to
be brought together in unity as the true form of Christianity will focus
on the actualization of life in unity with God though union with
Christ. Toward this church we find ourselves in the midst of ecclesiastical agitation regarding the foundation and character of the church of
the future. In this study we will define the foundational attributes of
Christianity as spirituality, catholicity, and evangelical freedom, united
in the trinitarian unity that retains the character of the whole without
denying the uniqueness of the constituent parts.

This historically progressive theological revelation of Christ in the
world corresponds with the actual, bodily manifestation of Christ in
the church. This phenomenon is reflected in modern theology and has
been described as the successive historical stages: 1) as doctrine, 2) as
an ethical law, 3) as a system of redemption, and ultimately, though
not always in the same way, 4) as a religion based on real, actual union
with God. This progression involves a change from a merely outward
focus to an increasingly inward focus. How so?

---

one of the most prolific authors of Christian history ever.

8   What will prevail is Christian monotheism, which is trinitarian monotheism or
     monotheistic trinitarianism.

Christianity was naturally and historically conceived first as doctrine, following God's order of creation where God first spoke things
into existence. Next Christianity became interested in the application
of its doctrine and began to focus on ethical concerns. This process is
an example of Christian teleology, of how God declares a thing to be
so from the beginning, and then draws the thing into increasing conformity with His declaration. Christianity's highest moral expression is
found in the fact of redemption and atonement, which centers on the
person of Christ. The completion of the process focuses on the necessity for the Redeemer to be both divine and human for the redemption
and atonement to take effect. Humanity is reconciled with God, first
by manifesting actual forgiveness in the hearts and lives of his people,
and then by manifesting (or growing) Christ's righteousness in them.
God and man are only reconciled inasmuch as they are actually united
in these two ways as the foundation of actual redemption.

As might be expected these four stages of Christianity are closely
related to the various forms of religion in the world. And if Christianity is to be considered to be the absolute expression of the universal
religion, it must actually manifest in the character and lives of real people. When primarily seen as doctrine, Christianity finds support in the
idea of religion as a mode of knowing God. This can best be seen as
the prevailing definition of Christianity among the Orthodox, particularly preceding Kant.[9]

The next stage of development grew out of the philosophy of
Kant, who said that religion was no more than morality. Evangelical
Christianity defined redemption as a state or feeling of moral awareness. However, the actual relationship of man to God in religion does
not come from human understanding, will, or feeling alone. Rather,
real relationship with God includes them all as a whole in the actual
reality of one's personal life. Because of the reality of the wholeness of
thought and life, for Christianity to actually be real and not a mere
idea, it must actually produce the union of God and humanity. It is in

---

9   Immanuel Kant (1724-1804), German philosopher whose contributions to meta-
    physics, epistemology, ethics, and aesthetics had a profound impact on almost every
    philosophical movement that followed him. Kant ushered in The Enlightenment, a
    movement of the 18th century that emphasized the use of reason to scrutinize previ-
    ously accepted doctrines and traditions and that brought about many humanitarian
    reforms.

this way alone that Christianity can be said to actually be the only source of all light and holiness and salvation.

The first three stages have different measures of truth, different ideas about what religious truth is. For the fourth stage to actually be what it purports to be requires that all of the other three stages are also actually true, manifestly true in actual human life, all at the same time. In addition, this fourth stage must embrace and include the first three, in the sense that the biblical idea of perfection is wholeness or completeness.

Christianity can only be properly regarded as the actual union of God and humanity where its doctrinal, ethical, and soteriological character are constituent elements of its original, inalienable nature, and are not mere thoughts or ideas, but actual facts of history and life. This definition naturally excludes all religious pantheism because from the pantheistic perspective God has nothing to unite with.

Christianity is the unique revelation of the living God historically united in the person of Christ in order to redeem humanity from the power of sin. This redemption involves the union of God and man by definition. The proper expression of this union is not "the unity of the divine and human," which lacks historical specificity and is liable to be taken in a pantheistic sense. A more definite and concrete expression is "the union of God and *you*." God doesn't unite with some generic idea of humanity, but with specific individuals. If this union is not actually manifest in your own individual person, you cannot know if Christianity is actually real because Christianity is more than the mere idea of such union.

3. CONCEPTION OF CHRISTIANITY AS DOCTRINE

Modern theology first defined itself in terms of doctrine. This was done in two ways. The whole Bible was assumed to be true because God Himself accredited it so. It was received on His authority alone, without any regard to the historical character of the text or of the actual man, Jesus Christ. It was simply considered to be the first manifestation of a theory of rational religion as defined by logic and reason themselves, which when divested of its original temporary covering (Judaism) would reveal its proper everlasting truth. Judaism, understood to be natural religion, would give way to Christianity, understood to be supernatural religion. From this perspective, naturalism and supernaturalism, which first seemed to be opposed to one another, both serve to define Christianity as essentially doctrinal in character.

However, an important difference began to take shape. Supernaturalism infused the biblical texts and stories of miracles with a fantastic character that seemed to defy both logic and reason. It suggested that the Redeemer had a kind of ethereal, other worldly character. It posited some kind of spiritual realm that was different from the ordinary world of everyday life.

Naturalism, on the other hand, had a strong aversion, distrust, and disbelief in everything tainted with an ethereal, other worldly character. It dismissed the various stories of biblical miracles because they understood them to violate logic, reason, and common experience. Naturalists required religion to be concrete and historical, and could not retain a sense of supernaturalism in the person of Christ.

This early expression of theology suffered from a tendency to attribute to supernaturalism what should be attributed to the person of Jesus Christ, to think of Christ as ethereal and other worldly. Naturalism makes the opposite error, that of denying what should be attributed to the person of Christ because it denies the reality of what is supernatural. The naturalists went so far as to wish that Jesus' name might be concealed from the world, so that people could enjoy the benefit of the natural truths he taught, without being deceived by a superstitious misunderstanding of the teacher himself. They wanted to purge Jesus of any supposed supernatural characteristics, stories, or teachings—in order to understand Jesus as real.

From a supernatural or "religious" perspective, naturalism is thought of only as a spiritual curiosity that belongs to other times. The supernaturalists became the theological conservatives, but their perspective could fare no better. The supernaturalists completely failed to understand or explain the unique character of Christianity. They found the essence of reality to be found in an ideal, other worldly, Platonic realm of pure form, purely idealistic in character. Thus, they were particularly suited to define Christianity as doctrine—ideas.

However, the truest definition of religion and the whole history of Christianity contradict such a thought. Religion obviously includes knowledge (thoughts and ideas) as one of its essential elements, but to conceive of Christianity as nothing more than an intellectual endeavor is to completely miss the proverbial boat. Love of God and neighbor are central to Christianity, and actually loving God and neighbor require more than mere ideas. Real Christianity requires a pervading sense of dependence on God, communion with Him, and complete self-surrender to His presence and will.

The natural/supernatural division of reality is a false dichotomy. Reality itself is composed of no such division. Such ideas are simply a product of human imagination.

If religion consisted of doctrine alone, it might be fully imparted, like logic or mathematics, by definition and demonstration. It might simply be teachable. But this is impossible. Don't get me wrong, instruction is obviously required. However, the proper creative impulse of genuine religious life cannot be found in the mere teaching of thoughts and ideas. This creative impulse must come to individuals from outside of themselves. The desire for unity necessarily implies that there is something outside of one's self to be united with. And the idea of the reality of something outside of one's self can only come from outside of one's self. And as it is with the individual, so it is with the human race. The idea of humanity as a whole with God can only issue from outside of humanity as a whole.

Teachers of religion can only accomplish their commission through representation. They must actually represent what they intend to teach. They must teach by example, not simply by instruction. The heart of religion must be caught before it can be taught. People cannot teach what they do not know, neither can they show what they do not have. Compared to example and actual life experience, instruction is cold and dead.

Religion is real only inasmuch as it feeds and reproduces. Indeed, the definition of life is "the condition that distinguishes organisms from inorganic objects and dead organisms, being manifested by growth through *metabolism*, *reproduction*, and the power of *adaptation* to environment through changes originating internally." Only life can beget life.

Pack as much as you can imagine into a doctrine and it will always fall immeasurably short of what is meant by religion in its actual living character. To make doctrine synonymous with religion is completely contradictory. Thoughts and ideas about divine things cannot produce genuine piety, much less may they be taken for such piety itself. Genuine piety is to be distinguished from Pietism, the movement, originating in the Lutheran Church in Germany in the

seventeenth century, that stressed personal piety over religious formality and orthodoxy. Pietism has simply created another false dichotomy.
Clearly, genuine religion cannot be a matter of mere doctrine, for to
be such is to divest it of its actual life.

Of course, religion involves doctrine, but not in the modern sense
of being a system of abstract propositions and logical proofs. These
kinds of thought systems have founded various schools, as the Greeks
know, but never a church or world religion. Philosophies can neither
eat nor reproduce, though they corrupt and conflate. Religion is primarily proclamation or testimony that something inexplicable and
undeniable has actually happened. It is not an abstract thought about
what happened, as if it intends to fill people's minds with various
thoughts and ideas.

Religion is, rather, a communication about an actual, historical
occurrence. It is not a sterile, abstract occurrence without consequence
or effect in the world, but it requires and produces a response. Real
religion involves a transaction, such as the comprehension of a system
of religious truths that require assent and conformity because they circumscribe the reality of human existence. Religion provides the
context for existence, individual and corporate.

Religion as doctrine follows what God has actually done in order
to provide for the perfection of God's action, its wholeness and completeness. But still the doctrines, the ideas, the thoughts in-and-of-
themselves have no power to generate life. Ideas only produce more
ideas, only life can produce life. Therefore, the power of religion only
comes from the presence of life. And in this case, this life must be
greater than humanity, greater than any individual life and greater
than all corporate life. The unity is greater than what is unified for the
same reason and in the same way that the whole is greater than the
sum of its parts.

Christianity, being derived from Christ, describes or points to
something that must exist in the teacher himself. The teaching is simply the verbal, experiential expression of this life. Thus, the apostles
and evangelists, who were the heralds of Christian salvation, preceded
doctrine. They came before the working out of the intricacies of
Christian doctrine. And they preceded the teachers of doctrine.

In every stage, the church always begins with testimony, and only
later proceeds to analysis and instruction. The power of doctrine
always results from the actual life which originally belongs to the

founder of the religion, and proceeds directly from the founder to his people.

In the case of Christianity, the action of God through the incarnation of Christ doesn't only have historical significance as something that has actually happened, but has doctrinal significance as the realization of the highest expression of religious ideals. These ideals have been abstracted from the historical facts, and put into a system of interrelated ideas, both popular and scholarly.

So, for theologians in particular, because they are most occupied with thinking about religion, Christianity has the semblance of being a self-contained set of doctrinal propositions. Theologians, then, are particularly susceptible to the philosophical error of confounding doctrine with the actual object that the doctrine represents. Indeed, those who think for a living tend to think that thinking is life. But, indeed, life is more than mere thought. Obviously, doctrine is the means of Christian instruction, but the means and the end must not be conflated. In-and-of-itself, Christianity is life—living power, a revelation of the Spirit in the form of doctrine. Doctrine that is devoid of life only produces more doctrine. Only life can produce life.

Even if Christianity is mainly regarded as doctrine, we must still ask about what makes Christian doctrine in particular unique among all religious doctrine. It's uniqueness is not found in any of its many religious or moral propositions. In fact, Christianity has much in common with other religions. Rather, Christianity's uniqueness consists in what Jesus Christ says about Himself and His relationship with God. It also consists of humanity's new relationship with God that he brought the human family as a consequence of his death. It also consists of the testimony of the Apostles concerning his person and work. All of these things result from the nature and character of Jesus Christ, second Person of the Trinity. Among all of the world's religions, Christianity alone is Trinitarian.

With the mention of the Trinity we immediately find ourselves beyond the realm of ideas and doctrine. In the light of the Trinity we are brought to the reality of religion, to the creative power of life—God Himself, revealed in and as Jesus Christ. The most essential aspect of Christ's mission in the world is His self-revelation, his self-exhibition of his humanity in unity with his divinity. This revelation concerns His whole life—birth to death to resurrection to ascension. It includes His testimony concerning Himself, and the account of the impression (likeness) He made on others.

Consequently, words and doctrines do belong to Christianity. But the *part* must not be mistaken for the *whole* because it is the holistic wholeness[10] of Christianity that makes it unique among the world's religions. This wholeness does not consist of Christian doctrine alone —though it is part of it. Rather, the uniqueness of Christianity is found in the Trinitarian Life of its founder, Jesus Christ. Only inasmuch as Christ actually is the God of creation, is Christianity the light of the world. Jesus did not say that His doctrine is the truth that He brought to the world. He said: I AM—

- "Jesus said to them, "I am the bread of life; whoever comes to me shall not hunger, and whoever believes in me shall never thirst." (John 6:35).
- "I am the light of the world. Whoever follows me will not walk in darkness, but will have the light of life" (John 8:12).
- "Truly, truly, I say to you, before Abraham was, I am" (John 8:58).
- "Truly, truly, I say to you, I am the door of the sheep" (John 10:7).
- "I am the good shepherd. The good shepherd lays down his life for the sheep" (John 10:11).
- "I am the resurrection and the life. Whoever believes in me, though he die, yet shall he live" (John 11:25).
- "I am the way, and the truth, and the life. No one comes to the Father except through me" (John 14:6).
- "I am in my Father, and you in me, and I in you" (John 14:20).
- "I am the true vine, and my Father is the vinedresser" (John 15:1).
- "All mine are yours, and yours are mine, and I am glorified in them" (John 17:10).

---

10 Holistic: Emphasizing the organic or functional relation between parts and the whole. Wholeness: An undivided or unbroken completeness or totality with nothing lacking.

4. CONCEPTION OF CHRISTIANITY AS MORAL LAW

The next historic development in Christian understanding placed the distinctive character of Christianity in the realm of ethics, emphasizing its power as a rule of life. This closely followed Kant's categorical division of reason, morality, and aesthetics into separate and distinct areas of inquiry. Rationalism followed in the train of Kant's work. Kant and the Rationalists taught that the human mind can have no certain knowledge of the supernatural or divine in a theoretical way, unlike the certainty of reason and logic. Moral certainty can only be presumed as an act of obedience to the demands of our moral nature.

What morality requires as a postulate for its own support may be relied upon as true, even though it is logically unknowable. In this regard moral law became an absolute measure of truth in its own realm. Morality became more reliable than religion, which became a secondary and subordinate concern, necessary only as required by morality for its own purposes. This change caused Christianity to be seen primarily as an ethical law, beginning as divine precepts, but in the final analysis religion was understood as the demand of morality, what Kant called practical reason.[11] Accordingly, Christ was the great lawgiver for humanity and the church was a platform for the grand struggle between good and evil in history. The ideas of faith and God's judgment were resolved into the mere confidence that virtue would prevail. Religion became faith in the moral order of the world.

We acknowledge the importance of this ethical idea in Christianity. It represents progress beyond the idea that Christianity is merely doctrinal and it puts Christianity's teleological character in a better light by suggesting that Christianity as a whole is bringing about a moral conclusion. It also put more attention on the author of Christianity as the center of the whole system, though still only in an idealistic way. It kept the age to which it belonged on good terms with Christianity by making Christianity more real because of its focus on morality. Nonetheless, Christian morality is only part of the reality of the whole of Christianity.

---

11 The *Critique of Practical Reason* is the second of Immanuel Kant's three critiques, first published in 1788. It follows on from his *Critique of Pure Reason* and deals with his moral philosophy, as his *Critique of Judgment* deals with aesthetics.

Thinking that Christianity is nothing more than morality produced a false idea because it overlooked what is most unique about Christianity—its Trinitarian character. Christian piety requires more than moral behavior because it is a means for an end beyond the believer. Christianity is not simply morality, it is creative. Its central concerns are redemption, atonement, and grace, which are overlooked by this moral understanding. Christianity is not simply a moral imperative, it is a fulfillment and satisfaction. It is not a request for God to do something, it's a divine gift that produces obedience out of gratefulness rather than duty. Duty, which was Kant's central concern, is nothing to the Christian because love is everything. And love obeys because of its own desire, without command or duty. The categorical imperative is irrelevant in the face of love. "We love him, because he first loved us" (1 John 4:19).

When understood either as doctrine or morality (law), the primary difference between Christianity and other religions cannot be seen. Were Christianity merely a system of doctrine, even if it was infinitely perfect, it would not be different from other religions or philosophies. Sure, Christianity provides a better system of law and morality, but if that is all there is to it, it would still be classified with Judaism and Islam as a biblical religion. At best it would be no more than a better version of Judaism or Islam, and not a different category of religion that is completely unique among religions.

In both cases the explanation of how Christianity is the foundation and source of the regeneration of human life would not be possible. Rather, we must agree with Paul and John that Christ is the source of a completely new order of humanity and world history. The explanation of how Christianity can provide new birth for believers and new forms of thinking, of how the Christian church and all that it includes is not simply a new idea or a higher morality, but is actually a new creation of the same kind as the creation of Adam in Genesis.[12]

5. THE RELIGION OF REDEMPTION

To see this unique character of Christianity as new, original, and different from all other religions, Schleiermacher,[13] who was more his-

---

12 From *homosapien* to *homochristos*; not mere wisdom (sapience) fused to flesh, but the incarnate Person of Christ fused to flesh, not perfectly, but adequately.

13 Friedrich Daniel Ernst Schleiermacher (1768-1834) was a German theologian and

torical than the Rationalists, sought to refer everything back to its ultimate ground or living root—the Person of Christ Himself. He
attempted to redeem the reality of the central orthodox beliefs of
Christianity from their complete dismissal by the Rationalists. In doing
so, he portrayed Christ, not simply as a teacher or lawgiver, but as
having the actual power of God to actually redeem the world through
the regeneration of humanity.

Schleiermacher did not deny that Christianity is doctrinal or ethical, but found it to be primarily teleological.[14] He thought that it was
necessary for Christianity to be completely and uniquely different
from all other religions, monotheistic or pagan, in order to have complete historical integrity. He found this uniqueness in the realization of

---

philosopher who attempted to reconcile the criticisms of the Enlightenment with
traditional Protestant orthodoxy. In Nevin's day he represented one of the highest
expressions of Christian theology. Because of his profound impact on subsequent
Christian thought, he is often called the "Father of Modern Liberal Theology." Had
Modern theologians been as influenced by Nevin, history would be quite different.

From Leibniz, Lessing, Fichte, Jacobi, and the Romantic schools of Idealists
Schleiermacher found a deeply mystical understanding of the inner depths of the
human personality. His religious thought found its expression most notably in his
book *The Christian Faith*, a systematic effort considered by many to be one of the
true classics of Christian theology.

He described the ego/individual as an individualization of universal reason, and
the primary act of self-consciousness as the conjunction of universal and individual
life, the union of the universe with reason incarnate. Thus, every person is a specific
and original representation of the universe and a compendium of humanity, a
microcosm in which the world is immediately reflected. Though individuals cannot
attain perfect unity of thought and being by either cognition or volition, they can
find it in their own personalities as a sort of immediate self-consciousness or feeling
(which are identical in Schleiermacher's terminology). This *feeling,* described as the
minimum of distinct antithetic consciousness or the cessation of the antithesis of
subject and object, constitutes the unity of our being. Because this feeling provides
the essential fact of self-consciousness, religion lies at the basis of all thought and
action.

At various periods of his life Schleiermacher used different terms to represent the
character and relation of *religious feeling*. In his earlier days he called it a feeling or
intuition of the universe, consciousness of the unity of reason and nature, of the
infinite and the eternal within the finite and the temporal. In later life he described it
as the feeling of absolute dependence, or, as meaning the same thing, the consciousness of being in relation to God.

14 Teleology: a necessarily theological explanation of phenomena by their ends or purposes. For instance, a flower is not pushed into the light by the biological character
of its roots, but is drawn into the light by God's definition (purpose) of what He
intends it to be. Similarly, God draws history into the future of His making.

redemption provided by the Person of Jesus Christ. Of course, this idea is also found in other religions, but those religions make redemption the result of various human accomplishments—purifications, penances, offerings, etc.—and an object of future realization, usually in another life.

The realization of Christian redemption is quite different. Christ doesn't simply order and prescribe the process of redemption, but actually accomplishes the whole work in Himself in the present, not merely in the future. Thus, Christian redemption is not merely accomplished *by* Him, but *in* Him and *through* Him. Furthermore, it is accomplished by the most perfect and all-sufficient form—His Person. He can do this because He alone is in complete, sinless, Trinitarian union with God. Thus, the Person of Jesus Christ is Himself the redemption He manifests in the world by His realization (making real) of the Christian Trinity. Moses was simply the medium through which God provided His law, and the law was for Moses as much as for others.

Not so with Christ! The religion of Christ is the Person of Christ. It was not merely given by Him, but is manifest *in Him*, and it remains in Him forever because He is its only perfect source. Christian redemption is the Person of the everlasting Redeemer, who alone is without peer. If the idea of religious redemption is true, it can only be true in the Person who Himself actually constitutes redemption in the real world in which people actually live. And if it is real, people will necessarily be conscious of it as an actuality in their own lives.

This definition of religion provides an important advance beyond the definitions of religion as mere doctrine or morality. Doctrine pertains to knowledge alone, law or morality pertains only to the will, but actual religious redemption must be more than mere thought, intention, feeling, or consciousness. Actual redemption necessarily includes the whole human being, head and heart, body and soul. This definition of religion involves a more complete, a more whole and satisfying definition of religion than any other.

Understood this way, Christianity takes on an actual, concrete historical character. It is not just an idea or an institution, but an actual Person. Christianity is not just an idea, not even an idea about someone who lived a long time ago. Rather, Christianity is a dynamic reality that actually exists as a Person in the lives of believers in this present world. It is not communicated through an imperial authority from on high (which it actually is), but it is communicated through the personal freedom and power it provides for its adherents. What is subjectively experienced as regeneration in the lives of believers is objectively manifest as historical fact in the world. These qualities of Christianity go far beyond all previous definitions of religion, and endue it with perfect and complete uniqueness in the annals of religious and philosophical history.

Indeed, the theology of Schleiermacher has provided a categorical advance beyond the previous definitions of Christianity in merely doctrinal or ethical terms. All serious seekers of Truth can now understand that the religion of Christianity is not simply a doctrine but is a Person. Christianity is the actual, living Person of Jesus Christ, alive in human history as the source of a renewed human kind that unfolds continuously, freely and in accordance with its own law. This renewed human kind exists in Christ, in the character of the only real Redeemer. No other religion before or since has ever exhibited anything like this, as the reader of this book will come to appreciate.

Yet, there remains a final requirement for a complete definition of human religion that is not yet clear. There is a serious defect in Sehleiermacher's theology regarding his understanding of the unique character of Christianity. His idea of Christian redemption does in fact provide a significant advance regarding the foundational character of Christianity, but his deficiency concerns his understanding and appreciation of the relationship between sin and atonement. Redemption assumes the effectiveness of atonement, and atonement assumes the seriousness of sin.

Actual reconciliation with God will always produce the personal confidence of actually being reconciled. Because actual reconciliation and redemption are the products of atonement, they follow where atonement has led. Atonement bridges the gap or amends for the wrong so that reconciliation and redemption may manifest. Therefore, the idea of atonement must take precedence over the idea of redemption regarding the definition of Christianity.

Notice also that redemption is subjective in that it effects individuals at the level of personal experience by delivering the person from the power of sin. In contrast, atonement is objective in that it happens outside of a person before it happens to the person. God must actually be atoned before that atonement can be applied to individuals. Atonement establishes a right relationship between God and humanity as a whole or class before it can be applied to specific, individual human beings.

Schleiermacher almost exclusively limits himself to the subjective character of religion by defining it as a form of feeling or individual consciousness. And it is completely inadequate to the character of religion to define its central characteristic in such subjective terms, to the near exclusion of the objective reality that paves the way for redemption to follow. Piety that is genuine, complete, and well-grounded embodies both understanding (doctrine) and will (morality) as essential elements of its constitution. Christianity obviously includes such piety in order to actually provide personal redemption.

But Christianity is infinitely more than mere piety. It is not merely the revelation of God's redemption, but is also and more-so the revelation of the character of God. Christianity reveals the character of God in the perfect wholeness of the Trinity. And that wholeness is shown to be more perfect by the fact of its actual reality. Christianity reveals God to be a merciful and just but loving Father, an obedient and sinless servant who is the Son of the Father, and a powerful, careful and Holy Spirit who actually accomplishes what God intends in human history.

This definition goes far beyond mere subjective individuality, and provides an infinitely more complete definition than that of mere redemption. This is the actual atonement that Christianity alone provides and which overflows the mere definition of religion with meaning and reality. Both redemption and atonement are the work of Jesus Christ on the cross for the world. They are spiritual works, of course. And for spiritual work to be real, it must manifest in a particular form of existence or some particular person in human history. If, for instance, redemption and atonement exist for God only with regard to humanity in general and not for any particular human beings, then it would fall short of actually being real in this world.

This requirement is also necessary in the case of Jesus Christ. His spiritual work on the cross is only real inasmuch as he Himself is real. It can only affect this world if he was an actual human being in this world. And because His work of redemption in the world rests on his prior work of atonement with God, it is necessary that Christ's character be such that it actually exists in the reality of human history and in the realm of God's divine existence. Thus, the Redeemer's particular character must necessarily touch both humanity and divinity if his work is to actually heal the breach between humanity and God.

And, indeed, Christianity reveals the character of the Redeemer to be equally and simultaneously human and divine, without confusion or conflation. And through the revelation of the character of Jesus Christ in history, we find the most complete, most full, and most perfect definition of religion ever provided. Thus, it is here that we find the true source and foundation of Christianity, and its most fundamental and most unique characteristic—the Trinity of God.

6. CHRIST'S PERSONHOOD IS ETERNAL LIFE

Jesus said, "I am the way, the truth, and the life" (John 14:6).

What is it in the Person of Christ that makes Him a perfect Savior, able to provide atonement and redemption? It is most certainly His nature, which is simultaneously human and divine. This nature gives Him all of the attributes of God, and simultaneously the characteristics of an actual human being. This dual nature makes Him complete and self-sufficient, unlike other human beings, but completely like God. Therefore, His Person is uniquely able to communicate both divinely and humanly because He knows both conditions subjectively, personally and intimately. This ability to communicate in both directions makes Him the perfect mediator between God and humanity.

The fact that His life is simultaneously comprehensive and individual, perfect and particular, universal and singular, without confusing or combining these characteristics makes Him unique in human history. In this regard faithful Christian theologians of every variation speak with one voice proclaiming that the character of Jesus Christ, His divinity and humanity in one Person, give Him the greatest significance possible. In Him alone deity and manhood somehow come together. They become unified as one, yet they can still be separately identified. This complex simplicity, this diverse unity stands at the center of the reality of the world in which we actually live as human beings and is an ultimate mystery. It is not that we cannot understand it, but that we cannot understand all of it completely. The mystery of our own unique individuality and wholeness as human beings is wrapped up in our own unity with the Person of Jesus Christ. In Him we are unified, both individually and corporately, but not identified. This is the mystery of the Trinity.

Theologians generally agree about this. But the amalgam of their particular explanations provides a range of views, some of which harmonize and some of which conflict. The central conflict is between Pantheism and ordinary[15] Christianity. Pantheism says that this uniqueness is universal, whereas ordinary Christianity specifies that it comes through Christ alone and is historically real in the character and/or Person of Jesus Christ. Pantheism turns divinity into a universally applied but "spiritual" abstraction, like Plato's ideal forms, whereas ordinary Christianity holds the ideal and the actual together in creative tension. The ordinary Christian view acknowledges that God in Christ is both universal and personal, both spiritual and actual.

This difference is stark. Whether the union of divinity and humanity is understood as an abstract spiritual ideal that is universally applied to all humanity, or as a particular individual actuality that is uniquely applied to Jesus Christ, these two conceptions accurately capture and reveal the conflict between these archetypal religions. These opposing religious views also produce opposing religious conclusions. Either God becomes human in the particularity of Jesus Christ as Christianity teaches, or humanity becomes conscious of its own eternal divinity as Pantheism teaches. Everything else in our understanding and explanations of human history and religion flow one way or another from this theological watershed. Many Christians still apply Pantheistic ideas to Christianity because they have not sufficiently experienced and understood the whole character of the actual new life in Christ. Thus, everything depends upon which of these views is regarded as true. Is the central fact of reality the manifestation of Jesus Christ in the flesh as God incarnate? Or is the central fact of history the evolution of human consciousness into the realization of its own divinity? If ordinary Christianity is true, then God is sovereign through Christ, and God is the principle cause of history and behavior. And if Pantheism is true, then humanity is sovereign through divine realization and humanity is the principle cause of history and behavior. Thus, Christianity's driving force is the Holy Spirit, and Pantheism's driving force is inspiration and moral influence.

---

15 Ordinary: having regulated jurisdiction. The ideal or correct understanding of Christianity without the historical baggage associated with the word *orthodox*.

7. HEGEL AND THE MODERN SPECULATION

Hegel[16] acknowledged Christianity to be the absolute truth of religion. He did so, because it has its essential nature in the incarnation, which exhibits the unity of the divine and human. On this basis he wanted to reconcile Christianity with the new philosophy that had grown out of Kant's work, and demonstrate their full identity in their last results. For both Christianity and transcendental philosophy[17] this unity represents the highest ideal.

However, what Christianity posits to be the actual, concrete form of the individual, historical God-man is abstracted by philosophy into the realm of speculative thought as something "spiritual," universal and idealistic. This line of thought further posits that it is the nature of the absolute or divine Spirit (God) to actualize in humanity as a whole, generically. The consequence is that the human spirit descends into the depths of its own being in order to recognize itself to be divine.

It is the nature and perfection of God to be human, or the other way around, it is the nature and perfection of man to be divine. This is a biblical idea that was realized in Christianity. Christianity has made known to man his divinity through the new birth in Christ. Christianity alone has ended the opposition between God and man, eternity and time. Christianity alone brings heaven down upon the earth. Christianity alone has overcome the dualistic antagonism of the finite and infinite. Christianity laid the foundation the unity of thought (*Monis-*

---

16 Georg Wilhelm Friedrich Hegel (1770-1831), a German philosopher, a creator of German Idealism. His historicist and idealist description of reality as a whole revolutionized European philosophy and was an important precursor to Continental philosophy and Marxism.

  Hegel developed a comprehensive philosophical framework of Absolute idealism to account for the relation of mind and nature, the subject and object of knowledge, including psychology, the state, history, art, religion and philosophy. In particular, he developed the concept that mind or spirit manifested itself in a set of contradictions and oppositions that synthetically integrated and united historically, without eliminating either pole or reducing one to the other. Examples include synthesis between nature and freedom, and between immanence and transcendence.

17 Transcendental Philosophy: any system of philosophy emphasizing the intuitive and spiritual above the empirical and material.

mus des Gedankens[18]), which forms the great triumph of modern speculation.

However, the later Hegelians were by no means satisfied. The
Hegelian peace made between Christianity and philosophy appeared
to them, who were on the political "Left,"[19] to be hollow and was not
allowed to stand. They denied that Christianity unifies the finite and
infinite as truth requires. They understood the requirement, but
denied that Christianity satisfies it. They carped that either Christianity
contradicted the necessity of God's immanence in the world, or the
unity of God and Jesus as an historic individual had no relevance
regarding the unity between humanity and God.

Therefore, they concluded, the dualism between God and man—
between the universal and the particular, between eternity and time—
remained unresolved. They did admit, however, that Christianity had
become an historical, worldwide movement because of the actual
union of God and Christ, though that union had no ability to affect
humanity as a whole, but only served to stimulate new ideas like nothing before or since.

The bottom line was that the union itself was understood to be
not real or historical, regardless of the historicity of Jesus the man. The
union was thought to be no more than a myth, a story, an idea or
abstraction intended only to stir the mere imagination of the church.
Because this unity was only a transcendental *idea*, Christianity fell
short of the truth because its unity did not actually connect humanity
as a whole with the divine. Indeed, Christianity's insistence on the
reality and universality of human sin seemed to create an unbridgeable
gulf between them. Sure, they thought, Christ attained to the requisite
unity, but he could not bring humanity as a whole into it. Christ's
unity was understood as an historic fact that was past and gone, or an

---

18 A reference to Hegelian synthesis. The triad *thesis, antithesis, synthesis* is often used to
describe the thought of Hegel, though Hegel never used the term himself. The
triad: The *thesis* is an intellectual proposition. The *antithesis* is simply the negation of
the thesis, or a reaction to the proposition. The *synthesis* solves the conflict between
the thesis and antithesis by reconciling their common truths, and forming a new
proposition, also known as a synthetic compromise.

19 Traditionally, the Left includes progressives, social liberals, social democrats, social-
ists, communists and anarchists. The Right includes conservatives, libertarians, plu-
tocrats, reactionaries, capitalists, monarchists, nationalists and fascists.

anticipated future event. But never as a present reality in the here and now.[20]

The Hegelians had three possible conclusions, all of which agreed that the identification of God with the world (pantheism and monism)[21] represents the highest truth. But the difference between them is very material. One concludes that Christianity and speculation are essentially the same—abstract. Another concludes the Christianity and speculation are mutually exclusive. And another allows the unity, but only for a single individual—Jesus Christ, who provided an abstract, ideational and isolated center for Christianity, a "spiritual" realm that has no empirical substance. This ideational realm of abstraction was then posited to be the synthetic domain of all truth, religious or otherwise. Thus, the Hegelian view created a synthetic, abstract, and unreal understanding of Christianity.

Generally speaking, Hegelian philosophy actually grasped the central element of Christianity—the actual divinity of Jesus Christ as an actual Person, but reduced it to a mere *caput mortuum*[22] by conceiving the most important element of Christianity as a mere speculation that is at best incomplete. What the Hegelians called the "unity of the divine and human" was understood to have happened only in the case of Jesus Christ, and was not transferable to anyone else except as an abstract thought or story. They denied the reality and extent of sin, Christ's mediatorial role, and Christ's headship of His body. Or if they did understand them, they considered them to be nothing more than mere thoughts and ideas, without empirical substance. All of this means that they also denied the reality of personal regeneration, or dismissed it as mere enthusiasm.

The vociferous, complex and emotionally laden arguments that followed Hegel's attempt to unite philosophy and Christianity produced a backwater of stagnant apathy. Christ was simultaneously considered to embody the highest expression of truth, but was impotent to carry it beyond his own hermetically sealed individual person.

---

20 This is the result of the failure to understand/conceptualize the actuality of the Christian Trinity, and its implications for humanity. See the work of Cornelius Van Til, R.J. Rushdoony, Peter Leithart, Phillip A. Ross, etc.

21 Monism is any philosophical view which holds that there is unity in a given field of inquiry, where this is not to be expected.

22 A Latin term whose literal meaning is "dead head" or "worthless remains," used in alchemy.

It remained for Modern philosophy to break the seal and find actual perfection in the speculative germ. But mere philosophy, concerned only about ideas, cannot break into the actual empirical realm. It can only think about it. Nonetheless, modern philosophy did fix its eye on the center or the very heart of Christianity—the divinity of Christ, but it could only more accurately train its deadly speculative arrows upon this vital point.

We will not consider those philosophies that conceive of God abstractly or beyond the world. Generally speaking, modern philosophy[23] teaches the simultaneous existence of God in the world and of the world in God. God is not identified as the world, but fills it with His actual presence and power. In this regard it understands Christianity to have put an end to the opposition of the infinite and the finite, the divine and human. But it acknowledges an absolute union of divinity and humanity in Christ alone, which casts a shadow of hopeless dualism every where else.

This kind of unity is not restricted to Christ as an individual human being, but proceeds from Him to affect the spiritual organism of which He is the head—the church, which became part of human experience. Here the heaven of personal salvation is not exclusively in the next world, but is involved in the present life as well. Nonetheless, Christianity was not understood to be monistic, in the Hegelian sense[24] Christianity allows for the reality of sin, which creates dualism. The fact that Christianity considers both sin and salvation to be real creates a gulf that must be bridged.

The reality of sin finds evidence in the conscience of every person. Sin puts every person in the untenable position of opposing a perfectly holy and just God. Yet, by nature every individual seeks union with God to bridge the gap created by sin. The various monisms must deny this dualism or deny their own validity. And the dualism can only be denied by denying either sin or God—or both. But to deny sin requires the sacrifice of moral awareness (produced by sin) or religious consciousness (produced by God)—or both. Any denial destroys spirituality. At the very least, denial of any kind destroys Christianity

---

23 Nevin didn't provide specific references.
24 Monism: The doctrine that reality consists of a single basic substance or element. Metaphysical monism produced both materialism and idealism.

because the central concern of Christianity is to bridge the gap between sin and God.[25]

Philosophical speculation solves this dualism problem through the use of logic, reason, redefinition, or bald assertion that simply posits that these opposites were originally one. However, logical redemption salves no conscience. Mere reason cannot turn duty into actual ability. The redefinition of sin changes nothing real. Nor can bald assertion create new life. Christianity alone fully accounts for the dualistic opposition as it actually exists. Christianity alone accounts for holiness and sin in such a way as to salve the one with the other. Christianity alone is both source and solution for the contradiction that God's created world lies in sin.

And Christianity alone overcomes this dualism, not by denial but by actually bringing God and humanity into actual, historical union through Jesus Christ. Christianity's solution is not mere thoughts and ideas, but is historically grounded in an actual human life. The actuality of this life is itself the actual power of redemption. Through this one, unique divinely human person humanity finds actual, historical, bodily participation in the divine through union with Christ.

This union comes to humanity, not through the evolution of human consciousness, nor by spiritual inspiration, nor by moral persuasion, but by the actual Person who mediates the grace of unity. Philosophy can only stimulate thought. It cannot change minds, renew hearts or restore lives. Christianity alone retains its true character of a genuine theistic religion, in which the dualism of God and sin is honestly acknowledged and actually bridged. Only Christianity acknowledges the absolute holiness of God, the comprehensive power of sin, and provides an eternal solution for a temporal problem.[26]

8. CONSTITUTION OF CHRISTIANITY AS THE UNION OF GOD AND HUMANITY THROUGH CHRIST

The best works of theology and philosophy agree that Christ Himself was in unity with God. And the testimony of Scripture and the church confirm that many people believed that Jesus Christ was divine. The divinity of Christ is the central defining idea of Christian-

---

25 Nevin is not arguing that Christianity is dualistic, but is pointing to what Cornelius Van Till calls the *antithesis* of Christianity or the opposition between flesh and spirit.

26 Neither religion nor philosophy can provide objective forgiveness or an actual new life.

ity. And Christianity has had such a real effect on the world that it cannot be dismissed as fiction. It is equally demonstrable that Christ intended to impart His Spirit and life to His people in order to continue and extend His existence in them, and theirs in Him, as the means of salvation and the cultivation of righteousness in the world.

The Gospel of John testifies particularly well about this. Christ, who was first glorified by the Father, will glorify Himself again in His people (John 17:22). Christians take the very life of Christ into themselves by actually eating His flesh and drinking His blood (John 6:53). Christians are symbolically cast into the ground by death through baptism (Romans 6:4), and like a grain of wheat, they themselves rise in the church in order to produce more seed, and multiply and perpetuate themselves through all time (John 12:24). John is very explicit that Jesus will draw people to God as He is lifted up in order to make them one with the Father.

> "that they may all be one, just as you, Father, are in me, and I in you, that they also may be in us, so that the world may believe that you have sent me" (John 17:21). "I in them and you in me, that they may become perfectly one, so that the world may know that you sent me and loved them even as you loved me" (John 17:23).

All that belongs to God also belongs to Christ, and with all of this divine fullness He communicates[27] Himself to His people. He makes His abode with them, and sanctifies them, or as the apostle Paul expresses it, only in reversed order: "all are yours, and you are Christ's, and Christ is God's" (1 Cor. 3:23).

The ground or root of the Christian faith is that to which it owes its origin and character. It is the actual unity of Christ with God. Because God is actually in unity with God He cannot lie. So, we must believe what He says, and He said that He intended to save the wholeness of the world (John 12:47). This ground or root of Christianity necessarily includes the salvation of the wholeness of the world, and is not simply focused on you or me as individuals. Rather, we are saved into the wholeness of the unity of God and humanity, as well.

Of course, Jesus Christ also knows the reality of human individuality. There is a wholeness of the individual just as there is a wholeness of humanity. Christ's unity with God is simultaneously individual and

---

27 Communicate: transfer to another, join or connect.

corporate, original, and complete. However, note that Christ's individuality is complex (John 17:21; 17:23, above).

In us Christ is not single but Trinitarian, nor are we single in Christ, but reflect "through a glass darkly" His Trinitarian character. The unity with God in Christ is some day to become, according to the measure of receptivity, the possession of the whole race.[28] A living head is not to be thought of apart from the body. There can be no redeemed church without a Redeemer, nor is there a perfect Redeemer without an actual redeemed church. Christ is made complete in His people, and in the same way, people are made complete in Christ.

There can be no deeper, higher, more meaningful, or more important understanding of the nature and character of true religion. The actual existence and fact of this Trinitarian unity in Christ and its necessary implications are themselves the actual composition, character, and constitution of Christianity itself. Therefore three things necessarily follow.

First, the religion that provides this revelation of the Trinitarian character of God in Christ provides the most important sign and seal of God, and is the truest religion in the truest sense.

Second, the truest religion will authenticate itself by actually manifesting in the world. It will realize itself—make itself real—in the actual, empirical world because its wholeness must necessarily include actual existence in humanity. Its wholeness requires that this unity of God and humanity actually exists as more than an abstraction. Life unified with life must actually be alive.

Third, everything that belongs to the wholeness of this religion must necessarily manifest its best and truest form as the singular holistic wholeness of a particular individual who actually lives in this actual world—Jesus Christ. It is endemic to the reality of wholeness to be more than a mere idea. Such a religion demands the participation of humanity to fulfill its holistic wholeness.[29]

---

28 There is Trinitarian multiplicity in the unity of the Godhead, and that multiplicity is also found wherever Christian unity exists.

29 This is not an expression of Universalism, but is a call for individual participation in the wholeness of humanity, available only in Christ. While it is God's intent to include all of humanity, it will take an eternity to complete. There are two meanings of this: 1) that it will never be complete in history (time), and 2) it will only be complete in eternity.

Finally, Christianity best meets the necessary criteria herein specified for such a religion.

9. CONTRAST WITH HEATHENISM AND JUDAISM

All religion is primarily about the communion of man (humanity,
both individually and corporately) with God. The most perfect form
of such communion is called *unity*. When individual personalities are
blended, merged, or melded in the process it produces *identity* rather
than *unity* or *union*. The fullest and most perfect form of unity does not
involve the loss of individual personality. When the individual personalities are actually alive a mutual interpenetration of spirit and nature
takes place, such that they may be said to live in each other freely and
sweetly, without resistance or prevention. There is a difference
between the unity of creature to creature and the unity of creature to
Creator. Creature to creature unity is analogous to cardinal numbers in
mathematics, and Creator to creature is more analogous to ordinal
numbers.[30]

Thus, religious or spiritual unity occurs when God comes into
formal relationship with an individual human being without any
obstruction or interference from the individual. In this way God can
communicate Himself—His love, His grace, His Spirit, His holiness,
etc.—to the individual fully, wholly, and completely. Such communication fills the individual to overflowing, but does not exhaust God of
His greater capacity for wholeness. The individual, by not resisting or
interfering, becomes submitted to God's dominion.[31] The individual
actively engages the effort to remove obstructions and resistance
through prayer and discipline, thus engaging his own subjectivity in
the service of God's objectivity.

The individual experiences this effort as doing his own will
because it requires his free, personal, active, passionate desire to serve
God in this way. Thus, the individual acknowledges the will of God
working in him to be his own personal desire. Thus, there is no conflict in such union between individual self-consciousness and universal
God-consciousness. Rather, human desire/will is absorbed in unity

---

30 Cardinal: Serving as an essential component. *Ordinal*: The order among the essential
    components. Thus, the whole (ordinal) is greater than the parts (cardinal).
31 Human dominion of creation is a poor reflection of God's dominion of man (Gen.
    1:28).

into God's desire/will. The various wills lose uniqueness as they identify as One, while the various personalities become more unique
through the increasing order and discipline of union.[32]

God alone accomplishes this union by actually changing the
innermost will or desire of individuals, through the power and presence of the Holy Spirit, to conform to the objective will of God,
manifest most perfectly in the person of Jesus Christ. How God
accomplishes this change is the subject of this book.

This union, though in seed form, belonged to Adam and Eve in
the Garden, when they enjoyed the innocence in which they were
originally created. But they yielded to the sin of the serpent, bringing
with it separation from God. The object of religion now is to restore
the perfect unity with God that has been derailed by sin. This can be
accomplished only through atonement. The purpose of atonement is
the renewal of communion and perfect union with God. This renewal
is not simply a return to the kind of semiconscious innocent communion enjoyed in the past by Adam and Eve in the Garden. Rather, the
renewal of communion sanctifies or ripens human consciousness that
has been dominated by sin, spiritual discord, and conflict.

The religions that historically preceded Christianity also aimed at
the central purpose of religion—union with God. Judaism, actuated by
the oneness or unity of God and plagued by the pervasiveness of
human sin, sought unity, atonement, and forgiveness symbolized
through sacrifice. Paganism essentially embraced the moral decrepi-
tude (sin) of humanity by imagining and worshiping various
perversions or partial reflections of the One True God through the
various establishments of polytheism. Their quest for divine unity led
them to embrace sin in their worship and practice, but to justify it
through the theological imagination of spirituality in abstract, other
worldly terms, thinking that their sin somehow satisfied the various
gods of their imaginations. But their denial of the unity of God and
their emphasis on sin denied them any kind of true communion, either
individually or corporately. The constitution of both Judaism and
Paganism made genuine union impossible.

Paganism as a religion cannot correctly conceive or realize union
with the only real God that actually exists because Paganism does not
reveal the Trinity. The gods of Paganism cannot reconcile eternity

---

32 A thousand personalities in union require greater order and discipline than two.

and time, infinity and finitude, the ultimate and the proximate, or the One and the many because union between divinity and humanity belongs to the Trinity alone. The idea of Pantheistic unity either identifies humanity with God or identifies God with nature.

The complex unity or singularity of reality[33] gets flattened through the ignorance or denial of the Trinity. The two ideas—divinity and humanity—are confounded, conflated, and/or flatly identified apart from the Trinity. With such lack of clarity, of particularity, there is no way to speak of real union with the only real Trinitarian God. It is true that Paganism speaks of unity with the divine, but apart from the conscious texture provided by the Trinity it can attain to nothing more than an imagined identity of humanity with an imagined divinity. Thus, it is not true unity with the only real Trinitarian God, but is an imagined unity with an imagined god. Genuine union with God only comes through union with the Son of God, the actual divine man Jesus Christ, who initiates and fulfills the union through the power and presence of the Holy Spirit.

Genuine unity can only be real on the basis of a constitutionally ethical, monotheistic, and Trinitarian religion,[34] in which a full, complete, and holistic distinction is made between God and his creation. Judaism set up the reality of such union through its Scripture and prophets, but could not actually bond (fully, holistically, wholly, completely, and perfectly) with human reality until the Son of God—the long awaited Jewish Messiah—actually manifested in the flesh as the Trinitarian Godhead. The unity that Paganism confounded and could not attain because of a faulty constitution, Judaism partly attained through its insistence on monotheism, but could not complete because it could only anticipate the Messiah apart from the perfection of the manifestation of the Trinitarian Godhead.

The Jewish Scripture did not deny that the reality of God's being in the world required Him to have feet of clay (*in weltlichkeit*) or a fully human nature, but until God manifest as Jesus Christ it was no more than an idea, a thought or abstraction. According to Jewish theology, God works in the realms of nature and humanity (history), but does so objectively, outwardly and/or visibly, but not subjectively, inwardly

33 The truth of reality for human beings is always, necessarily and delicately textured because God created us to be creatures of his Word.
34 Christian monotheism is Trinitarian and Christian unity is Trinitarian because they necessarily involved the Trinity, the plural One and only real God.

and/or invisibly. They understood God only transcendentally and objectively as the God who created the world, not the God who could be identified with the world—because their focus was exclusively on God's monotheistic character, which they correctly set against the false ideas of polytheistic gods.

Thus, the Jewish God worked exclusively in extraordinary, miraculous ways, in history and through nature, but not individualistically—not fully, not completely. Never were any Jewish people identified as being God incarnate. They saw God's acts as solitary, abrupt, and transient whether God was acting in history, in nature, or speaking to/through a particular individual. The Jews, particularly the Jews of the intertestamental period,[35] almost exclusively understood God as Lawgiver and Judge. Even when God worked with individuals or communities he called for change, but did not constitutionally or permanently change anyone. Jeremiah longed for the day that God would actually change hearts and minds (Jer. 31:33).[36] God's demand for changed hearts was made in the Old Testament (Deut. 6:5, etc.), but it remained for God to manifest as Messiah for that demand to be fully met, by grace, of course.

The perfect union of God and humanity requires a constant and consistent communication of the divine Spirit, a permanent indwelling of the divine nature, a fellowship in or on the basis of eternity on the part of man that would include the whole of his existence, personally, corporately, and historically. In Judaism we find the seed of such union. But only in Christianity does the seed come to flower and fruitfulness.

All of this is conceivable only on the basis of a perfect or complete religion in which God and humanity can be distinguished without being divided. Such union requires the recognition of God's grace as well as his holiness on the divine side, but also the human capacity for such union on the basis of man's original, created constitution apart from sin. Indeed, God is willing and humanity is able to enter this per-

---

35 The intertestamental period refers to the time between the writings of the Hebrew Bible and the Christian New Testament texts. Traditionally, it is considered to be roughly four hundred years, spanning the ministry of Malachi (c. 420 B.C.), the last of the Old Testament prophets, and the appearance of John the Baptist in the early 1st century A.D.

36 Of course, this point is overstated because God always saves people in the same way. Rather, this point should be understood as a tendency of the Old Testament and not a hard and fast rule.

fect union—apart from sin. In sin, man's subjective will became dis-
united from God's objective will. Thus, people began to serve their
own desires and concerns disassociated from God, whereas in the
absence of sin the subjective desires of humanity were identified with
the objective desires of God, both prior to the entrance of sin when
those desires existed in seed form, and after the breach of sin is healed
in glory. All of this is found in Christianity alone.

The Christian Triune God is the only self-existent Creator and
Preserver of all things, and is where and/or how Christians live, move
and have their being in Christ. Christian life in Christ bears witness to
the presence of this Triune God. He alone is to be infinitely exalted
because He alone is infinitely near, communicating Himself through
the condescension of boundless love.

Because perfect sinless holiness is actually found in the person of
Jesus Christ, who is Himself God by the mystical power of the Trinity,
so all humanity shares the actual humanity of Jesus Christ by the mystical power of the Holy Spirit through regeneration. The regeneration
of humanity as a whole reflects the process of creation in Genesis. Just
as humanity is born one person at a time, so humanity is reborn one
person at a time.

Thus, every Christian enjoys the privilege of conscious union
with God in Christ through the natural exercise of ordinary will,[37]
which is actually being regenerated by the Holy Spirit into union with
God's will through their own actual, individual, bodily participation in
Christ's Person, which necessarily includes His actual, individual body
—the church. Yet the wholeness of humanity is greater than any individual, and greater than the sum of individuals.

Here alone we have the true God, holy and boundless in His love,
a true Man who represents all humanity, people of every nation, race,
class, sect, and sex, in the most perfect way. Only in Christ is the
truest, most complete and perfect union of God and humanity in the
undivided and indivisible Oneness of a single living personality. Thus,
in Christianity alone is the One Universal Truth that all other religions
have struggled in vain to reach, teach, emulate, and manifest. Here is
the great crown of Christ, not merely distinguishing Christianity from
Judaism and Paganism, but setting Christian unity high above all reli-

---

37 Only Christian will is free will because it has been freed from slavery to sin. Unre-
generate will is tethered to sin through natural self-concern, the concern of the
flesh.

gions, even above the idea of religion itself, and revealing the mystery of actual Christian unity in the Triune God to be both the original seed of the religious urge revealed in antiquity, and the final purpose of religious fulfillment at the end of history.

10. THE ABSOLUTE RELIGION IN WHICH ALL OTHERS CULMINATE—THE RELIGION THAT IS JESUS CHRIST HIMSELF

It is the holistic wholeness of Christianity that shows it to be the absolute religion, the ultimate faith of humanity, and the form of piety in which the consciousness of an imperishable nature may take for its motto: "Jesus Christ, the same yesterday, today, and forever" (Heb. 13:8).

Religion is the bond of love between God and humanity. It begins as the expression of God's love for man (humanity, individually, and corporately), and culminates as man's love for God, which completes the circuit of the Holy Spirit. The perfect religion must be the perfect expression or manifestation of love, the greatest sacrifice of the greatest life for the greatest good of the greatest number of people. This is found only in Christ. His mission, to be given up to suffering and death, proceeds from God's everlasting love. God did not spare what He loved the most—His only begotten Son, in order to restore the lost wholeness of humanity that was broken by sin. That wholeness could only be restored as it has been broken, by both the archetypal man, Adam, and by each individual who lived in the likeness of Adam. The corporate whole was broken by the first individual or type, Adam, and the renewed corporate whole would be restored by succeeding individuals in the finest individual or type, Jesus Christ. Christ's love embraced the highest sublimity and the lowest simplicity in order to unify the grand diversity of humanity in Himself. His humanity is essential for His divine Oneness that is manifest in the Trinity.

The subjectivity of Christ's personal love, passion, and will on the cross is perfectly identified with the objectivity of God's justice and judgment for the cross. So, Christians follow Christ by the intentional imitation of the Master, by identifying our own subjectivity, our desires and will, with the objectivity of Christ's desire for His people, best exemplified in Scripture alone. As He unreservedly gives Himself to God for death through the power of God's love, He simultaneously gives Himself to humanity for life through the same power of love.

His death and resurrection is[38] our unity. They are distinct but not different. He Himself, His life, is the most perfect expression of love from God to man and from man to God, individually and corporately. He is the center of love that circumscribes regenerate humanity. His person is the "well of water springing up into everlasting life" (John 4:14). No other religion has any parallel or resemblance to the depth and height of Christianity.

Only in Christianity is God known as Love, where humanity's love for God is derived from God's love for humanity where love for one another is made identical with love for God. Only in Christianity is the lack of love for neighbor equivalent to the sin of murder. The world has not, nor can it ever, improve the perfection of Christianity, biblically conceived. Christ is simply without parallel in human history, nor will there ever be another like unto Him. Nor can Christ's work of atonement and redemption ever be repeated because He atoned for all sin and has redeemed the wholeness of humanity. Christianity, the utmost summit of religion, cannot be transcended.

Upon the full-orbed fellowship of this love rests the moral and spiritual union between God and man. In Christ, the Spirit of God functions without limitation or restraint. Christ's will was fully pervaded by the divine will.

> "I seek not my own will but the will of him who sent me" (John 5:30). "I and the Father are one" (John 10:30).

The unity between God and Jesus Christ is complete, perfect, whole, and holistic. And it is the character and reality of its wholeness that makes it available to others. It cannot be unavailable to any individual without losing its wholeness. Its wholeness necessitates its universal availability. However, universal availability is not equivalent to universal application. Because union with Christ involves the union of divine and human will, and will has a conscious element, Christian unity must be conscious unity in order to be whole and complete.

Speculative philosophy suggests that the consciousness of this unity is to be considered merely as a new point reached in the process of world-thought, either in the mind of Christ Himself or by the church in its zeal to glorify His person.[39] The human impulse for unity

---

38 Singular tense because of the oneness of unity, not a plural tense.
39 A reference by Nevin to German idealism, a philosophical movement that emerged in Germany in the late 18th and early 19th centuries. It developed out of the work of

with the divine was most perfectly actualized in the life of Jesus Christ. So, whether that impulse finds its origin in divinity or humanity, it remains uniquely satisfied in Christianity, and even as a conception it cannot be surpassed by anything higher in religion.

Even if religion is nothing more than thought devoid of empirical reality, it has reached its crowning height in Christianity. Were such a thought to actually achieve religious perfection, it would require actualization, for the very definition of perfection requires it. In this way, Christianity stands opposed to modern speculative philosophy because it exhibits the actuality of Jesus Christ as an historical fact.

Speculative philosophers can only imagine that their speculations correspond to the actuality of reality. In Christ, however, speculation must stop because mere speculation can never come to a right conception of actual unity. Speculative thought cannot actualize itself through speculation. Thus, speculation substitutes the idea of divine and human identity for the actuality of divine and human union in Christ.

If humanity is the manifestation of God in His essential nature, there is no room to speak of his becoming one with God. One cannot *become* what one already essentially is. Thus, the argument for divine/human identity cannot escape the fact that it is no more than an idea that is devoid of actuality. It is without substance or consequence. Of course, the reality of the idea is claimed for the human race as a whole, but the whole of the race is composed of individuals, which are thought to be copies that include the essence of divine identity. However, if even one such copy proves to be less than perfectly identical with the fullness of God's perfection, the theory ends up equating imperfection with perfection. Pure perfection cannot be plagued with such blatant contradiction. It is not possible for such an idea to be perfectly manifested in actuality.

Thus, speculation occludes the light of God in Christ that is actually shinning like the sun in the moral firmament, and offers candles of wax in its place. Regardless of their number, the totality of such candles cannot come anywhere near equaling the intensity of the sun. On

---

Immanuel Kant and was closely linked both with romanticism and the revolutionary politics of the Enlightenment. The best-known thinkers in the movement were Johann Fichte, Friedrich Schelling, and Georg Hegel, while Friedrich Jacobi, Gottlob Schulze, Karl Reinhold, and Friedrich Schleiermacher were also major contributors.

the contrary, if this idea of union between the divine and human is true, and the actualization of it is necessary for its perfection, then what is sought from cardinal totality can only be found in ordinal individuality. Because the whole is necessarily greater than the sum of its parts, the whole must be of a different order.[40] Furthermore, the ordinal individuality of the whole must be actual in order to be perfect.

Everything necessary for the union of divinity and humanity is present in the life of Jesus Christ. In His person the perfect consummation of actual union with God is evidenced, not merely in speculative thought, but in actual history. All that remains is that the theanthropic[41] life that is constituted in the Redeemer Himself is actually manifest in humanity in the actual world in which we live. In other words, His willing substitution of His life for ours on the cross needs to be met by our willing substitution of our lives for His in actuality. Because He initiated the process of substitution on the divine side, our substitution on the human side cannot fail to reach perfection in God because it began in perfection in God. On this ground Christianity is the ultimate human religion in which all other religions are mere sects that can realize their wholeness only in Christianity. Thus, the manifestation of Christianity restores the wholeness that is sought by other religions, including speculative philosophy. God and humanity are one only in the Trinitarian unity of Christianity, equally universal, equally particular, and equally eternal. This ultimate religion alone provides for the actual unity of the human race.

11. THE TRUE CENTER OF THE CHRISTIAN SYSTEM FROM WHICH ALL ITS PARTS GAIN THEIR RIGHT PORTION AND LIGHT

It is from this point of view that everything in Christianity can be best arranged and understood. This final conclusion regarding religion in general also serves as the central presupposition upon which to set each element of Christianity in order to understand it to the fullest degree, in its truest light, and in its proper position regarding both human history and individual fulfillment.

---

40 In set theory, an ordinal number is the order type of a well-ordered set. Two ordered sets X and Y have the same order type when they are order isomorphic. When two sets are order isomorphic, they are "essentially the same" in the sense that one of the orders can be obtained from the other by the substitution of one for the other.

41 Theanthropic: both divine and human in nature or quality.

Regarding Doctrine

This logical and historical conclusion or presupposition, as has been demonstrated, is not the *sine qua non* of Christianity. Though it is both important and significant, it is not the crucial element that actually makes Christianity true. The heart of Christianity is not doctrine, but actual visceral life. The purpose of doctrine is simply to represent and exhibit life. Like the statue of Mercury with which the Alcibiades[42] of Plato compares Socrates, doctrine is merely the shell or hull, in which vital Christian unity abides, both in the divine person of the God-man, Jesus Christ, and in the individual Christian. The seed of Christian unity or union in Christ grows roots in the divine reality and branches in the human reality, but is always only one vine.

Self-revelation is the main purpose and object of Christ's work in the world. Of course, this includes doctrine, for human beings are creatures of the Word. However, Christ's doctrine, which includes the whole of the Old and New Testaments, always serves genuine, actual, Christian unity in Christ. Thus, any doctrine that falls short of this purpose cannot itself be the true, pure, whole, and holistic doctrine of God in Christ. Doctrine only has significance or value inasmuch as it serves the visceral life and wholeness of Jesus Christ Himself. True doctrine represents Christianity objectively, while genuine personal piety represents Christ subjectively in the lives of individuals. But the holistic wholeness of Christian unity brings this subjectivity and this objectivity into actualized union in Christ.

Therefore, Christian revelation, the revelation of the Trinitarian reality of God in Christ, is more full than the revelation of doctrine alone, though intimately and constitutionally connected with it.

---

42 Alcibiades, an ancient Athenian statesman, was criticized by ancient comic writers and appears in several Socratic dialogues. He enjoys an important afterlife in literature and art, having acquired symbolic status as the personification of ambition and sexual profligacy. He continues to fascinate the world and appears in several significant works of Modern literature. Nevin's allusion suggests that doctrine plays a role in Christianity like Alcibiades played in Athens in that it thinks itself infinitely more important than it actually is. This is not to say that doctrine is not important, only that too many doctors of doctrine have overstated its role. Unnecessary doctrinal fences must not be built because Christian growth and maturity through sanctification must necessarily crisscross various doctrinal positions on the way to genuine doctrinal truth. Because doctrine can be corrected, insufficient doctrinal positions in and of themselves must not be anathematized.

Christian revelation is not simply the speculative expansion of the knowledge of God abstractly considered. Because we live in a world where sin continues to play a significant role, doctrine that relies on human interpretation and/or authority is always susceptible to sin and error.

Thus, human interpretation and religious authority will be liable to error until humanity as a whole has come to genuine, conscious unity in Christ. Until that time, both objective doctrine and subjective piety must serve the reduction and eventual removal of sin, which is also called *redemption*. Christian doctrine, therefore, must serve the unfolding of an actual economy of grace and power for this purpose, a real manifestation of God in Christ that actively educates, enlightens, redeems, and sanctifies both the wholeness of the human race, and each peculiar, individual manifestation thereof in the ultimate, objective truth of God in Christ.

Bare words, thoughts, ideas, plans, programs, strategies, and/or abstractions are not sufficient to this task. Obviously, revelation of this sort—revelation of the Word of God—is superior to the revelation of mere nature (Romans 2:14). But mere words fall far short of the visceral reality of life, regardless of their degree of conformity to objective Truth. Only as Christian redemption consciously unifies the subjectivity of personal will to the objectivity of divine will, through which the many individual Christians are also unified in Christ, is the living God in Christ fully revealed in actuality.

In the Old Testament we find a necessary, preparatory, but shadowy revelation through forms, writings, doctrines, and religious practices that have faithfully served the end purpose of human union with the only existing, Triune God.[43] However, the actual, personal manifestation of the grace and truth of this union, as came to dwell among us in Jesus Christ, was necessary to establish its actual perfection. In this sense Christianity alone serves the actual manifestation of the will of God for the salvation of humanity. Christianity alone provides the complete revelation of the wholeness of the person of Christ as the Son of the Father of the Trinity, in word and deed, in life and death, in resurrection and exaltation.

---

43 See: *The Jewish Trinity*, by Yoel Natan, Aventine Press, 2003, which traces the Trinity in the Old Testament.

This actual redemption required the complete identification of divine and human will, and its actuality in human history by the individual person of the Redeemer. But for this very reason, He Himself, His ordinary person[44] and not mere doctrine about Him, constitutes the visceral fullness of the revelation of Christianity. Because this revelation is *in* Him, rather than being something apart from Him that merely comes *through* Him, it is not anything other than His life itself, in the undivided wholeness of His personality and history, His being and work, His doctrine, life, death, resurrection, and glorification at the right hand of God. All that we know about Christ, plus His entire actual existence, constitutes His wholeness. This necessarily includes all that He was and is and ever will be, as well as all that He has done and is still doing, as the Head of his body—the church, to the end of time and into eternity.

Christianity is also Moral Law

If however Christianity were only the words of law or even the ideas of law, it would not have transcended the order of Judaism, ancient or modern. Were it only the abstractions of law it would at best only be a reformed, universal Judaism, that could accomplish no actual freedom or renewed life. Because Judaism does not manifest the fullness of union of God and humanity in an actual human being—which it forbids by law, it would leave Adam's race under the curse of sin and guilt.

Law, however refined or complete, always remains law. It can never be more than rules imposed by an external authority. It can only influence people with the threat of exaction, accusation, condemnation, imprisonment, and death. Only the Holy Spirit can express sufficient love for people such that those who are loved are actually changed subjectively so that they personally desire and will to respond in kind. True love is truly irresistible, and more so with divine love, which is perfectly catered to the uniqueness of each individual personality. True love for another person wells up from within. It cannot be imposed, nor can it be described or controlled by rules. True love must

---

44 Ordinary: Not exceptional in any way especially in quality, ability, size or degree, lacking special distinction, rank, or status (Gal. 3:28), having regular jurisdiction. Christ's ordinary person refers to his common humanity, not however of its lowest common denominator, but of a new common denominator—being *in Christ*.

truly issue from freedom of the will. God planted true love for the Father in the Son by the Holy Spirit.

Thus, Christ's love for the Father issued from His own individual, personal, subjective desire (John 10:17). The Old Testament law was not fulfilled merely by the identity of God's will with His own, but by the reality of His own personal, fleshly obedience in history. The identity of God's will with Christ's will required actualization in history in order to manifest the fullness of its perfection. Only then could the communication of that union be applied to anyone else. Only then was the substitution of Christ's ordinality applied to the cardinality[45] of other Christians. Only then was the archetype of Christ available to humanity for renewal and redemption.

In Christ, the law comes to be written in the hearts of individuals, thereby transmuting its objective authority into the subjective desire or will of its subject. By fulfilling God's Old Testament law, its objective demands are mystically transmuted into personal, subjective desires, first for Jesus Christ Himself, but also and necessarily for all who become consciously united with Christ—His body or church.

To see Christianity itself as being constituted by God's law is not completely wrong because there are legal and judicial elements of Christianity, particularly related to unrepentant sinners. That is to say that unrepentant sinners are condemned by the authority and jurisdiction of God's law because they themselves refuse to recognize the reality of Christ's wholeness, His ability to effect God's propitiation, or the reality of sin and their own need for redemption, or the truth regarding the place of religion in the life of humanity. Indeed, God does not treat all people, all sinners, the same. Repentant sinners, those who consciously recognize and respond with love of God's wholeness in Christ—however poorly, receive the wholeness of God's grace. Those who consciously deny God's wholeness in Christ—however lightly, receive the wholeness of God's judgment.

The wholeness of God's grace does not contradict or contravene the wholeness of God's judgment against sin precisely because the will of God is identified with the will of Jesus Christ, thereby allowing for the substitutionary atonement of the individuality of Christ for the wholeness of humanity. Consequently, only those who are included in

---

45 An intentional play on the idea of ordinal and cardinal numbers, and the reality of these categories.

the wholeness of humanity defined by God alone are included in the wholeness of humanity who are actually redeemed.

The cardinality of the number of redeemed individuals cannot be known by the redeemed themselves because they are redeemed into eternity, and eternity plays havoc with (is of a different order than) temporal mathematics and cardinal identities. Thus, the best and most productive way to describe the cardinal number of the redeemed is to say that it is without limit. Because the magnitude of the number is impossible to determine, the redeemed are filled to overflowing with their new ordinal identity regarding the wholeness of humanity with Christ.

Again, Christianity equals atonement plus redemption. Because Christianity alone actually frees people from sin and damnation, human freedom becomes real only in Christianity. Human freedom has its highest expression and deepest foundation in the unity of Christ with God. Judaism has no power to set people free in this way. Salvation in Judaism is a matter of community inclusion through symbolic provision, but could not actually remove or atone for sin or establish the wholeness of human life because of its less than universal conception of community.

Judaism is not to blame for the incompleteness of the Old Testament. Indeed, it is to be appreciated and held in high esteem for the preservation of the Old Testament and its steadfast commitment to God's law, because actual redemption could never manifest apart from these things. Nor could it manifest within the circumscription of these things because God himself is not circumscribed by them. The wholeness and perfection of God is greater than the Old Testament, greater than the Mosaic Law, greater than but not different from monotheism, greater than any human conception regarding the inclusiveness of the wholeness of humanity. Rather, the wholeness and inclusiveness of humanity can only determined by God in Christ alone because God in Christ alone is in unity with God.

Actual unity with God required the medium of an actual individual person, to enter freely into a communion of life through substitutionary atonement with the subjects of redemption. Such a communion could manifest perfectly only as the law of God that condemned humanity to damnation for Adam's sin was satisfied for all of humanity by the death of humanity as a whole, *or* by the One in whom the wholeness of humanity exists. Either of these deaths would atone for the sin because of the legal definition and practice of substitutionary atonement in the Bible.[46]

Christ being of infinite value as the Son of God propitiated God by his self-sacrifice, which canceled God's demand for the death of humanity, freeing humanity from the curse of God's law. Christ's own personal human self-sacrifice satisfied God because the wholeness of the ordinal Person of Christ includes the wholeness of human cardinality. Thus, the substitution functions in both directions across the equation. *Us in him*, and *him in us* are equivalent expressions of equivalent value. The substitution is bidirectional.

Thus, all of the curses that were abolished by Christ's redemption, and all of the blessings that it has and yet will produce are actualized through the wholeness of Christ's Person. Indeed, the actual life of Christ includes the whole of humanity from creation to eternity because of His divine nature. Divinity is not burdened or limited by temporality.[47]

Only one who is Himself morally free can represent or impart freedom to others. Furthermore, He who can set all humanity free, must necessarily be sinlessly perfect and fully united with God. He must have the jurisdiction, the authority, the power, and the will to do so. Such a person or life, overflowing with divine blessedness and love, must include in its essential constitution equivalency with the Person of God himself, equivalency with the wholeness of humanity, equivalency with the individuality of an actual human being. Only the constitution of Jesus Christ contains such equivalencies.

Only through these equivalencies can the wholeness of the divine will of God be substituted for the individuality of an individual will. Thus, this substitution of One will by another unites the subjectivity of human will with the objectivity of God's will through one act of substitution. And so, the conscious desire of Christ becomes the con-

---

46 According to Genesis 22:13, a ram was offered in place of Isaac. This was a substitutionary sacrifice. Further, there is a prophecy of the atoning work of Christ in Isaiah 53:4-5, where Jesus was prophesied to bear our sorrows, to be smitten of God (which is what is due us, the sinners), and that our chastening fell upon him. What was due to us, because of our sinfulness, is what fell upon Christ. Substitution is only valid when there is an equivalence of some kind between the thing and the substitute. Reconciliation requires that the thing and the substitute be of equal value to the account holder—God.

47 Temporality: The worldly possessions of a church. Christ possess His church like a head possesses a body.

scious desire of Christians such that Christians are self-motivated to conformity to Christ's will for His people to actually practice and manifest the character of Christ as it is revealed in the Bible. In addition, the divine constitution of Christ makes it impossible that Christ's wholeness can ever be impaired or exhausted.

Redemption requires atonement, pardon for sin, and peace with God, which is defined as human peace because of the composition of Christ's character. Such reconciliation can be effected only by an actual human individual in whom the love and grace of God are identical with God's desire for the holistic wholeness of life, which at every level and in every way provides a web of cooperative interactivity among the various parts, kinds, and creatures of life. It also provides individual communion with the divine person or life Himself.

Jesus Christ is in tangible unity or common union with God, and the ability to perceive that unity creates a sort of moral gravity that draws people into common union (communion) with Christ. The original unity of Christ with the Father in the Trinitarian Godhead is the basis and model for the atonement or restoration of union between humanity and God in Christ. By paying close attention to Paul's words we see that "God was in Christ, reconciling the world to himself" (2 Cor. 5:19). Paul clearly said that the existence of God in Christ was and still is the first cause of unity and atonement flows necessarily and completely from that first cause as an effect.

Everything else in Christianity finds its context and meaning from the unity of the Trinitarian Godhead. In the unity of the Trinitarian Godhead Christian theology and anthropology also find a model for unity, common cause, and common concern, so that they do not war against each other but find their common origin and purpose in Christology. In the unity of the Trinitarian Godhead God enjoys the highest and most unique glory for his condescending grace to lost sinners, and man enjoys the highest form of dignity and grandeur through growth in the likeness of Christ.

On both sides of the union (God's and man's) Christian revelation satisfies the deepest religious want (both lack and desire) of our ordinary human nature, restores to the spiritual world its inward harmony, and solves the mystical riddle of the universe.[48] The unity of God in

---

48   The mystical riddle must ultimately answer the question of God. What is God? What is life? How can anything exist? Nevin's age was flush with this concern and various answers were coming from Rationalism, science, Spiritualism, Theosophy,

Christ provides the only channel through which God works miracles because the actual contact or overlap of divinity and humanity involves the actuality of higher powers and laws.

Christianity is not remembering Jesus or using the stories of Jesus to motivate us to try harder or be better or avoid sin, etc. Christianity is the actual, living, visceral body of Christ in union with the Head of the body, Jesus Christ, such that the Head and the body (the church) constitutes one actual, living person.[49]

The resurrection of Christ in particular, the greatest miracle ever, can be understood as the natural and necessary consequence of the reality of divine perfection. God's eternal nature must be eternally actual in order to be perfect. Indeed, the life bond or covenant that unites the persons of the Godhead also unites Christ with his people, and provides the foundation for Christian eschatology, regeneration being the first stage of the resurrection of believers, which is the end or purpose of God's creation itself.

12. RECAPITULATION—MYSTICISM AND REFORMATION

What has been said here so far:

The specific, distinctive character of Christianity is not its doctrine, nor its morality, nor even its mere power of redemption. Rather, Christianity is the unique constitution, religious significance, and the actual life of its Founder, who alone unites divinity and humanity truly and perfectly in His Person. Doctrine, law, and redemption rest on the

---

etc. What these views all share is an underlying monotheism of one sort or another. Others who later contributed to this discussion include Friedrich Nietzsche, who suggested that the quest for meaning was futile; Ernst Haeckel, who promoted and popularized Charles Darwin's work in Germany and developed the recapitulation theory ("ontogeny recapitulates phylogeny") claiming that an individual organism's biological development, or ontogeny, parallels and summarizes its species' entire evolutionary development, or phylogeny; and William James, who denied the possibility of a unified answer, and thereby denied the possibility of absolute truth. These answers carried the day, and still enjoy popularity.

Nevin proposed that biblical Christianity alone can answer the question. And this book goes on to say that Nevin was right because Christianity alone is Trinitarian. The reality of the union of the Trinitarian Godhead is the answer that only regeneration in Christ provides.

49 While other Christian theologies agree in principle with much or all of this, Nevin goes on to say that the reality of Christianity is not the potential that Jesus Christ can work through His church, but that Christianity is the reality of Jesus Christ actually living through His church (1 Corinthians 12:12-14).

actuality of His life, both personally in Jesus Christ and corporately as the second Person of the Godhead.

In terms of doctrine Christianity appeals to human understanding. In terms of law, it appeals to human will. In both cases, it originates as something outside of people and is applied in a mechanical, cause and effect way. It works to change people by causing a secondary effect, an increase of knowledge and/or a change of behavior. In a sense, doctrine guides knowledge and law guides behavior, but in both cases the guide isn't natural to the person. In neither case (as doctrine or as law) does Christianity work to establish a primary cause that functions autonomously, such as changing personal abilities or desires. Neither doctrine nor law changes desires.

In contrast, the character of Christian redemption changes the soul, the heart or central purpose of individuals. It doesn't add to the old purpose, but revamps or replaces it so that the most fundamental desires, drives, and instincts become self-motivated to serve and achieve God's purposes. Prior to redemption the subjectivity of autonomy serves sin and selfishness. It remains subjective. But after redemption the subjectivity of autonomy serves the objectivity of Christ in God. The self-concern of a sinner is himself, but the self-concern of a Christian is the will of Jesus Christ.

Christ dwells in a person only inasmuch as everything in the person finds its primary reference in Christ. People are in union with Christ when they stop asking what Jesus would do as if they don't know, but they simply do what Jesus wants them to do because they do. People are in union with Christ when the habit of their ordinary behavior pleases the Lord. People are in union with Christ when they stop trying to please the Lord in order to gain his favor, as if they don't already have it in abundance. People are in union with Christ when they face an impossible task and say, "not what I will, but what you will" (Mark 14:36), or "not to do my own will but the will of him who sent me" (John 6:38), or "I seek not my own will but the will of him who sent me" (John 5:30).

Christianity is in the fullest sense organic,[50] in its nature. Christianity is a unique order or arrangement of life in Christ such that the self-concern of the individual is the genuine concern for the well-

---

50 Organic: being or relating to or derived from or having properties characteristic of living organisms.

being of humanity as a whole that reflects the integrity of Christ's desire, character, and behavior evidenced in the Bible. When the most fundamental self-concern of an individual actually serves the glory of God and His kingdom, his will is said to be unified with Christ's will.

From this center one's personal, subjective, self-centered desire is transformed into Christ's universal, objective, God-centered desires. Christ's objectivity then becomes fused to my subjectivity. At that point, doctrine becomes food, the threat of the law gives birth to the joy of obedience, the promise of reconciliation gives way to the confidence of redemption. In Christ Christians don't deny or degrade what is natural—body, appetites, pleasures. Nor do they oppose such things as if they are evil. Rather, in Christ such things are rightly ordered and related to God's purposes and enjoyed as sanctified fruit in God's kingdom. In Christ everything finds its proper orientation. In Christ the religion of humanity simply serves God's glory.

In any case, Christianity is both the only religion that actually redeems and the only religion that actually unites God and humanity. These two things both condition and complete each other. Redemption comes only through this unity, and the purpose of unity comes in redemption. The unity is subjective and personal, the redemption is objective and universal. Redemption is the heart and life of Christianity, unity is its head and mind. The understanding of Christianity as redemption comes more out of Paul's letters, the idea of union with God issues from John. Redemption is about overcoming obstacles and is more practical, unity looks to the end and purpose of humanity and is more mystical and theological. Redemption has to do with faith and hope—becoming, unity with love—being.

Because redemption starts from the union of God in Christ and leads to the unity of humanity in him as its ultimate purpose, and because redemption ceases when there is no more sin, while unity like love can never fail, and because redemption is tethered to time and the present state of the world, while union with God is eternal, bridging the alpha and the omega in its wholeness, unity is the *sine qua non*, the foundation and crown of Christianity. Unity outlives redemption and is therefore more fundamental.

In conclusion, only the religion of Christianity actualizes what all other religions can only hope for—the union of God and humanity in Christ. This union is the constitution of a new organic creation, a new creature that has a unique kind or type of life in the world. This new kind or type of life works its way into the world by working its way out from the heart of humanity, by doctrine and moral initiative, by redemption and reconciliation, utterly changing people as individuals and as a race in order to fulfill destiny—God's declarative will, into union with God in Christ. This is the substance of communion with Christ, whereby all life is sanctified and exalted into a higher order of existence.[51]

This view of Christianity is not completely new, though some of the texture and subtleties could not be articulated until the modern era. The origin of this view goes back to Genesis, and to God's decree prior to creation. So, it is no surprise that it can be found in bits and pieces from time immemorial, and in the early expressions of the ancient church. The idea that a mystery lies at the center of Christianity is original to Christianity itself.

While it is beyond the scope of the present volume to review it in its entirety, it is significant that it appeared in various forms of Christian Mysticism. Of particular concern is its expression in Germany during the Middle Ages. Its most serious and consistent expositor was Meister Eckhart.[52] For Eckhart the union of God and man through the incarnation of God and the deification of the man, provides the central concern of the religion of Jesus Christ. In this regard, as well as in its treatment of Christianity, Eckhart's Mysticism has a striking affinity with the modern speculative philosophy, except that Mysticism finds

---

51 The idea of higher order is at the heart of mysticism. It is also related to modern mathematical set theory, which applies to this discussion because we are discussing membership in the body of Christ, and said membership can be considered in terms of a well ordered set. The modern study of set theory was initiated by Georg Cantor and Richard Dedekind in the 1870s.

52 Eckhart von Hochheim (1260-1327), commonly known as Meister Eckhart, was a German theologian, philosopher and mystic. *Meister* is German for *Master*, referring to the academic title *Magister in theologia* he obtained in Paris. Coming into prominence during the decadent Avignon Papacy and a time of increased tensions between the Franciscans and Eckhart's Dominican Order of Friars Preachers, he was brought up on charges later in life before the local Franciscan-led Inquisition.

Tried as a heretic by Pope John XXII, his *Defence* is famous for his reasoned arguments to all challenged articles of his writing and his refutation of heretical intent. He purportedly died before the verdict was received, although no record of his death or burial site has ever been discovered. He was well known for his work with pious lay groups such as the Friends of God and succeeded by his more circumspect disciples of John Tauler and Henry Suso. In his study of medieval humanism, Richard Southern includes him along with Saint Bede the Venerable and Saint Anselm as representative of the intellectual achievement of the Middle Ages.

its source in Jesus Christ whereas speculative philosophy springs from the creative abilities of human thought. Speculative philosophy is secular, whereas classical Mysticism is necessarily Christian.

The general point of coincidence between the *Mystical Presence* and classical Christian Mysticism is that Mysticism transfers the objective elements of religion into the personal, subjective, human spirit. Doing so allows both aspects (human and divine) to lose their proper proportion and reality through the suggestion of ontological identity rather than moral union. In both, the objective, historical reality of Christ is mystically transformed into the actual, subjective reality of the individual. Here Christ is not simply the thought of an objective Savior who lived a long time ago, but Christ Himself actually becomes the Redeemer who actually lives in the redeemed person through regeneration.[53]

Here again, however, we must take care not to stray into heresy. There are three classic heresies to avoid:

1. The denial of Christ's Divinity—which lead to Ebonism, Arianism (Jehovah's Witnesses), Nestorianism, Socinianism, Liberalism, Humanism, Unitarianism.
2. The denial of Christ's two natures—which lead to Monophysitism, Eutychianism, Monothelitism. These all confuse the two natures of Christ by absorbing one of His natures into the other.
3. The denial of Christ's humanity—which lead to Docetism, Marcionism, Gnosticism, Apollinarianism, Monarchianism, Patripassianism, Sabellianism, Adoptionism, Dynamic Monarchianism.

Discussion of each heresy is beyond the scope of this book. Rather, we will focus on the general tendency of all heresy to collapse one or the other of Christ's natures into the other. Eutychianism leads to the divination of man. The other tendency, Apollinarism or Apollinarianism holds that Christ had a human body and a human "living principle," but that the Divine Logos was the "thinking principle," analogous but not identical to what might be called a *mind* today.

---

53 A human being is more than an individual human body. No individual human body can live apart from the social structures of human society. Thus, the structures of society are a necessary part of a human being, and these structures are necessary for actual life. Human beings reflect God's Trinitarian character, poorly and through a glass darkly—but actually.

Apollinarism leads toward framing Christianity as if it is no more than moral persuasion.

Meister Eckart was a pantheistic mystic, a Christian Neoplatonist and a Eutychist who understood God to be essentially fecund, creative, sort of like a seed. He saw Jesus as the "first of a kind" who was creating others just like himself. Evolutionary ascent into godhood is a very ancient idea that is found in many other religions. Eckhart was highly lauded by theistic minded philosophers and religionists involved in the various kinds of modern speculation that were proliferating in the nineteenth century.

From this perspective, union with God's divine nature is the product of thought or realization, which was a stage in the development of consciousness. Here Jesus Christ is understood to be only a human type or a Platonic form and without actuality. So, His history is only figurative and allegorical. Christ was thought to be the first who came to the sense of his Sonship in relation to God. So, by Christ people learn that they also partake of the same nature, and are in like manner (similarly, not identically) sons of God as Jesus was.

With Apollinarism the unity of Christ with God is regarded as the result of a free act of self-communication on the part of God, conditioned by the moral character of Christ, who accordingly carries with Him more significance as an historical prototype. His divinity is collapsed into His humanity. Here, union with God is brought about by Christ through His exclusively moral influence. Eutychianism, alternately, resolves the unity mainly into the exercise of abstract thinking. Apollinarism works to reach unity by an ethical and often ascetic practice. In Eutychianism the mystery involves the identification of God and man as a matter of nature or ontology. In Appolinarism, it is a matter of grace, made possible through the redeeming influence of Christ, by the self-discipline of mortification and a new inward life as a matter of moral commitment.

The pantheistic mysticism of Eckhart is the precursor and provides the pattern for modern philosophical speculation. Appolinarism, on the other hand, finds its pattern in the introspection and warmth of its religious life. It involves finding truth by looking within one's self, which prepared the way for the Reformation. In the Reformation emphasis on God's act of justification by grace alone, however, a new element was emphasized. The Mystics tended to overlook the darkness of human life: the pervasiveness and extent of sin and the need of redemption and atonement.

The consciousness of sin was powerfully awakened in Luther, and was emphasized heavily in the work of the sixteenth century. Consequently, deliverance from the power of sin, and reconciliation with God, were understood to be the main thing in Christianity because redemption in this Protestant theology could not be accomplished by an ideal image (speculation or abstraction), but only by a real person. Therefore, the historical Person of Christ was clothed again with new authority and prominence. And so the historico-ideal[54] was conceived to be the center of Christianity.

Still however, the Reformers overemphasized the fact that Christ was an actual redeemer and mediator in the flesh, but were not able to envision the wholeness of His Person or character, which alone accounts for His divinity or perfect unity with God. The uniqueness of Christ's perfect dual nature as human and divine allows Him alone to be the actual, human manifestation of the new prototype for the individual wholeness and integrity of human beings and the historical manifestation of God Himself who alone provides the mediation of redemption.

This brings us back to the fundamental insight and error of the mystics—the identification of God and man. The mystics were right that Christ enjoyed ontological identity with God Himself as the Son of God in the Trinitarian Godhead. Their error is in thinking that such ontological identity can also belong to other human beings—it cannot! The role and reality of Christ's person in human history is unique,[55] as is the role and reality of every individual person.

Nonetheless, as we reflect on the Truth of God from a twenty-first century perspective, which is more ripe and mature for the same reason that fruit matures on the vine over time, we do not want to lose the true and genuine insights of the Reformation. Reformation theology has made serious and genuine contributions toward human wholeness and the maturity of Christianity envisioned in Scripture. While heresy tends to collapse Christ's divinity into His humanity or

---

54 The unity of the historical and the ideal, the actual and the speculative, the real and the ideal.

55 See Aleph Null in *God Great Plan For The Whole World*, Phillip A. Ross, Pilgrim Platform Books, Marietta, Ohio, 2019, p. 231.

His humanity into His divinity, orthodox Christianity[56] holds that the uniqueness of Christ's Person consists in His eternal and historical role as the very Son of God in the individual Personhood of Jesus Christ by the power and presence of the Holy Spirit in His life.

The mystery of Jesus Christ is the reality of His humanity and His divinity in one historical yet eternal Person.[57] Therefore, we must hold and appreciate the historical contributions of Christ's church in every age as they contribute to its ripeness and maturity. Here, we will focus on two major streams and endeavor to consider their unique contributions to the Truth of Christianity without conflating or confusing them. There is value and a measure of truth in the mystical tradition of speculation, though it has erred on the one side. And there is value and truth in the more practical, earthy ordinariness of the Reformation, though it has erred on the other side.

We are endeavoring here to see Christ's Truth in such a way as to appreciate and unify what is true in both views without violating the uniqueness of Christ's divinity, Jesus' humanity, or the unity of God in Christ that is the church. In the same way that we can be united in Christ without becoming divine ourselves, and without devolving Christ's divinity into merely being a crutch of moral influence, so the truth and beauty of mystic speculation can be corrected by the truth and beauty of Reformation practicalities and applications. And simultaneously, the truth and beauty of the Reformation can be corrected by the wisdom and sensitivities of mystic speculation, rightly understood.

Thus, Christianity is the religion of unity with God in its Founder, and the union of believers with God in Christ. All of this, its wholeness, can be conceived and practiced rightly only when the true religion is found to rest on the inalienable Christian idea of a Personal

---

56 This is not a reference to the Orthodox Church of the East, but to the reality of a correct conception of Christianity that approaches errorlessness. It is a conception that does not collapse divinity into humanity or humanity into divinity. And therefore, it is both special in the sense of being unique and ordinary in the sense of being common, in the sense of establishing true Christianity as the model and basis for humanity through regeneration.

57 An ever present difficulty regarding the correct conceptualization of Christianity is the fact that it exists eternally in time. It brings the infinitude of eternity into the temporality of time, but any particular segment of time cannot contain the wholeness of eternity. So, all expressions of eternity in time and history fall short of the wholeness they intend to convey.

God, including Christ's personal propitiation, reconciliation, and redemption, and our personal repentance, faith, knowledge, and sanctification. All of these elements are of a whole cloth and must maintain their complete and unimpaired authority as dependent upon, but still indispensable constituents of the new creation in Christ Jesus.[58]

---

58 Nevin seems to be saying that there is an element of truth in the abstract speculation of the mystics, but that such speculation must be done in the light of the Reformation focus on human sin and the moral consequences of our redemption. In addition, Nevin seems to be concerned about the mystical emphasis of union with God apart from Christ, which tends to bring humanity into a divinity equal to that of Christ. The correction of this tendency is to emphasize a Trinitarian unity with Jesus Christ, which results in the fulfillment of our humanity rather than our elevation into divinity.

THE MYSTICAL PRESENCE

CHAPTER 1

Introductory Remarks

The *Question of the Eucharist*[1] is one of the most important belonging to the history of religion. It is central to the whole Christian system, including both doctrine and practice because Christianity is the living union of the believer with the person of Christ. This central fact of humanity is emphatically concentrated in the mystery of the Lord's Supper, which has always been central to the consciousness, history, reality, being, and practice of Christianity, and has always been celebrated with a character of sanctity (holiness) and solemnity (formality regarding promise-keeping), which is more important than any other Christian institution.

The sacramental controversy of the sixteenth century then was no mere war of words, nor the offspring of simple prejudice against Roman Catholicism, passion, or blind self-will, as some have thought. The Protestant Reformation belongs to the innermost sanctuary of theology, and has drawn from the central arteries of genuine Christianity. The spiritual heroes of the Reformation most certainly knew this. Because of this they had no right to overlook the question of the

---

1 Eucharist, from Greek εὐχαριστία (*eucharistia*), means "thanksgiving." The verb εὐχαριστῶ, the usual word for "to thank" in the Septuagint and the New Testament, is found in the major texts concerning the Lord's Supper, including the earliest: 1 Corinthians 11:23–24. The "Lord's Supper" (Κυριακὸν δεῖπνον) comes from 1 Corinthians 11:20–21. "Communion" is a translation of the Greek κοινωνία (*koinōnía*) in 1 Corinthians 10:16. Other translations are "participation," "sharing," "fellowship." Roman and Orthodox Catholics believe that Christ is actually present in the Eucharist, Protestants mostly don't. Nevin argued that the Catholics are right about Christ's presence, but wrong about how it happens. For a discussion, see the pertinent chapters in *Arsy Varsy—Reclaiming the Gospel in First Corinthians*, by Phillip A. Ross, Pilgrim Platform, Marietta, Ohio, 2006.

Eucharist which arose in their considerations, or to treat it as being of little importance. The Reformation left the question unresolved, and its lack of resolution has continued to agitate and disturb the unity of the faith.

The fact that this question seems to be so easily resolved by so many modern Protestants demonstrates that much of modern Protestantism has departed from the theological seriousness and depth of those Reformation heroes. The depth and commitment to the central issues of the Reformation is not a matter of academic clarification, as has been thought by too many, but is a matter of history, maturity, and sanctification that can be neither faked nor coaxed. With the ongoing revival of theology brought about by the various tools and perspectives of modernity,[2] there cannot fail to be a similar revival of interest in the sacramental question of the Eucharist. On the other hand, there can be no more certain sign of disease and/or rot in Christianity than the lack of interest in these things.

This question of the Eucharist, of the meaning and reality of Christian sacraments, divided the Reformation churches in two primary and as yet unreconciled camps. And what is more, both sections of the Reformation have seriously receded from the sacramental positions they originally took in the sixteenth century. This fact is most broadly and palpably apparent in the modern positions of the American Lutheran churches in the nineteenth century and since.

All who know that history are aware that the American Lutheran churches in their central character have entirely forsaken the sacramental position originally occupied by Martin Luther. Not only has the original Lutheran position been surrendered in favor of the now dominant Reformed position, but even the original Reformed position itself has deteriorated in the same way. We can measure the extent of this departure by learning that the original Protestant position was denounced in the days of Joachim Westphal[3] and Tilemann Hesshuss[4]

---

2   This is a reference to historical criticism, higher criticism, or the historical-critical method, a branch of literary analysis that investigates the origins of a text, that was born in Germany in the nineteenth century. But can also be extended today to its continuation in the work of Christians like Cornelius Van Til, R.J. Rushdoony, John Frame, James Jordan, Peter Leithart, etc.

3   Joachim Westphal (1510-1574) was a German "Gnesio-Lutheran" theologian and Protestant reformer. From 1571 to 1574 he served as Superintendent of Hamburg, presiding as spiritual leader over the Lutheran state church of the city-state.

4   Tilemann Heshusius (in German Hesshus or Hesshusen, 1527-1588) was one of the

as foul sacramentarian heresy. That original position is yet today considered by most Protestants to be no better than the Roman Catholic error of transubstantiation.

However, this falling away from the orthodoxy of the sixteenth century is not confined to the Lutheran churches. The position regarding the reality of the presence of Christ in the Eucharist that is still predominant in Protestant churches involves a similar departure. This can be seen in the various "symbolical books"[5] of these churches. Rationalism has undermined the high church understanding of the reality of the sacraments by treating them as allegorical or superstitious appendages unworthy of modern belief in the light of science. But since the high church understanding has deeper historical roots, the modern position must be seen as a novelty.

There is more to this issue than the simple substitution of one theory of the Lord's Supper for another. The doctrine of the Eucharist communicates the heart of Christianity as a whole, regarding both orthodoxy and orthopraxy. Consequently, any modification of the Eucharist in either doctrine or practice changes other elements of belief and practice as well, because of the organic relationship between doctrine (belief), liturgy (practice) and life.

Consequently, if the Reformation brought a new understanding of the Eucharist, that new understanding also changed other elements of Christian belief and practice. In fact, the whole of Christianity has been effected. There have been changes that have effected Christology, ecclesiology, and soteriology. It is not that changes in the doctrine of the Lord's Supper is the origin or cause of any such general theological revolution, but rather that the many changes brought about by the modern age have changed the way that various Christian

---

most energetic and pugnacious champions of scholastic orthodoxy. He identified piety with orthodoxy, and orthodoxy with *illocal con-insubstantiation* or "bread-worship," to use Melanchthon's expression. He stirred up strife everywhere, used the power of excommunication very freely, and was himself no less than seven times deposed from office and expelled. He tenaciously defended the literal eating of Christ's body by unbelievers as well as believers, and dissented from Westphal's coarse and revolting notion of a chewing of Christ's body with the teeth, and confined himself to the *manducatio oralis*. He rejected also the doctrine of Christ's ubiquity, and found fault with its introduction into the Formula of Concord.

5   This odd term used by Nevin can only refer to the various creeds and confessions that were written to sum and symbolize the faith. Consequently, "creeds and confessions" will henceforth replace it.

doctrines are understood, and the issues related to the Eucharist are the most significant.

This question of the Eucharist is therefore of great interest and importance. It is not a question of simple historical curiosity or of minor significance. It is a question of the utmost importance for theology and religion that no Christian is at liberty to ignore.[6]

To see and feel the truth of the assertion that the modern popular understanding of the Lord's Supper has seriously changed from the original Protestant position, we must know the original positions of the Protestant churches, both Reformed and Lutheran. Only then can we discern the differences.

However, our concern here is only with the doctrine of the Reformed Church. The Lutherans will have to sort out their own concerns. Our objective is to understand the doctrine the Lord's Supper as it was first taught in the sixteenth century. This will require a clear statement of the doctrine itself as found in the original sources, and secondarily we must see the evidence that this doctrine was in fact established authoritatively at that time.

---

6   "The eighteenth century came, and the same processes which were used for shutting out the invisible in every other direction were applied also in this. And yet tens of thousands of men and women in every part of Europe, would in that day have rather parted with their lives, or with any thing more dear to them, than with this feast. And now, in this nineteenth century, there are not a few persons, who, meditating on these different experiments, have arrived at this deep and inward conviction, that the question whether Christianity shall be a practical principle and truth in the hearts of men, or shall be exchanged for a set of intellectual notions or generalizations, depends mainly on the question whether the Eucharist shall or shall not be acknowledged and received as the bond of a universal life, and the means whereby men become partakers of it." Maurice's *Kingdom of Christ* (London, 1842.) Vol. ii., p. 72.

Section 1

Authority of Calvin in the Reformed Church

To obtain a proper view of the original doctrine of the Reformed Church on the subject of the Eucharist, we must study Calvin in particular. Not that he is to be considered the creator of the doctrine, he was not. It grew out of the general religious life of the church itself. It's Reformed manifestation opposed consubstantiation on the one hand, and the low Socinian[1] extreme on the other. Calvin, however, was the theological leader who first made the position most clear. The idea that Holy Communion is primarily symbolic came out of a misunderstanding of Calvin.

Relation of the doctrine to the view taken of Christ's union generally with his people

Calvin's profound, far-reaching, and deeply penetrating mind drew the doctrine from the heart of the church, exhibited it in its proper relations, proportions, and distinctions, provided a way that it could be understood, and clothed it with authority as a settled article of faith for belief and practice in the church. He is to be regarded as the accredited interpreter and expounder regarding it for all later times, and fortunately, there could be no better interpreter of its central importance. His instructions and explanations are quite complete and explicit. He treats the subject from all perspectives, and handles it

---

1   The ideas of Socinianism date from the element of the Protestant Reformation known as the Radical Reformation, and have their root in the Italian Anabaptist movement of the 1540s, such as the Antitrinitarian Council of Venice in 1550, and have developed into Unitarianism—though Nevin has more than Unitarians in mind.

under all forms, both didactically and controversially. So, we are left with no uncertainty about what he means at any single point.

Distinctions on the side toward Rationalism

Yet, Eucharistic theories tend to reflect the way that Christ is understood to be involved in the lives of His people. The liturgical structure of the Eucharist tends to follow and reveal the way that believers are understood to be related to Jesus Christ, and represents the significance and power of that relationship. Our understanding of the unity between Christ and His people informs our understanding and practice of Holy Communion. Thus, the original sacramental doctrine of the Reformed Church reveals the reality of a subjective, living union between believers and Christ by which they are incorporated into Christ's very nature. It is this vital existence in Christ that powers their common life in the church.[2]

The participation of the believer in Christ

Thus, salvation is a process by which believers are substantively, constitutionally, and mystically bonded together in unity literally *in* Christ as they grow into His likeness. It was understood that genuine, real and actual participation in Christ was bound up with the right use of the Lord's Supper. Eucharistic unity provided a demonstration of Christian unity such that participation in one was identical to participation in the other. The following distinctions may serve to define and more fully explain the nature of the communion linkage between Christ and his people first taught by Calvin and practiced in the Reformed churches in the sixteenth century.

1. Not common relationship only to Adam

The union of believers with Christ is not simply that of a common humanity, as derived from Adam. In this natural perspective, every individual shares in one and the same nature, and people commonly

---

2   "Moreover, lest by his cavils he deceive the unwary, I acknowledge that we are devoid of this incomparable gift until Christ become ours. Therefore, to that union of the head and members, the residence of Christ in our hearts, in fine, the mystical union, we assign the highest rank, Christ when he becomes ours making us partners with him in the gifts with which he was endued. Hence we do not view him as at a distance and without us, but as we have put him on, and been ingrafted into his body, he deigns to make us one with himself, and, therefore, we glory in having a fellowship of righteousness with him" (Calvin. Inst. iii. 11, 10).

share human nature with one another, bone of his bone and flesh of his flesh (Gen. 2:23). We all share common human genetics. Christ shared this nature as well, because He didn't take the nature of angels, but of men. He was born of a woman, and appeared in the likeness and fashion of a human being, only without sin.

However, our relationship with and likeness to Christ is not of the same order as our common human genetics, but it is just as important, and even more so, because in Christ Christians become new creatures. In the same way that the creation of Adam[3] was the creation of a new kind or species on the earth, so the new creation in Christ is the creation of a new kind or species on the earth. But clearly the Christian relationship to Christ's nature and mediatorial work is quite different from membership in the biological human race. We are "members of his body" (Eph. 5:30), of his flesh and of his bones, but not in a biological, DNA way, like we are related to Adam. Rather, our incorporation into Christ brings us into a higher order of life that is necessarily corporate and corporeal.[4] Our relationship with Jesus Christ is not abstract or a matter of mere association, rather it is a real, actual, existing, and spiritual connection with his Person.[5]

2. Not a merely moral union

Union with Christ is more than simple moral union. Moral union is found where two or more persons are bound together by inward agreement, sympathy, and interaction. Every common friendship is like this in some ways. Moral union is the relationship of the disciple to the master, whom he loves and reveres. It is the relationship of the devout Jew to Moses, his venerated lawgiver and prophet.

Moral union also exists between the believer and Christ. The Savior is alive in his thoughts and affections. He looks to Christ with an eye of faith, embraces Him in his heart, commits himself to His guid-

---

3   אָדָם, 'ādām: Strongs' H119: ruddy, a human being (an individual or the species, mankind), man (of low degree), person.

4   Christian unity in Christ is necessarily social and corporate. Individuals cannot have a relationship with Christ apart from the body of Christ, the church. See footnote 30, p. 33, regarding cardinality.

5   Nevin cites Calvin, De Vera Partic. Opp. Tom. ix., Amst. Ed.. p. 726. "For we are members of his body, of his flesh, and of his bones. First, this is no exaggeration, but the simple truth. Secondly, he does not simply mean that Christ is a partaker of our nature, but expresses something higher (καὶ ἐμφατικώτερον) and more emphatic" (Calvin, Eph. 5:30).

ance, walks in His steps, and endeavors to become increasingly clothed with His mind and passion. In the final analysis, however, an interaction like this only involves a human to human relationship. Communion is more than this because Christians become like Jesus in all respects, one with Him morally in the fullest sense of the word.

But Christianity includes more than a merely moral union. It includes moral union, of course, but goes beyond it. Union with Christ involves a relationship that is more inward, subjective, personal, and deep. Union with Christ is grounded in the common life shared by Christians, where Christ and His people are one even before they become assimilated to His character.

So in the sacrament of the Lord's Supper it is not simply a moral approach that the true worshiper is permitted to make. The glorious object of Christian worship is more than a moral guide. Communion with Christ is more than the good engagement of the Christian's own mind, more than faithful behavior, more than contrition, hope, and love. There is nothing wrong with such solemn reflections, or devotional feelings, or pious resolutions. Such things may well be part of the sacramental service.[6]

Nor is the sacrament only a sign or symbol that is to be used to encourage devotion or remember something in the past. It is not to be used simply like a picture of a friend to recall his image and revive our interest in his person when he is gone.[7] Nor is it simply a pledge of our own consecration to the service of Christ, or a pledge of the faithfulness of God to provide grace and salvation, like the rainbow was given

---

6   "And yet my writings everywhere proclaim, that eating differs from faith, inasmuch as it is an effect of faith. I did not begin only three days ago, to say that we eat Christ by believing, because being made truly partakers of him, we grow up into one body, and have a common life with him. Years have now elapsed since I began, and have never ceased to repeat this. How base then was it in Westphal, while my words distinctly declare that eating is something else than believing, impudently to obtrude, what I strenuously deny, upon his readers, as if it had been actually uttered by me?" (Calvin. Adv. Westph. Opp. Tom. ix., p. 669).

7   "Some one will say, that the symbol of bread does not shadow forth the body of Christ any otherwise than a lifeless statue represents Hercules or Mercury. This fiction is certainly not less remote from our doctrine than profane is from sacred. Does not he, then, who, pulling us from our place, precipitates us into the same condemnation, destroy the distinctions of things, as if by shutting his eyes he could pluck the sun from the sky?" (Calvin. Opp. T. ix., p. 667). "Nor is Christ a painter, nor an actor, nor any Archimides, who merely feeds the eyes when objects are seen, but truly and actually performs what the external symbol promises" Ib. p. 727).

to Noah after the flood.[8] If this is all it is, it would be nothing more than a moral communication with Christ through the sacrament. If this is all it is, it would have no power or virtue beyond what the worshiper would bring to it himself.

Thankfully, the ordinance is more than this. It is not simply an occasion for believers to arouse pious feelings and religious desires because it embodies the actual presence of the grace it represents. And this grace is not simply the promise of God upon which we rely, but the very life[9] of the Lord Jesus Christ Himself. In the Lord's supper we don't simply communicate with an abstract divine promise composed of thoughts or words or memories of what He has done and suffered for our account. It is not simply an intellectual connection to a vivid sense of God's all-sufficient salvation, but is an actual communication with the living Savior Himself, in the fullness of His glorified Person, made present to us by the power of the Holy Spirit.

3. Not a union in law alone

The relation of believers to Christ is more than a mere legal union, which means that it includes legal union, and something more. Christ is indeed the legal representative of his people, and what He has done and suffered on their behalf is legally counted to their benefit, as though it had been done by themselves. Christians have a legal interest in His merits, a legal title to all the advantages secured by His life and death. But this external, objective, theonomous imputation of legality is mystically transformed into an inward, subjective, autonomous infusion of the Holy Spirit who establishes a real unity of life such that believers, one with another and with Christ, are in union. Apart from such infusion, imputation has no power or authenticity.

The Christian's personal interest in Christ's legal merits and benefits issues only from a previous interest in His Person.[10] In the Lord's Supper, where the unity of objective imputation and subjective infusion are celebrated, Christians participate, not merely in the advantages

---

8 "...the spiritual mode of communion consists in our really enjoying Christ; that the bread is a symbol of Christ's body; so that those who receive the sign by the mouth, and the promise by faith, are truly made partakers of Christ. Does he, by these words, prove it to be my doctrine, that the fruition of Christ is nothing else than the look of faith?" (Calv. Opp. T. ix., p. 667).

9 Life: the experience of being alive; the course of human events and activities.

10 The origin and order of this interest is ultimately caught up in the mystery of Christ.

secured by Christ's mediatorial work—the rewards of His obedience, the fruits of His bitter passion, the virtue of His atonement, and the power of His priestly intercession—but also in His true, actual, extant and proper life itself. We partake of His merits and benefits only so far as we partake of His substance.[11]

4. Not communion with His divine nature alone or with the Holy Ghost as His mere representative, but a real communication with His substantial, personal mediatorial life

Again, the communion in question is not simply with Christ in His divine nature abstractly considered, or with the Holy Spirit merely as the representative of His presence in the world. Communion does not consist in the mere influences of the Spirit by enlightening the soul and stirring holy affections and purposes in it. Rather, it is *in* Christ, who is himself *in* the Spirit, that we, who are also *in* the Spirit, are united to Christ, whose very life animates all believers.

The new life of believers is *in* the Spirit as its element and medium. And it is always bound in this element to the person of the Lord Jesus Christ Himself. Christ is bound in identity to the Holy Spirit in the Godhead with God Himself. Similarly, each individual Christian is bound in union with Christ by the Holy Spirit to God, and bound in unity with all other Christians. Our fellowship is with the Father and with His son Jesus Christ, through the Holy Spirit. Our bond is not a bond of identity as is Christ's, but is the bond of union and unity in fellowship.

These bonds are real because they actually exist among real flesh and blood people, who also enjoy a real bond to God in Christ

---

11 "I say, then, that. by that body which hung on the cross our souls are invigorated with spiritual life, just as our bodies are nourished by earthly bread" (Calv. Opp. T. ix., p. 668). And, indeed, I see not how anyone can expect to have redemption and righteousness in the cross of Christ, and life in his death, without trusting first of all to true communion with Christ himself. Those blessings could not reach us, did not Christ previously make himself ours" (*Inst.* iv. 17, 11). "Nor in the present day, when bidding pious minds rise up to heaven, do we turn them away from Baptism and the holy Supper. Nay, rather, we carefully admonish them to take heed that they do not rush upon a precipice, or lose themselves in vague speculations, if they fail to climb up to heaven by those ladders which were not without cause set up for us by God" (Opp. T. ix.,p. 671). "He has said, more than an hundred times, that the Supper is the sacred bond of our union with Christ. In defending our Agreement, I openly maintain that Christ effectually uses this instrument, in order to dwell in us" (lb. p. 125). "...that the bread is substantially the body" (lb. p. 732).

through the Holy Spirit. So, it is a real communion with the Word made flesh, and not simply with the divinity of Christ but also with His humanity because both are inseparably joined together in His person. A living union with Christ from one perspective implies the necessity of a living union with Him in the other perspective. Indeed, God's Trinitarian nature/character demands that the wholeness of Christ's Person not be torn asunder.

Accordingly, in the Lord's Supper the believer communes not solely with the Spirit of Christ or with His divine nature, but with Christ Himself in His wholeness, His eternally living Person. Believers are therefore fed and nourished by the reality of Christ's flesh and blood. The communion is truly and fully with the individual who manifested on this earth as Jesus Christ, and not simply with the divinity of Christ as the Son of God.[12]

These distinctions by Calvin serve to define and keep the Reformed doctrine of the Eucharist from erring on the side Rationalism. Great effort was taken to keep the truth and mystery of Christ's presence in the sacrament from being rationally explained away on one side, and from being turned into magic or superstition on the other. These various ideas about the believer's union and communion with Christ were explicitly and earnestly rejected as being too low and inadequate for the majesty of this great mystery.

In opposition to all such representations it was constantly affirmed that Christ's people participate by faith in Christ's very life. The Lord's Supper both symbolizes this mystery and actually involves communi-

---

12 "I am not satisfied with the view of those who, while acknowledging that we have some kind of communion with Christ, only make us partakers of the Spirit, omitting all mention of flesh and blood" (Calvin. *Inst.* iv. 17, 7). "I openly maintain that Christ effectually uses this instrument, in order to dwell in us. While Westphal borrows my words to expound the faith of the church, he at least gives me some place in the church. What new asylum, then, will he seek for himself? For who will consent to his fiction in regard to a gross partaking of the body? We, too, admit as well as he, that Christ denies his Spirit to all who reject the participation of his flesh" (*Opp. T.* ix., p. 669). "It is true that believers are associated by the blood of Christ, so as to become one body; it is true, also, that this kind of unity is properly called *koinōnia*. I say the same thing of the bread. I hear also what Paul adds, as if by way of explanation, that we who communicate in the same bread are all made one body. And whence, I ask, is that *koinōnia* between us, but just that we are together made one with Christ, under the condition that we are flesh of his flesh and bones of his bones?" (Ib. p. 726). "Such is Augustine's idea of the integrity of a sacrament, viz., that it is an effectual instrument of grace to us" (Ib. p. 729).

cants in actual participation in the reality of Christ's Person. Their participation is not simply in His ethereal Spirit, but also in His flesh and blood. It is not merely and morally figurative, but is real, substantial, and essential.[13]

But it is not enough to settle the limitations of the doctrine by answering the Rationalists. To be understood properly, it must also be limited and defined on the other side by answering Roman Catholicism.

NOT TRANSUBSTANTIATION NOR CONSUBSTANTIATION BUT REAL CONJUNCTION WITH CHRIST, THROUGH FAITH, BY THE SPIRIT

1. It completely excludes the idea of Transubstantiation

According to the Church of Rome, the elements of bread and wine in the sacrament are literally transmuted into the actual flesh and blood of Christ. The sensible properties and qualities of the bread and wine remain the same, but the original substance is converted supernaturally and mystically into the true body of the glorified Savior, which is then exhibited and received in an outwardly way in the sacramental liturgy. In addition, this transmutation of the elements is not limited to the duration of the sacramental liturgy, but is believed to be permanent. The bread and wine continue afterward to be the true body of Christ, and continue to be proper objects of veneration, worship and care, as is the their tradition.

This explanation was rejected by the Reformers as a gross superstition, even by the Lutheran Church. The Reformed doctrine describes no change whatever in the elements. Bread remains bread, and wine remains wine.

---

13 "...as the sacred Supper consists of the earthly symbols of bread and wine, so Christ I hold to be, as it were, the spiritual material which corresponds to the symbols. But when we have grown into sacred union with Christ, the fruit and utility of spiritual gifts flows from this, that his blood washes us, the sacrifice of his death reconciles us to God, his obedience produces righteousness and all the benefits which the heavenly Father bestows by his hands" (Calv. *Opp. T.* ix., p. 743).

2. It excludes the Lutheran idea of Consubstantiation[14]

According to this view, the body and blood of Christ are not actually converted supernaturally from the elements. The bread and wine remain unchanged in their essence as well as in their sensual properties. But still the actual substance of the body and blood of Christ are present in the administration of the sacrament. Christ's presence is not bound to the elements permanently, apart from their sacramental use.

Lutherans believe that Christ's body and blood are actually present, not in the elements, but "with and under" them, but only in the proper administration of the sacrament. So, they maintain the idea of sacramental mystery transcending all the common laws of reason and nature. And they maintain a true, bodily presence of the Savior in the sacrament. They teach that Christ's body is received by the worshiper orally "with and under" the elements, but not as common food. Consequently, Christ is received by both believers and unbelievers, but unbelievers receive Him to their own condemnation.

This explanation ultimately involves the ubiquity of Christ's glorified body. The bread and wine retain their ordinary nature, but Christ is present in His human nature in all places and times that He desires through the *idiom of communication (communicatio idiomatum)*. But Christ imparts His true flesh and blood, in, with and under the outward signs to all communicants, with or without faith, by the inherent power of the ordinance itself.[15]

---

14 Consubstantiation: A technical term used by non-Lutherans to denote the Lutheran view of the elements of the Lord's Supper. According to Lutheran doctrine, the bread and wine remain bread and wine; though, after the consecration, the real flesh and blood of Christ coexist in and with the natural elements, just as a heated iron bar still remains an iron bar, though a new element, heat, has come to coexist in and with it—an illustration which Luther himself used in his letter to Henry VIII. Lutheran theologians repudiate the popular term *consubstantiation*, in the sense that it suggests a permanent connection of the elements with the body and blood of Christ, and confine this connection to the time period of the communion liturgy. They also reject the designation of their position as *consubstantiation* because they believe the term to be a philosophical explanation of the Real Presence, whereas "Sacramental Union," their preferred term, is a mere description of the doctrine.

15 "We believe, teach and confess that in the Lord's Supper the body and blood of Christ are truly and substantially present, and that together with the bread and wine truly distributed, and we take it. –We believe that the body and blood of Christ is not only spiritually by faith, but also the mouth, not naturally, but heavenly and supernatural way, by reason of the sacramental union, when bread and wine are taken. –We believe that not only true believers in Christ who come worthily to the Lord's Supper, but also the true body and blood of Christ are taken unworthily by

In opposition to consubstantiation, the Reformed doctrine taught that the participation of Christ's flesh and blood in the Lord's Supper is only spiritual, and in no sense corporeal. The idea of a local or imme-diate presence was utterly rejected. The elements did not comprehend or include the body of the Savior in any sense. It is not in the elements, but remains constantly in heaven, which they believe is according to the Scriptures. Christ's body is not handled by the minister or taken into the mouth of the communicant. The eating of the spiritual body is not oral, but is only by faith. Accordingly, it is present only to believers through the exercise of faith. The impenitent and unbeliev-ing receive only the naked symbols, bread and wine, without any spiritual advantage to their souls.[16]

Thus the doctrine is defined and limited on both extremes with proper distinctions to keep it from rationalistic tendencies on one side, and for the speculations of Rome on the other. The Reformed doctrine allows the presence of Christ's Person in the sacrament, including His flesh and blood, so far as the actual participation of the believer is con-cerned. Calvin was even willing to employ the term *real presence*, if it was understood as synonymous with true presence, by which he means a presence that brings Christ truly into communion with the believer in both His human nature and His divine nature.[17]

---

infidels" (*Form. Conc.* Art. vii. Hose, Lib. Symbol, p. 599, 600).

16 "He says, that all we preach about spiritual eating, goes to aggravate our crime, because, according to him, it shamefully sports with Christ's little ones. Our exposi-tion is, that the flesh of Christ is spiritually eaten by us, because he vivifies our souls in the very manner in which our bodies are invigorated by food: only we exclude a transfusion of substance. According to Westphal, the flesh of Christ is not vivifying unless its substance is devoured. Our crime then is, that we do not open our arms to the embrace of such a monster." Calv. *Opp. T.* ix. p. 668, 669.

17 "We share in the body and blood of Christ, none of us denies this. However, we ask: what is the required nature of the body and blood of our lord in this communi-cation? That it be in the flesh. I wonder how to assert this simply and openly. When we say *spiritual* there is murmuring, let us remove this common response because the voice is real. We, on the other hand, because what is received is real, are opposed to the fallacious or imaginary, and speak strongly in opposition to combat and end the matter. I would have testified to this with calm and moderation, because according to us we enjoy Christ by way of a spiritual communication. We are con-tent with this way of reasoning, which for us is the life-giving flesh of Christ. Beyond this no one except a quarrelsome man will rise up because Christ is given by the spiritual into the souls of our life for us to also eat. When the body is one with Christ as our friend, faith grows to communicate to all" (Calv. Opp. T. ix. p. 657, 658). "Westphalus urges the presence of the flesh of Christ in the Supper: we

The word *real*, however, was understood ordinarily to denote a local, immediate, corporal presence, and was not approved because of this. To guard against this it may be qualified by the word *spiritual* to better conform it to the doctrine, as explained here. It is a real presence unlike the idea that Christ's flesh and blood are not present at all. It is a spiritual real presence unlike the idea that Christ's actual body is *in* the elements. It is not merely real, and not merely spiritual, but is both *at the same time.*

The elements of communion are simply eaten as bread and wine, and the symbols are received in a symbolic way. Nonetheless, what the symbols symbolize, the body and blood of Christ, are at the same time personally and supernaturally communicated for the real nourishment of new life in the believer. This new life in Christ is dependent upon the elements of this communication as much as the physical body is dependent upon food. The concern here is not with the material particles of Christ's body, but with the Spirit apart from which the particles are dead.[18]

The communion is spiritual, not merely material. It is a participation of the Savior's life, as a human being, existing in a true bodily form. The living energy, the vivifying virtue of Christ's flesh, as Calvin says, courses into the communicant and sanctifies the believer into deeper and deeper unity. Thus, the immortal heritage of Christ is brought to light and possession in the person of the believer.

Objective Grace of the Sacrament, including the actual life of Christ, particularly in His human character

There are two points that need further clarification. The first is, that the sacrament carries an objective power regarding its design. This power is not merely subjective, suggestive, commemorative, or representational. This power is not a sign or picture that derives significance from the mind of the beholder. The virtue of this power is not put into it by the faith of the worshiper, as if the virtue or right-

---

simply do not deny, as long as faith is engaged" (Ib. p. 668).

18 "Now, should any one ask me as to the mode, I will not be ashamed to confess that it is too high a mystery either for my mind to comprehend or my words to express; and to speak more plainly I rather feel than understand it. The truth of God, therefore, in which I can safely rest, I here embrace without controversy. He declares that his flesh is the meat, his blood the drink, of my soul; I give my soul to him to be fed with such food" (Calv. *Inst.* iv. 17, 32). "There remains, however, the man Christ in heaven" (Id. Opp. T. ix., p. 699)

eousness belongs to the believer. Nor is there any communication of this virtue or righteousness without the faith of the believer, either. Grace is not conferred mechanically or automatically. There is no *opus operatum*,[19] nor is the style of the liturgy sacred.

The faith of believers is merely receptive, not generative. Faith is the condition of its efficacy for the communicant, but not the principle of the power itself. The principle of the power belongs to the divinity of Christ which the elements represent. The signs are bound to the objective reality of what they represent. They are not simply in the subjective thought of the worshiper, but exist objectively because of the objectivity of Christ's divinity. The union is not natural, but sacramental and supernatural. The sacramental grace is imposed on the elements by the instruction of Jesus Christ, who imbued the sacrament with the power of His person. The grace is not *in* the elements like a nut is in a shell. Rather, the grace is in the nut like the life of the oak tree is in the acorn.

The grace cannot be separated from the sign. Whatever abstraction can be imagined about a thing and its essential properties happens only in our minds, not in reality. The reality of God's grace is whole and is truly present for all who receive it. In the case of the Eucharist, the sign carries the potential grace, like the oak tree is carried in the acorn, and the seal confirms the actual grace upon its delivery. Thus, the power of the Lord's Supper is objective because it continues to operate regardless of who receives it. The power does not depend upon the faith of the believer, the believer's faith simply serves as a conduit for the power and this, we say, is one point that must always be kept in view, in looking at the doctrine that is now the subject of our attention.[20]

---

19 Literally "the work wrought," a Latin phrase used to denote the spiritual effect in the performance of a religious rite which accrues from the virtue inherent in it, or by grace imparted to it, irrespectively of the administrator.

20 "Westphal cannot prove that Christ is prostituted indiscriminately to dogs and swine that they may eat his flesh. God ceases not to send rain from heaven, though the moisture is not received by stones and rocks (Calv. *Opp. T.* ix., p. 674). "Westphal's clear argument finds what no man would have suspected to be contained in my words. Beginning thus shrewdly, he calumniously misrepresents my doctrine to be, that if a wicked man approaches the table, virtue is no longer connected with the signs, though I have never said any thing of the kind. When he asks, what, then, will become of the word of the Lord which sets the same sacrament before all, whether good or bad, the same page contains an answer, which any man who has eyes may see, nay, which even the blind may feel. Besides, in the Agreement it is

The other point to keep in mind is that the spiritual grace of the sacrament is in the life of the Savior Himself, and particularly in His human nature because apart from His human nature that grace would not reach humanity. He became flesh for the life of the world, and our communion with Him involves a real participation in that life. The mystery of the Supper is that His flesh and blood are present with power that is received by communicants.

This is the doctrine of the Reformed Church as it stood in the sixteenth century, but labors under serious difficulties today. However, today's difficulties have no bearing upon the origin of the doctrine. The purpose so far has been to describe and define the doctrine itself. It remains now to show that this was in fact the accredited, established doctrine of the Reformed Church in the sixteenth century.

---

distinctly stated that the unbelief of men does not overthrow the faith of God, because the sacraments always retain their virtue; that thus, on the part of God, nothing is changed, whereas, in regard to men, every one receives according to the me sure of his faith. How careful I am to guard against any idea that the truth of God depends on men" (Ib. p. 699).

SECTION II

Reformed doctrine gradually established

The Reformed Church position, as distinguished from Lutheran consubstantiation, was not the product of any single man or any particular country. The great Protestant movement took root in different countries independently. At the same time, the differences between competing Reformed doctrines and confessions were not clearly and fully developed from the beginning. Rather, the doctrines grew in response to one another.

The Lutherans had a fairly developed system by the end of the century—the *Form of Concord* (1577). Similarly, the Reformed doctrine must be considered, not as it was at its outset, but as it was after its true substance and contents had come to be properly understood and defined, with proper antithesis to all the questions and issues that it raised.

Relation of Zwingli to the church

This being the case, we will not trouble ourselves with the opinions about the Lord's Supper of Zwingli, or Oecolampadius, or of the Swiss Reformed Church. The Reformed Church as a whole was not historically derived from Switzerland in any sense that it could be said to be legitimately bound by the theological views of the Swiss. Nor are we under obligation to consider the great Reformer of Zurich (Zwingli). With all his merits, entitling him as they do to the respect of the Protestant world through all ages, the relationship of Zwingli to the doctrinal life of the Reformed Church was mostly accidental.

79

This is shown by the fact that he left behind him no creed or confession of significance for any portion of the church. Therefore, we may not appeal to his authority as carrying any decisive weight.

Zwingli's view of the sacrament

Zwingli was not always consistent regarding to the Lord's Supper. Sometimes he appears to take the Reformed position, but we can doubt that he was satisfied with it because of his insistence that it was no more than a lifeless ceremony to induce memory and inspire commitment. His understanding of the sacraments was quite low, being without divine power, compared with the doctrine of Calvin, or the Heidelberg Catechism. Yet, sometimes he speaks of them in a way that sounds perfectly rational. He tells us:

> "We believe that Christ is truly present in the Lord's Supper; yea, we believe that there is no communion without the presence of Christ."

But at the same time Zwingli resolves the Eucharist into a common moral influence. For the sacraments have their value and efficacy, he says, a) they are venerable institutions of Christ, b) they are testimony to great facts, c) they are made to stand for the things they represent and to bear their names, d) these things are of vast worth, and reflect their own value on their signs, as a queen's wedding ring, for instance, is more than all her other rings, however precious besides, e) there is an analogy or resemblance between the signs and the things they signify, f) they serve as sensible helps to our faith and lastly, g) they have the force of an oath.

See his *Christianae Fidei brevis et clara Expositio*, addressed to the King of France shortly before his death, and published afterward in 1536: quoted by Hospinian, ii., p. 239-241. "I believe, therefore, that a sacrament is a sign of a holy thing, that is, of grace given already." Ad. Car. Imp. Fidei Ratio. "That it cannot be proved from the Holy Scriptures that the body and blood of Christ are corporeally present in the bread and in the wine of the Lord's Supper." De Vera et Falsa Hel. This is low enough, certainly, and in full contradiction to the true Reformed doctrine. Calvin went so far as to call it profane. See a quotation from a letter to Viret, in Henrys Leben J. Calvin's, vol. i., p..271: "Never his (Zwingli) law of all things. Perhaps at the end of life he revised and corrected that which first cut against his will. But in the earlier writings, I remember, were a profane opinion of the sacraments."

The Helvetic (Swiss) Church in the early years of its history had a similarly low view of the sacrament. They, too, were chaotic and contradictory. Theological investigation and discussion were needed to give them proper shape and form. This work was accomplished gradually and was completed about the middle of the century, through Calvin's work in Geneva.

To learn the true character of the Eucharistic doctrine of the Reformed Church in the sixteenth century, we must examine it after it was properly defined and settled in terms of church practice. Rather than interpret the later views in the light of the earlier, we should interpret the earlier views in light of the later because these later views had become more mature. This later form of the doctrine, as developed and enforced by Calvin, is the view found in the creeds and confessions of the church generally. And this view carried the day, maintained its authority, and is the view considered here.

However, this is not to suggest that the doctrine of the Reformed Church regarding the Eucharist was essentially different at the beginning from what it later became. The doctrine has been substantially the same from the beginning. Calvin did not bring in a new doctrine to supplant that which had previously prevailed. He simply contributed to its right understanding and full enunciation, which was already in practice. It is true that the process of clarification generated some confusion.

It is difficult to say exactly what Zwingli believed. His view was probably not clearly fixed in his own mind. Uncertainty and contradiction both appear in the Helvetic doctrine, which was completed after his death. But it is still sufficiently plain that the doctrine itself included more than the idea of mere symbolism in the sacrament. It has cried for a higher, more consistent expression, such as the doctrine brought forward by Calvin.

EARLY HELVETIC CHURCH

With all their opposition to Luther's idea of a bodily presence, the old Helvetic divines clearly taught that the sacraments have an objective force. The signs exhibit in fact what they signify. And this involves a real connection with the power of his whole life, by which believers are nourished with his very body and blood. This is a view that is much higher than that commonly entertained in our own time by those who pretend to agree with the faith of the original Swiss Church.

Confession of Basel

In illustration and proof we turn to the *First Confession of Basel,* published January, 1534, in compliance with Bucer's request to show the world that the Swiss were not liable to the reproach of "having the Supper without Christ." Produced originally by Oecolampadius, it was revised and improved by his successor, Oswald Myconius. *On the subject of the Lord's Supper,* Art. VI. (*Hospinian, Hist. Sacrum. Pars Altera*, p. 221,) it uses the following language:

> "In the Lord's Supper, (in which with the bread and wine of the Lord are represented and offered to us by the minister of the church the true body and blood of Christ,) bread and wine remain unchanged. We firmly believe, however, that Christ himself (*ipsummet Christum*) is the food of believing souls unto eternal life; and that our souls, by true faith upon Christ crucified, are made to eat and drink the flesh and blood of Christ; so that we, members of his body as of our only head, live in him, as he also lives in us; whereby we shall at the last day, by him and in him, rise to everlasting joy and blessedness."

The strength of this language can be reduced by two or three qualifying explanations in the margin. They remind us that it is only the soul that is fed and nourished in a spiritual way by the apprehension of Christ, and that the true, natural, and substantial body of the Savior is not present. The wording is ambiguous compared with later statements. But still it reveals something deeper in the doctrine than is intelligible by the words. The elements are more than mere signs and outward pledges. They actually offer what they signify, a real communication with the human Christ.

First Helvetic Confession

The *Second Confession of Basel,* more commonly known as the *First Helvetic Confession* was clearer. Written by Bullinger, Myconius, and Grynacus (1536) under the appointment of an ecclesiastical convention which had assembled in the name of the different Protestant cantons at Basel for this purpose. Authorized and made public, it speaks to the subject of the sacraments:

> "The signs called sacraments are two, namely baptism and the Lord's Supper. These sacraments are expressive of holy signs of high secret things; not however naked and empty signs; but they consist of signs and real things. For in baptism the water is the sign, but the thing itself is regeneration and adoption into the family of God. In the Lord's Supper or Eucharist the bread and wine are the signs, but the spiritual realities are the communion of the body and blood of Christ, the salvation procured on the cross and the forgiveness of sins. These real spiritual things are received by faith, as the signs are in a bodily way." Art. 20.

Here we see that the sacraments are not simply signs, nor merely pledges of grace unbound to their particular constitution. But they consist of real things as well as signs. There is an actual exhibition of these real things in the ordinances themselves. They are there independently of all thought or feeling on the part of the worshiper. Although, of course, they can only be owned by faith. Thus, baptism is described in the next article as the "laver of regeneration, which the Lord extends, by a visible sign, to his elect, through the ministry of the church." And then of the Lord's Supper, it says again:

> "Concerning the mystical Supper we thus judge, that the Lord in it truly offers to his people his own body and blood, that is himself, to the end that he may live more and more in them, and they in him. Not that the body and blood of the Lord are naturally united with the bread and wine, or locally included in them, or are made carnally present in any way; but that the bread and wine are, by divine appointment, symbols under which, by the Lord himself, through the ministry of the church, the true communication of his body and blood is exhibited, not as perishable food for the belly, but as the aliment of eternal life." Art. 23. (Niemeyer's Col. Cunf. p. 112.)

This Confession was later examined by Luther, Bucer, and Capito at Wittenberg the same year. The Strasburg divines sought reconciliation between the two confessions, and produced the *Wittenberg Concord*. Strangely, Luther pronounced the Confession to be orthodox, though it contradicted his own system, and falls short of Reformed doctrine, which was made clear later.

CALVIN

To better understand the doctrine under examination we must
consult Calvin. No authority has greater respect. He was emphatically
the greatest theologian of his age. More than others, he was able to
speak and clarify the mind of the church, in whose bosom he stood.
Calvin did not propose the private ideas only of a single man regarding the Lord's supper. Clearly, the history of the time demonstrates
that Calvin represented the authority and views of the vast majority of
Reformed Church in the sixteenth century.

It is not necessary to cite detailed quotations to show the true
character of the view he held, or its agreement with the doctrine previously described as the true and proper doctrine of the Reformed
Church in the beginning of its history. That is precisely what Calvin
himself did, and it is supported by copious references at every point
already. The difficulty here is not finding proofs and illustrations, but
to choose between the multitude that are available.

Calvin has written much on the Lord's Supper, and he is always
clear, consistent and true to Scripture. Time and again in every way,
he tells us that Christ's body is located in heaven only, and is not
included in the elements. Christ can be apprehended only by faith, and
not by the hands or lips. Nothing is to be imagined like a transfusion
or transmission of the material particles of His body into our physical
persons. And yet our communion with Christ by the power of the
Holy Spirit involves a real participation—not merely in His doctrine,
nor merely in His promises, nor merely in the feelings love, nor
merely in His righteousness and merit, nor merely in the gifts and
endowments of His Spirit—but in His own true substantial life itself.
And this not as understood to be merely in His divine nature, but His
presence is most immediately, peculiarly, and embodied in His
humanity itself for our salvation.

The Word became flesh, not simply for the purpose of effecting a
salvation that might become available in a demonstrable way, but to
open the fountain of life in our human nature itself, that will continue
to drench other people by streaming new life to the end of time. The
flesh of Christ, His humanity, is the medium, and the only medium by
which we are incorporated into His life. To have part in Him at all, we
must be joined to Him in the flesh—His and ours, and this relationship
with Christ is not like our common relationship to Adam, but is by the

power of the Holy Spirit a connection to the Person of Jesus Christ Himself.

Extracts from Calvin's Institutes

"That Christ is the bread of life," he says in his *Institutes* IV. 17, 5,

> "by which believers are nourished to eternal salvation, there is no man, not entirely destitute of religion, who hesitates to acknowledge; though all are not equally agreed respecting the manner of partaking of him. For there are some who define in a word, that to eat the flesh of Christ and to drink his blood, is no other than to believe in Christ himself. But I conceive that in that remarkable discourse in which Christ recommends us to feed upon his body, he intended to teach us something more striking and sublime; namely that we are quickened by a real participation of him, which he designates by the terms of eating and drinking, that no person might suppose the life which we receive from him to consist in simple knowledge. For as it is not seeing bread, but eating it, that administers nourishment to the body, so it is necessary for the soul to have a true and complete participation of Christ, that by his power it may be quickened into spiritual life. At the same time, we confess that there is no other eating than by faith, as it is impossible to imagine any other; but the difference between me and those whose opinion I now oppose is this. An evasion of the point of an argument by raising irrelevant distinctions or objections. They consider eating to be the same thing as believing; while I say, that in believing we eat the flesh of Christ, because he is made ours actually by faith, and that this eating is the fruit and effect of faith. Or to express it more plainly, they consider the eating to be faith itself; but I apprehend it to be rather a consequence of faith."

Again, (IV. 17. 8,) he tells us that Christ was from the beginning that life giving Word of the Father, from which all things have derived their existence. "In him was life," the source and fountain of all creaturely existence, even before he appeared in our nature. But this "life was manifested," when he assumed our flesh, to restore the ruin produced by the fall.

> "For though he diffused his influence over the whole creation before that period, yet because man was alienated from God by sin, had lost the participation of life, and saw on every side nothing but impending death, it was necessary to his recovery of any hope of immortality, that he should be received into the communion of

that Word. For what confidence can it raise in anyone, to hear only that the fullness of life is comprehended in the Word of God, a great way off, whilst in himself and all around nothing but death is presented to his eyes! Now, however, since that fountain of life has come to dwell in our flesh, it is no longer thus hidden from us by distance, but open to our reach and free use. The very flesh moreover in which he dwells is made to be vivific for us, that we may be nourished by it to immortality. 'I am the living bread,' he says, 'which came down from heaven; and the bread that I will give is my flesh, which I will give for the life of the world.' (John 6: 48, 51.) In these words he teaches, not simply that he is Life, as the everlasting Word descending to us from heaven, but that in thus descending he has infused this virtue also into the flesh with which he clothed himself, in order that life might flow over to us from it continually."

Again, sect. 10:

"We conclude that our souls are fed by the flesh and blood of Christ, just as our corporeal life is preserved and sustained by bread and wine. For the analogy of the sign would not hold, if our souls did not find their aliment in Christ; which however cannot be the case, unless Christ truly coalesce into one with us, and support us through the use of his flesh and blood. It may seem incredible indeed that the flesh of Christ should reach us from such immense local distance, so as to become our food. But we must remember how far the secret power of the Holy Spirit transcends all our senses, and what folly it must ever be to think of reducing his immensity to our measure. Let faith embrace then what the understanding cannot grasp, namely that the Spirit unites things which are locally separated. Now this sacred communication of his flesh and blood, by which Christ transfuses his life into us, just as if he penetrated our bones and marrow, he testifies and seals also in the holy supper; not by the exhibition of a vain and empty sign, but by putting forth there such an energy of his Spirit as fulfills what he promises. What is thus attested he offers and exhibits to all who approach the spiritual banquet. It is however fruitfully received by believers only, who accept such vast grace with inward gratitude and trust."

The following passage, sect. II, is worth particular attention because it brings some of the leading points of the doctrine clearly into view in a way that cannot be misunderstood or contradicted.

"I say then, (what has always been held in the church, and is still taught by all of sound belief,) that the sacred mystery of the Supper consists of two parts; the corporeal signs, which being placed before our eyes represent to us invisible things according to the infirmity of our apprehension; and the spiritual truth, which these symbols typify and exhibit. This last I am accustomed to describe in a familiar way, as including three things; the signification, the matter answering to this, and the virtue or effect which follows from both. The signification holds in the promises, which are in some sense interwoven with the sign. What I call the matter or substance, is Christ, with his death and resurrection. By the effect I mean redemption, righteousness, sanctification, eternal life, and all the other benefits which Christ confers upon us. Moreover, though all these things have a relation to faith, I allow no room for the cavil,[1] that, in representing Christ to be received by faith, I make him an object simply of the understanding or imagination. For the promises present him to us, not that we may rest in contemplation merely and naked notion, but that we may enjoy him in the way of real participation. And truly, I see not how any one can have confidence, that he has redemption and righteousness by the cross of Christ, and life by his death, if he have not in the first place a true communion with Christ himself. For those benefits could never reach us if Christ did not first make himself ours. I say, then, that in the mystery of the Supper, under the symbols of bread and wine, Christ is truly presented to us, and so his body and blood, in which he fulfilled all obedience to procure our justification; in order that we may first coalesce with him into one body, and then, being thus made partakers of his substance, may experience the virtue also which belongs to him, in the participation of all blessings."

Catechism of Geneva

The *Catechism of Geneva* was written by Calvin in 1536, (enlarged and improved in 1541,) for the use of the Geneva Church. Observe the following extract on the subject of the Lord's Supper:

Q. Why is the Lord's body figured by bread and his blood by wine?

A. To teach us, that such virtue as bread has in nourishing our bodies for the support of the present life, the same is in the body of the Lord for the spiritual nourishment of our souls; and that as by wine

---

1   Cavil: an evasion of the point of an argument by raising irrelevant distinctions or objections.

the hearts of men are exhilarated, their strength refreshed, the whole man invigorated, so our souls receive like benefits from the Lord's blood.

Q. Do we then eat the body and blood of the Lord?

A. We do. For since the whole hope of our salvation consists in this, that his obedience, which he rendered to the Father, may be placed to our credit as though it were our own, it is necessary that he himself should be possessed by us. He does not communicate his benefits to us except as he makes himself ours.

Q. But did he not give himself to be ours at that time, when he exposed himself to death, that he might reconcile us, being redeemed from the sentence of death, to the Father?

A. That is true. But it is not enough for us unless we receive him now, in order that the efficacy and fruit of his death may reach us.

Q. Is not the mode of receiving him, however, by faith?

A. This I allow; but add at the same time, that this takes place, not only as we believe that he died to redeem us from death, and rose again to acquire life for us, but as we acknowledge also that he dwells in us, and that we are joined to him with such union as holds between members and their proper head; in order that by the grace of this union, we may become partakers of all his benefits." (Sect. v., *Niemeyer's Coll.* p. 164, 165.)

Tract De Vera Participatione, Against Hesshuss

One more extract from Calvin will suffice. It is taken from a short appendix to his tract, *Of the true participation of the flesh and blood of Christ in the holy supper*, written against the virulent Hesshuss in 1561, near the close of his life. The object of the appendix is to set forth distinctly the points of agreement and disagreement, in the case of the sacramental question, with a view to ultimate concord. After stating the points with regard to which both sides were agreed, and touching upon the sacraments in general and the Lord's supper in particular, it states that Christ in the Supper really and efficaciously fulfills all that the analogy of the signs demands, so as to provide a true communication with His body and blood. He goes on to say:

"It remains to notice the points with regard to which it is still unsettled, in what light they are to be viewed or represented. All however, who are possessed of sound judgment, and approach the subject at the same time, without passion, must allow that the controversy is simply on the mode of eating; since we openly and ingenuously affirm, that Christ becomes ours, in order that he may afterward impart to us the benefits he possesses; that his body also was not only once offered for our salvation, when he was slain upon the cross to expiate sin, but is daily extended to us for our nourishment; so that while he himself dwells in us, we may have an interest also in all his blessings. We teach finally, that he is vivific because he inspires his life into us, just as we derive strength from the nutriment of bread. It is in fixing the method of eating then, that contentions arise. Now our definition is, that the body of Christ is eaten, inasmuch as it forms the spiritual aliment of the soul. We call it aliment again in this sense, because by the incomprehensible power of his Spirit, he inspires into us his own life, so that it becomes common to us with himself, in the same way precisely as the vital sap from the root of a tree diffuses itself into the branches, or as vigor flows from the head of the body into its several members. In this definition, there is nothing captious, nothing obscure, nothing ambiguous or deceitful.

That some, not satisfied with this clear simplicity, require the body of Christ to be swallowed, is agreeable neither to the authority of Scripture nor the testimony of the ancient church; and it is astonishing that men possessed of moderate judgment and learning, should contend so pertinaciously for the new comment. What the Scriptures teach is not at all called by us into question, namely, that the flesh of Christ is truly meat and his blood truly drink; since they are truly received by us, and avail to solid life. We profess also that this communication is exhibited in the Sacred Supper. Whoever insists on more, certainly exceeds proper limits."

Again:

"It is a vain dispute moreover that is made about the twofold body. The character of Christ's flesh was indeed changed when it was received into celestial glory; whatever was terrene,[2] mortal or perishable, it now put off. Still however it must be maintained, that no other body can be vivific for us, or may be counted meat indeed, save that which was crucified to atone for our sins; as the sound of the words also indicates. The same body then which the Son of God once offered in sacrifice to the Father, he offers to us daily in the Supper, that it may be our spiritual aliment. Only that

---

2   Terrene: of or relating to the earth; earthly.

must be held which has been already intimated as to the mode, that it is not necessary that the essence of the flesh should descend from heaven in order that we may be fed by it; but that the power of the Spirit is sufficient to penetrate through all impediments, and to surmount all local distance. At the same time we do not deny, that the mode here is incomprehensible to human thought; for flesh naturally could neither be the life of the soul, nor exert its power upon us from heaven, and not without reason is the communication, which makes us flesh of Christ's flesh and bone of his bones, denominated by Paul a great mystery. In the sacred Supper then we acknowledge it a miracle, transcending both nature and our own understanding, that Christ's life is made common to us with himself, and his flesh given to us as aliment. Only let all comments be kept at a distance that are repugnant to the definition already given, such as those concerning the ubiquity of the body, or its secret inclusion under the symbol of bread, or its substantial presence upon the earth.

These things being disposed of, a doubt still appears with respect to the word *substance*; which is readily allayed, if we put away the crass imagination of a manducation of the flesh, as though it were like corporal food, that being taken into the mouth is received by the belly. For if this absurdity be removed, there is no reason why we should deny that we are fed with Christ's flesh substantially; since we truly coalesce with him into one body by faith, and are thus made one with him. Whence it follows that we are joined with him by substantial connection, just as substantial vigor flows down from the head into the members. The definition must stand then, that we are made to partake of Christ's flesh substantially; not in the way of any carnal mixture, or as if the flesh of Christ drawn down from heaven entered into us, or were swallowed with the mouth; but because the flesh of Christ as to its power and efficacy vivifies our souls, not otherwise than the body is nourished by the substance of bread and wine.

Another subject of controversy is the word *spiritually*, to which many are averse, because they think that it implies something imaginary or empty. On the contrary however, the body of Christ is said to be given to us spiritually in the Supper because the secret energy of the Holy Spirit causes things that are separated by local distance to be notwithstanding joined together; so that life is made to reach into us from heaven out of the flesh of Christ; which power and faculty of vivification may be said not unsuitably to be something abstracted from his substance, provided only it be taken in a sound sense, namely that Christ's body remains in heaven, while nevertheless life flows out from his substance and reaches to us who sojourn upon the earth." (Calv. Opp. edit. Amslehd. Tum. xx. p. 743, 744.)

Common misrepresentations against Calvin's view

It seems strange in the light of these quotations that anyone should still think of calling in question Calvin's faith in the doctrine of a real communication with Christ's life in the Lord's Supper. It will not do to talk of figurative language, and to remind us that this matter is resolved by him into a spiritual feeding that is different from an oral and physical feeding. This is understood by everyone. He was no Roman Catholic nor Lutheran.

But if there ever was a clear case, we have one here. We affirm that Calvin's spiritual feeding was intended to include full communication as much as was involved in the Lutheran doctrine. It is a true participation of the substantial life of Christ's body and blood, according to the faith of the universal church[3] from its beginning.

To guard against carnal misconstructions, Calvin spoke of the ascent of the soul to Christ in heaven, through the power of the Holy Spirit, rather than by Christ's descent to the earth in the sacrament. But this doesn't change the substance of his doctrine. In whatever way it occurs, he held and taught the fact of a real presence of the Savior's human life in the sacramental transaction.[4] The sacrament was the true supernatural vehicle and bearer of the presence and communication of the Spirit.

The Lutherans pretended that Calvin acknowledged no inward connection between the institution and the grace it represented. But this is manifestly false. He does in fact say that the signs have no virtue or force in themselves as such. Augustine says the same thing. But both Calvin and Augustine hold the transaction to be more than what falls upon the senses.

---

3   Ancient Church, Roman Catholic Church, Orthodox Church and Reformed Church.
4   Nevin's use of "sacramental transaction" is of interest because it is historically understood to be a term of Roman Catholicism, not Protestantism. Rome's position is that the sacraments are material transactions which symbolize and effect a spiritual result. Nevin seems to be arguing for a spiritual rather than a material transaction, but a transaction nonetheless.

Calvin's statement clear and full

It is held to be truly and properly the form, under which and by which, Christ is made present through the Spirit. Thus on 1 Cor. 10:3, Calvin says:

> "The Papists confound sign and thing; profane men, such as Schwenkfeld and others like him, rend them asunder; let us keep the middle; that is, let us hold the conjunction established by the Lord, but with proper distinction, so as not to transfer rashly to one what belongs to the other."

So, still more clearly, on 1 Cor. 11:24.

> "Why is the appellation *body* attributed to the bread? All will allow, I presume, for the same reason that John denominates a dove the Holy Ghost. Thus far it is agreed. But now the Holy Ghost was so called, because he had appeared under the form (*sub specie*) of a dove; whence the name is transferred to the visible sign. And why should we deny a similar metonymy[5] here, by which the name of the body is attributed to the bread, because it is its sign and symbol."

Next he speaks of the meaning of the metonymy itself, and it is more than a figure or a picture.

> "The dove is called the Spirit, as being the sure pledge (*tessera*) of the Spirit's invisible presence. So the bread is Christ's body, as it assures us certainly of the exhibition of what it represents, or because the Lord in extending to us that visible symbol, gives us in fact along with it his own body; for Christ is no juggler, to mock us with empty appearances. Hence it is to me beyond all controversy that the reality is here joined with the sign, or in other words that, so far as spiritual virtue is concerned, we do as truly partake of Christ's body as we eat the bread."[6]

---

5   Metonymy: Substituting the name of an attribute or feature for the name of the thing itself.

6   F. D. Maurice, of King's College, London, in his late work entitled *The Kingdom of Christ* (1838), which has attracted some attention, falls grossly into the same error with regard to Calvin, which it is here attempted to expose. The Calvinist, he says, (vol. ii., p. 105,) "requires that we should suppose there is no object present, unless there be something which perceives it; and having got into this contradiction, the next step is to suppose that faith is not a receptive, but a creative power; that it makes the thing which it believes." He admits, at the same time, "that there were characteristics in the creed of the Calvinist, which ought especially to have delivered him" from the general tendency of Protestantism to run into this false view. So far as

TESTIMONY OF SCHLEIERMACHER

According to Schleiermacher (*Der. chr. Glaube*, § 140), Calvin's view of the Lord's Supper does not pertain to the elements as such, but to the act of eating and drinking, not simply the spiritual enjoyment of Christ that was taught by Zwingli. Rather, Calvin taught that the real presence of His body and blood had to be nowhere else. Both views, the Lutheran and Calvinistic, acknowledge a real presence of Christ's body and blood.

It cannot be imagined that such a theologian as Schleiermacher has misunderstood Calvin. It deserves to be noted that this great thinker, with all of his theological research, finds no absurdity or contradiction whatsoever in the Calvinistic doctrine itself. In fact, he prefers it to the view of Luther, though he also thinks the truth may still require a higher reconciling theory. The Zwinglian doctrine he says has the advantage of being very clear and easy to be understood, but it is far too worldly and unspiritual.

FAREL AND BEZA—COLLOQUY OF WORMS

At the Colloquy of Worms, 1557, various delegates came from the Reformed Gallic Churches, namely, William Farel, pastor at the time in Neufchatel, John Budaeus, a citizen of Geneva, Caspar Carmel, minister of the church in Paris, and Theodore Beza, then professor at Lausanne. They brought an important Confession of Faith that embodied, not simply their own views, but also the views of the

---

Calvin himself is concerned, it must be perfectly plain from the testimony which has now been presented, that the charge quoted is utterly erroneous. *He taught clearly an objective presence of Christ's life in the sacramental transaction as such, which could become available only through faith, but which faith could not be said, in any sense, to create;* since the very guilt of the unworthy communicant proceeds mainly from this, that he treats the actually present grace as though it were a mere figment, not discerning the Lord's body. That the "Calvinist" of modern date has too often fallen into the contradiction of making faith creative, in the sacrament, rather than receptive, is indeed most painfully true. But in doing so he has fallen away entirely from the standpoint of the man whose name he professes to honor. Whether this standpoint is to be held itself responsible for the apostasy, is another question, perfectly legitimate and of immense practical importance; which it becomes the friends of the Reformed Church to look steadily in the face. If Calvinism—the system of Geneva—necessarily runs here into Zwinglianism, we may, indeed, well despair of the whole interest. For most assuredly no church can stand, that is found to be constitutionally unsacramental.

diverse religious communion they represented. In the article of the Lord's Supper it employed the following language, which will be found to closely follow Calvin's:

> "We confess that in the Supper of the Lord not only the benefits of Christ, but the very substance itself of the Son of Man; that is, the same true flesh which the Word assumed into perpetual personal union, in which he was born and suffered, rose again, and ascended to heaven, and that true blood which he shed for us; are not only signified, or set forth symbolically, typically or in figure, like the memory of something absent, but are truly and really represented, exhibited, and offered for use; in connection with symbols that are by no means naked, but which, so far as God who promises and offers is concerned, always have the thing itself truly and certainly joined with them, *whether proposed to believers or unbelievers."*

This last clause deserves especially to be noted, as affirming in the strongest way the objective force of the institution.

> "The power which it carries, as the medium of a real communication with the flesh and blood of Christ, is in no sense the product of our piety and faith."

It exists in the divine constitution of the ordinance itself, though it can be of no value where no faith is at hand for its reception. The article proceeds:

> "As it regards the mode now in which the thing itself, that is, the true body and true blood of the Lord, is connected with the symbols, we say that it is symbolical or sacramental. We call a sacramental mode not such as is figurative merely, but such as truly and certainly represents, under the form of visible things, what God along with the symbols exhibits and offers, namely, what we mentioned before, the true body and blood of Christ; which may show that we retain and defend the presence of the very body and blood of Christ in the Supper. So that if we have any controversy with truly pious and learned brethren, it is not concerning the thing itself, but only concerning the mode of the presence, which is known to God alone, and by us believed.

> "Finally, as to the mode in which the thing itself, that is, the natural and true substance of Christ, is truly and certainly communicated to us, we do not make it to be natural, nor imagine a local copula-

tion,[7] or a diffusion of Christ's human nature, or that crass and dia-
bolical transubstantiation, or any gross mingling of the substance of
Christ with ours; but we say that it is a spiritual mode, that is, such
as rests on the incomprehensible energy of God's Spirit, as unfolded
to us in that word of his own, *This is my body*. And we now all
brethren beg dispassionately to consider, whether it is proper that
those who thus think and teach concerning the sacraments of
Christ, should be branded as infidels and heretics." (Hospinian,
Hist. Sacram. Para All. p. 433.)

BEZA AND PETER MARTYR—CONFERENCE AT POISSY

In the year 1561 a conference was held on the subject of religion
at Poissy, France, in the presence of the king of Navarre, and many
other distinguished guests. Beza, who was then a settled minister at
Geneva, and Peter Martyr, professor of divinity in Zurich, were also
there by special invitation to represent the interests of the Reformed
faith. Beza made a long speech of great eloquence and power that presented the leading articles of the new confession. The court was filled
and everyone accepted it with the highest admiration. On the subject
of the Eucharist, he reiterated the view which has been previously provided, namely that the communion of the believer with Christ in this
ordinance involves a real participation in his flesh and blood.

> "We do not say what some, through misapprehension of our lan-
> guage, have supposed us to teach: that there is in the holy Supper a
> commemoration only of the death of our Lord Jesus Christ. Nor do
> we say, that we are by it partakers only of the fruit of his death and
> passion; but we join the ground also with the produce, (*fundum
> cum fructibus*,) which it is found to yield; asserting with Paul, that
> the bread which we break by divine appointment, is the commu-
> nion, that is, the communication of Christ's body for us crucified,
> and the cup which we drink, the communication of his true blood
> for us poured out; yea, in that same substance, which he took in the
> womb of the virgin, and which he carried up into heaven. And
> what is there then, I pray, which you can find in this sacrament,
> that we too may not seek and find!" (Hosp. II. p. 515.)

After this clear statement, he went on to exclude the idea of transubstantiation from the doctrine, in terms equally clear, and then

---

7   Copulation: coupling or joining.

excluded all suggestion of a local presence of Christ's body *in, with,* or *under* the elements, as taught by Luther. In opposition to every sort of imagination he said:

> "We affirm that his body is as far removed from the bread and wine, as heaven is exalted high above the earth," though he immediately added, that the reality of the communion is in no respect impaired by this consideration; since by the power of faith, in a spiritual way, we still partake of his body and blood" as truly as we see the sacraments with our eyes, touch them with our hands, take them into our mouths, and are nourished and supported by their substance in our corporal life."

The remark that Christ's body and the elements, regarding their locality, are as far apart as heaven and earth caused a general murmur in the assembly, according to the record, and was later made the occasion of no small reproach. In response Beza found it necessary to address a letter to the queen of Navarre desiring an opportunity to explain himself more fully on this point. In this he says:

> "I was led to the remark which has given offense, in meeting the objection of some who, through misunderstanding, charge us with wishing to exclude Christ from the sacrament; which would be indeed manifestly impious. Whereas the fact is we hold it sure from the word of God, that this precious sacrament was instituted by the Son of God, for the purpose of making us more and more partakers of the substance of his true body and his true blood, in order that we may thus become more closely united to him, and coalesce with him unto eternal life. If this were not the case, it would not be the Supper of Jesus Christ. So far are we then from saying Jesus Christ is absent from the Supper, that we of all men abhor that blasphemy. But we say it makes a great difference here, whether we hold Jesus Christ to be present in the Supper, in so far as he gives us in it truly his own body and his own blood, or make his body and blood to be included in the bread. The first we affirm; the second we deny, as repugnant to the truth of Christ's nature, to the article on the ascension, and to the doctrine of the fathers." (Hasp. II. p. 516.)

This colloquy of Poissy ran from the first part of September until the end of November. It was thought best, however, as it progressed to move it from being a public event to a private event. Five delegates were appointed from the Roman Catholics, including two doctors of

the Sorbonne, and five from the Reformed, to confer together freely
regarding the various subjects in debate. The representatives of the
Reformed Church were Beza, Martyr, Gallasius, Marloratus, and
Espinreus. Of course, much of their attention was given to the sacramental question. As the result, they finally agreed to the following
formula, which expressed their common belief.

> "We confess that Jesus Christ in the Supper offers, gives, and truly
> exhibits to us, the substance of his body and blood, by the opera-
> tion of the Holy Ghost; and that we receive and eat, spiritually and
> by faith, that true body that was slain for us; that we may be bone
> of his bones and flesh of his flesh, and so be vivified by him and
> made to partake of all that is wanted for our salvation. And whereas
> *faith, resting on the divine word, makes what it perceives to be present*;
> and we by this faith receive truly and efficaciously the true and
> natural body and blood of Jesus Christ, by the power of the Holy
> Ghost; we acknowledge in this respect the presence of the body
> and blood themselves in the Supper." (Hosp. II. p. 519-521.)

To this formula both the Roman Catholic delegates and the
Reformed delegates declared themselves willing to subscribe. In addition, most of the prelates in attendance were also satisfied with it,
when it was first submitted for their approval. However, the higher
Roman Catholic authority of the Sorbonne led to its defeat because
they thought it betrayed the Catholic faith. So, the five Roman
Catholic representatives fell under much reproach as a result. They
were charged as having conspired with heretics to wrong the orthodox doctrine of the church.

With all of this in mind, we can bring forward the testimony of
the several Confessions that were written for their own use during this
time by the different national branches of the Reformed Church.
Among them all we find a truly remarkable agreement, but nowhere is
that agreement more striking than in the articles on the Lord's Supper.
The language they use is sufficiently clear, for the most part, to
exclude all doubt as to their true meaning on the point under consideration. But if there is any room for hesitation, it must be abandoned
in the light of the following view of their actual opinion at the time
these creeds and confessions were written. The more fully we become
acquainted with the historical connections and relations under which
they began, the more we will see that they don't mean anything less

than what they clearly say. And it is unnecessary to add that their historical sense is their only true sense.

THE GALLIC CONFESSION

This was written by an assembly of delegates from the Reformed churches of France, who were called together in Paris, in 1559. It closely follows the doctrine of Calvin and Beza, previously presented. Some have supposed that Calvin wrote it, but there is no historical evidence, and the supposition is not necessary to account for the agreement. The agreement simply shows that the doctrine of Calvin was the doctrine of the Reformed Church, and was being incorporated into its creeds and confessions. This Confession teaches that Christ

> "...truly feeds and nourishes us with his flesh and blood, that being made one with him, we may have with him a common life. For although he is now in heaven, and will remain there also till he shall come to judge the world; we believe, notwithstanding, that through the secret and incomprehensible energy of his Spirit, apprehended by faith, he nourishes and vivifies us by the substance of his body and blood. We say, however, that this is done spiritually, not as substituting thus an imagination or thought for the power of the fact, but rather because this mystery of our coalition with Christ is so sublime, that it transcends all our senses, and so also the whole course of nature." (Art. 36.)

> "We believe, as before said, that in the Supper, as in Baptism, God in fact, that is, truly and efficaciously, grants unto us all that is there sacramentally represented; and so we join with the signs the true possession and fruition of what is thus offered to us. We affirm, therefore, that those who bring to the Lord's table the vessel of a pure faith, truly receive what the signs there testify; namely, that the body and blood of Jesus Christ are not less the meat and drink of the soul, than bread and wine are the food of the body." (Art. 37., Niemeyer Coll. Omf. p. 338.)

OLD SCOTCH CONFESSION

The overthrow of Roman Catholicism took place in Scotland in 1560, when this Confession was produced under the auspices of the distinguished Reformer, John Knox. On the point of Christ's presence it says:

"We do then utterly condemn the vanity of those who affirm that the sacraments are nothing else but mere naked signs. Rather, we surely believe, that by baptism we are inserted into Christ, and made partakers of his righteousness, by which all our sins are covered and remitted. And also, that in the Lord's Supper, rightly used, Christ is so united to us as to be the very nutriment and food of our souls. Not that we may imagine any transubstantiation of the bread into the natural body of Christ, and of the wine into his natural blood, as the papists have perniciously taught, and believe to their own damnation. But this union and conjunction which we have with the body and blood of Jesus Christ, in the right use of the sacrament, is effected by the operation of the Holy Ghost, who carries us by true faith above all that is seen, and all that is carnal and terrestrial, and causes us to feed upon the body and blood of Jesus Christ, once broken for us and poured out, but now in heaven, appearing for us in the presence of the Father. And though the distance be immense in space between his body now glorified in heaven and us mortals still upon the earth, we do notwithstanding firmly believe that the bread which we break is the communion of his body, and the cup which we bless the communion of his blood; and so we confess that believers in the right use of the Lord's Supper thus eat the body and drink the blood of Jesus Christ, and we believe surely that he dwells in them and they in him, yea, that they become thus flesh of his flesh and bone of his bones; for as the eternal Deity has imparted life and immortality to the flesh of Jesus Christ, so likewise his flesh and blood, when eaten and drunk by us, confer upon us the same prerogatives." (Sri. 21., Niemeyer, p. 352, 353.)

BELGIC CONFESSION

This dates from 1563, and is of great authority and force as a standard for the faith of the Dutch Reformed Church both in Holland and America. It was officially approved by the Synod of Dort, as well, and has a distinctive ecumenical character, and it models the beliefs of the entire Reformed Church at the beginning of the seventeenth century. Its testimony is particularly clear.

"The sacraments are signs and visible symbols of invisible internal realities, through which as means God himself works in us by the power of the Holy Spirit. Those signs then are by no means vain or void; nor are they instituted to deceive or disappoint us. For the

truth of them is Jesus Christ himself, without whom they would be
of no force whatever." (Art. 33.)

"He has instituted terrene and visible bread and wine to be the
sacrament of his body and blood; by which we are assured, that as
truly as we receive and hold in our hands this sacrament, and eat
the same with our mouth, to the sustentation of our natural life, so
truly also do we by faith, which is as it were the hand and mouth
of our soul, receive the true body and true blood of Christ, our
only Savior, in our souls, to the promotion of our spiritual life.
Moreover, it is most certain that Christ commends his sacrament to
us so earnestly not without cause, as himself performing in us really
all that he represents to us in those sacred signs; although the mode
is such as to surpass the apprehension of our mind, and cannot be
understood by any; since the operation of the Holy Spirit is always
secret and incomprehensible. We may say, however, that what is
eaten is the very natural body of Christ, and what is drunk, his true
blood; only the instrument of medium by which we eat and drink
these is not the corporeal mouth, but our own spirit itself, and this
by faith." (Art. 35., Niemeyer, p. 383, 385.)[8]

---

8   I (Nevin) translated from the Latin; and there are frequent variations in the text of
    the Confession itself, as given in different editions. This may explain any deviations
    from the letter of the English version, as used by the Dutch Reformed Church in
    this country. For anyone who is at all familiar with the view of Calvin, or with the
    true character of the sacramental question in the sixteenth century, the sense of the
    Confession is too clear to be mistaken. Christ, it is true, is held to "sit always at the
    right hand of his Father in the heavens;" but notwithstanding all this, he "doth not
    cease to make us partakers of himself by faith." And to guard against the idea of a
    mere moral communication in the case, it is added, that he conveys to us, at his
    table, not simply his benefits or merits, but these as inhering in his person; "both
    himself, and the merits of his sufferings and death." Christians have a two-fold life;
    one natural, the other spiritual, beginning with their second birth "in the commu-
    nion of the body of Christ." This last life is supported by a living bread, sent from
    heaven for the purpose, "namely Jesus Christ, who nourishes and strengthens the
    spiritual life of believers when they eat him, that is to say, when they apply and
    receive him by faith in the spirit." A spiritual reception, of course, but still a real
    reception of Christ's true human and heavenly life; otherwise the article must be
    held guilty of the most egregious trifling, in the case of one of the most solemn and
    perilous points in theology. The Form for the administration of the Lord's Supper,
    in the Liturgy of the Dutch Reformed Church, corresponds fully with the doctrine
    of the Confession. "That we may now be full with the true heavenly bread, Christ
    Jesus," the service exhorts, "let us not cleave with our hearts unto the external bread
    and wine, but lift them up on high in heaven, where Christ Jesus is our advocate at
    the right hand of his heavenly Father, whither all the articles of our faith lead us; not
    doubting but we shall as certainly he fed and refreshed in our souls, through the
    working of the Holy Ghost, with his body and blood, as we receive the holy bread

SECOND HELVETIC CONFESSION

What is called the *Second* or *Later Helvetic Confession*, was written by Henry Bullinger, in 1562, though it did not become public until 1566. It then became the standing, universally acknowledged exposition of the faith of the whole Helvetic Church, and was also well received in other countries. Its treatment of the Lord's Supper is particularly replete. Regarding the subject at hand the following extract is provided:

> "Believers receive what is given by the minister of the Lord, and eat the Lord's bread and drink of the Lord's cup; inwardly, however, in the mean time, by the work of Christ through the Holy Spirit, they partake also of the Lord's flesh and blood, and are fed by these unto eternal life. For the flesh and blood of Christ are true meat and drink unto eternal life; and Christ himself, as delivered up for us and our salvation, is that which mainly makes the Supper, nor do we suffer anything else to be put in his room." (Art. 21.)

The article then goes on, in explanation of this statement, to describe different forms of eating. There is first a corporal eating, such as the Capernaites[9] have in mind when they strove among themselves saying, *How can this man give us his flesh to eat?* Then there is a spiritual eating, where Christ is appropriated by ordinary faith so that he lives in us and we in him.

---

and wine in remembrance of him."

9   *Expository Thoughts on Mark*, by Pastor J.C. Ryle describes the dwellers of Capernum and warns us against following in their way: "It is good for us all to mark well this case of Capernaum. We are all to apt to suppose that it needs nothing but the powerful preaching of the Gospel to convert people's souls, and that if the Gospel is only brought into a place everybody must believe. We forget the amazing power of unbelief, and the depth of man's enmity against God. We forget that the Capernaites heard the most faultless preaching, and saw it confirmed by the most surprising miracles, and yet remained dead in trespasses and sins. We need reminding that the same Gospel which is the savor of life to some, is the savor of death to others, and that the same fire which softens the wax will also harden the clay. Nothing, in fact, seems to harden man's heart so much, as to hear the Gospel regularly, and yet deliberately prefer the service of sin and the world. Never was there a people so highly favored as the people of Capernaum, and never was there a people who appear to have become so hard. Let us beware of walking in their steps. We ought often to use the prayer of the Litany, 'From hardness of heart, good Lord, deliver us.'" (*Capernaitical* has been defined as "believing in the Roman Catholic doctrine of transubstantiation." Thus, *Capernaites* was used by Nevin to suggest those who believe it.)

"By this is not meant a merely imaginary, undefinable food, but the body of the Lord itself delivered up for us, which however is received by believers, not corporeally, but spiritually by faith."

Still different from this is the sacramental eating,

"by which the believer not only participates in the true body and blood of the Lord spiritually and internally, but outwardly also by coming to the Lord's table receives the visible sacrament of the Lord's body and blood."

The sacrament adds something of its own to the ordinary life of faith.

"He that partakes of the sacrament outwardly with true faith, partakes not of the sign only, but enjoys also, as already said, the thing itself which this represents." (Niemeyer, p. 519, 520.)

When this confession became public, a spirit of the most violent intolerance came to prevail on some of the Lutherans against all who professed the Reformed doctrine by such men as Westphal, Timann, and Hesshuss. They particularly directed their attention towards the elector of the Palatinate, Frederick the Third. It was feared that he would be excluded from the peace between the Catholics and Protestants. At that time it became quite important to bring all the Reformed churches into common belief and teaching. Frederick had his heart set upon this agreement.

At the end of 1565 he wrote to Bullinger and begged him to send a confession of faith that might serve to repress the cavils of the Lutherans as soon as possible. He also had his eye on the imperial diet which was close at hand. Bullinger forwarded him the confession which he had prepared three years earlier. It so pleased the elector that he wanted to have it translated and published in German. To give it greater importance and authority, it was submitted to the other Helvetic churches, who approved it and it later became known as the official *Swiss Confession*.

Its history is important because it shows the substantial harmony of Switzerland and the Palatinate on the sacramental question at the time it was published. Its harmony rested on the foundation of the Calvinistic doctrine, as has been already explained. Indeed, Calvin's doctrine was the reigning view of the Reformed Church in the Palatinate, beyond all shadow of doubt.

THE HEIDELBERG CATECHISM

Next comes the venerable symbol of the German Reformed Church, the Catechism of the Palatinate drawn up in response to the Elector, Frederick, III. It was written by Caspar Olevian, a disciple of Calvin, and Zacharias Ursinus, a friend of Melancthon, and approved and ratified by a general ecclesiastical synod at Heidelberg and published as an official confessional standard in 1563. It has been translated into all modern languages, honored with countless commentaries, and exalted by general agreement to have symbolical authority for the whole Reformed Church.

To see it in its proper light, it is necessary to explain the sacramental controversy in Germany at the time. Only in this way, can we come to learn why it was written and its true value.

Circumstances of its Formation

After the death of Luther, 1540, the sacramental controversy remained at rest for some years. However, before long it began to appear that Calvin's high ground was being abandoned by many who still considered themselves true to the Augsburg Confession. A violent counter movement was gradually created, which turned against Calvin, and later against Peter Martyr. Both had declared themselves to be in open and offensive hostility against extreme views because the mind of the church had come to rest on Calvin's moderate view.

But the extremists would have no peace. The war began in 1552 by Joachim Westphal in Hamburg. His *Farrago* was intended to challenge the Swiss churches, with Calvin at their head, and call to arms all who thought that the strong towers of Lutheran orthodoxy were in danger of being overthrown. This was followed by a second attack the following year, and again the year after by a third. Other influences were used in an attempt to dislodge Calvin's doctrine. In self-defense Calvin began writing. A war of words had been unleashed on all sides.

The Lutheran church was torn with dissension and distraction. The strict Lutherans, "fierce for orthodoxy," had their hands full suppressing heresy at home. That horrible sacramentarian doctrine[10] was

---

10 During the Protestant Reformation the Sacramentarians denied not only the Roman Catholic transubstantiation but also the Lutheran sacramental union. There were two factions: 1) the followers of Capito, Carlstadt and Bucer, who at the diet of Augsburg presented the *Confessio Tetrapolitana* from Strassburg, Konstanz, Lindau and Memmingen, and 2) the followers of the Swiss reformer, Zwingli, who to the

found everywhere lifting up its head, or at least struggling to do so, under the very shadow of the *Augsburg Confession* itself. And what is worse still, the venerable author of the Confession, still living at Wittenberg, refused to lift a finger in opposition to the mischief; nay, is more than suspected of being himself in league with it in his heart. No wonder that all Protestant Germany was mad with theological excitement and passion.[11]

But what was the nature of the question at issue with regard to the Lord's Supper? It was not at all concerned with the reality of the sacramental presence, but only and wholly with its mode. The controversy was not between the high view of Luther and the low theory commonly attributed to Zwingli. All agreed that the sacrament involves a real participation in the substance of Christ's flesh and blood, that it concerns his true human life, and is the only ground of our salvation.

However, the strict party was not satisfied with this confession.[12] They insisted on certain other definitions and admissions, which appeared to them to be necessary to put the doctrine in its truest sense. They contended for the formula, "In, with, and under," as indispensable to a complete expression of the sacramental presence. The communication must be allowed to be by the mouth. It must be granted to all who eat, whether with or without faith. And lastly, the ubiquity of Christ's body and the *communicatio idiomatum* in its full extent must also be accepted as the foundation of the doctrine.

---

same diet presented his private confession of faith. The doctrinal standpoint was the same—an admission of a spiritual presence of Christ which the devout soul can receive and enjoy, but a total rejection of any physical or corporeal presence. After holding their own view for some years the four cities accepted the *Confession of Augsburg*, and were merged in the general body of Lutherans. Zwingli's position was incorporated in the Helvetic Confession. It is a curious inversion of terms that in recent years has led to the name *Sacramentarians* being applied to those who hold a high view of the efficacy of the sacraments.

11 A full account of these agitations and conflicts, may be found in Planck's "*Geschichte tier Protestantischen Theologie*," vol. v., Second Part. They form one of the most strange and interesting chapters in the church history of the Sixteenth Century.

12 The Radical Reformation was a sixteenth century response to both the corruption in the Roman Catholic Church and the expanding Magisterial Protestant movement led by Luther, Calvin, and many others. Beginning in Germany and Switzerland, the Radical Reformation birthed many radical Protestant groups led by Thomas Müntzer, Andreas Karlstadt, the Zwickau prophets, and anabaptist groups like the Hutterites and the Mennonites. Although their numbers were small at the time, the literature of the Radical Reformation is vast today, partly as a result of the success of the Radical Reformation in the United States.

It was for refusing to admit these extreme positions that the Calvinists were branded with the *Sacramentarian* title, and held up to odium in as being social pests. It was not the Zwinglian view of the Lord's Supper, but the Calvinistic view, in all its length and breadth that had been recognized as the official doctrine of the Reformed Church. And as such it was pursued with unrelenting hate by the high-toned orthodoxy of the day. It is important to keep this in mind.

The intestine war broke forth first in the city of Bremen, where it quickly became violent and gradually involved the whole country in commotion. The first target was the distinguished preacher, Albert Hardenberg, a man of learning and piety, and who was considered to be a key person. Unfortunately for him, he was suspected of being more Reformed than Lutheran in his view of the Lord's Supper. It was not the least consideration in his prejudice, that he was known to be in regular correspondence with Melancthon, as one of his most intimate and confidential friends.

The movement against Hardenberg began in 1555, and was led by John Timann, one of his ministry colleagues in Bremen, who came forward with great zeal to the assistance of Westphal in his crusade against Hardenberg's supposed heresy. In time, many other preachers joined in the process of persecution. Every effort was made to bring Hardenberg into discredit with the magistracy and the people, labeling him an enemy of the true Lutheran faith.

Pulpits rang with reproaches hurled upon his head. Conspiracy and intrigue dominated Bremen for years. Timann died in the midst of the controversy, but others picked up his mantle to continue the fight. Other cities and states—Hamburg, Lubeck, Lunenburg, Saxony, Mecklinburg, Wirtemburg, Denmark—were quietly engaged to interpose and provide mediation. But in the end, Hardenberg had to retire. Nonetheless, the controversy continued for thirteen years holding Bremen in continual violent disturbance. But it came to a more favorable result than was expected.

Bremen was the first of many such attacks of the religious revolution of the Palatinate that stormed across Lutheran Germany like lightening. The struggles were long and arduous, and took place under the following circumstances.

One of the most violent, unsettled men of this turbulent period, was Tilemann Hesshuss. He is most memorable for the strong admonishment inflicted upon him by Calvin in his last tract on the

Sacrament.[13] Hesshuss was a man of inordinate ambition, fond of money, intolerant, and overbearing; and a perfect zealot in the cause of Lutheran orthodoxy.

In 1558, he was appointed the First Professor in the University of Heidelberg and General Superintendent of all the churches in the Palatinate. But before six months had elapsed he became very generally disliked, which had happened everywhere else he had ever lived. In particular, he was drawn into vehement controversy with William Klebiz, a deacon in Heidelberg at the time. Klebiz was a man of the most unpastoral temper, and little inclined to maintain friendly relations with the new superintendent. In short order, an open, violent rupture between them flared up about the sacramental question.

Hesshuss charged Klebiz with heresy because Klebiz favored the Calvinistic view of Christ's presence in the Lord's Supper, rather than the strict Lutheran view. The critical point of his apostasy was found mainly in the fact that he affirmed the participation of Christ's body in the Supper to be by faith and not by the mouth. Hesshuss was savage in his denunciations, and poured forth his indignation every Sunday from the pulpit. He described Klebiz as the new Arius in the Heidelberg Church. Nor did Hesshuss spare the university and the authorities of the city for their supposed indifference to the portentous mischief of this new Arian threat.

Klebiz returned violence for violence, and soon the whole city was in commotion. During this same time, Frederick III succeeded to the Electorate. Frederick's moderate measures to quell the dispute failed. In the end, Frederick resorted to a more vigorous solution. Both Hesshuss and Klebiz were dismissed from office. And finally public rest was restored.

---

13 *Sound explanation of the Clear Doctrine of True Participation in the Flesh and Blood of Christ in the Holy Supper, and Discussion of the Clouds that Envelop Heshuss (Dilucida Explicatio Sana Doctrina de Vera Participatione Carniset Sanguinis Christi, in Sacra Cana. Ad discuticndas Heshusii nebulas)*. Published 1561. In this tract, Hesshuss is handled, without gloves, showing that he was incited by ignorance, stupidity, and reckless delirium, etc. Such epithets like impure as a buffoon, epileptic, obscene, beastly, etc., are plentifully sprinkled throughout. In conclusion, the writer excuses himself from farther controversy with Hesshuss because he is destitute of all modesty and reason, delivering him over at the same time to the discipline of Beza. "There is in the beast such ingenuousness and docility, to be cleansed from his slandering me, but because a bull in which too much wantonness rejoices cannot be not broken, Beza abandoned the effort to subdue him." (Odd. ix. p. 723-742.)

Frederick wanted this controversy settled in his dominion in order to preserve a lasting peace. He came up with a plan to establish a rule of faith for the Palatinate, and all would be required to conform to it. To help him formulate such a rule he asked Melancthon for counsel and advice. This produced the celebrated response of Melancthon, which became public after his death, and made Frederick an object of reproach to the strict Lutherans, whose views it opposed.

It accomplished Frederick's purpose and silenced the sacramental controversy by requiring everyone to submit to some common confession, and condemned the teachings of Hesshuss and his followers. The Elector had made up his own mind in favor of the moderate or Calvinistic view of the sacrament. He also found that position to be predominant among his people. His Election was confirmed and it was resolved that the Palatinate should become Reformed.

This, of course, became news across all of Germany. And soon, the son-in-law of the Elector, Duke John Frederick of Saxony, became disturbed and troubled when he heard it. He immediately went to Heidelberg, taking a pair of his best theologians with him, Morlin and Stossel. He was determined to rescue Frederick III from the dangerous snare of Calvinism. To do this, he purposed a public disputation to be held between Morlin and Stossel on his side, and anyone Frederick III wanted to nominate to defend his side. The proposal was accepted, and the disputation lasted five full days during June, 1560, in the presence of the two princes.

The Calvinist doctrine was defended by Peter Bocquin, a distinguished theologian from Heidelberg. The crux of the debate was the mode of the Eucharistic presence. The divines of John Frederick argued for the high Lutheran doctrine of a true corporeal presence, *in, with,* and *under* the bread that was received orally and not simply in a spiritual way. It was received by both believers and unbelievers.

Bocquin, on the other hand, maintained the view that Christ is present by the power of the Holy Spirit only to those who believe. He allowed, however, not only "that the body is presented with the bread," but also "that the true substance of the true body is received by believers." And he argued convincingly that this does not make it necessary to suppose an oral communication, or to hold that the body is either *in* the bread or *under* it. The final result of the disputation was that the elector found himself even more confirmed than before that he was right in his resolution to establish the Reformed doctrine in the Palatinate.

During this same time, the Heidelberg Catechism was produced, and was made the official public expression of Christianity, as previously stated. From the nature of the case, we may easily understand the perspective that the doctrine of the Lord's Supper must be grounded. Calvin provided the correct foundation, which is different from the Lutheran position on one side and Zwinglian position on the other. Again, Calvin explicitly rejected the idea of an oral feeding, but, as Planck remarks, he also clearly teaches that the soul of the believer is truly fed in this sacrament by an actual participation of the body and blood of Christ.

We turn now to the Heidelberg Catechism itself.

Extracts

In answer to Question 75, it is said that Christ, "feeds and nourishes my soul to everlasting life, with his crucified body and shed blood, as assuredly as I receive from the hands of the minister, and taste with my mouth, the bread and cup of the Lord, as certain signs of the body and blood of Christ."

> "*Q76:* What is it then to eat the crucified body and drink the shed blood of Christ?"

> "*A:* It is not only to embrace with a believing heart all the sufferings and death of Christ, and thereby to obtain the pardon of sin and life eternal; but also, besides that, to become more and more united to his sacred body, by the Holy Ghost who dwells both in Christ and in us; so that we, though Christ is in heaven and we on earth, are notwithstanding, 'flesh of his flesh and bone of his bone;' and that we live and are governed forever by one spirit, as members of the same body are by one soul."

> "*Q 79:* Why then doth Christ call the bread his body, and the cup his blood, or the new covenant in his blood; and Paul the communion of the body and blood of Christ?"

> "*A:* Christ speaks thus, not without great reason; namely not only thereby to teach us that as bread and wine support this temporal life, so his crucified body and shed blood are the true meat and drink whereby our souls are fed to eternal life; but more especially, by these visible signs and pledges to assure us, that we are as really

partakers of his true body and blood, (by the operation of the Holy
Ghost,) as we receive by the mouths of our bodies these holy signs
in remembrance of him; and that all his sufferings and obedience
are as certainly ours as if we had in our own persons suffered and
made satisfaction for our sins to God."

Commentary on The Meaning

Here we have all the characteristic positions and distinctions of
Calvin's theory plainly brought into view. And with the knowledge of
this doctrine firm in our minds, and the historical conditions under
which the Catechism was created in our sight, we must simply and
honestly accept Calvin's plain meaning without unnecessary speculation. True to the general form of the controversy at the time, Calvin
affirms a real communion with Christ's flesh and blood. He allows the
fact of it, but refuses to acquiesce to the Lutheran speculation regarding the mode. The presence of Christ is not "in, with, and under" the
bread, but only *with* it. Christ's presence is not for the mouth, but only
for faith. And consequently, though not explicitly mentioned, Christ's
presence is not for unbelievers but for believers only.

However, in every way this is a true presence. The believer partakes in Christ, not merely figuratively, but in actual fact; not simply
of His benefits, but of His actual life; not merely in His divine life, but
of the substance of His human life, which is denoted as "his body and
blood." The sacramental signs not only testify to the general truth that
Christ is our life, but they seal this truth as a fact that is actualized with
their exhibition and use. To say that by the participation of Christ's
body and blood the Catechism means only a moral union with Him
through our faith and creates a mere interest in the benefits of His
death is to charge it with the most wretched tautology.

Where it says "besides that" and "more especially" it intends an
important point to be made. The second proposition, in each case,
must not be considered to simply be a meaningless repetition of the
sense of the first, in terms more obscure and difficult to understand.

No such poor tautology must be be allowed. The Catechism
counts it not enough, that we embrace the offer of salvation, as if it is
something separate from Christ himself. No! We must be incorporated
into His life, we must have part in the very substance of His flesh and
blood in order that we may truly have part in all the blessings He has

procured. It is as though "we had in our own persons suffered and made satisfaction for our sins unto God."

We may be told that the language of the Catechism and of the other Confessions herein quoted must be understood in a figurative sense, since it is understood that the body and blood of Christ are not actually corporeally present in the sacrament, and therefore they cannot be taken literally into the believer's person. Allowing this objection, however, doesn't necessarily mean that the words have no actual meaning or application, or that they have no spiritual reality. If by eating the flesh and blood of Christ the framers of these confessions meant the words to be merely figurative, they have written quite carelessly. And it would be all the more incredible that those who rejected Rome's confusion of real presence with an empirical presence, that they would revert to the same error made in a slightly different way—consubstantiation rather than transubstantiation.

The thought is absurd. By *flesh and blood* they meant the true body of Christ, the same body that was born of Mary, and hung upon the cross, and is now enthroned in heaven.[14] Believers feed upon the words "flesh and blood of Christ," not carnally, but spiritually. And the words point to a reality, not an abstraction. So, however it is true, whatever its proper substance, the reality clings to the words as life clings to our physical bodies. And Jesus' human life is conveyed to the lives of believers. In this way he "becomes united more and more to his sacred body, by the Holy Ghost," so as to be truly "flesh of his flesh and bone of his bone," even as limb and head are filled and ruled with the same life in the physical body.

But this "sacred body" of the Savior is sometimes said to be the church. Fine, allow this to be part of the greater reality of Christ's body. It follows, then, that the holistic wholeness of Christ's life, including the reality of His humanity, *includes* the church in an organic way because of Christ's headship of the church. In the final analysis we come to the same conclusion. To be incorporated into the church, in this sense, is to be incorporated into Christ at the same time, which must include His true human life.

Of course the Catechism has no reference to the church in this regard, and especially not to the church in any way that is external to

14 They were not trying to define how this could be possible, only that this is what Scripture says. They were standing in the tradition of Augustine, who said, "Seek not to understand that you may believe, but believe that you may understand."

the believer, as Calvin's interpretation is now understood to imply. The "sacred body" to which His people are united is simply Christ's own person in human form, crucified for our sins and now gloriously exalted for our justification in heaven.[15] This was the view of the Reformed Church at this time, and this is the sense of the Catechism.

However, should any doubt still linger with regard to the sacramental doctrine of the Catechism, as now defined, it must be completely abandoned in the light of our next authority: the testimony of Ursinus himself.

URSINUS, THE AUTHOR OF THE CATECHISM

The works of this divine include a good deal on the subject of the sacraments. Hospinian (*Hist. Sacram. Pars Altera*, p. 659, 660) mentions a tract of his pen, published in 1564, on behalf of the theological faculty of Heidelberg, titled "The True Doctrine of the Holy Supper of our Lord Jesus Christ, faithfully expounded from the principles and sense of the divine Scriptures, the ancient and orthodox church, and also of the Augsburg Confession."

In the third chapter he proposed to settle the question regarding this controversy in the Protestant churches. The issue "is not whether the flesh of Christ be eaten; for this none of us deny; but how it is eaten." The Lutherans said that it is eaten *corporeally* and *orally* by both the godly and ungodly. The Reformed churches, on the contrary, said that it was eaten spiritually only by believers.

The earliest commentary we have on the Heidelberg Catechism is that by Ursinus, published in his divinity lectures after his death by David Parous, titled the "Summe of Christian Religion," London, 1645.[16] The following quotations will serve to provide an understanding of the author's doctrine of the Lord's Supper.

His Sacramental Doctrine as Exhibited by Himself

"These two, I mean the sign and the thing signified, are united in this sacrament, not by any natural joining, or corporal and local

15 "Calvin expressly rejects the idea, that by the body of Christ, to which we are united in the sacrament, is to be understood *merely* as the church. He repels as slanderous, the attempt to fasten on his view this consequence." (Opp. ix., p. 701.) Emphasis added to suggest that it includes the church but is not exhausted by the church.
16 This has been translated from the original Latin into English. Not having the Latin work at hand, I can only appeal to the translation—Nevin.

existence one in the other; much less by transubstantiation, or changing one into the other; but by signifying, sealing, and exhibiting the one by the other; that is by a sacramental union, whose bond is the promise added to the bread, requiring the faith of the receivers. Whence it is clear, that these things in their lawful use, are always jointly exhibited and received, but not without faith of the promise, viewing and apprehending the thing promised, now present in the sacrament; yet not present or included in the sign as in a vessel containing it; but present in the promise, which is the better part, life, and soul of the sacrament. For they lack judgment who affirm, that Christ's body cannot be present in the sacrament, except it be in or under the bread; as if the bread alone without the promise, were either the sacrament, or the principal part of a sacrament" (p. 434).

"There is then in the Lord's Supper a double meat and drink. One external, visible and terrene, namely, bread and wine; and another internal. There is also a double eating and receiving; an external and signifying, which is the corporal receiving of the bread and wine; that is, which is performed by the hands, mouth, and senses of the body; and an internal, invisible, and signified element, which is the fruition of Christ's death, and a spiritual ingrafting into Christ's body; that is, which is not performed by the hands and mouth of the body, but by the spirit and faith. Lastly, there is a double administrator and dispenser of this meat and drink; an external, of the external, which is the minister of the church, delivering by his hand the bread and wine; and an internal, of the internal meat, which is Christ himself, feeding us by his body and blood" (p. 470).

"As therefore the body of Christ signifies both his proper and natural body, and his sacramental body, which is the bread of the Eucharist; so the eating of Christ's body is of two sorts; one sacramental, of the sign to wit, the external and corporal receiving of the bread and wine; the other real or spiritual, which is the receiving of Christ's very body itself. And to believe in Christ dwelling in us by faith, is, by the virtue and operation of the Holy Ghost, to be ingrafted into his body, as members to the head and branches into the vine; and so to be made partakers of the fruit of the death and life of Christ. Whence it is apparent that they are falsely accused who thus teach, as if they made either the bare signs only to be in the Lord's Supper, or a participation of Christ's death only, or of his benefits, or of the Holy Ghost, excluding the true, real, and spiritual communion of the very body of Christ itself" (p. 470, 471).

In the appendix is the following brief summary of the leading objections made by the "Consubstantiaries" against the "sincere doctrine of the Lord's Supper" as held by the "Sacramentarians," together with proper answers.

"*1st Obj.* The errors of the Sacramentarians are, that there are but bare signs and symbols only in the Supper."

"*Ans.* We teach that the things signified are, together with the signs in the right use exhibited and communicated, albeit not corporeally, but in such sort as is agreeable unto sacraments."

"*2d Obj.* The Sacramentarians say that Christ is present only according to his power and efficacy."

"*Ans.* We teach that he is present and united with us by the Holy Ghost, albeit his body be far absent from us; like as a whole Christ is present also with his ministry, though diversely according to the one nature."

"*3d Obj.* The Sacramentarians affirm that an imaginary, figurative, or spiritual body is present, not his essential body."

"Ans. We never spake of an imaginary body, but of the true flesh of Christ, which is present with us, although it remain in heaven. Moreover, we say that we receive the bread and body, but both after a manner proper to each."

"*4th Obj.* The Sacramentarians affirm, that the true body of Christ which hung on the cross, and his very blood which was shed for us, is distributed and is spiritually received of those only who are worthy receivers; as for the unworthy, they receive nothing besides the bare signs, to their own condemnation."

"*Ans.* All this we grant, as being agreeable to the word of God, the nature of sacraments, the analogy of faith, and the communion of the faithful" (p. 472)."

In conclusion, a statement is given of the general points "wherein the churches which profess the gospel agree or disagree in the controversy concerning the Lord's Supper." Among the points of agreement, the third one mentioned is "that in the Supper we are made partakers not only of the Spirit of Christ and His satisfaction, justice, virtue, and operation, but also of the very essence and substance of His true body and blood, which was given for us to death on the cross, and which was shed for us; and are truly fed with the self-same unto eternal life: and that this very thing Christ should teach and make known unto us, by this visible receiving of this bread and wine in his Supper." The disagreement is about the three following particulars.

"1. That one part contends that these words of Christ, *This is my body*, must be understood as the words sound, which yet that part itself does not prove; but the other part, that those words must be understood sacramentally, according to the declaration of Christ and Paul, according to the most certain and infallible rule and level of the articles of our Christian faith.

"2. That one part will have the body and blood of Christ to be essentially *in* or *with* the bread and the wine, and so to be eaten that together with the bread and wine, out of the hand of the minister, it enters by the mouth of the receivers into their bodies; but the other part will have the body of Christ, which in the first Supper sat at the table by the disciples, now to be and continue, not here on earth, but above in the heavens, and without this visible world and heaven, until he descend thence again to judgment, and yet that we notwithstanding here on earth, as oft as we eat this bread with a true faith, are so fed with his body, and made to drink of his blood, that not only through his passion and blood shed, we are cleansed from our sins, but are also in such sort coupled, knit, and incorporated into his true, essential human body, by his Spirit dwelling both in him and us, that we are flesh of his flesh, and bone of his bones; and are more nearly and firmly knit and united with him than the members of our body are united with our head, and so we draw and have in him and from him everlasting life.

"3. That one part will have all, whosoever come to the table of the Lord's Supper, and eat and drink that bread and wine, whether they be believers or unbelievers, to eat and drink, corporeally and with their bodily mouth, the flesh and blood of Christ, believers to life and salvation, unbelievers to damnation and death; the other holds, that unbelievers abuse indeed the outward signs, bread and wine, to their damnation, but that the faithful only can eat and drink, by a true faith, and the fore-alleged working of the Holy Ghost, the body and blood of Christ unto eternal life" (p. 480).

Calvin himself is hardly more explicit, in the statement of his own doctrine. We seem to hear in these quotations the very echo of the words we have already heard from Calvin's own lips. However, it is the testimony of Ursinus, the principal author of the Catechism of the Palatinate, speaking *ex cathedra* of the doctrine it contains. Where shall we find an expositor of its sense more worthy to he trusted and believed?

Hospinian

Omitting all other testimony that might be brought forward from the sixteenth century that merely repeats what has already been presented, we will examine the work of the Helvetic divine, Rodolph Hospinian. He is the distinguished author of the great work on the history of the Sacrament. He lived in Zurich from 1563 into the following century. His sympathies were all with the Helvetic Church. His analysis of this issue in the sixteenth century simply assumed that the Reformed doctrine of the Eucharist had always been what we have found it to be in the authorities already quoted. Furthermore, it was not merely in complete conformity with Calvin's teaching, but even in harmony with the official sense of the Augsburg Confession, as understood by Melancthon and a large part of the Lutheran Church.

General Testimony

He refers to Calvin's statements always with approbation, as a true representation of what was held and taught in the Reformed communion, and of what Zwingli himself taught. He misunderstood some of Hospinian's ideas, but that doesn't undermine his views on the Eucharist. In fact, it makes them more worthy of attention. He was defending the sacramental orthodoxy of the Helvetic church as having always been Calvinistic, as distinguished from Ubiquitarianism.[17] He takes it for granted that Calvin's view, and nothing lower than this, was, and had always been the true and proper doctrine of the Reformed Church.

He argued that the controversy between Calvin and the Lutherans was not about the fact of Christ's presence, or the power of the sacra-

---

17 The Ubiquitarians, also called Ubiquists, were a Protestant sect started at the Lutheran synod of Stuttgart, 1559, by Johannes Brenz (1499-1570). They believed and taught that the body of Christ is omnipresent and therefore exists in the Eucharistic bread.

ments, but only about the mode—how it worked. Speaking of the Augsburg Confession, he highlighted the article on the Eucharistic presence in the Wittenberg German text, 1531, "that the body and blood of Christ are truly present, and with the bread and wine distributed to them that eat, in the Lord's Supper." He explained that "these words contain nothing contrary to our view."

Later he reported still more explicitly:

> "Ours do not reject the tenth article of the Augsburg Confession, in its sound, true, right, pious, and catholic sense, as held by the fathers, and all the true Christian saints always in the church; namely, that in the Lord's Supper, along with the bread and wine, that is, while the sacrament of the Lord's body and blood is received, there is truly exhibited also the body and blood itself of the Lord, to be received by faith. For whilst the ministers distribute the sacrament of the body and blood of Christ, Christ communicates himself to be spiritually enjoyed, that the pious may have communion with him and live by him" (Hosp. Hist. Sac. Part II. p. 157, 158).

THE SYNOD OF DORT

This venerable council was convened in 1618 with particular concern to the errors introduced by Arminius. It was composed of delegates from the United Provinces, England, Switzerland, the Palatinate, Hessia, Nassau, East Friesland, and Bremen. So it was an ecumenical council of the entire Reformed Church. It was not called to deal with the sacramental question, but it did indirectly by endorsing both the Belgic Confession and the Heidelberg Catechism as being true and faithful expositions in their entirety regarding the faith of the church.

The Belgic Confession, having been submitted previously for examination by the various national delegations was unanimously approved in the 146th session as containing nothing at variance with the word of God, nor requiring any changes. The Heidelberg Catechism was later put before the council, with the request that it might be tried in the same way. The result was a declaration filed in the name of all present that

> "the doctrine contained in the Catechism of the Palatinate was found to be in conformity at all points to the word of God, nor requiring any changes."

In addition, they said that it was

> "a completely accurate compendium of the orthodox Christian faith, being with singular skill not only adjusted to the apprehension of tender youth, but so framed also as to serve the purpose of instruction at the same time in the case of older persons" (Ada Syn. Nat. Dort. Stss. CXLVI. p. 302).

Westminster Confession

This belongs to the middle of the seventeenth century. It has a different character in some respects, from the older confessions of the Reformed Church because of the influence of the Puritan principle. The Puritan principle tended toward the subjective and was unfavorable to the idea that Christianity involves any objective and mystical aspects, as was held in the original Reformed doctrines. The Puritan tendencies have in fact contributed largely to the false ideas about Christianity that are currently in vogue.

But notwithstanding all this, the doctrine of the real presence in the Westminster Confession appears full force. The testimony of the Westminster Confession is not as authoritative as the symbolical authorities of the sixteenth century, which were closer to the original. Nonetheless, it shows how deeply the old Calvinistic doctrine was incorporated in the heart of the church, and how complete and clear it was in the beginning. After a hundred years its basic tenets remained in the bosom of the Puritan Revolution. Let the Confession speak for itself.

> "Worthy receivers, outwardly partaking of the visible elements in this sacrament, do then inwardly also by faith, really and indeed, yet not carnally and corporeally, but spiritually, receive and feed upon Christ crucified and all benefits of his death; the body and blood of Christ being then not corporeally or carnally in, with, or under the bread and wine; yet as really but spiritually present to the faith of believers in that ordinance, as the elements themselves are to their outward senses" (Chap. 29, § 7).

Compare this with the following questions from the Larger Catechism, which confirms and illustrates the same view.

Q168: What is the Lord's Supper?

A: The Lord's Supper is a sacrament of the New Testament, wherein by giving and receiving bread and wine, according to the appointment of Jesus Christ, his death is showed forth; and they that worthily communicate, feed upon his body and blood, to their spiritual nourishment and growth in grace; have their union and communion with him confirmed; testify and renew their thankfulness and engagement to God, and their mutual love and fellowship with each other, as members of the same mystical body.

Q. 170: How do they that worthily communicate in the Lord's Supper, feed upon the body and blood of Christ therein?

A: As the body and blood of Christ are not corporeally or carnally present in, with, or under, the bread and wine in the Lord's Supper; and yet are spiritually present to the faith of the receiver, no less truly and really than the elements themselves are to their outward senses; so they that worthily communicate in the sacrament of the Lord's Supper, do therein feed upon the body and blood of Christ, not after a corporal or carnal, but in a spiritual manner; yet truly and really, while by faith they receive and apply unto themselves Christ crucified, and all the benefits of his death."

It must be admitted that this is not entirely free from ambiguity, as compared with the language of the sixteenth century. Taken by itself, it might be held to mean that the presence of Christ's body is involved in the lively conception of it in the worshiper's mind, as a mere idea. But doing so involves a strange abuse of language to express so plain a thought. Those who are tolerably familiar with Calvin's doctrine of the Lord's Supper, as it was held before this time in the Reformed Church, will agree that such poor linguistic construction found here doesn't deserve respect. It is not simply a *real spiritual* presence that is here affirmed as belonging to the sacrament, but a *spiritual real* presence,[18] an actual communication by faith with the body and blood of Christ that involves union and communion with His actual Person. Only as Christ's presence is as real as our own bodies can believers find a full interest in all the benefits of His death.

The term *spiritual* is not opposed to the idea of substance, nor does it refer to the Person of Christ simply as a spirit, and not a body. On

---

18   The difference between *real spiritual* and *spiritual real* is the subject of each phrase. The first lies in the spiritual dimension and the latter lies in the real dimension. A real spirit is more like a disembodied ghost, whereas what is spiritually real is also corporeal.

the contrary, it has regard to the most real substance of His body itself. The idea of Christ's flesh intermingling with our flesh is simply imaginary and must be abandoned. Rather, the meaning conveyed here asserts even more positively that we are speaking of a real participation in the fleshly life of Jesus, which cannot be separated from its effects. Our communion is with the Savior's body and blood, the life-force coursing through His veins and the historical result of His bodily sacrifice, all of which are part of His spiritual form. The wholeness of His life is brought into the wholeness of the believer's life.

If this is not the meaning of the Westminster Assembly, if in the use of the language that has been borrowed so freely from the creed of Calvin and the Reformed Church in the sixteenth century, then the assembly intended a meaning quite different from that creed. Unfortunately, the language of the Westminster Confession opened the way to understand this communion to be a mere moral union with Christ, a communication with Him in His abstract, other worldly, divine nature alone, or only a moral appropriation of the merits of His life and death. It is quite difficult to make any intelligible sense whatever of their words, and more difficult still to vindicate the interpretation as worthy either of their wisdom or their truth.[19]

CHURCH OF ENGLAND

So far no notice has been taken of the Thirty-nine Articles of the Church of England. As this branch of the Protestant communion is considered by many to be somewhat tainted with the errors of Rome in its very constitution, it seemed best not to lay much stress on its testimony regarding the question at hand. It is remarkable that what is called by many *high sacramental doctrine* has had such little prominence in the teachings of the Reformed Church, compared with the original view of the sixteenth century.

We find that the doctrine has been clearly proclaimed. How could it be otherwise, in the period to which we refer? "Sacraments ordained of Christ," it is said, "be certain sure witnesses and effectual signs of grace, and God's good will towards us, by the which he doth work

---

19 In the interest of satisfying all factions and forging a position regarding the presence of Christ in communion that would be universally acceptable to all Protestants at the time, the Westminster Assembly crafted language that suggested the reality of both opposing views, which can only be resolved by resorting to intellectual abstractions and deeming them to be "spiritual."

invisibly in us, and doth not only quicken, but also strengthen and confirm our faith in him" (Art. xxv). However, it is only in a heavenly and spiritual manner, as distinguished from a mere corporeal eating. Nonetheless, "the body of Christ is given, taken, and eaten in the Supper" (Art. Xxviii).

In the Communion Service believers receive the elements and are represented as partaking of Christ's most blessed body and blood, at the same time. Undoubtedly the doctrine of the real presence of Christ by the Spirit in the Holy Eucharist is plainly taught by the English Church. So it is odd that any question should ever be made with regard to the point in the church itself. But it is no less certain that it has no claim to be considered a distinctively Episcopal doctrine in any sense, as far as the history of the Reformed Church is concerned. Among all the early Reformed Confessions, all more distinctly affirm it than the Thirty-nine Articles. The Confession of the Dutch Reformed Church, in particular, is decidedly more highly sacramental here than that of the Church of England. Even the Westminster Confession does a better job of it.

HOOKER AND OWEN

Lastly, we refer to the authority of two of the most eminent English divines who lived near the age of the Reformation, and who may be taken as the most prominent representatives of the two contrary tendencies found in the Reformed Church—Hooker and Owen. How different are their spiritual views, and yet how closely bound together they are regarding the ultimate ground of their religious life. Hooker seems to be the most earnest, most learned, and most indefatigable champion of the church as a whole. Owen is no less the indefatigable champion of the idea of religious freedom and individual responsibility. Hooker was the great ornament of the English Episcopacy. Owen was the prince, the oracle, and the metropolitan of the English Independency (Congregationalism) and Puritanism.

Hooker belongs to the close of the sixteenth century, Owen flourished amid the revolutionary storms of the period that followed. Both are considered witnesses only, and not as sources of authority in themselves. Hooker was an Episcopalian, with high views of the church. But as a man of learning, he must have understood the doctrine of the Reformed Church, as it was in his own time. Owen was a Puritan, with low views of the church. But this only makes his response to the same truth more striking because its last echo had nearly ceased to be heard among the Puritans of a later day.

The following passages are extracted from Hooker's *Ecclesiastical Polity* (emphasis added):

> "It is too cold an interpretation, whereby some men expound our being in Christ, to import nothing else, but only that the self-same nature which maketh us to be men, is in him, and maketh him man as we are. For what man in the world is there, which hath not so far forth communion with Jesus Christ? It is not this that can sustain the weight of such sentences as speak of the mystery of our coherence with Jesus Christ. *The church is in Christ as Eve was in Adam.* Yea, by grace, we are every one of us, in Christ and in his church, as by nature we are in those our first parents. God made Eve of the rib of Adam. And his church he frameth out of the very flesh, the very wounded and bleeding side of the Son of man. His body crucified and his blood shed for the life of the world, are the true elements of that heavenly being, which maketh us such as himself is of whom we come. For which cause the words of Adam may be fitly the words of Christ concerning his church, 'flesh of my flesh, and bone of my bones,' a true native extract out of mine own body. So that *in him even according to his manhood*, we according to our heavenly being, are as branches in that root out of which they grow" (Book V. chap. lvi. § 7).

> "These things St. Cyril duly considering reproveth their speeches, which taught that only the deity of Christ is the vine whereupon we by faith do depend as branches, and that neither his flesh nor our bodies are comprised in this resemblance. For doth any man doubt, but that even *from the flesh of Christ our very bodies do receive that life which shall make them glorious at the latter day, and for which they are already accounted parts of his blessed body*? Our corruptible bodies could never live the life they shall live, were it not that here they are joined with his body which is incorruptible, and that his is in ours as a cause of immortality, a cause by removing through the death and merit of his own flesh that which hindered the life of ours. Christ is therefore, both as God and as man, that true vine, whereof we *both spiritually and corporally* are true branches. The mixture of his bodily substance with ours is a thing which the ancient Fathers disclaim. Yet the mixture of his flesh with ours, they speak of, to signify what our very bodies, through mystical conjunction, receive from that vital efficacy which we know to be in

his; and from bodily mixtures they borrow divers similitudes rather to declare the truth than the manner of coherence between his sacred and the sanctified bodies of saints" (Book V. c. lvi. § 9).

"This was it that some did exceedingly fear, lest Zwingli and Oecolampadius would bring to pass, that men should account of this sacrament but only as of a shadow, destitute, empty, and void of Christ. But seeing that by opening the several opinions which have been held, they are grown for aught I can see on all sides at the length to a general agreement concerning that which alone is material, namely the real participation of Christ, and of life in his body and blood by means of this sacrament; wherefore should the world continue still distracted and rent with so manifold contentions, when there remaineth now no controversy saving only about the subject where Christ is? Yea, even in this point no side denieth but that the soul of man is the receptacle of Christ's presence. Whereby the question is yet driven to a narrower issue, nor doth any thing rest doubtful but this, whether when the sacrament is administered Christ be whole within man only, or else his body and blood be also externally seated in the very consecrated elements themselves; which opinion they that defend, are driven either to consubstantiate and incorporate Christ with elements sacramental, or to transubstantiate and change their substance into his; and so the one to hold him really but invisibly molded up with the substance of those elements, the other to hide him under the only visible show of bread and wine, the substance whereof, as they imagine, is abolished, and his succeeded in the same room" (Book V. c. lxvii. § 2).

"It is on all sides plainly confessed, first, that *this sacrament is a true and a real participation of Christ, who thereby imparteth himself, even his whole entire person as a mystical Head unto every soul that receiveth him, and that every such receiver doth incorporate or unite himself unto Christ as a mystical member of him,* yea of them also whom he acknowledged to be his own; secondly, that to whom the person of Christ is thus communicated, to them he giveth by the same sacrament his Holy Spirit to sanctify them as it sanctifieth him which is their head; thirdly, that what merit, force, or virtue soever there is in his sacrificed body and blood, we freely, fully, and wholly have it by this sacrament; fourthly, that the effect thereof in us is a real transmutation of our souls and bodies from sin to righteousness, from death and corruption to immortality and life; fifthly, that because the sacrament being of itself but a corruptible and earthly creature, must needs be thought an unlikely instrument to work so

admirable effects in man, we are therefore to rest ourselves altogether upon the strength of his glorious power, who is able and
will bring to pass that the bread and cup which he giveth us shall
be truly the thing he promiseth.

"It seemeth therefore much amiss that against them whom they
term Sacramentarians, so many invective discourses are made, all
running upon two points, that *the Eucharist is not a bare sign or figure only, and that the efficacy of his body and blood is not all we receive
in this sacrament.* For no man having read their books and writings
which are thus traduced, can be ignorant that both these assertions
they plainly confess to be most true. They do not so interpret the
words of Christ, as if the name of his body did import but the figure of his body, and to be were only to signify his blood. They
grant that these holy mysteries received in due manner do instrumentally both make us partakers of the grace of that body and
blood which were given for the life of the world, and besides also
impart unto us even in true and real though mystical manner the
very person of our Lord himself, whole, perfect, and entire, as hath
been showed" (Book V. c. lxvii. § 7, 8).

Extracts from Owen, the oracle of the Independents

It is easy to feel ourselves to be in a different element from that
which formed the inward life of Hooker. The whole system of Owen
tended to carry him towards an incorporeal spiritualism in religion,
that might be thought to be particularly unfavorable to a right understanding of the sacraments. Still, however, when we contrast his
language with the frigid, rationalistic style of the present day (1850s),
we should not be surprised at the difference. The following passages
are taken from Owen's "Sacramental Discourses," Vol. XVII, of his
Works, Russel's London edition (emphasis added).

"Christ is present with us in an especial manner in this ordinance.
One of the greatest engines that the devil ever made use of to overthrow the faith of the church, was by forging such a presence of
Christ as is not truly in this ordinance, to drive us off from looking
after that presence which is true. I look upon it as one of the greatest engines that hell ever set on work. It is not a corporeal presence;
there are innumerable arguments against that; every thing that is in
sense, reason, and the faith of a man, overthrows that corporeal
presence. ... Christ is present in this ordinance in an especial man-

ner in three ways: by representation; by exhibition; by obsignation[20] or sealing." Disc. x. p. 209, 210.

"Christ is present with us by way of exhibition; that is, *he doth really tender and exhibit himself unto the souls of believers in this
ordinance*, which the world hath lost, and knows not what to make
of it. They exhibit that which they do not contain. This bread doth
not contain the body of Christ, or the flesh of Christ; the cup doth
not contain the blood of Christ; but they exhibit them; both do as
really exhibit them to believers, as they partake of the outward
signs. *Certainly we believe that our Lord Jesus Christ doth not invite us
unto this table for the bread that perishes, for outward food; it is to feed
our souls.* What do we think then? Doth he invite us unto an
empty, painted feast? Do we deal so with our friends? Here is
something really exhibited by Jesus Christ unto us to receive, be-
side the outward pledges of bread and wine. We must not think
the Lord Jesus Christ deludes our souls with empty shows and ap-
pearances. That which is exhibited is himself, it is his 'flesh as meat
indeed, and his blood as drink indeed;' it is himself as broken and
crucified that he exhibits unto us." ... "Christ doth exhibit himself
unto our souls, if we are not wanting unto ourselves, for these two
things, incorporation and nourishment; to be received into union;
and to give strength unto our souls" (Ib. p. 211, 212).

"As it is plain from the sign and the thing signified that *there is a
grant, or a real communication of Jesus Christ unto the souls of them
that believe*, so it is evident from the nature of the exercise of faith in
this ordinance; it is by eating and drinking. Can you eat and drink
unless something be really communicated? You are called to eat
the flesh and drink the blood of the Son of Man; unless really communicated, we cannot eat it nor drink it. We may have other
apprehensions of these things, but our faith cannot be exercised in
eating and drinking, which is a receiving of what is really exhibited and communicated. *As truly my brethren as we do eat of this
bread and drink of this cup, which is really communicated to us, so every
true believer doth receive Christ, his body and blood, in all the benefits of
it, that are really exhibited by God unto the soul in this ordinance, and it
is a means of communicating to faith*" (Disc, xxiii. p. 265).

"It is a *common received notion among Christians, and it is true, that
there is a peculiar communion with Christ in this ordinance, which we
have in no other ordinance*; that there is a peculiar acting of faith in
this ordinance which is in no other ordinance. *This is the faith of*

---

20   Obsignation: the act of sealing or ratifying, the state of being sealed or confirmed.

the whole church of Christ, and has been so in all ages. This is the greatest mystery of all the practicals of our Christian religion, *a way of receiving Christ by eating and drinking*, something peculiar that is not in prayer, that is not in the hearing of the word, nor in any other part of divine worship whatsoever; a peculiar participation of Christ, a peculiar acting of faith towards Christ. *This participation of Christ is not carnal, but spiritual.* In the beginning of the ministry of our Lord Jesus Christ, when he began to instruct them in the communication of himself, and the benefit of his mediation, to believers, because it was a new thing, he expresses it by eating his 'flesh and drinking his blood, John vi. 53, 'Unless ye eat the flesh and drink the blood of the Son of man, ye have no life in you.' This offended and amazed them. They thought he taught them to eat his natural flesh and blood. 'How can this man give us his flesh to eat? They thought he instructed them to be cannibals. Whereupon he gives that everlasting rule for the guidance of the church, *which the church forsook, and thereby ruined itself*; saith he, 'It is the Spirit that quickens; the flesh profits nothing. The words that I speak, they are spirit, and they are life.' I*t is a spiritual communication, saith he, of myself unto you; but it is as intimate, and gives as real an incorporation, as if you did eat my flesh and drink my blood"* (Disc. xxv. p. 268).

"The fourth thing is the mysteriousness, which I leave to your experience, for it is beyond expression, the mysterious reception of Christ in this peculiar way of exhibition. There is a reception of Christ as tendered in the promise of the Gospel, *but here is a peculiar way of his exhibition under outward signs, and a mysterious reception of him in them really, so as to come to a real substantial incorporation in our souls"* (Ib. p. 270).

All this is not without some measure of ambiguity as it regards a real participation in the substance of Christ's humanity. It falls short of the firm, clear utterances of Calvin and the church of the sixteenth century. But it still provides important testimony of Christ's real presence in the sacrament from such a man as Owen, in the age of Cromwell and the English Commonwealth. Owen at least writes in strong terms his testimony of the objective power and true exhibition of Christ's presence in the sacrament.

Moreover, the communion is specific, mystical, bound to the ordinance as its medium and instrument, not merely spiritual, empirical, and theological. It involves a real incorporation into a real Christ, and it is plainly understood that this includes a special respect to His human nature, His flesh and blood, as was given for the life of the world.[21]

But it is at this particular point that Owen's representation wavers. The truth that struggles for utterance is still embarrassed by its flight into abstraction that colors the understanding, and is not permitted to come to a clear, complete, and unfaltering expression.[22]

---

21 To deny the corporeal reality of Christ's body and blood in the sacrament is to undermine the reality of the efficacy of Christ's bodily and bloody sacrifice on the cross.

22 It seems that the more that science became the driving perspective of intellectual and scholastic endeavors, the more embarrassing the plain statement of the doctrine of Christ's presence became. Of course, the reigning scientific perspective of the time was Newtonian, and the struggles to hold the truth of Scripture to the truths of Newtonian physics is clearly seen. The development of quantum physics and modern linguistics appear to have paved the way to maintain the integrity of science and the integrity of Scripture in the original Reformed position of Christ's presence in the Eucharist.

CHAPTER II

The Modern Puritan Theory
Section I.

It cannot be denied that the view of the Lord's Supper at the present time in the Protestant church involves a serious departure from the faith of the sixteenth century with regard to the Eucharist. The fact must be immediately clear to anyone familiar with Christianity today (1850s). This difference can be seen only when contrasted with the views that have been herein described and detailed.

Falling Away from the Creed of the Reformation

The departure from the original Reformed sacramental doctrine is not confined to any particular country or religious confession (denomination). It can be most widely seen among the continental churches of Europe, which have succumbed to a rampant faith in Rationalism, which has replaced the old orthodoxy even among theologians. It is also widely prevalent in Great Britain and America, as well.

Most Striking in the American Lutheran Church

It is especially striking in the Lutheran Church, in the light of this study, because of the Lutheran's supposed high view of the Lord's Supper, and the zeal it exercised in opposition to what it saw as the sacramentarian error. In this regard, the current Lutheran position can hardly be recognized as the Lutheran position of the Reformation. The original words remain, but their original distinctive character is gone.

This is particularly true regarding the Lutheran Church in America. It is not true that it has only moderated the old sacramental doctrine of the church as is seen in the *Form of Concord*. Clearly, it has abandoned its own previous doctrine altogether. Not only is the original Lutheran position that was occupied so violently against the Calvinists in the sixteenth century, openly and fully renounced currently, but the Calvinistic foundation itself, which was originally opposed as being the very threshold of Godless infidelity, has now come to be considered to be in too close agreement with Rome. In no other denomination is the anti-mystical, pro-rationalistic tendency that was originally charged upon the Reformed doctrine, more decidedly developed in the folds of its own bosom.

This involves a strange contradiction that has not always been true on their part. It must not be assumed that the abandonment of the original Lutheran principle of Christ's presence in the sacrament can be limited to this doctrine alone. As Christ's centrality in the sacrament goes, so goes the whole Christian theological system, in that the whole system follows the centrality of Christ and/or the lack thereof. Where Christ is not bodily present in the sacrament, He is not bodily present in the atonement or redemption, which must then necessarily nullify the whole idea of Christ's atonement and redemption.

The whole life of the Reformed Church in its various branches regarding the Eucharistic question has been brought into contradiction to the original Reformed position. Reformed churches today cannot be true to themselves. This of course we regard as a fit subject for lamentation. Never was there a time when it was more important, that this church should understand and fulfill her own mission; and in no part of the world perhaps is this more needed than just here in America, where the tendency to undervalue all that is sacramental and objective in religion has become unhappily so strong.

Note on the Lutheran Observer

It is not intended, of course, to indiscriminately involve all who are connected with the church in this admonishment. There are, no doubt, many excellent pastors who belong to it who are concerned and deplore the errors that are revealed here. And it is to be trusted that these will yet bring their influence to the situation, in order to deflect to some degree the reproach now resting upon these churches. For the fact of the reality of the situation herein described cannot be seriously questioned by anyone acquainted with current trends in Christianity. Nor can it be denied that these matters must be subject to public treatment.

It is well known that the American Lutheran Church has altogether abandoned the sacramental doctrine of Luther, and the original
genius and life of the Lutheran Confession, regarding Christ's presence
in the sacrament. This condition is regarded by others as an evangelical improvement in the character and state of the church. Such a view
necessarily judges both modern Puritanism and Methodism to be
superior, and work to supplant these ideas into the bosom of their
respective churches.[1]

We have an obligation to see the *Lutheran Observer* as a measure of
the prevailing thinking and practice of the Lutheran Church. The
Observer is not under any ecclesiastical direction and control. The editor's views are simply his own. Nonetheless, the mere fact that this
denominational newspaper represents the Lutheran Church before the
world, makes it an organ of the church, and a credible interpreter of
the church's views. So, it is important to notice that the *Observer* has
been characteristically un-Lutheran in other respects as well, and now
openly derides the doctrine of Christ's real presence in communion
through the humanity of Christ as an unnecessary superstition!

For instance, referring to the Reformed or Calvinistic view as
asserted at Mercersburg, the editor of the *Observer* does not hesitate in
the Dec. 5, 1845, issue to say that:

> "Dr. Nevin's doctrine of Con-corporation, alias his semi-Roman-
> ism in relation to the Eucharist...." ... "The Mercersburg effort to
> revive the errors of bygone ages, from which it was fondly hoped
> our American churches had finally and forever escaped." ... "That
> figment of the imagination, that poor, low, mystical, confused, car-
> nal, and antiquated doctrine, yclept (sic) con-corporation! Only
> think of it—the literal communication of Christ's glorified human-
> ity to the believer, thus confounding the natures of believers and of
> Christ, and actually predicating ubiquity of humanity! The glori-
> fied body of Christ received by the believer with the bread and
> wine!"

---

1   This idea was worked out in more detail in Nevin's treatment of the *Anxious Bench*,
    which shows that the New Measures of Finney were not actually new, but were
    simply advancements on the errors of the Puritans and Methodists. The central error
    that concerned Nevin was the loss of the objective character of Jesus Christ in the
    life of the church, and the emphasis on the subjectivity of the individual's personal
    Christian experience.

"If this is not a corporeal presence, what meaning is there in language? If (Nevin's analysis) is not Puseyism,[2] and an immense stride toward Romanism, we would like to know what is?" ... "It grates upon the ear, jars the feelings, offends the understanding, and unhinges the holiest associations of many of the best and most spiritual [sic!] men, in the most evangelic churches."

This is how, not the old Lutheran, but the old Reformed doctrine of the Lord's Supper, is profanely abused by the principal voice of the American Lutheran Church! Of course, multitudes in that church have been pained and mortified by such bare-faced ecclesiastical infidelity. They disclaim all sympathy with it in their hearts, and protest against it quietly as downright treason to all true Lutheranism. Still, the paper is endured as the principle organ of the church, and until something more effective than silent protest is practiced, we must mourn over fact that the Lutheran Church is faithfully represented by the *Lutheran Observer*.[3]

Same in the Reformed Church
Unfortunately, it is not the Lutheran Church alone that has fallen away from its original creed regarding the Lord's Supper. Though the defection may not be as immediately palpable and open to observation, it exists with equal certainty in the Reformed churches. It is worse in Europe, but not much better in America.

Sect system
The very nature of our sect system[4] is necessarily unfavorable to all proper concerns regarding the sacraments. This may be taken, and

---

2   Edward Bouverie Pusey (1800-1882) was an English churchman and Regius Professor of Hebrew at Christ Church, Oxford. He was one of the leaders of the Oxford Movement. Puseyism was a derogatory term for the Oxford Movement used by its contemporary opponents. The Oxford Movement, within the Church of England, originated at Oxford University in 1833, and sought to link the Anglican Church more closely to the Roman Catholic Church.
3   Whether this accusation is true and enduring must be left in the hands of the Lutherans. However, the modern fracturing of the Lutheran Church in America and the ongoing existence of the Missouri and Wisconsin Synods of the Lutheran Church suggest that the problem persists.
4   The proliferation of Christian denominations, which now (2011) are themselves obstacles of the true, ancient, proper, reformed, and universal doctrine and practice of the Eucharist.

indeed must be taken, as a just evaluation of the spirit of sect, as distinguished from the true spirit of the Christian church.

Baptists

As the Baptistic spirit continues to divide and proliferate a variety of Baptistic sects, it will be found that Baptism and the Lord's Supper are increasingly viewed as mere outward signs, without the efficacy that is supposed to be in the inward state of the person by whom they are received. It is this idea that leads to the rejection of infant baptism on the part of those who think that they can improve historic Christianity by schismatic division. It is particularly significant, moreover, that the sum of the Baptistic schisms is numerically larger than any other denomination in the country.

Prevalence of the Baptistic Principle

But the Baptistic Principle[5] prevails more extensively than simply in Baptist churches. It is very plain that all true sense of the sacramental value of infant baptism is lacking in large portions of the church where the ordinance is still retained. And in consequence, it follows the pattern of being merely an outward, traditional, lifeless form. Because of this general sacramental attitude, the Lord's Supper also is shorn of all its significance and power. Methodism, though not technically Baptist, has the same attitudes about the sacraments, and their doctrine of the church is almost as seriously flawed as the Baptist system is.

The general Baptistic sacramental error, however, is more extensive. It even reaches into various Reformed churches, i.e. the various Presbyterian branches, and Dutch Reformed, show evidence that they have fallen away, to some extent, from the original position of the Reformed Church regarding the sacraments. Remains of the original teachings can be found in the private piety of many such church members today, probably because of their early catechical education, and partly because of their personal piety.

---

5   Baptistic Principles: 1) Baptism by immersion, 2) salvation is essential to baptism, 3) all of the New Testament is the Law of Christianity; the New Testament is all of the Law of Christianity, 4) individualism, 5) freedom of individual conscience, 6) salvation is essential to church membership, 7) the church is a spiritual body, and none but the regenerate should belong to it (Source: Benajah Harvey Carroll, 1843-1914).

Note on Mystical Union

There is much comfort in the idea of union with Christ. The same idea in stronger terms is made by Prof. Tayler Lewis, of New York in an article on the church question, published in the *Biblical Repository*, January, 1846. The idea of mystical union, he says correctly, is, and ever must be, a living principle in the hearts of all evangelical Christians. He appeals to the devotional books of the Scottish church, and even to the common phraseology of Wesleyan prayer meetings to show this is the form of the truth of life itself. It is the truth behind all the outward displays that are required by the various tenets of Rome or Oxford, though they are usually practiced as dead relics of antiquity.

> "The life may be stronger than the dogma. Even in the absence of definite conceptions, the extreme fondness of a certain class of minds for this language, manifests the current of the affections in distinction from the speculative views maintained, and a consciousness, that even if there be a figure, it is figurative of a reality more precious and glorious than was ever set forth in any form of rationalism."

This is very true. Dr. Lewis admits, however, that there has been a great falling away by the church at large from the faith of the Reformation, as well as from primitive Christianity with regard to this point. He says that even as a dogma, this truth is no longer maintained. He overrated the extent to which it was practically felt. It is always to be kept in mind that every Christian truth finds its counterfeit and shadow in the religious practices of a lower view. Rationalism and abstraction tend to prevail wherever people strain too hard to peer behind the mysteries of reality.

The very idea of religion, no matter how defective, always involves a demand or quest for union with God. Of course, when people get excited and especially in connection with Christianity, this need for union will prevail. And all this certainly constitutes a strong argument for the truth of religion and unity with God. But there is a constant human tendency to substitute the thought for the reality. It is common for people to think a thing and by thinking it think that they have done it, as seen among the Anabaptists[6] and Quakers.[7] In addition, much of the experience of Methodist prayer meetings labors under the same defect of unreality. There is a universal danger of this where religion is allowed to focus only or primarily on its subjective experience and/or expression, which always disregards or undervalues the sacraments and the idea of the holistic wholeness of the church, or the people of God in Christ.

The piety of the old Scotch divines is far more substantial in contravening this tendency, and we should be thankful that the life and power of the sacraments and the church are still felt among the old Scots. The assumptions of mystical union are far more extensive than the doctrine is understood or acknowledged among the Scots. This lack of understanding regarding the mystery at the heart of life and doctrine is itself a great evil. And it is especially difficult to hold to the mystical truth against a strong tide of Rationalism and its errors. And it is particularly difficult when Rationalism arrogates to itself the title of Protestant orthodoxy, because it threatens to rarefy and spiritualize the whole of the truth into a moral abstraction, at best.

As long as Rationalism masquerades as Christianity among the populous—and particularly among church leaders and theologians, all doctrine of any kind can be suppressed in a variety of ways. Such sup-

---

6   Anabaptists: (re-baptizers) are Protestant Christians of the Radical Reformation of sixteenth century Europe, and their direct descendants, particularly the Amish, Brethren, Hutterites, and Mennonites. The Anabaptists insist upon the free course of the Holy Spirit in worship, and maintain that all must be judged by Scripture alone. While the original Reformers understood *sola scriptura* to mean that the Bible was the highest and *final* authority of worship and polity, the Anabaptists understood it to mean the Bible was the *only* authority.

7   The Religious Society of Friends (Quakers) began in England in the late 1640s amidst social upheaval and dissatisfaction with the established church, the execution of the king, and the rise of Nonconformist movements. George Fox, a prominent Quaker in the seventeenth century, taught that Christ had come to teach his people himself. This is the basis of modern Quaker faith and practice. Fox was convinced that it was possible to have a direct experience of Jesus Christ without mediation. He spread this message as an itinerant preacher and found several existing groups of like-minded people. In the first few years of the movement, Quakers thought of themselves as part of the restoration of the true Christian church after centuries of apostasy. While the theological beliefs of different Quaker groups do not correspond exactly their style of worship, the groups that use programmed worship (liturgy) tend to be more evangelical, and those with unprogrammed worship tend to be more liberal. Quakers also believe in continuing revelation, where God speaks directly to individuals today, which classifies them as Charismatic.

pression is done *theoretically* by Rationalists. It is a common error for Rationalists to mistake the description of a thing for the thing itself. This is how they approach our systems of theology, biblical exposi- tions, sermons, and religious teaching generally, and more so regarding the sacramental question. This rationalistic tendency is more damaging to the Christian sacraments because the sacraments require an objective spiritual operation that is outside of the subjective reality of the individual.

When it comes to the sacraments, this rationalistic substitution of idea for reality is accomplished *practically*. Or perhaps it would be bet- ter to call it an *impractical* application because it substitutes a mere idea for what must be a reality in practice. The orthodox ideas and feelings regarding the sacraments are maintained on the part of professing rationalistic church attenders, but they are equally denied by their practice. For instance, the authority of church elders is maintained in doctrine, but too often disregarded in actual practice. This undermines the old doctrines by taking the wind out of their proverbial sails, and leads to the ultimate rejection of such doctrines and their loss to the general knowledge of the church.

When all of this is brought into view, it is most often denied. And sometimes it is denied that the Reformed Church ever held or taught any doctrines of the sort. Or if at length, it is admitted that Calvin and some other old church divines maintained some such view, it is sum- marily argued that the work of the Reformation was to disabuse the church of such primitive superstitions.

Of course it is true that old religious superstitions have clogged the arteries of human development for too many millennia and that the Reformation did, in fact, remove many of them as it also brought a newfound interest in science and technology. Indeed, science and technology are the fruit of Christian rationalism, which posited reason and consistency as characteristics of the natural realm because they are characteristics of God. So, it is to an extent understandable. The great thinkers did not want to get dragged back into the darkness and bondage they had just left behind.

So, from their Newtonian scientific perspective, they considered the older doctrines to have no relevancy whatever for the church because it was being flooded with new light and liberty regarding the gospel and because of God's grace that had been newly rediscovered by Luther. The very ideas of a spiritual reality were unintelligible and absurd, savoring of the dead doctrine of transubstantiation, which exalted the flesh at the expense of the spirit because it insisted on the empirical, corporeal reality of the Holy Spirit.

A real presence of the wholeness of Christ in the Lord's Supper in or under any form was simply not to be endured by human reason because the rationalists thought that it was contrary to God's truth, and therefore to his Word. Thus, Rationalism remains the dominant perspective that guides the thinking of our churches generally. Even in the Episcopal Church, with all the account it professes to make of the sacraments, few are willing to adopt all of the necessary implications of the Eucharistic presence that were made clear either by Hooker or Calvin.

To see the stark contrast between these two views we need only seriously attend to the differences made apparent by this study, particularly to the doctrines and practices of the Eucharist. Compare the language of your church position with the language of the church on the same subject in the original Reformation, prior to, say, 1625.

Compare the old doctrines to the following extracts taken from several popular modern theological writers (1850s), which provide a fair representation of the view that is now too commonly entertained among Christians and their churches.

Extracts from Ridgely's Body of Divinity

"The sacraments are also said to seal the blessings that they signify; and accordingly they are called not only signs but seals. It is a difficult matter to explain, and clearly to state the difference between these two words, or to show what is contained in a seal that is not in a sign. Some think that it is distinction without a difference."

"If we call them confirming seals, we intend nothing else hereby but that God has, to the promises that are given to us in his word, added these ordinances; not only to bring to mind this great doctrine, that Christ has redeemed his people by his blood, but to assure them that they who believe in him shall be made partakers of this blessing; so that these ordinances are a pledge thereof to them, in which respect God has set his seal, whereby in an objective way he gives believers to understand, that Christ and his benefits are theirs; and they are obliged at the same time by faith, as well as in an external manner, to signify their compliance with his covenant, which we may call their setting to their seal that God is true."

(Ridgely's *Body if Divinity,* Philadelphia edition of 1815, Vol. IV. p. 163, 165.)

Extracts from President Edwards[8]

"Thus concerning Christ's death, showed forth or signified in this ordinance. We are farther, under this head, to consider how he is present, and they who engage in it aright feed on his body and blood by faith. *We are not to suppose that Christ is present in a corporal way,* so that we should be said to partake of his body in a literal sense; but he being a divine person, and consequently omnipresent, and having promised his presence with his church in all ages and places, when met together in his name; in this respect he is present with them, in like manner as he is in other ordinances, to supply their wants, hear their prayers, and strengthen them against corruption and temptation, and remove their guilt by the application of his blood, which is presented as an object for their contemplation in a more peculiar manner in this ordinance."

"*As for our feeding on, or being nourished by the body and blood of Christ, these are metaphorical expressions,* taken from and adapted to the nature and quality of the bread and wine by which it is signified; but that which we are to understand hereby is, our graces being farther strengthened and established, and we enabled to exercise them with greater vigor and delight; and this derived from Christ, and particularly founded on his death. And when we are said to feed upon him in order hereunto, it denotes the application of what he has done and suffered to ourselves; and in order hereunto we are to bring our sins, with all the guilt that attends them, as it were, to the foot of the cross of Christ, confess and humble our souls for them before him, and by faith plead the virtue of his death, in order to our obtaining forgiveness, and at the same time renew our dedication to him, while hoping and praying for the blessing and privileges of the covenant of grace, which were purchased by him." (Ibid. p. 245.)

"There is in the Lord's Supper a mutual solemn profession of the two parties transacting the covenant of grace, and visibly united in that covenant; the Lord Christ by his minister on the one hand, and the communicants (who are professing believers) on the other. The administrator of the ordinance acts in the quality of Christ's minister, acts in his name, as representing him; and stands in the place where Christ himself stood, at the first administration of this

---

8   Jonathan Edward's son.

sacrament, and in the original institution of the ordinance. Christ, by the speeches and actions of the minister, makes a solemn profession of his part in the covenant of grace; he exhibits the sacrifice of his body broken and his blood shed; and in the minister's offering the sacramental bread and wine to the communicants, Christ presents himself to the believing communicants as their propitiation and bread of life; and by these outward signs confirms and seals his sincere engagements to be their Savior and food, and to impart to them all the benefits of his propitiation and salvation. And they, in receiving what is offered, and *eating and drinking the symbols of Christ's body and blood*, also profess their part in the covenant of grace; they profess to embrace the promises and lay hold of the hope set before them, to receive the atonement, to receive Christ as their spiritual food, and to feed upon him in their hearts by faith."

"The sacramental elements in the Lord's Supper do represent Christ as a party in covenant, as truly as a proxy represents a prince to a foreign lady in her marriage; and our taking those elements is as truly a professing to accept Christ, as in the other case the lady's taking the proxy is her professing to accept the prince as her husband. Or the matter may be more fitly represented by this similitude:—it is as if a prince should send an ambassador to a woman in a foreign land, proposing marriage, and by his ambassador should send her his picture, and should desire her to manifest her acceptance of his suit, not only by professing her acceptance in words to his ambassador, but in token of her sincerity, openly to take or accept that picture, and to seal her profession by thus representing the matter over again by a symbolical action." (President Edwards. *On Full Communion. Works*, New York, 1844, Vol. I. p. 145, 146.)

Extracts from Hopkins

"The elements of this ordinance are bread and wine. The bread consecrated and broken represents the broken body of Christ, in his death on the cross. The wine poured out represents his blood in his death, which was shed for the remission of sins. The professed followers of Christ, *by eating the bread and drinking the wine, when consecrated and blessed by prayer and thanksgiving, and distributed to them by the officers of the church, do by this transaction profess cordially to receive Christ by faith*, and to live upon him, loving him, and trusting in him for pardon and complete redemption, consecrating themselves to his service. And by the ministers of the gospel consecrating those elements, and ordering them to be distributed to the communicants, Christ is exhibited as an all-sufficient Savior, and the promise of salvation is expressed and sealed to all his friends. *This is therefore a covenant transaction*, in which those who partake of the bread and wine express their faith in Christ, that they are his friends, and devoted to his service, and their cordial compliance with the covenant of grace, and solemnly seal this covenant by partaking of these elements. And at the same time they are a token and seal of the covenant of grace on the part of Christ." (Dr. Samuel Hopkins. *System of Theology*, Second edition, Boston, 1811. Vol. II. p. 343.)

Extracts from Bellamy

"At the Lord's table Christ, by the mouth of his minister says, *This is my body, take ye, eat ye all of it. This is my blood, take ye, drink ye all of it.* Hereby sealing to the truth contained in the 'written instrument.' But it is therein written in so many words: 'I am the living bread that came down from heaven. If anyone eats of this bread, he will live forever. And the bread that I will give for the life of the world is my flesh.... Whoever feeds on my flesh and drinks my blood abides in me, and I in him' John 6:51, 56. Thus it is written, and thus it is sealed on Christ's part. On the other hand, the communicant by his practice declares: 'I take his flesh, and eat it; I take his blood and drink it;' and seals the covenant on his part. And thus the 'written instrument' is externally and visibly sealed, ratified, and confirmed, on both sides, with as much formality as any 'written instrument' is mutually sealed by the parties in any covenant among men. And now if both parties are sincere in the covenant thus sealed, and if both abide by and act according to it, the communicant will be saved." (Bellamy. *Works*, Vol. III. p. 166.)

Extracts from Dwight's Theology

Dr. Dwight has much to say of the Lord's Supper. In speaking of its design, he tells us that it is intended, first, to represent the great sacrifice of Christ on the cross. Sensible impressions go far beyond those made directly on the understanding. In no other ordinance is this truth so fully realized as in the Lord's Supper.

"The breaking of the bread, and the pouring out of the wine, exhibit the sacrifice of Christ with a force, a liveliness of representation, confessed by all Christians, at all times; and indeed by most others also; and unrivaled in its efficacy even by the Passover itself. All the parts of this service are perfectly simple, and are contemplated by the mind without the least distraction or labor. The symbols are exact, and most lively portraits of the affecting original, and present to us the crucifixion, and the sufferings of the great subject of it, as again undergone before our eyes. We are not barely taught; we see and hear, and of consequence feel, that Christ our Passover was slain for us, and died on the cross that we might live."

"So those doctrines of the Christian system, which are most intimately connected with it, are here exhibited with a corresponding clearness."

"In this solemn ordinance, these truths are in a sense visible. The guilt of sin is here written with a pen of iron and with the point of a diamond. Christ in a sense ascends the cross; is nailed to the accursed tree; is pierced with the spear; and pours out his blood to wash away the sins of men. Thus, in colors of life and death, we here behold the wonderful scene in which was laid on him the iniquity of us all."

The other purposes of the institution, treated of at length, are as follows: It is a standing proof of Christ's mission; it exhibits the purity of Christ's character; it admonishes Christians of the second coming of Christ; it unites them in a known, public, and efficacious bond of union; it is a visible and affecting pledge of Christ's love to His followers; it is suited also to edify Christians in the divine life.

"The edification of Christians is the increase of justness in their views, of purity and fervor in their affections, and of faithfulness in their conduct, with regard to the objects of religion. To this increase, in all respects, the Lord's Supper naturally and eminently contributes." (Dwight's *Theology*, Serm. CLX.)

The motives which should influence us to the celebration of the Lord's Supper are stated to be: 1. The command of Christ; 2. The honor of Christ; 3. The benefits derived from it by the church; and 4. Our own personal good.

"At the table of Christ chiefly, after their baptism, Christians are seen, and see each other, as a public body, as mutual friends, and as followers of the Lamb. Here, mutually, they give and receive countenance and resolution; worship together as Christians only; rejoice together; weep together; and universally exercise the Christian graces, invigorated, refined, and exalted by the sympathy of

the gospel. Here the social principle of the intelligent nature ascends to the highest pitch of dignity and excellence, of which in
this world it is capable. Mind here refines, enlarges, and ennobles
mind; virtue purifies and elevates virtue; and evangelical friendship
not only finds and makes friends, but continually renders them
more and more worthy of the name."

"No exercises of the Christian life are ordinarily more pure, vigorous, and evangelical, than those which are experienced at the
sacramental table. The sense which we here feel of our guilt, danger, and helplessness, is apt to be vivid and impressive in an unusual
degree. Equally impressive are the views which we form of forgiv-
ing, redeeming, and sanctifying love. Here godly sorrow for sin is
powerfully awakened. Here are strongly excited complacency in
the divine character, admiration of the riches of divine grace, and
gratitude for the glorious interference of Christ in becoming the
propitiation of our sins. Here brotherly love is kindled into a flame;
and benevolence, warm, generous, and expansive, learns to encircle
the whole family of Adam. Here, more perhaps than anywhere
else, Christians have *the same mind which was also in Christ*, and prepare *themselves to walk as he walked*. Every evangelical affection
becomes vigorous and active, virtuous resolutions stable, and the
purposes of the Christian life exalted."

"The ends proposed in the institution of the Lord's Supper by the
Redeemer of mankind, are certainly of a most benevolent and glorious nature, and peculiarly worthy of the All-perfect Mind. They
are the enlargement and rectification of our views concerning the
noblest of all subjects, the purification of our affections, and the
amendment of our lives. The means by which these ends are accomplished, are equally efficacious and desirable. They are at the
same time simple, intelligible to the humblest capacity, in no respect burdensome, lying within the reach of all men, incapable of
being misconstrued without violence, and therefore not easily susceptible of mystical or superstitious perversion. In their own
proper, undisguised nature, they appeal powerfully to the senses,
the imagination, and the heart, and at the same time enlighten, in
the happiest manner, the understanding. Accordingly, Christians in
all ages have regarded this sacrament with the highest veneration;
have gone to the celebration with hope; attended it with delight;
and left it with improvement in the evangelical character."
(Dwight's *Theology*. Serm. CLXI.)

Extracts from Dick's Theology

Dr. Dick endorses and accepts in full the opinion of Zwingli on the Lord's Supper, which he affirms to have been this:

"That the bread and wine were *no more than a representation of the body and blood of Christ*; or in other words, the signs appointed to denote the benefits that were conferred upon mankind in consequence of the death of Christ; that therefore *Christians derive no other fruit from the participation of the Lord's Supper, than a mere commemoration and remembrance of the merits of Christ*, and that there is nothing in the ordinance but a memorial of Christ."

There seems to have been a disposition in that age, he thinks, "to believe that there was a presence of Christ in the Eucharist, different from his presence in the other ordinances of the gospel; *an undefined something which corresponded to the strong language used at the institution of the Supper*, 'This is my body, this is my blood.' Acknowledging it to be figurative, many still thought that a mystery was couched under it. It was not indeed easy for those who had long been accustomed to the notion of the bodily presence of Christ, at once to simplify their ideas; and perhaps too they were induced to express themselves as they did, with a view to give less offense to the Lutherans. Whatever was their motive, their language is not always sufficiently guarded."

"Calvin was one of the brightest ornaments of the Reformation, and in learning, genius, and zeal, had few equals, and no superior. Yet, he too falls into this condemnation. A passage is quoted, which it is found impossible to understand. 'It supposes a communion of believers in the human nature of our Savior, in the Eucharist; and endeavors to remove the objection arising from distance of place, by a reference to the almighty power of the Spirit, much in the same way as Papists and Lutherans solve the difficulty attending their respective systems.'"

"If Calvin had meant only that in the Sacred Supper believers have fellowship with Christ in his death, he would have asserted an important truth, attested by the experience of the people of God in every age; but why did he obscure it, and destroy its simplicity, by involving it in ambiguous language? *If he had any thing different in view; if he meant that there is some mysterious communication with his human nature, we must be permitted to say that the notion was as incomprehensible to himself as it is to his readers.*"

"Stripped of all metaphorical terms, the action must mean, that in the believing and grateful commemoration of his death, we enjoy the blessings which were purchased by it, in the same manner in which we enjoy them when we exercise faith in hearing the gospel. Why then should any man talk as Calvin does, of some inexplicable communion in this ordinance with the human nature of Christ; and tell us that although it seems impossible, on account of the distance to which he is removed from us, we are not to measure the power of the Divine Spirit by our standard? I am sure that the person who speaks so, conveys no idea into the minds of those whom he addresses; and *I am equally certain that he does not understand himself.*"

"There is an *absurdity* in the notion, that there is any communion with the body and blood of Christ, considered in themselves; that he intended any such thing; or that it could be of any advantage to us."

"When our church therefore says, that 'the body and blood are as really, but spiritually, present to the faith of believers in that ordinance, as the elements themselves are to their outward senses,' and that they 'feed upon his body and blood to their spiritual nourishment and growth in grace,' it can mean only, that our incarnate suffering Savior is *apprehended by their minds*, through the instituted signs; and that by faith they enjoy peace and hope; or it means something unintelligible and unscriptural."

"This looks to the Westminster Confession. The language of the Gallic or French Confession is then quoted, only to be condemned in still more explicit terms. Still the presence of Christ in the Eucharist must be admitted. But then it is only as he is present in religious services generally."

"In all these ordinances he is present; and he is present in the same manner in them all, namely, by his Spirit, who renders them effectual means of salvation." (*Lectures on Theology*, by the late Rev. John Dick, D. D., Lect. XCI. XCII.)

Extracts from Dr. Green

"By the body and blood of Christ, figuratively represented in the Lord's Supper, we are undoubtedly to understand his whole work of satisfying the justice of God in behalf of his peculiar people, which was consummated or completed, when his body was broken and his blood shed on the cross of Calvary; together with the privileges and blessings resulting, both in this life and that which is to come, from their Savior's finished work. All these rich and inestimable gifts of divine grace, faith receives and applies in the proper celebration of this holy rite."

"Justly does our Confession of Faith declare, when speaking of this sacrament, that 'the body and blood of Christ are as really, but spiritually, present to the faith of believers, in this ordinance, as the elements themselves are to the outward senses.' O, my young friends! what blessed visions of faith are those, in which this precious *grace creates an ideal presence* of the suffering, bleeding, dying, atoning Savior. When Gethsemane, and Pilate's hall, and the cross, the thorny crown, the nails, the spear, the hill of Calvary are in present view; when the astounding cry of the co-equal Son of the Father, 'My God, my God, why hast thou forsaken me,' thrills through the ear to the heart; when the joyous voice quickly follows, proclaiming, 'It is finished! Father, into thy hands, I commend my spirit.' Yes, it is here that faith sees the sinner's ransom amply paid, &c. &c. Well may it be added, that 'spiritual nourishment and growth in grace' must be the result of views and exercises such as these." (*Lectures on the Shorter Catechism*, by Dr. Green, vol. ii. p. 338-340.)

Extracts from Barnes

"John 7:53-56. The plain meaning of the passage is, that by his bloody death, his body and his blood offered in sacrifice for sin, he would procure pardon and life for man; and that they who partook of that, or had an interest in that, should obtain eternal life. He uses the figure of eating and drinking because that was the subject of discourse, because the Jews prided themselves much on the fact that their fathers had eaten manna; and because, as he had said that he was the bread of life, it was natural to carry out the figure, and say that that bread must be eaten, in order to be of any avail in supporting and saving men."

"Is meat indeed. Is truly food. My doctrine is truly that which will give life to the soul."

"Dwelleth in me. Is truly and intimately connected with me. To dwell or abide in him is to remain in the belief of his doctrine, and in the participation of all the benefits of his death."

"I in him. Jesus dwells in believers by his spirit and doctrine. When his spirit is given them to sanctify them, and his temper, his meekness, humility, love, pervades their hearts; and when his doctrine is received by them and influences their life, and when they are supported by the consolations of his gospel, it may be said that he abides or dwells in them."

"Matthew 26:26. This is my body. This represents my body. This broken bread shows the manner in which my body will be broken; or this will serve to call my dying sufferings to your remembrance."

"So Paul and Luke say of the bread, 'this is my body broken for you; this do in remembrance of me.' This expresses the whole design of the sacramental bread. It is by a striking emblem to call to remembrance in a vivid manner the dying sufferings of our Lord." (Barnes, Notes on the Gospels.)

These are respectable authorities, and they are quoted with respect. They will be acknowledged generally no doubt to be a fair representation of the predominant modern view, with regard to the Lord's Supper, particularly as it prevails in New England, and throughout the Reformed Churches in America in general. The extracts are various and complete, and are the best means of producing a clear and distinct idea of the sense that runs through them as a whole.

It would be easy of course to multiply them almost to any extent. But this is not necessary. All that the case requires is simply such a picture as may be acknowledged to furnish a proper exhibition of the general view it is intended to represent. For this, the extracts now offered are sufficient.

Section II

Difference Real and Seriously Important

The first point requiring attention is the difference between the view here exhibited and the Reformed doctrine of the sixteenth century, as has been described. It is not necessary to suggest that the two systems are absolutely different. But it is sufficient to notice that there has been a change, whether better or worse may not yet be clear. But the plain fact of the difference surely is clear. *The theology of New England, regarding the sacramental question, is not the theology of the Reformed Church of the sixteenth century.* This Puritan theory of the power and virtue of the sacraments is not the theory that was held by Calvin and that appears in the creeds and confessions of the first Calvinistic churches.

We need only to be familiar with the opinions of the sixteenth century, as presented for instance in Hospinian or Planck, and then contrast that to the thinking of our own time (1850s), as revealed in those works quoted in the previous chapter, and the difference should be clear. It reveals a transition into an entirely different spiritual perspective. The difference is not simply in the words and forms employed. It penetrates to the central ideas themselves. A different perspective prevails between the two cases regarding the nature and purpose of the sacraments. And underlying this, differences regarding the nature of Christian salvation and the relationship between believers and Christ is starkly revealed.

Calvin could not possibly have approved what appears to have been the sacramental doctrine of Jonathan Edwards. Ursinus would have openly condemned the way the subject is presented by Ridgely. Dr. Dick virtually pronounces himself at variance with all the early

145

Reformed doctrines. Even Owen himself could hardly have patiently endured the language of Dr. Dwight. The difference suggested here is real and serious. *The doctrine of the Lord's Supper that runs through these extracts, is not the original doctrine of the Reformed Church.* The corrections of the Reformation were more difficult to bring about than has been previously thought.

To make the difference more clear we will examine in detail some of the characteristics of the modern Puritan view in the light of the old Reformed view. They will reveal that there is more to this concern than mere words.

1. The Eucharist as Related to Other Services

In the old Reformed view the communion of the believer with Christ in the Supper has a specific purpose that is different from everything else that takes place in worship. The sacrament, *not merely the elements in themselves, but the union of element and Word through the procedure of the liturgy and the context of participation as a whole*, exhibits the saving grace of Jesus Christ to the faithful, who are the church, like nothing else.

It is not simply that the Word is brought to mind like a common memory of some past event. The objective fact of God in Christ in history is not simply an idea that is subjectively considered by the communicants, as if the communicants are objective observers of history. But rather, the subjectivity of the communicants finds its home in the objectivity of God in Christ, such that the subjectivity of the believers belongs to the objectivity of God without doubt. The subjective and objective are united without loss of their essential characteristics, rather than melded into a common identity that washes away their essential differences. Thus, they are held in union by the power of the Holy Spirit as they are joined together through the common life of the church, the body of Christ. The practice and context of the Eucharistic liturgy exerts a particular, peculiar, and altogether extraordinary power that benefits believers.

"There is a peculiar communion with Christ," says Dr. Owen, "which we have in no other ordinance." And this, he adds, *has been the faith of the whole church in all ages.* "A way of receiving Christ by eating and drinking; something peculiar, that is not in prayer, that is not in the hearing of the word, nor in any other part of divine worship whatever; a peculiar participation of Christ, a peculiar acting of faith towards Christ." Owen surely got this right!

However, in the Modern Puritan view this specific, peculiar virtue of the sacraments is not recognized. Christ is present in all ordinances, we are told by Dr. Dick, "and he is present in the same manner in them all, namely by his Spirit, who renders them effectual means of salvation." Similarly for Dr. Dwight the entire force of the institution consists in the occasion it provides for the personal affections and subjective involvement in the other elements of religious worship—the passion of singing hymns, the intellectual engagement of Scripture and sermon, the empathy of corporate prayer.

But the idea of a peculiar, objective sacramental power that is beyond the subjectivity of the believer, that is uniquely and powerfully exhibited in the Eucharist, seems to have no place at all in his understanding. Of course, he is aware of and celebrates the glory of God in Christ, and he is personally moved by the story and passion of Christ. But whatever union he finds with Christ is intellectual and abstractly "spiritual," such that whatever else it is, it is most certainly not actual, physical, or corporeal.

2. Mysteriousness of the Ordinance

In the old Reformed view, the sacramental transaction is mysterious and in some sense is an actual miracle. The Spirit works through the Eucharist in a way that transcends, not only human understanding, but the ordinary functioning of the world in every other way. Something happens in and through the sacraments that, on the one hand, belongs to the regular order of life that is exercised in the church, but on the other hand, it involves something supernatural. The Eucharist is uniquely miraculous, not simply as compared with nature, but even as compared to everything else about Christianity.

Calvin confirms it:

> "Not without reason, is the communication, which makes us flesh of Christ's flesh and bone of his bones denominated by Paul a great mystery. In the sacred Supper, therefore, we acknowledge it a miracle, transcending both nature and our own understanding, that Christ's life is made common to us with himself and his flesh given to us as aliment."

The miracle of the Eucharist that involves the union of believers in God in Christ is the central mystery of Christianity. And while it is uniquely exhibited in the Eucharist, it is everywhere present in Christian history, experience, understanding, and participation because it fixes the objectivity of God to the subjectivity of believers. It is historically objective and personally subjective.

"This mystery of our coalition with Christ," says the Gallic Confession, "is so sublime, that it transcends all our senses and also the whole course of nature."

"The mode is such," according to the Belgic Confession, "as to surpass the apprehension of our mind, and cannot be understood by any."

"The mysteriousness," we are told by Dr. Owen, "is beyond expression; the mysterious reception of Christ in this peculiar way of exhibition."

Now contrast this with the Eucharist as it has been represented by Puritans quoted above. Yes, the Eucharist is spoken of with great respect, as being full of interest, significance, and power. But there is *no mention of any mystery or miracle*. According to Dr. Dwight it has as much miracle and mystery as a fourth of July celebration. The ends contemplated in the one are religious, in the other, patriotic. But the institutions in both cases are spoken of in purely material respects of the same order. They simply serve to remind people of past events.

The ends proposed in the Supper,

> "the enlargement and rectification of our views—the purification of our affections—the amendment of our lives. The means are efficacious and desirable; at the same time simple; intelligible to the humblest capacity; in no respect burdensome; lying within the reach of all men; incapable of being misconstrued without violence; and therefore not easily susceptible of mystical or superstitious perversion. In their own proper, undisguised nature, they appeal powerfully to the senses, the imagination, and the heart; and at the same time enlighten in the happiest manner, the understanding."

All this is said to show "the wisdom of this institution," as if Christian wisdom purges all sense of mystery and miracle from Christianity, or at least from the symbolism and reality of its central institution.

"There seems to have been a disposition in that age," says Dr. Dick, with reference to the sixteenth century,

> "to believe that there was a presence of Christ in the Eucharist different from his presence in the other ordinances of the gospel; an undefined something, which corresponded to the strong language used at the institution of the Supper: 'This is my body, this is my blood.' Acknowledging it to be figurative, many still thought that a mystery was couched under it."

Dr. Dick himself finds no mystery in the Eucharist, probably because he considers himself to be enlightened and therefore beyond all ancient and gross superstitions. He is a victim of the Newtonian scientific rationalism of his age. And while there were most certainly a host of scientific and cultural advances that issued from Newtonian physics, the suggestion that humanity in general or some particularly intelligent individuals are able to rationally understand the deepest depths of the universe, much less God himself, is the very height of unmitigated pride!

Accordingly, Calvin's doctrine was rejected because it was deemed incomprehensible, not even understood by himself—as Calvin humbly admits—and most certainly beyond the understanding of his readers.

> "Plain, literal language is best, especially on spiritual subjects, and should have been employed by Protestant Churches with the utmost care, as the figurative terms of Scripture have been so grossly mistaken."

Dr. Dick simply cannot abide the fact that God can do something that he (Dr. Dick) cannot understand, and then require that very thing to be accepted by faith alone. Dr. Dick might wonder why God would require of us something that we cannot understand. To which we must then inquire of Dr. Dick why the central commitment to Christianity is a matter of faith rather than ratiocination.

To this we may add, that the very reason why the kind of plain, simple language that would suit Dr. Dick was not employed by the Protestant churches in their creeds and confessions is that these Protestant churches believed and intended to assert the presence of a mystery in the sacrament. But the perspective of Kant's enlightenment had replaced the original Reformed perspective and would not allow the reality of any mystery in Dr. Dick's understanding. Dr. Dick's position was more enlightened Rationalism than biblical Christianity, in that Dr. Dick was forced to deny anything that could not be rationally explained in order to be consistent to his underlying Rationalistic mindset.

3. Idea of its Objective Value or Force

The old Reformed doctrine always includes the idea of a real and objective element in the sacraments that is properly denoted as spiritual. The sacramental union between the sign and the thing signified is real, objective, and spiritual. And its reality exists in the objective, holistic wholeness of the ordinance itself, not merely in the subjective faith or mind of the communicant. Without faith this objective and mysterious power that belongs to the sacrament cannot benefit the communicant. Without faith this objective and mysterious power that belongs to the sacrament actually harms the communicant (1 Cor. 11:29). Subjective faith, the personal willingness created by unimpeded trust, establishes the necessary condition that fulfills the promise of Christian union to become actual. However, this condition is not the thing that it provides.

Note on the Difficulty of Understanding

It is strange how much difficulty some people seem to find in making this distinction. Because faith is necessary to the right use of the Lord's Supper, they mistakenly think that it is the power of personal faith that draws God's grace to the believer. So, when they hear about the objective virtue of the sacrament itself, or the actual presence of an objective spiritual energy that belongs to the institution of the sacraments that is apart from the faith of believers, they are quick to call it the *opus operatum* of Roman Catholicism.

Because the central mystery of transubstantiation involves a priestly incantation that functions not unlike the superstition of alchemy that supposedly changes one substance into another, they classify the mysterious presence of Christ in the sacraments with alchemy and transubstantiation, and categorically reject it. They don't realize that they have made an error by putting Christ's mystical presence into the same category as alchemy and transubstantiation.

Christ's mystical presence in the Eucharist makes no substantial changes, either to the elements or to the communicants. The bread and wine remain bread and wine, and the communicant remains a communicant. There is no substantial identity that is magically or mysteriously made between the communicant and Christ. The communicant does not become Christ, nor does Christ become the communicant. All personal identities are maintained.

There is, however, a unique and real union of wills that the institution of the Eucharist facilitates. Union with Christ involves the fusing or welding of the will of the communicant to the will of God in Christ. God's will remains God's and the will of the communicant remains his own, but their covenantal union is acknowledged and reaffirmed—and actually strengthened thereby. We can think of it as if each celebration of the Eucharist brings additional welds to the union. Some of those welds involve new relationships with other believers, and some of them involve the establishment and development of a deeper relationship with Christ.

Each new weld (participation in the Eucharist) brings additional strength to the union. All welding is done by the divine Welder, not by the communicants themselves. The divine Welder provides both the torch of the Holy Spirit and the welding rod (or filler metal), which is derived from the subjective experience of the believer. There is no transmutation of any elements in the believer or in God, but there is a gradual and progressive transformation of the will of the believer as it increasingly reflects and imitates the will of God. Forgive this poor analogy regarding the objective reality of the covenantal union that is forged between God and believers in Christ, which is both facilitated and celebrated in the sacrament of the Eucharist.

Precisely how this works is and will eternally remain a mystery because it is not under human scrutiny or control. Like birth, we only become aware of it after the fact. Thus, whether apprehended by the communicant or not, it requires faith, but is independent of that faith because it is willed and accomplished by the holistic wholeness of God in Christ alone.

The difference between condition and principle meets us everywhere. The plant cannot vegetate and grow without the presence of certain conditions required for its development: earth, moisture, heat, light, etc. Are these conditions the principle or ground of its life? Does the seed have no life in it until it begins to grow? No, life is in the seed objectively, even if it never germinates. And so it is with the sacrament of the Lord's Supper—not regarding merely the elements, of course, but the whole of the liturgical exercise has objective life.

The sacramental mystery makes the true and whole life of Christ objectively present, and when an individual who has had sacramental contact with Jesus Christ meets with the proper conditions in his soul, Christ will manifest himself as something quite different from the mere working of the conditions themselves by which this is accomplished. It's like the Tree of Christ attaches or deposits a seed into the will of the sacramental subject, and when that seed is exposed to the right conditions, it germinates.

Unbelievers receive Christ in the sacrament in the same way. But when Christ doesn't meet with the proper conditions, He exercises a different judgment. That seed has a different destiny,

> "some fell by the way side, and the fowls of the air came and devoured it up. And some fell on stony ground, where it had not much earth; and immediately it sprang up, because it had no depth of earth: But when the sun was up, it was scorched; and because it had no root, it withered away. And some fell among thorns, and the thorns grew up, and choked it, and it yielded no fruit. He eats and drinks judgment to himself, not discerning the Lord's body" (Mark 4:4-7).

The grace of the sacrament comes from God to Christ, and it comes to humanity generally through Christ, but it comes to individuals specifically as individuals are in Christ, in the body of Christ. And if that grace is going to make contact with the actual life of an individual, it must be received, not just individually but in some actual, fleshly way. Thus, it comes in the sacrament because that is the true and proper institution that Jesus provided for this purpose.

It is at best silly to think that God's grace inheres in or under or even above the elements of bread and wine. And it is pure nonsense to think that the bread and wine are morphed into the body of a man (or a divine man or a divine body). Such a thought involves a categorical error. Rather, Christ's presence is mysteriously involved in the sacramental transaction as a whole through the power of the Holy Spirit.

Furthermore, the grace is truly present, according to Calvin, even where it is excluded from the soul by unbelief, like when the life nurturing qualities of rain falls fruitless on barren rock. Unbelief has no interest or ability to receive it, but the intrinsic virtue of the sacrament itself is still there. The bread and wine are still the sure promise of

Christ's presence, and when they are presented as such in Eucharist, they become the fulfillment of that promise.

"The symbols," said Beza and Farel,

> "are by no means naked; but so far as God is concerned, who makes the promise and offer, they always have the thing itself truly and certainly joined with them, whether proposed to believers or unbelievers."

> "We do utterly condemn the vanity of those who affirm, that the sacraments are nothing else but mere naked signs" (Old Scotch Confession).

> "Those signs then are by no means vain or void" (Belgic Confession).

> "We teach that the things signified are together with the signs in the right use exhibited and communicated" (Ursinus).

Thus, the sacrament not only signifies, but seals the grace it carries in its constitution to believers. It is not simply a pledge that the blessings it represents are theirs in a general way, apart from this particular engagement. It is not like a man by some outward promise binds himself to fulfill the terms of a contract in another place and at another time. *The sacramental transaction certifies and makes good the grace it represents. It actually communicates it at that time.* Of course, God's grace is not bound to time, so it is not complete at that moment, but it is real. So it also exhibits the thing signified. The thing is actually there, not the name of the thing alone, and not its sign or shadow. Rather, the actual substance itself is present.

"The sacrament is no picture," said Calvin, "but the true, veritable pledge of our union with Christ." To say that the body of Christ is adumbrated by the symbol of bread, like a dead statue is made to represent Hercules or Mercury, is completely inadequate.

The signs, Owen tells us,

> "exhibit that which they do not contain. It is no empty, painted feast. Here is something really exhibited by Jesus Christ unto us, to receive, besides the outward pledges of bread and wine."

How different from all this is our modern Puritan theology. Here too the sacraments are said to seal and to exhibit the grace they represent. But plainly the older, proper sense of these terms has been changed. For the Puritans, the seal simply ratifies a covenant, in virtue of which certain blessings are made sure to the believer, on certain conditions, under a wholly different form.

For the Puritans, the two parties in the transaction, Christ and His people, agree to be faithful to each other in fulfilling the engagements of a mutual contract. And in doing so, they both affix their seal to the sacramental bond. This is the view presented by Edwards, Hopkins, and Bellamy. The contract of salvation according to Bellamy is in the Lord's Supper,

> "externally and visibly sealed, ratified, and confirmed, on both sides, with as much formality as any written instrument is mutually sealed by the parties, in any covenant among men. And now if both parties are sincere in the covenant thus sealed, and if both abide by and act according to it, the communicant will be saved."

So the sacrament is allowed to be exhibited, but *not of any actual present substance, as the old doctrine always held, but like a figure, shadow, or sign.* Without the substance being present the seal remains a mere sign. A picture or statue may be said to exhibit their original in the same way and to the same extent. The sacramental elements are Christ's proxy.

> "Or the matter may be more fitly represented by this similitude: it is as if a prince should send an ambassador to a woman in a foreign land, proposing marriage, and by his ambassador should send her his picture, etc." (J. Edwards).

With Dr. Dwight the sacrament is reduced to a mere occasion by which religious affections are excited and supported in the breast of the worshiper. He seems to have no idea at all of an objective force that belongs to the institution in its own nature. *Everything is subjective, and subjective only.* Everything turns on the adaptation of the rite to instruct and affect. He measures its wisdom and power by this standard alone. It is admirably contrived to work upon "the senses, the imagination, and the heart," as well as to "enlighten the understanding." *Its whole force, when all is done, is simply the amount of the good thoughts, good feelings, and good purposes that are brought to it, and made to go along with it, on the part of the worshipers themselves.*

4. Communion with Christ's Person

According to the old Reformed doctrine the invisible grace of the sacrament includes a real participation in His person. That which is made present to the believer is the very life of Christ Himself in its true power and substance. The doctrine proceeds on the assumption that Christian salvation only exists in an actual union between Christ and His people. It is mystical, of course, but also real in the highest sense. In that union believers are as closely joined to Christ as the limbs are to the head in the natural body. They are in Him, and He is in them, not figuratively but truly, like a growing process that will finally become complete in the resurrection.

The power of this fact is mysteriously concentrated in the Holy Supper. Here Christ communicates Himself to His church, not simply as a right to the grace that resides in His person, or as an interest in the benefits of His life and death. But as a person to person communication, which is the ground and fountain from which all these other blessings may be expected to flow. This idea is found in all of the various forms in which the sacraments can be presented, and in terms that are clear and explicit.

Christ first, and then His benefits. Calvin will hear of no other order but this. The same view runs through all the Calvinistic creeds and confessions. The efficacy of His atonement is not a title to Christ in His benefits or the work of His spirit, but a true and real participation in or relationship with Him. On this basis alone can any title or right legitimately come.

> "We are quickened by a real participation of him, which he designates by the terms eating and drinking that no person might suppose the life which we receive from him to consist in simple knowledge" (Calvin).

> "A substantial communication is affirmed by me everywhere" (Ibid.).

> "He nourishes and vivifies us by the substance of his body and blood" (Gallic Confession).

> "It is not only to embrace with a believing heart all the sufferings and death of Christ, and thereby to obtain the pardon of sin and life eternal; but also besides that to become more and more united to his sacred body, by the Holy Ghost, etc." (Heidelberg Catechism).

"We teach that he is present and united with us by the Holy Ghost, albeit his body be far absent from us" (Ursinus).

"In the Supper we are made partakers, not only of the Spirit of Christ, and his satisfaction, justice, virtue, and operation; but also of the very substance and essence of his true body and blood, etc." (Ibid.).

"Christ crucified, and all benefits of his death" (Westminster Confession).

"It is on all sides plainly confessed, that this sacrament is a true and a real participation of Christ, who thereby imparteth himself, even his whole entire person, as a mystical head, unto every soul that receiveth him, and that every such receiver doth incorporate or unite himself unto Christ as a mystical member of him" (Hooker).

A peculiar exhibition of Christ under outward signs, "and a mysterious reception of him in them really, so as to come to a real substantial incorporation in our souls" (J. Owen).

As *the modern Puritan theory eviscerates the institution of all objectivity,* so it must more decidedly refuse to admit the idea of any such virtue belonging to it. It makes the union of the believer with Christ to be nothing more than morality, or at best, an abstract incorporation into his Spirit!

The insufficient and contradictory character of the idea of a real union with Christ on the basis of Puritan theology will be discussed elsewhere. Mostly, this idea is not acknowledged at all. The whole thing is described as a sort of biblical figure, more imagination than actual reality.

The sacred Supper provides an occasion for piety to be considered, and the contents of salvation are reviewed and reflected upon, as the story of the Redeemer's life and death describes. This is how the Puritan participates in the fruits of Christ's love, the benefits of His mediatorial work, His imputed righteousness, His heavenly intercession, the influences of His Spirit, etc. He thinks about it! *But he has no part whatever in the substantial life of Christ Himself.*

"A mutual solemn profession of the two parties transacting the covenant of grace, and visibly united in that covenant" (J. Edwards).

"Sensible impressions are much more powerful than those which are made on the understanding, etc." (Dr. Dwight).

"The ends proposed in the institution of the Lord's Supper are, the enlargement and rectification of our views concerning the noblest of all subjects, the purification of our affections and the amendment of our lives" (Ibid.).

"Stripped of all metaphorical terms, the action must mean that in the believing and grateful commemoration of his death, we enjoy the blessings which were purchased by it, in the same manner in which we enjoy them when we exercise faith in hearing the Gospel" (Dr. Dick).

"No man who admits that the bread and wine are only signs and figures, can consistently suppose the words, 1 Cor. 10:16, to have any other meaning, than that we have communion with Christ in the fruits of his sufferings and death; or that receiving the symbols we receive by faith the benefits procured by the pains of his body and the effusion of his blood" (Ibid.).

Christ's "doctrine is truly that which will give life to the soul" (Barnes).

"To dwell or abide in him, is to remain in the belief of his doctrine and in the participation of all the benefits of his death" (Ibid.).

"The whole design of the sacramental bread, is by a striking emblem to call to remembrance, in a vivid manner, the dying sufferings of our Lord" (Ibid.).

5. Participation in His Body and Blood

In the old Reformed view of the Lord's Supper, the communion of the believer with the true person of Christ, in the form stated herein, is actual because the Word was made flesh in and through Christ. His humanity provides the medium of His union with the church. His life is the fountain of all life, and it flows from Him only as He is the Son of Man—human. To have part in it at all, we must ourselves have a real part in Him as a real human person. We must eat His flesh and drink His blood in order to take into us the real, fleshly substance of what He was as man, in order to become flesh of His flesh and bone of His bones, as the old doctrines teach.

"The very flesh in which he dwells is made to be vivific for us, that we may be nourished by it to immortality" (Calvin).

"This sacred communication of his flesh and blood, in which Christ transfuses his life into us, just as if he penetrated our bones and marrow, he testifies and seals also in the Holy Supper" (Ibid.)

"I do not teach that Christ dwells in us simply by his Spirit, but that he so raises us to himself as to transfuse into us the vivific vigor of his flesh" (Ibid).[1]

"The very substance itself of the Son of Man" (Beza and Farel).

"That same substance which he took in the womb of the Virgin, and which he carried up into heaven" (Beza and Peter Martyr).

"As the eternal deity has imparted life and immortality to the flesh of Jesus Christ, so likewise his flesh and blood, when eaten and drunk by us, confer upon us the same prerogatives" (Old Scotch Confession).

"That which is eaten is the very, natural body of Christ, and what is drunk his true blood" (Belgic Confession).

"Flesh of his flesh and bone of his bone.... We are as really partakers of his true body and blood, as we receive these holy signs" (Heidelberg Catechism).

"We are in such sort coupled, knit, and incorporated into his true, essential human body, by his Spirit dwelling both in him and us, that we are flesh of his flesh and bone of his bones" (Ursinus).

"They that worthily communicate in the sacrament of the Lord's Supper, do therein feed upon the body and blood of Christ—truly and really" (Westminster Catechism).

The modern Puritan view utterly repudiates all of this as being semipopish mysticism. It allows for no real, bodily participation of Christ's person in the Lord's Supper under any form, and least of all under the form of His humanity. Whatever actual communion Puri-

---

1   "The spiritual life that Christ bestows is not only to be confessed in his spirit which gives life, but also the spirit of his life-giving power makes us partakers of his flesh, which includes participation in the life that is fed upon. So, communion with Christ is more than believing and speaking, but is not less than what we understand them to communicate through the spirit of his flesh and blood, in order to keep Christ whole. But Christ's self-communion of flesh and blood, in the bread and wine used as sacred symbols of his holiness exhibits and offers food to all who celebrate it properly and legitimately according to its institution." *A confession of the Faith of the Eucharist*, exhibited by Farel, Calvin and Viret, a. 1537.

tanism is willing to admit is limited to the presence of Christ in His divine nature, or with regard to the energy of His Spirit.[2] Everything said in Scripture and the confessions about His body and blood is understood to be figurative, intended to express the value of His sufferings and death. With regard to Christ's body in the limited sense of His life as incarnate, formerly on earth and now in heaven, no communion is possible. Communion is limited to remembering what He endured for our salvation. The Puritans find that Christ's "flesh is no help at all. The words that I have spoken to you are spirit and life" (John 6:63).[3]

The language of the Calvinistic confessions on this subject is resolved into a stark, disassociated metaphor that means nothing.

> "If he (Calvin) meant that there is some mysterious communication with his human nature, we must be permitted to say the notion was as incomprehensible to himself as it is to his readers" (Dr. Dick).

> "There is an absurdity in the notion that there is any communion with the body and blood of Christ, considered in themselves" (Ibid.).

> "Justly does our Confession of Faith declare, that the body and blood of Christ are as really, but spiritually present to the faith of believers, etc. What blessed visions of faith are those, in which this precious grace creates an ideal presence of the suffering, bleeding, dying, atoning Savior! Then Gethsemane, and Pilate's hall, and the cross, the thorny crown, the nails, the spear, the hill of Calvary, are in present view!" (Green).

> "This broken bread shows the manner in which my body will be broken; or this will serve to call my dying sufferings to your remembrance" (Barnes).

Claims of the Question to its Earnest Attention

Let this suffice in the way of comparison. *The two theories, as it should now be evident, are entirely different.* And it is not a small difference. It is not simply a formal or accidental difference. The modern Puritan view or theory involves a material falling away, not merely

---

2   This is an important insight that retains the value of the Puritan contribution, that value being the spiritual connection with Christ's divinity and not limited to His humanity.

3   This is not what John was talking about in this verse.

from the form of the old Calvinistic doctrine, but from its inward life and power.

It makes a great difference whether the union of the believer with Christ is regarded as the power of one and the same life of Christ, or if it is just a matter of one's own thoughts and feelings. It makes a difference whether the Lord's Supper is only a sign and seal of God's grace in a general way, or also the pledge of actual grace present in the transaction itself. It makes a difference whether we are united by means of this grace to the person of Christ, or only to His merits and blessings. It makes a difference whether we communicate with the whole Christ in a real way in the ordinance, or only with His abstract divinity. These are the differences that stare us in the face from the comparison made above. We must see and acknowledge that these differences exist, and that they are serious.

These concerns are entitled to our earnest attention. Apart from all judgment of the character of the change which has taken place, the fact of the change deserves our consideration. *We have no right to overlook it, or to treat it as though it did not exist.* We have no right to think that it is unimportant, or to take it for granted that the Christian truth is all on the modern Puritan side.

This is a serious concern because the doctrine of the Eucharist lies at the very heart of Christianity, and the chasm that divides these two doctrinal systems here is both deep and wide. For churches that claim to best represent the Reformation because of their true and legitimate succession, the subject is worthy of careful consideration. Only ignorance or frivolity can allow themselves to make light of it.

SECTION III

The Modern Puritan View as a Departure from the Faith of the Orthodox Church in all Ages

A strong doubt comes against the modern Puritan doctrine, compared with the Calvinistic or Reformed, because it has a much shorter history than the whole history of the church. In contrast, the Calvinistic view of Christ's presence in Communion has been the view of almost all of Christianity from its very beginning. Calvin's view included a strong protest against the errors that had captured the church at Rome. And it rejected transubstantiation and the sacrifice of the mass, and refused to agree with Luther in his suggestion regarding a local presence. But *in spite of all this, it did not rupture from the original doctrine of the church.*

The central idea of this doctrine from the beginning, even under the perversions that have just been named, continued to guide the church. It is precisely this central idea, *the true and proper substance of the ancient church's faith* that created the difference between the Reformed and the modern Puritan doctrines. In the Reformed system Christ is actually present in all His power, but in the Puritan system He isn't. The voice of antiquity is on the side of the sixteenth century regarding its high view of the sacrament. But it lends no support whatever to the low view, which has since come to prevail.

It is readily granted that the view taken of the Lord's Supper in the early church, represented in the writings of the fathers, is by no means free from obscurity and contradiction. *We are not to look for clear and satisfactory statements of theological truth from the infancy of the church,* anymore than we are to look for eloquence from children. The early fathers provide no binding authority for the faith of later times in the

Puritan view, although it does not follow from such a concession that we are at liberty to despise or overlook their authority either. It would be just as irrational for an old man to divorce himself from his own childhood because of its imperfections and foolishness.

The doctrines of the church have an independent history from the overall life of the church. The life and power of the doctrinal truths have always been present from the beginning. But *centuries of careful consideration have been needed to give them their proper, balanced and full shape for their mature expression.* Of course, testimonies from the early fathers can be gathered that seem to contradict various orthodox doctrines of the later church. Time and consideration were required to come to the full, mature understanding of the doctrine of total depravity and free grace, for instance. Clearly, the later views are more balanced and mature.[1]

The Eucharist Involves a Real Communion with Christ's Life

All such confusion and contradiction about this only serves to show that the article in question had not yet come to its clear theological formulation. The confusion doesn't impair the validity of the doctrine, nor does it bring reproach on those who witness to its truth. It is sufficient that they are true to the soul and substance of the whole Christian faith. Sure, earlier expressions may fall short of the full and mature doctrinal clarity, but the later statements must always preserve the substance of the earlier creed.

In this case, the full weight and significance of the Lord's Supper are not found in full flower in the early church. Nor should we be surprised to find some confusion and contradiction regarding the nature and design of the ordinance in the testimony of the early fathers. The doctrine of the Eucharist, like every other Christian doctrine, has a long history. Moreover, its history has proceeded through various very early errors. All this is to be taken into consideration as we examine this issue.

But all this can never provide a sufficient reason for treating the authority of the early fathers with indifference or contempt. Allowing that their testimony is imperfect, confused, and not always consistent, and seeing the advances of the fourth and fifth centuries, we can see that transubstantiation represents a significant error. Nonetheless, we still have no

---

1   It is also true that all later views are not always superior. It is not the earliness or lateness of a view that makes it right, but the orthodoxy of the view broadly considered.

right to assume that the early church had no real and substantial faith regarding the Eucharist. Nor can we conclude that this faith was completely different than that of the church now. *In the midst of all errors and contradictions, the early church must have been in possession of the truth, here as at other points, at least in its essential power and life.* In hindsight, there must be a certain fundamental substratum in which the true idea of the sacrament has always been at hand, and to which the church is bound through all ages.

Only Faith in Christ's Real Presence could have been Turned into the Error of Transubstantiation

It is quite certain that the early fathers did not teach either transubstantiation or consubstantiation. There is not a single passage which can be quoted from the first three centuries that provides the least support for either of these dogmas. However, the general testimony of the period explicitly contradicts them both.

In the following period, during the time of Paschasius Radbert,[2] in the ninth century, the case is the same. Radbert's writing style introduced what often seems to endorse and affirm the superstition that was later openly proclaimed as the truth of transubstantiation because of his emphasis on sacramental efficacy. The sacramental doctrine of the early church recognized no local presence of Christ's body in the elements, no simple oral communication, and nothing like a magical virtue attached to the elements. But neither did it take the opposite extreme of making the ordinance into a mere representation of spiritual blessings to the mind of the worshiper.

From the beginning it was understood to be more than a representation or thought. It was regarded as a substantial mystery that involved the innermost life of the communicant with the Savior Himself as a unique and extraordinary person. Accordingly, the Eucharist was exalted and honored as the central service in Christian worship, around which all other services were made to revolve, and from which they might be said to receive their light. The elements were much

---

2   St. Paschasius Radbertus (785-865), a Frankish Benedictine monk, theologian, and Abbot of Corbie. He wrote numerous treatises, expositions and biographies during the Frankish Carolingian era. His most influential work, *De Corpore et Sanguine Domini* (831-833), is an exposition on the nature of the Eucharist, and was an instruction manual for the monks under his care at Corbie. It is the first lengthy treatise on the sacrament of the Eucharist in the Western world.

more than simple memorials and signs. They were called the Lord's body and blood, which could not have been the case if they had not been regarded as the actual exhibition of His person, though mysterious.

The same thing is clear from the extant records of the institution. All of the earliest documents show that the Eucharist was the heart of the church and that the Eucharist included in a real communion with the whole person of Christ as the source of all interest on the part of the believer regarding His benefits. In the course of time, this idea grew into the absurdity of transubstantiation as a way to preserve the real presence, and serves to illustrate the importance of Christ's bodily and mystical presence from the beginning.

If Christianity had not included in its very nature the idea of a true substantial union with the human life of Christ that not only signified but embodied and made actual in the mystery of the Supper, such a superstition as transubstantiation could never have prevailed. The simple fact that the early sacramental doctrine was brought to such perversion as this extraordinary and unreal idea provides satisfactory evidence that the doctrine always contained the idea of Christ's actual presence. Had the low view of the sacraments prevailed in the early church, such an error as that which supposes an actual change of the elements into the body and blood of Christ could never have appeared.

The Idea of an Offering for Sin

The early fathers spoke of the Eucharist frequently as an offering or oblation, *never, however, in the sense in which it came to be regarded in the later Roman Catholic Church.* It was seen merely as an act of Christian worship, in which the congregation joyfully recognized the goodness of God displayed in the natural creation. They rendered praise to Him for the grace of redemption that was bestowed upon the world through His Son Jesus Christ.

In the Roman Catholic Church communion was also regarded as a memorial of the Savior by which to remember Christ and His sufferings and death that is to be perpetuated in the church to the end of time. But this only accounts for one side of the sacrament. Even as an act of thanksgiving and commemoration, the service included a special reference to the death of Christ as a propitiation for sin, *something to be appropriated by the worshiper as the indispensable condition of his own life.* It is understood to be more than a mere occasion for the exercise of ordinary recollection or imagination. This aspect demands faith on the part of the worshiper, and embodies an objective exhibition of Christian sacrifice by both an actual pledge and seal for the benefit of the faithful.

Real Atonement Apprehended in Christ's Person

This relationship in Christ always involves the whole church, which makes it both more intimate and more objective at the same time. To have part in His atonement, *there must be a real participation also in the life of His person.* This is the objective side of Christian consciousness, and both conceptions must be joined together for the relationship to be real and whole.

The view of the Eucharist held in the early church also includes this idea of *a real communication with His person as the only way that the other benefit can become available.* In some cases this idea is not as clear, but it is never out of sight. For the most part it stands out with such prominence that it leaves no room whatever to question its presence.[3]

---

3   For an able and full exposition of this point, the reader is referred to a recent work, *Das Dogma vom keiligen Abendmahl und seine Geschichte*, von Dr. August Ebrard. Frankfurt a M. 1845. Dr. Ebrard is a Reformed Professor of Theology, at Zurich. His work is intended to be a vindication of the substance of the Reformed or Calvinistic theory of the Eucharist, as distinguished from the Old Lutheran view. It is polemical, but the ultimate design is irenic. The author argues for reconciliation, and that all that is needed for this purpose is a statement of the doctrine that relieves it from appearing as merely accidental objections. He maintains a real communion with Christ's whole life in the new nature of the Christian generally, and in the transaction of the sacrament in particular. His perspective is that of the original Swiss Reformation, and of Zwingli himself. It shows how powerfully the tide of evangelical thinking has already been set in the direction here taken. I need not say that it has been particularly encouraging to me to meet with this publication in the course of the present work; maintaining as it does, substantially, the same view of Christ's presence in the Eucharist, though constructed on a wholly different plan, and in view also of altogether different relations, I regret, however, that the second volume, which was to have appeared some months ago, exhibiting the history of the doctrine since the Reformation, has not yet come into my hands—J.E.N.

(Johann Heinrich August Ebrard [1818-1888] was a German Reformed theologian. Besides his theological works Ebrard published legal, scientific and political writings. In addition, he also wrote works of fiction under the pseudonyms Gottfried Flame Mountain, Christian German and Sigmund Storm. He is still considered one of the most important Reformed theologians 19th Century).

Testimony of Ignatius

Ignatius speaks of the Eucharist (*ep. ad Smyrn.* c. 7.) as the flesh of Christ that suffered for our sins and was raised again by the goodness of the Father. This does not imply that he thought that the body of Christ is in the bread. We know he did not. But the language he employed is true to the general view of the church at the time, and serves to show how much the idea prevailed that the things represented by the signs in the Lord's Supper were bound to them such that in some sense were one and the same presence.

So when he said that the bread was "the medicine of immortality, the antidote of death" (*ep. ad Ephes.* c. 20), it does not imply that he considered the reception of Christ's body into the believer's person was the physical means of his resurrection. Rather, it simply shows that something more was involved in the sacramental service than the mere thinking about Christ and His mediatorial work. *The sacrament was understood to carry the power objectively in itself to unite us with the atonement of Christ,* by making us one with Him in His life. It is the antidote of death because it causes us to "live always in Jesus Christ."

Testimony of Justin Martyr

Justin Martyr (*Apol.* I. c. 66,) tells us that the Eucharist was not received by Christians as common bread or common drink, but that as Jesus Christ Himself became flesh for our salvation. Christians simply believed that the consecrated food in this solemnity was His flesh and blood. This meant that in partaking of the one, we partake of the other also but mysteriously in a way that sustained the new life which is communicated to us by Christ.

Testimony of Irenaeus

Some scholars think that Irenaeus went even farther to teach that the bread and wine in the Eucharist are so pervaded with the very body and blood of Christ that by physical incorporation they become the source of immortality to the body of the believer. Comparing one passage with another, however, it appears that this could not have been his meaning. Nonetheless, it is certain that he considered the participation of the sacramental bread and wine to be a simultaneous participation of the person of Christ in the body of the true Christian such that it becomes his nature. Thus, Christ is the fountain of his eternal life.

"As the bread out of the earth," he said,

> "after its consecration, is no longer common bread, but the Eu-
> charist, consisting of two things, an earthly and a heavenly: so also
> our bodies, when they partake of the Eucharist, are no longer mor-
> tal, having the hope of the resurrection to life everlasting" (*Adv.
> haer.* IV. 18, 5,).

> "As the slip of the vine inserted in the ground has in its own time
> brought forth fruit, and the grain of wheat falling into earth and
> undergoing dissolution has been raised up with multiplication by
> the Spirit of God, through whom all things consist; and these,
> made meet afterward, in God's wisdom for man's use, and having
> added to them the word of divine consecration, become the Eu-
> charist, which is Christ's body and blood; so in like manner our
> bodies are nourished by this, and after they are buried and dissolved
> in the earth, shall in their own time rise again, the divine word im-
> parting to them the resurrection" (Adv. haer. V. 2, 3).

Here he seems to identify the elements with Christ's body and
blood, and has been supposed by some to teach that the mere oral or
corporeal reception of them served to convey into the bodies of
believers in a physical way the virtue of immortality. But other passages show that such was not his meaning. Nonetheless, even in these
quotations, it is clear that everything is referred to the word of God,
the presence of a higher life that is felt to be mystically joined with the
sacramental symbols. Hence he styles the bread and wine elsewhere
the antitypes[4] of Christ's body and blood, in the participation of which
we are made to receive the remission of sins and life everlasting. This
term (ἀντιτυπα—*copies*) was frequently applied to the elements in the
early church.

Tertullian and Cyprian
The view represented by Ignatius, Justin Martyr and Irenaeus was
that which prevailed most generally, according to Neander, in their
time.[5]

Neander tells us that the view represented by these fathers
involved the supposition of an actual corporeality assumed by the
Logos immediately in the sacrament itself, in conjunction with the

---

4   A person or thing represented or foreshadowed by a type or symbol.
5   *Allg. Gesch. der Chr. Religion imd Kirch.* 2d edit. Hamburg, 1843. Vol. ii., p. 1117-
    1120.

elements, and in such a way as to be carried over with them into the bodies of believers as a *pabulum of immortality,* an idea which he admits, however, was not distinctly used till a later time. It lies, he thinks, particularly in a passage of Justin, to (Apol. i. 66,)

> "For not as common bread and common drink do we receive these; but in like manner as Jesus Christ our Savior, having been made flesh by the Word of God, had both flesh and blood for our salvation, so likewise have we been taught that the food which is blessed by the prayer of His word, and from which our blood and flesh by transmutation are nourished, is the flesh and blood of that Jesus who was made flesh."

It must be confessed, however, that this is very obscure evidence of any such opinion. Ebrard, in the work already quoted, shows very clearly that these early fathers, in the use of such language, did not intend to assert what their language at times might seem to imply, an actual corporealization of Christ in any way in the elements, but simply the actual presence of His body, but mystically, in the sacramental transaction. The elements were constituted the "body and blood" of Christ by consecration, and were described in the liturgical phraseology. They received a new character in the Eucharistic benediction, to become the down payment of what they represented. But still, they remained substantially bread and wine.

It shows, however, how deep the ordinance understood it to be a real communion with the human form of the life of Christ. For even the idea mentioned by Neander would resolve into this, that Christ's humanity must extend itself, not by any division of His individual person, but by organic reproduction in all whom Christ will raise up at the last day. In this form, His life is the true bread of heaven, as He expressly says in John 6:51-54.

In the north of Africa, as represented by Tertullian and Cyprian, we find a more guarded phraseology in relation to the subject. The bread and wine are described as symbols, and no room is given for the imagination to confound them with the actual body and blood of Christ. But they are not dead symbols. Along with their sacramental use, a real communication with the body and blood they represent is also emphasized. The visible and the invisible elements are comprehended in the same transaction.

The practice of the church may itself be taken as evidence that a high view was taken regarding the objective virtue of the sacrament. It was in northern Africa particularly, that daily communion prevailed and for a while also the custom of extending the ordinance to infants.

Tertullian tells us that the words "My body," in the words of institution mean, "The figure of My body." This is sufficient to show that he had no thought of any thing like an actual inclusion of Christ's body in the bread.[6] But he tells us elsewhere that we partake in the Supper of "the fatness of the Lord's body" (*De pudic, cap.* 9). And that our flesh is fed with the sacramental body and blood of Christ in order that the soul also may be fat from God" (*De resur. earn. Cap.* 8). While elsewhere he makes this spiritual nourishment to be the very life of Christ himself (*De orat. c.* 6), when he teaches that the petition for daily bread must be taken mainly in a spiritual sense because Christ is the proper bread of life, and according to His own word is signified in the bread of the Eucharist. So when we pray, "Give us our daily bread," we require the perpetuity of Christ, and the liberty of the individual from his body.

Testimony of Clement & Origen

The Alexandrian fathers, Clement, and more particularly Origen, separate more widely the subjective and the objective elements of the sacraments. Their tendency always moved toward an extreme spiritualism, which Origen came too close to making the whole of Christianity into nothing more than a philosophical allegory. He continually disparaged the letter in order to exalt the spirit. Regarding the Eucharist, he went so far as to make the body and blood of Christ nothing more than His word.[7] "His great object," says Neander, "was

---

6   Rudelbach, in his work, "*Reformation, Lutherthum und Union*," Leipzig, 1839, devotes a special excursus to Tertullian's doctrine of the Lord's Supper in which he labors with all his might to make him out to be a sound Lutheran of the old stamp. He will have it that the term *figure* in the passage here referred to (*Adv. Marc.* iv. 40), denotes the actual form of the body itself, in the sense of its reality! This, however, would be nothing less than transubstantiation itself. Ebrard exposes the extravagance of Rudelbach with just severity, (p. 294-208.) The whole method of Tertullian's thinking is opposed to every such construction of his words. He, Cyprian, and Augustine, the founders and fathers of Western Latin theology, occupy the same ground that was later taken by the Reformed Church, in distinction from both the Lutheran and the Church of Rome.

7   "Pursuing his allegorical exegesis, he makes the body to be the word of the Old Testament, and the blood the word of the New!" See Ebrard, *Das Dogma vom keiligen*

to withstand the idea of a magical efficiency in the Supper, separately considered—which however the other church teachers were far from holding; but his view opposed in fact every conception of any sort of higher meaning or force in the outward signs, even such as was admitted by the African church."

It is hardly necessary to say that this view found comparatively small acceptance in the church. The tendency was already moving the other way. We cannot say, that the presence of Christ was confounded with the presence of the symbols, which represented it, but that the two were mystically bound together. The language that expressed this mystical bond became increasing bold and absolute until the liturgical use of the terms "body and blood" applied were to the bread and wine rather than to Christ's actual body. This was probably happening here and there long before the time of Paschasius Radbert adopted the practice.

Testimony of Cyril of Jerusalem

So we hear Cyril of Jerusalem in the fourth century discussing the words of institution:

> "When he himself has plainly said in relation to the bread, *This is my body*, who will presume to have any farther doubt? And when he has solemnly assured us, *This is my blood*, who will hesitate ever to say that it is his blood? He changed water before into wine resembling blood in Cana of Galilee; and shall we distrust him here as changing wine into blood?"[8]

This sounds like transubstantiation itself in the fullest sense, and yet there is good reason to believe that this was not the intended meaning of Cyril, in the final analysis.

Abendmahl und seine Geschichte, p. 274-277.

8   *Cateches.* 4. The terms μεταβολή, μεταμορφόω, μετασχηματίζω (*change, transform, transforms*) etc. were familiarly applied at this time to the change which was supposed to take place in the elements by their consecration. A new character was thought to be imparted to them by the influence of the Holy Spirit, which made them to be what they were not before, in a sacramental sense. Still no idea was entertained of an actual transmutation of the bread and wine into Christ's body and blood. They were regarded only as having a supernatural character communicated to them, in virtue of which they served to bring those who partook of them into communion with Christ's true body and blood.

Testimony of Chrysostom

Chrysostom uses very strong language in the same way, but he is more guarded and less liable to misconstruction. He makes the sensible elements in the Supper to be the form in which its proper spiritual grace is brought near to the believer, like the washing with water in Baptism is the objective exhibition of the grace of regeneration. But still the objective and subjective are not made to necessarily adhere together. The first is something, *looking* (αναζητούν) for the senses, the other is *conceiving* (νοητόν), not a mere thought, but something to be received by the soul and not simply by the mouth. "If thou hadst been without a body," he says, "the grace might have come to thee in the same naked form; but since the soul is interwoven with the body, he gives thee the spiritual in forms of sense."[9]

Testimony of Ambrose

Among the Latin Fathers of the same period we find Ambrose almost as bold in his representations as Cyril.

> "The sacrament you receive is wrought by the word of Christ. The word of Elijah had power to bring down fire from heaven; and shall not the word of Christ avail to change the character (*speciem*) of the elements? You have read, in relation to the whole work of creation, He spake and it was done, he commanded and it stood fast; and shall not the word of Christ, which could thus call out of nothing that which was not, be able also to change things that are into what they were not before?"[10]

And yet he says, in his exposition of Luke, again, "*Not a corporeal Christ, we touch, but by faith only.*" The change that he supposed to be wrought in the bread by its consecration was not to actually transmute it into Christ's body, but it simply served to clothe it with a new power or virtue by the Holy Spirit, (Cyril's divine μεταβολή—*change*) so that for the recipient it became the true medium of an actual communication with the body of Christ that it represented.

Testimony of Augustine

We have a much better representative of the faith of the Western Church during this period in Augustine, the great theological succes-

---

9   Hom. 82, in Matthaei evangelium.
10   De initiandis, cap. 9.

sor of Cyprian in north of Africa. He distinguished clearly between the objective and subjective elements of the sacramental transaction, between the form of the sacrament and its substance. He said that the bread is simply the sign of Christ's body.[11] In the sacraments, "*one thing is seen, nothing else is meant.*" He will hear of no oral communication: *"for the grace of the bites thereof is not consumed."*

Still, as Neander remarks, Augustine held a real conjunction in the case of the Lord's Supper between the signs and the things signified; in virtue of which believers (not unbelievers), along with the outward form were made to partake of its proper contents, the "*res sacramenti*" (*reality of the sacrament*) itself. And this *res sacramenti* he held to be the union of believers with their one head, Christ, and their closer union thus with one another, as members of his glorious mystical body, the church. He asserts as clearly as Calvin that the local circumscription of Christ's proper body is in heaven; and of course makes our communion with Him to be wholly by the Spirit. Still he represents it to be always a real communion. "*Have faith, in whom is with you, whom you do not see*" (Augustine)[12]

Rejecting Transubstantiation, the Reformers Acknowledged the Authority of the Early Church

It is not necessary here to refer to other authorities. Nor does the subject call us to trace, even in a general way, the course of the sacramental doctrine as corrupted by the Roman Catholic Church in later times.[13] As previously remarked, the confusion regarding bodily pres-

---

11 "For the Lord does not hesitate say: This is my body, as a sign of his body."
12 See Neander's *Kirchengesch.* Bd. 2, Abth. 3, p. 1399-1401.
13 This is done at length by Prof. Ebrard in the work previously mentioned. The progress of this error was very slow and insidious. It may be traced particularly in the gradual differences of representation that appear in the different ancient liturgies. In time, the false view, which at first only existed in the form of feeling, began to also claim authority in the logical expressions regarding its understanding. Even up to the Ninth Century this drew a very active protest. The doctrine of Paschasius Radbert initially caused much commotion and was strongly opposed by the monk Ratramn, Rabanus Maurus, John Scotus Erigena and many others. "They did not deny," says Knapp, "the presence of the body and blood of Christ; but they taught that this *conversio* or *immutatio* (*conversion* or *change*) of the bread and wine is not of a carnal, but of a spiritual nature; that these elements are not transmuted into the real body and blood of Christ, but are signs or symbols of them. In many points they approximated to the opinion of the Reformed theologians" (*Chr. Theol. Wood's Trans, vol.* ii. p.571). That is, they insisted on what had been the general doctrine of

ence and transubstantiation in the sacrifice of the Roman Catholic
mass only serves to show the error of the position more clearly. The
fact that the sacrament was originally understood to involve not simply
a memorial of Christ's sacrifice, but the power of the sacrifice made
present in his glorified life. To the consciousness of the early church,
the solemn ordinance was an immediate (sometimes called *local*) exhibition of the atonement for sin provided by Christ's death. The
believer was thought to receive the full benefit of it as a living atonement brought before God through participation in the sacrament. This
involved an actual reception of the life itself, in whose presence alone
such living and enduring virtue resided.

The mere recollection of the atonement as a past fact was not
enough. It must be apprehended and appropriated as a present reality
in a living way. Christ Himself must animate the sacrament and be
received, Soul to soul, in the sacrament. The sacrament spiritually and
actually provided what it represented, according to the understanding
of the early church. There was no transubstantiation of the elements
into Christ's body and blood, as later taught by the Church of Rome.
The bread and wine are called His body and blood, but only in a
sacramental or liturgical sense—not in a literal sense. We hear of no
material or local presence of His flesh in the Lutheran sense, no tactile
communication with His glorified body, no reception of His life in a
merely oral way. But the fact of a real communication with His life,
His humanity, as defined in the sacramental transaction (*actio in actione*
—*in the doing of the action*) is more distinctly asserted for this very reason.

All Christian antiquity has been opposed to the low rationalistic
idea of a merely moral virtue in the Eucharist. The faith of the church
later became the occasion for the superstitious error of transubstantiation. The doctrine of the real presence *in spirit* (εν πνεύματι)
degenerated into transubstantiation, or the real presence *in flesh* (εν
σαρκί).

The living memorial of Christ's one sacrifice was later converted
into the new, repeated sacrifice of the mass. Nonetheless, the corrup-

the church from the beginning, namely, that the elements were the body and blood
of Christ, not literally, but mystically, which served after their consecration to make
them present to the communicant in fact, though in a spiritual way. Any view lower
than this was out of the question, as the church then stood, and even this was borne
down at last by the force of the corruption that had now begun to usurp its place.

tion of a great truth may never be reasonably sought against the authority of the truth itself. And of all forms of fanaticism, there is none more pathetic than the zeal that seeks to rectify a gross error in one direction, by throwing itself blindly into the arms of an error equally gross in the other. We must not seek revenge for this acknowledged abuse by demolishing the truth out of which error has developed.

It is not necessary to strip the sacrament of all mystery, and refuse to allow it any objective power whatever to be free of transubstantiation and the mass. This is what the Reformers thought, as we have seen—and not only Luther and Melancthon, but Calvin, Beza, Ursinus, and the fathers of the Reformed church generally. They sought to save the substance of the primitive faith, while they endeavored to rescue it from the errors with which it had become overlaid in the Church of Rome. They honored the authority of the ancient fathers, and the life of the early church. And they took pains to show, as best as they could, that this testimony, rightly interpreted and understood, was on their side, and not on the side of Rome.

Only at a later time, when a theology of a different spirit from that which generally prevailed in the sixteenth century, was the ancient church charged with corruption and superstition by constructing the entire truth of Christianity *de novo* from the Scriptures alone, without any regard to the primitive faith and with a presupposition against Christ's real presence.

SECTION IV

Second General Presumption Against Modern Puritanism

The modern Puritan theory of the Lord's Supper involves a falling away from the general faith of the original Reformation, and finds no sanction whatever in the faith of the primitive church. This of itself is quite condemning. What right had Puritanism to depart from the original creed of the sixteenth century, and the Reformed correction of Rome in favor of ancient Christianity? Answer: the right of private judgment against the established authority of tradition. Doing so they abandoned the tradition of Reformed hermeneutics and the work of the early church. Why should Puritan doctrine carry sufficient weight to overcome the judgment of the universal church from the beginning in this matter?

Because of the centrality of the sacraments only the strongest grounds and best arguments can justify such a modern departure from what has been accepted from Christian antiquity. Modern Puritans presumptively over reacted to real errors in their effort to undermine the political power of the Roman church, which turned the Reformation into a revolution.

But this is not all. Another error of modern Puritanism came to the fore when they departed from the faith of the Reformation in that their new position is in harmony with the errors of Pelagianism, the very error the original Reformers refused to make. The modern Puritan view of the Lord's Supper, therefore, is constitutionally rationalistic.

Socinianism of the Sixteenth Century

As a matter of course, the Socinians of the sixteenth century took sacramental theology to support their false theological system. As the Socinians denied the divinity of the Savior, and reduced Christian salvation to a mere system of morality, they could see nothing more in the sacraments than external influence, and merely human ceremonies. Their idea was that Christianity, as merely spiritual, had no dependence on religious forms and rites, so they took no account whatever of any objective virtue or power that belong to the sacraments themselves, as divine institutions. They counted it mere Jewish ritualism to attribute any objective value to them.

"For how," it is asked,

> "can that serve to confirm us in faith, which we do ourselves, and which though commanded of God is still our own work, including or exhibiting nothing remarkable, and having no fitness to convince or persuade us of the truth of any of those things, by which our faith is confirmed."[1]

The sacraments are made to be a "*mutually sacred union between God and men.*" The idea of a real presence of any sort in the Lord's Supper is thought to be a mere superstition. Everything is turned into a naked commemoration of Christ's benefits.[2]

> "In the Lord's Supper, we receive according to the Lord's own word, nothing from the ordinance itself save bread and wine; but we commemorate past favors and give thanks for them" (*F. Soc. Opp. I.* p. 753).

> "Q What is the Lord's Supper?

> "*A*: The appointment of Christ that his saints should break and eat bread and drink of the cup, in order to show forth his death; which is to continue till his advent.

> "Q: But what is it to show forth the Lord's death?

> "*A*: Publicly and solemnly to give thanks to Christ, that out of his ineffable love towards us, he suffered his body to be tortured, and in a sense broken, and his blood to be shed; and to extol and mag-

---

1   F. Soc. Opp. I. p. 753.
2   Here are the seeds of American pragmatism.

nify the kindness he has shown to us in this way" (*Mac. Oat. Qu.* 334, 335).

"Q: Is there no other reason for the institution?

"A: There is no other *(absolutely none—nulla prorsus)*; though many have been imagined, etc." (*lb. Qu.* 337).

"Q: What is the meaning of the words, *This is my body?*

"A: They are variously understood, for some suppose that the bread is actually changed into the body and the wine into the blood; which they call transubstantiation. Others imagine the body of the Lord to be in the bread, under the bread, with the bread. There are those finally, who believe that they partake of the Lord's body and blood in the Supper, though only in a spiritual way. But all these opinions are fallacious and erroneous" (lb. Qu. 340).

Arminianism in the Seventeenth Century

With the rise of Arminianism in the following century in the bosom of the Reformed church, we find a similar undervaluation of the Sacraments that reduced them in the end again to mere signs.[3]

"We hold the sacraments to be sacred and solemn rites, by which as covenant signs and seals, God not only represents and adumbrates, but in a certain sense also exhibits and confirms, his benefits promised especially in the gospel covenant" (Confess. Remonst. xxiii. 1. Drawn up by Simon Episcopus, Jt. D. 1622).

"We may say that God exhibits his grace to us through the sacraments, not as conferring it by them actually, but by employing them as clear signs to represent it and set it before our eyes. They operate upon us as signs, that represent to our mind the thing whose signs they are. Nor should any other efficacy be sought in them. They promote piety besides on our part, as involving an

---

3   Dutch Arminianism was originally articulated in the Remonstrance (1610), a theological statement signed by 45 ministers and submitted to the Dutch states general.
The Synod of Dort (1618–19) was called by the Dutch states general to pass a judgment upon the Remonstrance. The five points of the Remonstrance asserted that: 1)
election (and condemnation on the day of judgment) was conditioned by the rational faith of man; 2) the Atonement, while qualitatively adequate for all, was efficacious only for those who believe; 3) unaided by the Holy Spirit, no person is able to
respond to God's will; 4) grace is not irresistible; and 5) believers are able to resist sin
but are not beyond the possibility of falling from grace. The crux of Remonstrant
Arminianism lay in the assertion that human dignity requires an unimpaired freedom of the will.

obligation to duty, of the same nature with a soldier's oath" (Lim-
borch Theol. Chr. v. 66, 31, 32).

"The Lord's Supper is the other sacred rite of the New Testament,
instituted by Jesus Christ, on the night in which he was betrayed,
for the Eucharistic and solemn commemoration of his death; in
which believers, after proper self-examination and assurance of
their own faith, eat sacred bread publicly broken in the congregation, and drink wine publicly poured out, to show forth with
solemn action of thanks, the Lord's bloody death endured for our
sake, (by which our hearts, as the body is nourished by meat and
drink, are fed and strengthened to the hope of eternal life); and also
to testify publicly before God and the church, their living spiritual
communion with Christ's crucified body and shed blood, (or with
Jesus Christ himself as crucified and dead for us), and so with all the
benefits procured by his death, as well as their love to one another"
(Conf. Remonst. Xxiii. 4).[4]

Neological Rationalism in the Eighteenth Century

The triumph of Rationalism,[5] during the eighteenth century in
Germany and throughout Europe generally brought with it a still
more extensive degradation of religious views. It is not necessary here
to trace the rise of this apostasy and its connection with the previous
state of Protestantism.[6] It is enough to say that it grew out of a tendency involved in the very nature of Protestantism from the
beginning. The opposite tendency of that by which the Roman
Catholic Church previously had been carried into an equally false
extreme. As Romanism had sacrificed the rights of the individual to the
authority of the universal, the claims of the subjective to the overwhelming weight of the objective, so the tendency of Protestantism
asserted these same rights and claims by a violent reaction, which
swallowed the opposite interest.[7]

---

4   "In this matter," says Bishop, "the consent of the Reformed themselves have many,
    among whom Zwingli is a primary teacher and the very best on this ceremony."
    Limborch expressly opposes the Calvinstic theory.
5   The doctrine that reason alone is a source of knowledge and is independent of God.
    In theology it is the doctrine that human reason, unaided by divine revelation, is an
    adequate or the sole guide to all attainable religious truth.
6   For a brief but clear sketch of this, the reader is referred to Prof. Schaff's *Principle of
    Protestantism*, p. 98-102.
7   The issue here is Plato's philosophical problem of the "One and the many." The
    issue cannot be solved apart from the doctrine of the Trinity, previously cited.

The Reformation was deeply imbued with the positive life of truth and faith, and was kept within the limits of logic. With Luther, Calvin, and the Reformers generally, the principle of individual freedom was still held in check by the principle of social responsibility. Subjective, individual reason was required to bend to the idea of objective, divine revelation as something broader and more sure than itself. It never was able to reconcile these polar forces.

The old Lutheran orthodoxy involved the necessity of such a process of inward conflict and ultimate resolution in order that the contradiction which was lodged in its bosom could come into view, and the way be opened thus for its reconstruction, in a form that was more perfect and more true to its own nature.[8]

The errant tendency of Protestantism finally burst through all the countervailing efforts, which had restrained it in the beginning. Protestant religion became pure subjectivity, first in the form of Pietism, and later in the desolation of Rationalism, which reduced everything to natural morality. As such, eighteenth century Protestantism was characteristically apostate. As an age, it had no room for the supernatural. Everything was reduced to the dimensions of the human spirit in its isolated, subjective character.

Theology of course was drained of all objectivity. Even the super-naturalism of the period was rationalistic, and it occupied a false position with regard to the truth, in that the occult was thought to reflect spiritual truth, and was granted a kind of equal standing with biblical truth. The ideas of rationalism infected the whole of the theology of this period, and into the next, and were openly heretical and professedly orthodox alike.[9]

These ideas showed themselves in low views of the sacraments, in Baptism and the Lord's Supper. Rationalism was too spiritual to make much account of liturgical forms and services of the church. Everything was resolved into the exercise of the worshiper's own mind. The subjective was everything, the objective was next to nothing. So, the

---

8   The doctrines of transubstantiation and consubstantiation were liturgical efforts to solve the philosophical problem of the one and the many, transubstantiation falling to the side of the one (or universal and objective) and consubstantiation falling to the side of the many (or particular and subjective).

9   Nevin himself struggles here to indicate that there is some truth to the subjectivity of rationalism, but at the same time it fails to account for the objectivity of universal truth.

supernatural was simply folded into the moral. The sacraments become abstract signs, and signs only. Any power they may have was not found in them, but merely in their use that pious souls made of them. They were occasions for quickening one's own devout thoughts and feelings. The sacraments were thought to have no objective validity or reality, but are only useful subjectively.

General Lack of Faith in this Period (1850s)

Under the power of this subjective, individualist spirit even the better theologians of the period were defective in their understanding of the Lord's Supper, as compared with the original Protestant fathers of the sixteenth century. Such men as Zachariä, Mursinna, Döderlein, Knapp, Sleudel, etc., no longer venture to speak of a real communication with Christ's body and blood in the old sense. For the old doctrine, they substitute at best a simple *praesentiam operativam (presence of an operative),* which became mere heavenly efficacy. It is true that it was supernatural in that it referenced heaven, but actually it was still only moral because it was no more than an occasion for the exercises of piety on the part of the worshiper.

The more consistently rational theologians didn't worry about orthodoxy, and for this reason were more consistently rationalistic in their thinking. Men like Henke, Eckermann, the elder Nitzsch, Hase, De Wette, Wegscheider, etc. simply discard the idea of a celestial substance—something objective—being involved in the sacrament, and found its whole meaning apart from the divine.

Note

Nor can any exception be made, with regard to this point, even in favor of Storr and Reinhard. They do indeed employ language, which seems at times to imply a participation in the very substance of Christ's life; but this is so qualified and modified again by a different phraseology, that everything runs out at last into the idea of mere supernatural influence or power. Reinhard pretends, indeed, to censure the Reformed view as too low; but he misrepresents it by charging it with the error of holding the elements to be mere signs; whereas they should be regarded, he says, as exhibitive also of what they represent. This, however, as we have seen, was always the true doctrine of the Reformed church itself. Then he affirms that we receive in, with, and under the bread and wine, the true body and blood of Christ; but immediately explains this to be, in other words, "that the exalted God-man Jesus works (exerts an influence), by his body and blood, on all who make use of this ceremony." Again, by "presence," he understands simply, "nothing more than the power to exert an influence at a particular place," *Dogmatik*, § 162. Storrt in the judgment of Bretschneider, does not get beyond the same view; and to be satisfied of this, we need only to read attentively all that he says on the subject, in § 114 of his *Dogmatik*. The words of institution mean, he tells us, "This bread makes you participant of my body—this wine hands over to you my blood," and argues at large against the figurative interpretation of Zwingli and Oecolampadius. But all comes at last to this, that the Lord Jesus, in whose Person humanity and divinity are inseparably united, is actually present at the celebration of the Supper, and "exerts his influence there in an incomprehensible manner." The believer derives actual nourishment from Christ, more than is comprehended in the simple exercise of his own faith and trust; but still it is in the form of a "salutary influence," mysteriously proceeding from his person, rather than by an actual participation in His very life itself. In this respect, the doctrine of Storr and Reinhard, undoubtedly falls short of the doctrine taught by Calvin; for it is not to be questioned that this last had in his mind always, as much as Luther himself, the idea of a true reproduction of Christ's life in the believer, an actual extension of its very substance into the believer's soul, and not simply an operation proceeding from this life, under however high a form. — Professor Schmucker, of this country, in his translation of the *Biblical Theology* of Storr and Flatt, 1826, has an appendix to this section on the Eucharist, in which he brings forward the concurrent view of Reinhard, backed by the authority of Mosheim, as a fair exhibition of the proper Lutheran doctrine. And yet it was considered by many an evidence of the strong power of sectarian prejudice, that the American Lutheran Professor should have allowed himself at the time, to go so far as to endorse, apparently, the doctrine of the real presence, even in the convenient sense of these "sober and judicious" divines!

Extracts from Mursinna, Doederlein, Knapp

"The design of the Holy Supper is this; that all who profess the name of Christ, while they partake of the broken bread as a sign of his crucified body, and of the wine as the symbol of his shed blood,

may thankfully remember the benefits which they owe to their Redeemer, and so be incited to fulfill all the duties to which they are
bound. Along with this main end Paul mentions another also, 1
Cor. 10:17, namely, that when we come to the table in common,
we call to mind the natural love that is required of those who profess the same religion, and show ourselves ready to maintain it"
(Mursinna. Lehrb. der Dogm. p. 267, 268).

"Nor is it difficult to understand and show, what force this sacrament has in itself to affect the mind. Its efficacy, in the way of
exciting and quickening faith, and for the purposes of piety, is
clear. Some however may say, if the Eucharist furnish nothing
more than this opportunity of calling to mind Christ's benefits, as
already before us in the word, it seems to be a superfluous rite. So
far am I however from thinking any institution to be superfluous
which brings the truth, though otherwise known, with new force
before the mind, it appears to me suitable to the gravity and dignity of the subject rather, that it should be presented to the
understanding and memory, not in one way only, but in manifold
ways. The virtue of the Lord's Supper, therefore, like that of Baptism, does not differ from the power of the divine word. Like this it
is logico-moral, worthy thus of the divine wisdom and of the
Christian religion, including also the influence of the Holy Spirit,
who makes use of the bread and wine as instruments to excite such
affections as are pious and pleasing to God" (Döderlein. Inst.
Theol. Ch. p. 691-694).

"The Holy Spirit acts upon the hearts of men through the Supper,
or through the bread and wine, and by this means produces faith
and pious dispositions. But he produces this effect through the
word, or through the truths of Christianity, exhibited before us and
presented to us in this ordinance. The effect of the Lord's Supper is
therefore an effect, which is produced by God and Christ, through
his word, or the truths of his doctrine, and the use of the same. In
this sacrament of the Supper, the most important truths of Christianity, which we commonly only hear or read, are visibly set
before us, made cognizable to the senses, and exhibited in such a
way as powerfully to move the feelings, and make an indelible impression on the memory" (Knapp. Led. on Chr. Theol., Wood's
Translation, vol. ii. p. 562).

"Hence it appears that the internal efficacy of the Lord's Supper, or
of the word of God through the Supper, is two-fold.

1. This ordinance is the means of exciting and strengthening the faith of one who worthily celebrates it, etc.—For we are reminded by it, 1st. Of the death of Christ, etc., 2d. Of the causes, etc.

2. In this way does this ordinance contribute to maintain and promote piety among believers, etc." (Ibid. p. 563).

"The better way, therefore, in exhibiting either the Lutheran or Reformed doctrine, is, to avoid these subtleties, and merely take the general position, that Christ, as man and as the Son of God, may exert his agency, may act, whenever and in whatever manner he pleases. He therefore may exert his power at his table, as well as elsewhere. This is perfectly scriptural; and it is also the sense and spirit of the Protestant theory. And this doctrine concerning the nearness of Christ, his assistance, and strengthening influence, in his present exalted state, secures eminently that proper inward enjoyment, which Lutheran and Reformed Christians, and even Catholics, with all their diversity of speculation on this point, may have alike in the Lord's Supper. Christ, when he was about to leave the world, no more to be seen by his followers with the mortal eye, left them this Supper, as a visible pledge of his presence, his protection, and love" (Ibid. p. 577).

Extracts from Henke, Wegscheider, Bretschneider

"The meaning of Christ seems to have been, that the close intimacy which had subsisted thus far between him and his friends, should not be interrupted by his death; but that it was his desire now especially to give himself to them as he was, to be and remain wholly theirs in the most intimate conjunction. As therefore they were now taking bread and wine, so he ought to be himself received by his disciples, his whole discipline, his spirit and example, with all the benefits about to be procured by his death, so as to be converted as it were into their very flesh and blood, etc." (Henke. Lin. Fid. Chr, p. 252).

"The sacred Supper is the solemn participation of bread and wine, as symbols of Christ's death, by which such as attend upon it, being impressively reminded of this death and of the general merit of Christ, but especially of his instruction and example, are excited and engaged to true piety towards God and Christ, as also to kindness towards others, and are imbued at the same time with the hope of obtaining by their virtue the pardon of sin and everlasting felicity. Thus the bread and wine in the Eucharist, are not only

properly called signs significant, but also signs or symbols exhibitive, inasmuch as they do in a certain moral way represent to
communicants the whole Christ, such and so great as that divine
teacher was who sealed his doctrine with his blood, and forcibly
press upon them the duty of following him with decision, so as not
to shrink even from enduring death, after his example, for what is
true and right. Although the rite, regarded as a manducation (eating) of human flesh and potation (drinking) of human blood,
whether really or symbolically, is not so suitable to the views and
manners of the Modern world, as to those of antiquity; still, even
for our age, if administered with becoming regard to its advanced
cultivation, it is capable of being turned to excellent moral account.
Hence it is greatly to be wished, that its more frequent use might
be encouraged, etc." (Wegscheider. Inst. Theol. § 180).

Even the more sound theologians of this period, Reinhard, Knapp,
etc., hold that the salutary influence of the sacrament does not depend
at all on the view that may be taken of its nature; a judgment that may
be allowed to be correct within certain limits, though not in the form,
nor to the extent exactly, in which it is to be understood, probably,
with these divines. Bretschneider, according to whom the original
institution was simply a solemn covenant meal, designed to proclaim,
symbolically, the introduction of the new dispensation, to which other
references and uses were subsequently attached, considers that the benefit to be derived from it is not suspended absolutely even on a full
faith in Christ's death as the ground of our salvation.

"For one who does not honor Jesus as a Mediator, but simply as a
teacher of divine truth and a benefactor of mankind, who sacrificed
his life to the noblest ends, may still, by the celebration of his death,
be excited to like zeal for truth and virtue, to improvement, and to
perseverance in the conflict with superstition and vice, and be filled
thus with the presentiment also of a better world. The great design
of Christianity, which is to free men from sin and to prepare them
for a higher life, is in that case advanced in him as well as in others,
though in a different way; and hence the Lord's Supper becomes
for him too a salutary sacrament" (*Dogmatik*, § 200).

Rationalistic Supernaturalism and its Purpose
These extracts may suffice to illustrate the genius of Rationalism,
as it regards Christianity. Let us rejoice in these recent developments
in theology, where previously it had tremendous influence, and that a

new and brighter era has begun to dawn auspiciously on the history of
the Protestant church (1850s). The authority of interpreters, like
Paulus and Quinol, and theologians such as Amnion, Wegscheider,
and Bretschneider have come to be little regarded. Along with this
development relative orthodoxy has also passed away. John David
Michaelis is not as worthy of confidence as Semler. The cool, mechanical, abstract supernaturalism of Ernesti and Morus is almost as unreal
and unsubstantial as the openly infidel theology it struggles against.
Who now will take the Rosenmullers, or Koppe and his followers for
guides in the study of the scriptures? Who still sits at the feet of such
men as Mursinna, Doderlein, Flatt, Storr, Reinhard, and Knapp for
instruction in the mysteries of the Christian faith? They are all indeed
venerable names, and they are entitled to the lasting respect of the
church for their fidelity to Christ in a time of general apostasy and
defection.

The results of their work will always continue to be of value for
Christianity, at least in an indirect way. But they stood themselves in a
false position with regard to the truth, and they were not able to stem
the tide that was bearing all thought and all life in the contrary way.
So far as any better order of religion has come to prevail, it must be
referred to other influences altogether.

The salvation of theology has sprung from a different quarter. The
very orthodoxy of the school now noticed was itself rationalistic, and
we may say that it served only to precipitate the catastrophe it sought
to avert. For its conception of the supernatural was always external and
abstract, putting it in the same false relationship to nature and humanity that was established by Rationalism itself.

Much has been done to justify the wrong issue by making false
assumptions which established common cause with the enemy. How?
By consenting to meet him on his own ground, in the arena of the
mere finite understanding.[10] No wonder that such a defense of the
supernatural was unable to sustain itself against the reigning tendency
of the age. No wonder it yielded to this tendency more and more, and
was ultimately swept away by the flood of popular individualism.[11]

---

10 For more on this insight see the work of Cornelius Van Til.
11 This rationalistic period has been driven by German scholarship, which has been
    imported into American theology. Those acquainted with German scholarship, and
    to whom we are indebted for translations of German theological works are fifty
    years behind current scientific developments. Thus, we follow trends that have

Sect Principle and its Affinity with Rationalism

Parallel with the development of the subjective principle in the false way of spiritual abstraction is the realization that the same principle can operate in the equally false way of Sectarianism and schism.[12] No one can attentively study this principle, without being led to see that the two tendencies of spiritual abstraction and schism are but different phases of one and the same spiritual obliquity.[13] No one reading the history of the church can fail to see the many points of correspondence that hold between the two results of this principle, in spite of the apparent differences that seem to superficially separate them.

The spirit of sect or denomination is full of religious pretension. And when people profess to make religion their first and highest value they turn it into something personal and experiential, which turns it into something hyper-spiritual and tends toward restlessness and hyperactivity (2 Cor. 11:5). Hence what often begins in fanaticism and wild ideas, usually in opposition to liturgy and the existing order of church organization and practice. In this it conforms to rationalist ideas in the sense that rationalism appeals to individual opinion regarding unanswerable questions, and ends in the worst errors of Rationalism itself.

Both systems (rational abstraction and schism) are antagonistic to the historic church. Both trample under foot the authority of history and tradition. Both make objectivity to be nothing, and subjectivity to be everything. Both undervalue objectivity in favor of their own sub-

---

already been proven wrong. Nor does it help to distinguish between the orthodoxy of the period and its avowed religious infidelity. The whole posture of the period has been rationalistic. Ernesti, for instance, is entitled to no confidence whatever, as a guide to the true sense of God's word, as it is spirit and life. Knapp, with all his orthodoxy, comes perpetually short of the true depth of Christianity as a science. When the German school of theology is recognized and honored by a wide section of the American Church as the best and only safe form of German religious thinking, while the far deeper and infinitely more spiritual efforts of Dorner, G. A. Meier, Julius Muller and others of like spirit is struggling to overcome the contradictions of the old standpoint, are superciliously condemned as transcendental nonsense. It is certainly not easy to possess one's soul in proper patience. Alas, it is but too plain that with all our boasted orthodoxy, the coils of Rationalism have fastened themselves with a deadly embrace on the thinking of hundreds, who are the last to dream of any such thing.

12   Nevin points to the problem of Denominationalism, which he associates with revivalism and the New Lights.

13   Obliquity: The quality of being deceptive. On this subject, the reader is referred again to Schaff's *Principle of Protestantism*, p. 107-121.

jectivity. Both despise formality under the pretense of exalting the spiritual informality. Both reduce the sacraments to mere outward rites, and often deny their necessity. Both make much of the Bible, but often submit it to some supposed superior but imaginary inward light that is received directly from God, which always forces biblical interpretation and understanding to submit to the subjectivity of individual interpretation, apart from the tradition and history of the church.

Both of these forms of thinking eschew historic Christianity as a permanent order of life and a real supernatural constitution unfolding itself historically in the world. The entire emphasis and concern is for the flesh, the natural life of humanity. Of course, the flesh and its individualism are exalted, and while there is much talk about the spirit it is never more than the subjectivity of their own spirit or experience of the spirit. While the sect principle speaks in lofty tones of heavenly divinity that is completely removed from all that belongs to the present world, but in reality it never escapes the limitations of the flesh.

Hyper-Spiritualism Always Devolves into Feshly Concerns

Hyper-spiritualism is nothing more than fleshly pseudo-spiritualism, and sooner or later always falls back impotent and self-exhausted into the very thing from which it vainly pretends to escape. It's ultimate concern always resolves to individual performance, works, or personal experience and enthusiasm. Anabaptism led to the excesses of Munster[14] in the same way that Mormonism[15] led to the excesses of Nauvoo. There is an apparent difference between the inspiration of

---

14 Thomas Müntzer (1489-1525) believed and taught of the "living word of God" (continued revelation and prophecy), the banning of infant baptism, and that the bread and wine of the Eucharist were only emblems of Jesus Christ's sacrifice. Luther disagreed with all of these doctrines. He was one of the founders of the Anabaptist movement.

15 Mormonism or the Latter Day Saint movement arose in western New York, where its founder, Joseph Smith, Jr., had been raised during the Second Great Awakening. This "awakening" was a response to the secularism of the Age of Enlightenment. A large camp meeting in 1801 at Cane Ridge, Kentucky, found participants exhibiting charismatic gifts such as glossolalia, prophecy, and heavenly visions. Joseph Smith's father, Joseph Smith, Sr. also had several visions or dreams, as had Smith's paternal and maternal grandfathers. Joseph Smith, Jr. and several of the church founders were Freemasons, and were founding members of a lodge in Nauvoo, Illinois, in March 1842. There are some similarities between Mormon temple worship and symbolism and the stories and symbols of Freemasonry. Modern-day revelation from God continues to be a principal belief of the Mormon faith.

George Fox,[16] and the cold infidelity of Elias Hicks[17]. And yet Hicks was a true spiritual descendant of Fox. The inner light of Hicks and the light of reason as held by Fox are actually the same thing. Both of them contradict the central tenet of Christianity. Both are supremely subjective and supremely rationalistic at the same time. Thus, both issue from the same principle.

Anabaptists

It is no coincidence that the sectarian spirit (or denominationalism) since the Reformation (and after) shared a close affinity with the spirit of theoretical rationalism, especially in its low regard for the sacraments. The relationship between the two systems of abstract speculation and sectarianism is their common subjectivity and focus on individualism. The Anabaptists and Socinians of the sixteenth century go hand in hand with the Mennonites and Arminians of Holland in the century following. They all hold the sacraments to be nothing more than signs for the understanding and heart of the pious communicant, that they are without any objective value or force in and of themselves.

Quakers

The Quakers also reduce the sacraments to matters of memory and moral influence for the true Christian life. They don't view them as having or communicating anything living, vital, or historically objective. They are more consistent about this than all the other sects. No other group holds more tenaciously to the abstract, spiritual theory of sectarianism. Consequently, they agree with infidelity itself in their utter rejection of the sacraments.[18] They have no sense of the objective

---

16 George Fox (1624-1691) was an English Dissenter and a founder of the Religious Society of Friends, commonly known as the Quakers or Friends.

17 Elias Hicks (1748-1830) was an itinerant Quaker preacher from New York, who promoted doctrines that embroiled him in controversy and eventually led to the first major schism within the Religious Society of Friends. Hicks considered "obedience to the light within" the primary tenet and the foundational principle of the Religious Society of Friends. He downplayed and reputedly denied the virgin birth of Christ, the complete divinity of Christ and the need for salvation through the death of Christ. He also was reported to have taught that the leading of the Inner light was more authoritative than the text of the Bible.

18 "Does nothing elude our heritage? The sign and pledge (seal) are like Scripture and the Spirit of God." *Bard. Apol.* The Lord's Supper, originally observed, "*imbecillium causa*" (*the cause of the imbecile*) was only a shadow, he tells us, that is no longer

historical Christ revealing Himself in the church and exhibiting Himself in the sacraments. They only know the Christ within, the interior, subjective spiritual life of the believer himself. Can any true salvation be expected if they only seek for Christ within themselves?

> "Whenever the soul is turned towards the light of the Lord within, and is thus made to participate in the celestial life that nourishes the interior man (the privilege of the believer at any time), it may be said to enjoy the Lord's Supper, and to partake of his flesh and blood."

To insist upon the outward sacraments, performing them as spiritual works, is to fall back to Judaism, and to magnify rites and forms at the cost of that spiritual worship, which alone is worthy of our own nature, or suitable to the character of God.

The anti-sacramental tendency of the sect spirit (denominationalism) is clearly revealed in its true rationalistic nature by its rejection of infant baptism. The rejection of infant baptism is the rejection of its mystery. If the sacraments are regarded as ceremonial rites only, that have no objective value or force, except what is experienced by the subjectivity of the worshiper, then infants are rightly excluded. But since infants have no demonstrable knowledge, faith, or experience, their baptism can only rely upon the mysterious presence of Christ in the sacrament. If there is no objective historical, reality in the life of the church that is deeper and more comprehensive than the mere life of the individual believer alone, infant baptism can only be an unnecessary, meaningless contradiction. But if Christ is actually alive in the church as an ongoing, historical reality, then infant baptism exhibits His grace, mercy and power to regenerate the infant whenever He chooses, or not.

Baptistic Principle as and Index of Schism and Heresy

As already remarked in the first part of this chapter, where the consciousness of the true church is dominated by the spirit of sectarianism (denominationalism), the tendency to deny and/or devalue the objectivity of the sacraments prevails to the same extent. Thus, there is no more sure criterion and measure of the presence of sectarianism, as opposed to the true spirit of the universal, historical church, than commitment to the baptistic principle. This principle, whether carried out

---

needed for those who have the substance.

fully in practice or not, constitutes the sure mark of sectarianism all the world over.[19]

Because this perspective is rooted in moral persuasion and influence, and is easily kept in place by outward social pressures, it tends to drain and enervate the vigor of faithfulness because it requires church members to be rationally driven. And because Rationalism itself is a denial of the mystery of Christ's presence, it does not avail itself of the fullness of God's power and grace that does not submit to human understanding.

However, inasmuch as sectarianism comes to full flower, the baptistic principle asserts its authority to the same degree. In discarding infant baptism as a relic of Roman superstition, the Anabaptists and Mennonites increase their connection with Socinians and Arminians, who share the same evaluation of the sacraments. According to the Racovian Catechism,[20] the baptism of infants is without authority and without reason, and to be tolerated only as a harmless inveterate prejudice.[21]

The Remonstrants of Holland (original Arminians) also condemn infant baptism, but find baptism itself to have no binding authority or significance.[22] At the present time in America there is widespread

---

19 "Why are the Congregationalists or Baptists any better than the German Reformed or the Episcopalians?" Thus asks the Biblical Repertory in its review of Schaff on Protestantism (Oct. 1845), charging the author with being vague in what he says on the subject of sectarianism. The question is certainly odd because of the quarter from which it comes. Imagine Baxter or any sound Presbyterian of the seventeenth century asking such a question in relation to Congregationalism! But here the Baptist schismatics themselves, whom the New England Congregationalists of that period could not tolerate, are classified equally with the churches of the Reformation. Such a classification betrays a low conception of the church, in that a sect or subgroup is equated with the whole, which Scripture denounces. Neither Calvin nor Luther could have endured such a spirit so utterly uuhistorical, unchurchly, and unsacramental from beginning to end as that of the Anabaptist schism.

20 The Racovian Catechism (pol. Katechizm Rakowski) is a nontrinitarian statement of faith from the sixteenth century. The title Racovian comes from the publishers, the Polish Brethren, who had founded a sizable town in Raków, Kielce County, where the Racovian Academy and printing press was founded by Jakub Sienieński in 1602. The Polish Brethren or Ecclesia Minor were an antitrinitarian minority of the Reformed Church in Poland who had separated from the Calvinist majority, or Ecclesia Major in 1565.

21 We are persuaded to tolerate old and famous errors because of Christian charity. Rac. Cat.

22 "Remonstrantes believe that the willing rite of the baptism of infants in the ancient church was not likely, and doing so could not have been done without great offense

acceptance of denominational sectarianism. The Baptists, including all the sects that reject the baptism of infants, comprise the most numerous religious profession in the United States. In addition, baptistic practice prevails even more widely among churches that have not traditionally forsaken it.

Thus, the spirit of heresy and schism are identical. Both are equally unchurchly and anti-sacramental. It is not simply an accidental or superficial resemblance that unites them, but the subjective power of common experience. Indeed, it belongs to the genius of sectarianism to express itself through common human rationality.

Note

Ronge, the famous head of the "German Catholic" movement, now garnering so much attention reveals his true theological perspective. Christ laid down His life, according to this man, to open the way for the spread of His beneficial doctrine in the world. He argued that the Supper was instituted to preserve His memory, and to be the universal "brother meal of humanity" in all times. There was a notice of the Easter Service held last year (1850s) in Berlin, by Rouge and Czersky, in Krummacher's *Palmblatter*, June, 1845. The rationalistic and sectarian spirit always betrays itself in the same ways! Ronge, it will be remembered, was first hailed by our religious papers generally to be a second Huss or a Luther. However, such a thought dishonors the Reformation.[23]

---

and scandal; it would have been unlawful, rejected and condemned as criminal." *Apolog. Remonst.*

23 The German Catholics (Deutschkatholiken) were a schismatic sect formed in December 1844 by German dissidents from the Roman Catholic Church, under the leadership of Johannes Ronge. The Bible was made the sole rule, barring all external (papal) authority. Many of the "New Catholics" were involved in politics. Their membership dominated the parliament in Worms. With their view of rational or enlightened religion, the council proclaimed that the sole basis of Christian faith was to be in the Bible, interpreted "by each for himself in the light of reason." They were later forced to change their name from "New Catholics" to "German Catholics." A Protestant group analogous to the New Catholics was the Friends of the Light. In 1849, these two groups combined to form the Free Congregations. The term, "Old Catholic Church," is a common way of describing a collection of Ultrajectine Christian national churches that originated with groups that split from the Roman Catholic Church over certain doctrines, most importantly that of Papal Infallibility. Ultrajectine defines the tradition of the Old Catholic Church of the Netherlands headquartered at the city of Utrecht. It is used to describe the anti-Papal Primacy and Jansenist tendency of those independent churches, which were

Ronge was no Reformer, but only a Radical of the worst stamp. Like Luther, he had cast off the authority of Rome. But further resemblance is superficial. Luther was full of positive life, Ronge was wholly negative and destitute of all faith in Christianity as a real, historical, life-revelation in the world. Luther was objective and felt himself to be only a passive instrument regarding the true and proper historical life of the church itself. Ronge was completely subjective, unhistorical, and full of blind self-will. Luther was a primary, central, and original product of a vast spiritual revolution that came into being with deep, convulsive personal struggles in Luther before it revealed itself in the rest of the church, which was ripe for the change.

Ronge stood in no such relation to the personal religious piety of his time, yet he wants to play the spiritual hero. But no spiritual convulsion has manifest in his own soul. His religious vocation is superficial and feigned in the fullest sense. And the movement over which he presides has the same character. God may yet bring that movement into subjectivity at some point in order to advance His kingdom, but it actually belongs not to God's kingdom, but to the world. There is an excellent article on this subject by Professor Ullmann, characterized by his usual caution, moderation, and profound historical wisdom, in the *Studien und Kritiken*, for the last year (1845?).

Association of Modern Puritanism with this Errant Tendency

The modern Puritan theory of the Lord's Supper, as presented here in contrast with the original Reformed doctrine, is in harmony with sectarianism and denominationalism. This will be obvious to anyone, who will only take the time to review the examples of the Puritan theory quoted above, and to compare them with the modes of thought and language employed by the rationalistic school regarding the sacraments.

To date, American theology is dominated by the rationalistic supernaturalism of Germany, which could not defend itself against German neology.[24] It borrows the orthodoxy of Ernesti, Morus, Rein-

---

founded in later centuries. These churches are not in communion with the Holy See of Rome, but their Union of Utrecht of Old Catholic Churches is in full communion with the Anglican Communion and a member of the World Council of Churches today.

24 The coining or introduction of new words or new senses for established words, related to equivocation, the art and habit of liberalism.

hard, and Knapp, but concerns itself with a very small part of their learning. American theology cannot see its own contradictions. Consequently, the errors work themselves out in many practical ways that create difficulties for theology and piety.

It is not necessary to establish any overt connections between speculative Rationalism and sectarianism to see their similarities. It is enough that they are connected by their subjectivity, a false tendency regarding Protestantism itself. This tendency has always manifested heresy and schism. They always go together. Differences in core Christian doctrine always produce differences in practice. The concern for purity always moves toward separation from what is less than pure.

From the beginning, Puritanism represented a further advance of the sectarian spirit of the Reformed church. It showed itself more independent of all authority but its own, and was more inclined toward abstract spiritualism in religion. The original Reformed church could not defend itself against the secular individuality of the Enlightenment that appeared in the guise of ultra-Protestantism, and was hostile to the theology and structure of the church. Because it thought that it was the cure for the errors of history, it was irreverent towards history.

Indeed, Puritanism, denominationalism, and sectarianism have yet to furnish any reason or evidence that this spirit has had a change of character in this regard.[25] On the contrary, it is clear that its initial impetus has confirmed and consolidated itself from its beginning, in that its central concern was purity. This concern is the curse of sectarianism, as evidenced by the growth of sects in both Great Britain and America. The leaven of rationalism was baked into its theology, which has produced expected results. Of course, we must take care not to deny what is good and valuable in Puritanism because of its errors.

Be all this as it may, the Puritan presumption of its intellectual rigor and beneficence was a departure from the original sacramental doctrine of the Reformation. And it has a strikingly similarity with the apostasy of Rationalism, which has similar tendencies. It might be quite startling to see that Puritanism sundered itself from the universal faith and doctrines of the Eucharist as Christendom defined and developed it from the beginning of the church. But still more startling is the

---

25 This spirit is in harmony with the Serpent in the Garden who tempted Adam and Eve to subject God's intention to human reason and their own personal, individual judgment.

fact that it was accepted by such seemingly knowledgeable and otherwise distinguished company.

This much is clear. The Reformation included in its original documents two different and conflicting elements, tendencies or theologies. And many Reformed theologians believed that they could be true to themselves and Scripture only by acknowledging the authority of both. Each new sect could see the errors of the old sects, but their corrections only produced yet another sect. However, their corrections created a powerful liability which became increasingly ultraistic[26] and extreme as they tried to separate themselves from the errors of Roman Catholicism. It eventually came to be understood that these opposites were mutually necessary for the perfection and proper support of the other.

Over time, this became increasingly and undeniably clear, as we have seen. The simple tendency to protest against authority gradually sundered Protestantism as a movement from the historic, sacramental unity of the church that had been won at so great a cost. And the growth of science out of Rationalism seemed to affirm the success of theoretical and practical rationalism in theology, and the church generally.[27]

The low view of the sacraments, which treats them as memory aids and moral influences, came in with this unfortunate obliquity.[28] It belongs historically and constitutionally to the bastard[29] form, under which the original life of Protestantism has become so widely defined by heretics and schismatics. Its affinity with Rationalism in one respect and with Sectarianism in another (two different phases of the same modern spirit of Antichrist) is too clear to be called in question. It created a departure from the historic faith—not only from the Lutheran,

---

26 Ultraistic: extremism, especially in politics or government; radicalism.
27 Nevin struggled here to say some hard things. The Protestant tendency toward subjectivity has severed itself from the counterbalancing influence of the objectivity found in both the earliest catholic tendencies of the early church and of the earliest Protestant tendencies of the Reformation. Both extremes (subjectivity and objectivity) are held in balance and in tension by the doctrine and practice (liturgy) of the Trinity.
28 In large degree Western Christianity, and particular Protestantism, has failed to understand the connection between theology and liturgy.
29 Fatherless, even Godless in the sense of not representing the fullness of the Triniarian God.

but from the Reformed church as it stood in the sixteenth century. It involves a very serious perversion of the true Protestant doctrine.[30]

Unlike the Catholics and the Magisterial Lutheran and Reformed (Zwinglian and Calvinist) Protestant movements, the Radical Reformation abandoned the idea of the visible church as distinct from the invisible church. The consequence was that they came to believe that the church only consisted of the tiny community of believers of their particular sect, those who accepted Jesus Christ and demonstrated this by "believer's baptism," which almost always meant baptism into their sect. Such ideas and practices sunk the objective virtue of the sacraments and the church itself wholly out of sight. For them the faith was entirely subjective. This subjectivity was also the result of making the worship service spiritual and rational, rather than liturgical.[31] In this way, both rationalism and sectarianism damage Christianity's claim to involve the supernatural and deny Christ's divinity (and His body's participation in His divinity because He and His body are in unity). The Radical Reformation proceeded on the same false abstraction, by which soul and body, objectivity and subjectivity, are mutually exclusive, and even antagonistic, spheres of existence. Such abstract theology is the ancient heresy of Gnosticism in new garb.

Both rationalism and sectarianism show the same utter disregard for the authority of all previous church history, and work to construct a whole new idea of the church—doctrine, sacraments, etc.—as the product of independent judgment. They create an abstract idea of the church and substitute that abstract idea for the reality of the continuity of the historic church, and call their idea the invisible church. And this invisible church has only an abstract, philosophical connection with the historic church because they also deny the possibility of any actual connection. Such actual connection must be ultimately mystical

---

30 The Radical Reformation was a sixteenth century response to what was believed to be both the corruption in the Roman Catholic Church and the expanding Magisterial Protestant movement led by Martin Luther and many others. Beginning in Germany and Switzerland, the Radical Reformation birthed many radical Protestant groups throughout Europe. The term covers both radical reformers like Thomas Müntzer, Andreas Karlstadt, groups like the Zwickau prophets and anabaptist groups like the Hutterites and the Mennonites.

31 It cannot be denied that Puritan Protestantism involved the rejection of ritual and liturgy. However, ritual and ceremony are very much a part of human life. Liturgy is not just the order of the worship service at church, but is the actual work of the people in their ordinary lives.

because it is ultimately beyond human explanation or understanding. In addition, the idea that the invisible church does not overlap the visible church defies both the Bible and common sense. The Radical Reformation involves a defection from the original creed of the Reformation. It would have been understood in this way by Luther, Zwingli, Calvin, Beza, and Ursinus, and the fathers of the Reformed church generally. It was treasonable to the original interest and efforts of the Reformation.

This concern is not to be decided by church authority or blind tradition. Of course, it is possible that the ancient church may have gone astray from the very beginning. The fathers of the Reformation were not infallible, and it must be understood that the original Reformation was the spiritual product and was birthed out of the Catholic Church. It has an organic connection to the earlier church. The original Reformation was not a sectarian idea or effort, but was a reconstitution of the catholicity or wholeness of the church.[32] If the later Reformers had maintained the original doctrines of the Reformation, Protestantism generally would have been something vastly different from what it is now.

What is born is not radically different from its mother. The original, catholic Reformers may have been wrong about the things we have discussed, and possibly in many other points. That's not the issue. It is simply contrary to God's promises and Christian history that the whole of Christendom could have been so wrong for so long about such a central doctrine of the church. Yet, the Radical Reformers want us to believe that Christianity had been completely lost until modern Protestantism discovered sectarianism and rationalism. This is what Protestantism teaches, based on its claim to superior evangelical theology and practice.

The coincidence may be accidental (circumstantial) only, and not natural or necessary. With regard to all this, we are troubled by the conclusion that we cannot deny. Nonetheless, we simply wish to exhibit the facts as we understand them, weighty though they be. They stand as a judgment against modern Puritanism, and impose an obligation upon all Christians not to acquiesce in it without examination.[33]

---

32 The Reformers went back to the original sources of Christianity and not to the corrupt sources of the Middle Ages, which they hoped to correct.

33 In these last paragraphs Nevin sum up his findings, and indicate that he is not will-

CHAPTER III

The need for some Formal Modification in the Statement of the Doctrine

It has been already admitted that the Calvinistic theory of the Eucharistic presence, as presented in all the Reformed creeds and confessions of the sixteenth century, has some difficulties. These concern the true and proper substance of the doctrine. From time immemorial Christ's presence has been understood to be an ultimate mystery that cannot be reduced to any complete explanation, but still it became necessary in the controversy to define and describe the limits of the fact itself at every point. With Romanism and Lutheranism on the one side and the Socinanizing tendencies of sectarianism and rationalism on the other, it is also necessary to defeat various popular objections, and meet the demands of common sense. It is, however, a difficult argument to make because there is a lot of history and the theological issues are subtle, and widely ignored.

The success of such an effort necessarily depends upon the general theological and philosophical culture of the time. There have been some enormous intellectual and scholastic advances coming out of Germany. And in light of these it is surprising that they have not brought more clarity to the subject, but those advances have yet to penetrate popular culture. This we find to be the case in fact.

---

ing to make a private judgment about what he has found, because to do so would make him guilty of the very problem under consideration. He simply published his findings for the consideration of others. He said, in essence, "Here I stand. Prove me wrong." But neither did he want to discard everything that Puritanism had brought to the table. He simply wanted to correct the errors and retain the truths in order to strengthen the whole church.

Section I

PRELIMINARY POSITIONS

The Calvinistic Theory not Sufficiently clear regarding the Organic Nature of Life

Calvin's theory seems to labor at three particular points, and all are connected with a false psychology that is applied either to the Person of Christ or the persons of His people. This false psychology provides an inadequate understanding of the meaning and extent regarding the definition, idea, and reality of *person*.

First, Calvin does not make a sufficiently clear distinction between the reality and fullness of a person based upon its organic nature and the mere idea of a person that is derived from our human senses. A real body is always composed of organized matter. If we consider the man-ifestation of a body as the result of the application of an organic law of nature, the body itself is real enough, but the law is merely an idea and has no dimensional or bodily existence in time. Only when a body is transfused and inseparable from such a law at every point can it be said to be manifest in reality. And even then we can say that the body is a medium for the law to be exercised, or that the law is a medium for the manifestation of the body. The point is that a subjective and invisi-ble medium[1] is required for the true manifestation of objective existence.[2]

The idea of the body of Christ as the whole of life itself is not material. Because the origin of life is beyond scientific materialism, the

---

1 Medium: An intervening substance through which signals can travel as a means for communication.
2 Nevin speaks about the role of law with regard to personal identity, and the abstract universalism of the law versus the concrete particularity of the individual, which can only be resolved by a Trinitarian perspective.

identity of life is not bound to materialism, either. Human bodies continually absorb and expel all sorts of material elements for life—air, water, food, waste—and yet they remain the same in the sense of not losing their identity over the course of life. And since, the body is not air, water, food, or waste none of these things encompass or impact the identity of the body. Yet, the body is dependent on these things. This suggests that the whole of the human body is greater than the sum of its parts, and that the "whole" is not located in any particular, material part of the body. Certainly, the idea of the whole of the body is an intellectual abstraction, but the actual whole of the body is not merely intellectual. The most important aspects of it will always remain an ultimate mystery in that its wholeness, like the source of life itself, lies beyond human comprehension—though we can understand some of it.

Real communication between the body of Christ and the bodies of His saints does not necessarily imply any transfer of His flesh, Jesus' flesh, into their persons. Such an idea is absurd and superstitious. It has no real meaning or value. The flesh of Christ's body remains connected to His fleshly body, and has no power to be supernaturally transferred across space and time. Rather, the supernature of Christ is the holistic wholeness of humanity because Christ functions as the archetypal or prototypical model[3] of the new humanity in God's image that he inaugurated. Thus, he is the model of humanity's parts (individuals) as well. Thus, the communication between Christ and people is real and is not limited or bound to any particular individual, but belongs to each individuation of His type.

John said that "the flesh is no help at all" (John 6:63). This clearly brings into view one of the most valid and powerful objections to the false teaching of transubstantiation, and impacts the doctrine of consubstantiation, as well. Both transubstantiation and consubstantiation suggest a physical, material, tactile element of Christ's body that participates in the sacrament. In contrast, Calvin suggested that the element of Christ's body that participates in the sacrament is spiritual, which does not simply mean an abstract idea but rather points to the real, immediate, holistic wholeness that is unique to Christ and is available to each Christian in such a way that it is the central defining

---

3   See https://wiki2.org/en/Aleph_number. Set Theory and the role of the Aleph Null helps to explain a lot of biblical mysticism. Jesus was able to fulfill God's law because Jesus was more than a mere individual. He was both fully human and fully divine.

characteristic of their own person or individual identity. Thus, both transubstantiation or consubstantiation err by imagining Christ's influence or communication to be something material that is intimately related to the bread and wine.

Calvin objected most strenuously to these false, absurd, and superstitious theories. He was not unaware of the idea of the distinction as described above, though his descriptions were not as clear as we need them to be today. It was more of an intuition to him because his era did not have access to the language of science, as we do. So, he was not able to bring this idea forward directly or clearly. He simply allowed for it by not closing off its possibility with fruitless speculation.[4]

Thus, too much emphasis has been put on the idea of the flesh of Christ being materially connected to the bread and wine, whether by way of *becoming*, or simply *in* and *under* the elements. By focusing on the spiritual element, Christ's wholeness and archetypal role, we see that it is the power of God as the seat and source of new life in Christ that is given to His people as they participate in the Eucharist.

Here there is no need to imagine or invent any material connection between Christ and His church, because the connection is powered and maintained by God Himself. There is no awkward or violent denial of common sense or science. No wonder that men of less intellectual power and subtlety than Calvin were at a loss to understand such a seeming contradiction in terms. Calvin simply held on to both ends of the opposition because Scripture presents both ends without trying to speculate about their connection. And by holding to both ends he held them together in a kind of knot, without speculating about how such a knot was possible. It was enough that Scripture clearly assumes and teaches their connection.

There is no doubt that Christ's body is in heaven. So, how can its vivific virtue be involved in believers? By the miraculous power of the Holy Spirit. However, it is not so much that Christ's life comes down to believers, but that believers are raised up by grace into the exercise of faith to the presence of the Savior on high. The connection or communication always results in a real participation in the wholeness of

---

4   Calvin failed to solve the philosophical problem of the one and the many, which is
     resolved only by the doctrine of the Trinity. See *The One And The Many: Studies in
     The Philosophy of Order and Ultimacy*, by R.J. Rushdoony, Ross House Books.

humanity, which includes the fall of Adam and the redemption of Christ. Both are necessary to the fullness of the history of humanity.

Nonetheless, Calvin's treatment of the mystery, the paradox of holding together what sometimes seems to be mutually exclusive ideas of individual subjectivity and Christ's objectivity, is incomplete. If Calvin had used the language of organic human wholeness as the aspect of Christ that is communicated in the sacrament, his theory would have been much more consistent and intelligible. But the language in vogue during his time made him speak of the "vivific virtue" (life giving power) of Christ's flesh, which isn't wrong, though it does not allow for the overlap of unity between individual subjectivity and Christ's objectivity. From this perspective local, material contact between Christ and believers is not necessary for true and accurate continuity of existence, either in the sphere of nature or in that of grace.[5]

Calvin Failed to Properly Understand what is Involved in Personal Unity

Secondly, Calvin failed to consider the full extent of what is denominated a person. One's skin is not a hard and fast border between one's body and the environment. Life requires a physical exchange between one's individual body and various aspects of the environment through breathing, eating, and reproduction, for instance. Thus, life requires communication between individual subjectivity and the objectivity of the environment. And life in Christ capitalizes upon a similar spiritual communication between archetype and individual instance, Christ himself and His people. Calvin dwelt too much on the life-giving virtue of Christ's flesh as he sought to correct both transubstantiation and consubstantiation, as if Christ's flesh was not necessarily and *inseparably* knit to his soul and his divinity, as a single indivisible manifestation of the wholeness of life. Calvin failed to realize that where the wholeness of existence is present in a real way, the flesh is a necessary part of that wholeness, though it may not be immediately or locally obvious. Where an objective connection

---

5   Again, Calvin's problem of holding subjectivity and objectivity together by having the Holy Spirit mysteriously mediate between the wholeness, universality, and spirituality of Christ and the partness, particularity, and materiality of the individual has been greatly resolved by R.J Rushdoony, who was applying the insights of Cornelius Van Til.

is real, like that between Christ and believers, the connection establishes the reality of the subjective unity, to the same extent.[6]

When I read about or think about the planet Saturn, the act
involves my whole person. No, my body does not go to Saturn, of
course, but mind and body are inseparable so there is a bodily reality
involved, though it is subjective. Reading and thinking involve the
single, unitary, and absolutely unique life which is myself as the unity
of soul/body. And if it were possible in any way that the thought
which carries me to Saturn, could be made to assume there a real concrete existence, holding an organic connection with my own life, it
must appear as a human existence under a human form, which in such
a case would be as strictly a continuation of my bodily as well as spiritual being, as though it had sprung immediately from the local
presence of my body itself.[7]

In a similar way, the acts of the incarnate Word—Christ—belong
to His person as a whole, and He is God so His wholeness is all inclusive. We are not saying that His humanity separately considered could
be said to exercise the functions of His divinity separately considered.
Such a statement would make a false distinction. Similarly, there is just
as little reason to say that Christ's divinity separately considered always
exercises the same functions. They are exercised by the anthropic or
archetypal Person of the Mediator, who is one and indivisible.

If then Christ's life is communicated to the persons of His people
in a real and not merely a figurative way, His life must be involved in
its human form, not only His humanity and His divinity, but His body
and soul. In addition, His extended bodily existence must not be
dependent on local physical connections as we commonly know them.
And yet there is a strict continuity of Christ's bodily life by implication. Because Christ is whole in a holistic sense, His wholeness as a
person must always include His material body. A disembodied human
spirit cannot be whole, nor can a material body that is devoid of spirit.
The "anthropic person of the Mediator" is referred to by Calvin as

---

6   This is another hashing of the same concern. Nevin seems to be trying to say that
    the wholeness of a particular individual is of the same relationship as Christ to
    humanity.

7   Here Nevin insists that the wholeness of the body is always experienced in the
    mind. The mind is where the wholeness of the body is found, and every experience
    that the mind has is always necessarily attached to the body, even though it seems
    abstract.

being a type or archetype, but the way that Christ brings His type to influence or communicate with individuals is not always clear.

This point does not appear to have been understood with sufficient distinctness by Calvin or the Reformers generally. So, there is more or less confusion, and at times some seeming contradiction involved in tracing the derivation of Christ's human life into the person of the believer. Bound as he felt himself to be to resist everything that looked or smelled like the idea of a *local presence* (because of the Catholic and Lutheran errors), Calvin found it necessary to resolve the whole process into a special supernatural agency of the Holy Spirit, as a medium to fill in the missing blanks. Indeed, this is usually the way that mysticism functions. As more things become clear there is less and less mystery, but there will always be an element of mystery to life, Christ and the sacraments—and it will always be significant.

Thus, our usual biological understanding of Christ's human nature becomes both too small and too abstract, and it makes it difficult to maintain the idea of a true (actual) organic connection between the wholeness of Christ's life and that of His people. It is not easy to maintain a clear distinction between the organic communication of Christ's substance, His life (or being), and a spiritual influence abstractly conceived. Calvin's concern for the real, organic bodily existence of Christ always fared poorly in comparison to the high-minded, spiritual tones of his Lutheran adversaries.

Nonetheless, he never failed to protest against their unrealistic and abstract spirituality as grossly perverse and unjust, and indeed he took the greatest pains to save himself from being misunderstood at this point. And Calvin's insistence upon the fact that the wholeness and unity of Christ always included in some sense His own biological body was the source of constant and serious conflict. Calvin was excoriated for holding body and soul or body and spirit together as not being sufficiently "spiritual."

Note

The pertinacity of those who misrepresent Calvin at this very point is amazing. Narrow-minded Lutherans have charged him with theological duplicity, thinking that he differed from Zwingli in this regard, while in fact he agreed with him.[8] Modern Calvinists, who

---

8   Today we think that Zwingli taught that the sacraments were nothing more than

have themselves fallen away from Calvin's sacramental doctrine of the
sixteenth century fain to bring Zwingli down as well. They neglect
the quotations used above that demonstrate Zwingli's actual position.
Even the *Form of Concord* is liable to injustice because it divides the
Sacramentarians into two classes: the more gross who openly profess
that they believe that Christ is actually present in the Eucharist, and
the political who use high sounding Lutheran language to speak of
Christ's presence.

These last, who represent the Calvinistic, proper, and original
Reformed view are made to be "*omnium nocentissimi sacramentarii*" (*the
harmful sacramentarians*) because they themselves pretend to allow a
"true presence of the true substantial and living body and blood of
Christ in the Lord's Supper," and yet declare it to be only or merely
spiritual, and by faith, as if faith is the result of moral persuasion.
Under these high sounding terms, they will have nothing present in
the Eucharist but mere bread and wine. "For the term *spiritually*, signifies with them only Christ's Spirit, or the virtue of his absent body, and
his merit," etc.

Writers such as Guerike, (*Symbolik*, p. 452-455,) Rudelbach, (*Ref.
Luth. und Union*, p. 188 ff.) and Scheibel, (*Das Abendmahl*, p. 331 ff.)
spare no pains in their Lutheran zeal to establish the same misrepresen-
tation. They insist that Calvin only plays with words by pretending to
go beyond Zwingli in his theory of Christ's presence in the Supper,
and that it all boils down to the *idea* of mere power and effect, as if the
sacrament simply signifies the grace it represents, and nothing more.
They disregard the reality of sacramental sealing.

They simply presume that communion with Christ is only spiritual and has nothing to do with His body. They assume that the life of
Christ's body, in order to be real, has nothing to do with His soul.
When such an assumption is granted, it leaves no room in Calvin's
theory for any actual or real communion at all. But this is not what
Calvin taught. On the contrary he taught that to make the Eucharist
separate Christ's divinity from His humanity, or His body from His
soul was to deprive it of all reality or value. Calvin refused to make any
such division, and taught that the more spiritual a thing is, the more
real it is.

---

memorials, but we forget that biblically speaking a memorial is not an abstract
thought but a concrete shrine that is built to induce memories. Biblical memorials
are always grounded in concrete existence.

Everything that Luther intended to secure by his doctrine of an oral or physical communication with Christ, Calvin offered a more satisfactory answer by holding Christ's spiritual communication to be inseparable from His bodily communication. He declared himself to be of one mind with Luther regarding this, and the only difference between them pertained to the mode. This was the position taken also by the Reformed church in general.

Did Calvin not understand what Luther meant by his doctrine? And shall we not believe him when he says he agrees with the reality of Christ's actual body and blood present in the bread and wine, but understands it to take place in a different way? Is there anything less real in Calvin's understanding of Christ's actual but spiritual presence in the Eucharist than in transubstantiation or consubstantiation?

There is no reason to question that he believed and taught a real sacramental communication, not by the power and operation of Christ's Spirit alone, but with Christ's true, substantial and bodily life because they cannot be separated. The communion elements are signs, and might be physically separated from the *reality of the sacrament* (*res sacramenti*), as Augustine also explicitly taught. But the sacramental transaction as a whole was not a mere sign or symbol. It actually exhibits what is represented, not unlike the dove in whose form the Holy Spirit descended upon the Savior at His baptism.

"It is perfectly plain," said Bretschneider, "that Calvin's theory includes the true, full participation of Christ's body and blood for the strengthening and quickening of the soul," which was Luther's main concern. But Luther's analysis of whether this takes place *under* the bread, or at the same time as the bread is eaten, or by the mouth or by the soul, does not get at the substance of the issue. It is a shallow analysis from our modern standpoint. For unless we conceive of the body of Christ as something sensible, and understand communion as a Capernaitic (cannibalistic) eating as Jesus taught in John 6:63, our own oral participation must become the power of the Holy Spirit in the final analysis. But even in this case there is a real communication with Christ's body, though it confuses mystical identity with mystical union.

All of this transcends all known analogies and claims the virtue of an extraordinary divine power that is present in the sacrament for the purpose. It is not a natural and necessary result of a new life that exists in the human soul. All natural explanations are unsatisfactory. Christ's person is one (unified, holistic, and whole), and the person of the believer is one in the same way but to a lesser degree. So, to secure any kind of real communication of the whole human life of Christ into the whole personality of the believer, it is only necessary that the communication originates from the center of Christ's life and reach to the center of ours.

Such a thing can only be done by the Holy Spirit. But the Holy Spirit is not to be sundered from the person of Christ because the doctrine of the Trinity forbids it. We must say rather that this is the only form and/or way that Christ's life is made present in the church for salvation.

Calvin's Doctrine comes to no clear Representation of the Distinction Between Life as Something Individual and Life as Something Universal

The third source of embarrassment belonging to the form in which Calvin presented his doctrine of the Eucharist is found in the fact that he made no clear distinction between the individual personal life of Christ the individual man and Christ the Savior God. In every sphere of life the individual (or particular) and the general (or universal) are closely united in the same subject. Thus, in the vegetable world the acorn that is planted into the ground is transformed into an oak tree. And yet the life from acorn to oak tree is only a single life.

But from another perspective, the same oak tree includes the power of life that is capable of reaching far beyond all of the individual limits of the particular acorn that was planted. For the oak may produce ten million other acorns, and so repeat and extend its own life in a forest of trees for thousands of years. Still, in the end, the life of such a forest is nothing more than an expansion of the life that at one point lay dormant in a single acorn. In a similar way, the whole of humanity, which has enjoyed a similar kind of existence, is bound together inwardly and organically in unity, similar to that of any individual existence (acorns).[9]

Every parent may be regarded as the bearer, not only of the single individual life that constitutes his own person, but of a more universal aspect of life that reveals itself in his children. As the first acorn is to the forest, so the archetypal man is to society. Thus especially, in an emi-

---

9   This is an important analogy because it shows that the unity of a biblical kind is contained in its DNA, the archetypal pattern created in reproduction.

nent sense, the first man Adam is always exhibited in this kind of twofold character.[10] In one respect he is simply an individual man, to be counted as one among his sons. In another sense he is the arche-typal man or federal head of humanity in whose single person was included the whole life of the human race. Thus he bears the Hebrew name of the race itself—אדם (Adam), and in this generic title particu-larly he is presented to us in the sacred history of the Bible.

His individual person was limited wholly to himself, of course. But a whole world of similar but separate persons are involved in his life as a generic or universal principle, root, or archetype. And all of these individual persons, whose existence is part and parcel of Adam's one life, are caught up in his seed. Adam lives in his posterity as truly as he has ever lived in his own individual person. Indeed, Adam as a race or kind lives more fully through population expansion. Each indi-vidual since Adam participates in the wholeness of humanity because of the indivisibility of soul and body. Each are truly bone of his bone and flesh of his flesh.[11]

The life of Christ is to be understood in a similar way, but fuller. Christ's character includes the individual, the universal, and the union of both through the mystical power of the Holy Spirit. The individual and universal in Christ don't have the same form as they do in Adam because in Christ is the fullness of the Spirit, which mends the broken wholeness of humanity in the sin of Adam. Thus, in Christ humanity becomes a renewed species, as important and unique as the old species. The relationship of the single oak to its offspring forest is not com-pletely the same as that of Adam and his posterity. Nor is humanity in Christ completely commensurate with the relationship of Christ to His church (Rom. 9:6). This will soon be clarified, but for the point now in hand the cases are parallel.

The distinction between an individual and the universality of life in the Person of Christ is just as necessary as the same distinction in the Person of Adam. And the analogy is sufficient to show that there can

---

10 While Nevin argues for a twofold human character, I suggest a trifold or trinitarian character. See footnote 4, p. 7.

11 How might this work? Consider the *Fractal*: a rough or fragmented geometric shape that can be split into parts, each of which is a reduced-size copy of the whole through a property called self–similarity. The term *fractal* was coined by Benoît Mandelbrot in 1975 and was derived from the Latin *fractus* meaning broken or frac-tured. While fractals are a mathematical construct, they are found in nature.

be a real communication of Christ's life to His people, without any sort of local contact with His individual Person. From one perspective the Savior is a man, Jesus of Nazareth, who Himself partakes of the same flesh and blood as other men, even though He is mysteriously in union with the everlasting Word. But from another perspective the Savior is the archetypal or universal Person, though in a higher and more complete sense than Adam was. Christ is the Son of Man, in whose Person is revealed the truest archetype or model of humanity, in the ultimate and comprehensive form.

Without any loss or change of character in the first perspective, Christ's life is extended into this last perspective with continuity into the individual persons that constitute His people. He lives in Himself, and yet He lives in them and through them—through His people—actually and truly at the same time. Calvin did not account for this distinction between the individual and the universal character of the life of Christ as well as he might have. Then again, language, science, and history would not have been able to accommodate such distinction during his time. Nonetheless, it is clear that the idea of it was in some measure present to his mind. But it was not brought out clearly, distinctly, or fully, which caused his theological system to labor some on this account, and infused the ranks of the Calvinists with critics who were not as able as Calvin to hold the opposing forces of subjectivity and objectivity in creative tension.

These Three Points are of Great account, as it Regards the Apprehension of the Doctrine

It is easy to see that the three more nuanced determinations—the organic nature of life, personal unity, and the individual/universal aspects of life—modify and materially improve Calvin's doctrine of Christ's union with His people. These three nuances help us better understand the mode of unity by relieving it of some of its difficulties and providing an explanation better suited to our scientific mindset. Even those who prefer intellectual abstractions will be satisfied because our further analysis is neither arbitrary nor hypothetical.

We are simply engaging the current science and philosophy of the present time to better explain what Scripture plainly says. No inquiry can be taken seriously if it fails to bring the best scholarship into play.[12]

---

12 Nevin is a creature of his own time and was filled with the hope of 1850s science.

At the same time it should be clear that we are not allowing science or scholarship to take the lead in this inquiry, but that we are preserving the true and proper substance of the old Reformed doctrine in the light of modern science and scholarship.

In this regard our effort differs from that of the Rationalists and modern Puritans. We agree with them that the doctrine as originally proposed has difficulties. And we agree that they had a right to quarrel with it. But we disagree that the solution is to abort the entire original doctrine. We find that they have thrown out the proverbial baby with the bath water, which can never be right. Too often the attempt to correct one kind of error is done by overemphasizing the opposite error.

Thus, we must hold fast to the central truths of the original doctrine by placing them in a better, fuller, and more biblical context. How can anyone complain of our effort to understand these things in the better light of current science and scholarship? Surely this kind of effort is better than simply abandoning the whole doctrine. Those who have abandoned it are reactive and negative, whereas our effort here is proactive and positive. Our effort is to preserve original truth, both biblical truth and scientific truth, regarding the wholeness of life and Spirit without being slaves to a dead and lifeless reading of God's Word.

We need to discern between the dynamic power of God's Word and a narrow-minded dogmatism that idealizes some romantic view of the past at the expense of the reality of the present. Life in Christ can never issue from dead traditions. But neither can it be disjoined from the life of the past. Its true form is found in the flow of history, where the past, though left behind from one perspective, is always taken up by the present from another perspective. Thus, past truth is reborn as it is both corrected and nourished by present truth. Present truth that requires the wholesale abandonment of past truth can never be the whole truth.

However, when we speak of putting the doctrine of the Eucharist into a form that is more satisfactory to our understanding, it is not to be imagined that we consider it to be any less a mystery on this account. The mystical union of Christ with His church transcends all analogies we are capable of imagining. It is vain to expect, therefore, that our finite understanding can ever fathom or grasp the mystery of existence in its fullness. However, we must not abandon orthodoxy simply because we do not have a perfect understanding of it.

We find that our modern, scientific understanding recoils from that which it cannot absolutely comprehend, as if our knowledge can be equivalent to God's. Sometimes the best that we can do is to understand the limits of our understanding, rather than fabricating ideas and trusting our own fabrications as if they are true. When we substitute our own fabrications for God's ultimately mysterious truth we have already turned from trusting God and begun trusting ourselves. So, we fall back for ultimate relief on human reason, as if it provides a deeper and more comprehensive power than God Himself. Indeed, this is the lure of rationalism.

It is imperative that false ideas be abandoned and that we do not confuse representations of truth for truth itself. It is also important that we not mistake ultimate truth for various analogous truths regarding the organic character of Christ's life. Jesus Christ, who is imbued with supernatural character and divinity cannot ever be separated from the organic character of His humanity.

Though regeneration in Christ results in a new creation, it must still be regarded as a continuation of the natural creation. New life in Christ does not make us anything other than human beings. Only by holding the wholeness of Christ in unity can we comprehend the doctrine of unity in Christ forged by the original Reformers, as taught in Scripture. Increased understanding comes from holding Christ's humanity and divinity in unity, and not by separating them or denying one for the sake of the other. There should be no radical break or departure from the substance of true doctrine nor any break or departure regarding its form of communication. However, change in both depth and breadth should be expected as Christ's revelation continues to unfold in history.

We must take advantage of modern scientific truths that Calvin did not or could not apply, and hold fast to the authority of God's most holy revelation of Himself engaging humanity as a man. We must not neglect Christ's humanity because we cannot understand or explain how that aspect of His character can be present in the Eucharist. I (Nevin) will now endeavor to put the doctrine comprehensively into a better form. This will then be available so that we can test the veracity of the doctrine by the Scriptures themselves. Scripture, of course, provides the last and only conclusive measure of truth. But before we look to the Scriptural proofs, we must clearly understand what it is that we intend to prove.

Perhaps the best procedure will be to present successive theses or propositions, accompanied with illustrations as each case may require. We will first examine the doctrine of Christ's Mystical Union generally, and then to the specific question of the Eucharist.

SECTION II

1. The Race Hopelessly Lost in Adam

The human world in its present natural state, as descended from Adam, has been sundered from its proper life in God by sin, and is completely incapable of mending the breach on its own. The fall of Adam was the fall of the entire race. It broke the holistic wholeness of humanity, which was created to live in relationship or union with God. It was not simply because Adam represented the human race, but because the human race was itself encompassed in his individual Person. The terrible fact of sin revealed itself in him as an objective fact that is now incorporated into the universal life of humanity itself through the particular and subjective lives of human individuals. And from Adam's fall forward in history sin has interfered with the progress of human maturity and development, in the sense that maturity and development require the conscious integration of human wholeness.

The ruin under which humanity lies is an organic[1] ruin. Sin brought an organic disruption to human nature. It broke humanity's organic wholeness. This disruption occurred, not simply because all men were created sinners, but rather because the disruption *made* all men to be sinners in fact—objectively. Men do not make their own nature, rather their nature makes them. To have part in human nature after the Fall, we can only have part in it as a fallen nature, a spiritually impotent nature. Because life requires organic unity with the original source of life—because life only comes from life, and that organic unity requires wholeness, and because sin broke human wholeness, humanity is not in organic unity with the principle or fountain of life.

---

1 Organic: Constituting an integral part of a whole; fundamental.

The mend that sin requires is organic, which means that it is both sub-jective and objective, particular and universal.

Sin is not a consequence of accident or bad example, as Pelagians and their ilk vainly dream. We are all under the same condemnation. We are all born into sin, into a humanity that is separated from God by sin. Because sin is an objective human fact, all individuals are born into the objective fact of sin, and cannot overcome it subjectively or individually. There is a law of sin at work in us from our birth. The whole Pelagian view of life is shallow in that it understands humanity only as a vast aggregation of particular individuals, outwardly put together[2] like a huge sand-heap, and nothing more. But the human race is not a sand-heap. Rather, humanity is unified by the power of a single life, a special life, an archetypal life that has one foot outside of time. Thus, humanity is bound and organized in unity, not merely outwardly, but inwardly. Man (Adam) was one (Gen. 1:26) before he became many (Gen. 1:27). Thus, every particular individual proceeds from and shares in Adam's original seed nature.

It is quite correct to say that Adam's sin is imputed to all his pos-terity. Only let us not imagine such imputation to be a mere outward transfer like handing a rock to a friend. Arguments against this kind of imputation (as a merely outward transfer) are legitimate. This kind of idea of imputed sin substitutes a fiction for a fact. No imputation of this sort is taught in the Bible. This is not how it works, the imputa-tion of Adam's sin to his posterity involves no such fiction.

Rather, sin is attributed to individuals simply because it belongs to the class before the consideration of any specific individuals of the class. Individuals are born into Adam's nature. We are what Adam was because Adam was the archetype or model for all individual existence. And for this reason alone individuals are born also into his guilt, not because they have already sinned as individuals, but because as individ-uals made in Adam's mold they can do nothing else.

---

2   "Outwardly put together" is an important phrase that suggests that from this per-spective people don't sense any personal, subjectivity that is beyond human under-standing. Because freewill means conscious choosing, all human unity is created and maintained by personal, individual volition. In contrast to this Nevin argues for what we might call a structural unity like the unity of the acorn and the forest.

2. This Ruin Includes Soul and Body

The union in which we stand with Adam in his fallen state extends to his entire Person, body and soul, because they always appear together in unity. He did not fall only in his soul, nor only in his body, but in both at once. Adam's whole Person fell. The humanity of which he was the prime root also fell in him and with him, and to the same extent. The whole became wholly fallen or corrupt. And so it now includes in all of Adam's posterity, all who constitute a real and true perpetuation of his life in its wholeness, in both body and soul, to the end of time. Humanity is modeled on his body/soul life.

Both are carried by ordinary generation, the same identical organic life-stream that continues over time. We are bone of his bone, flesh of his flesh, and blood of his blood. And still there is no material communication, no immediate contact between us and the Person of Adam. Not a particle of Adam's individual body has come into ours. The communication resolves into law or principle. And it is not one law or principle for the body and another for the soul, but one and the same law or principle impacts both through the commonality of what may be called biblical *kinds*. Where the law works, there Adam's life is reproduced, body and soul together.[3]

And still the individual, Adam, is not merged with his posterity in any way. He does not lose his own personality nor is he swallowed up by theirs. Rather, his unity with his posterity is generic in that it applies to the class or kind called *Man*—אדם *(Adam).* Of course, generic unity is none the less real though it differs from class identity. Everyone is familiar with this kind of thing because it is the context of our individuality, and needs no explanation. We all simply assume it as a common fact of our existence. And yet it is an important truth about us (and every biblical *kind*). It is something very wonderful, very astonishing, and ultimately very mysterious because its full explanation goes quite beyond our understanding.[4]

---

3   This appears to be an overstatement because we now know that various physical characteristics are carried by DNA in family lines, "each according to its kind" (Gen. 1:11) and DNA has physical properties. DNA is essentially a pattern or fractal. In the very next sentence Nevin admits that body and soul are one. So, whatever is communicated is done so body and soul. The point is the organic unity of body and soul, and I (Ross) insist that it is an organic unity of body, soul and Christ, a kind of trinitarian whole.

4   Inherited similarity does not change the fact of individual identity. Individual identity is not swallowed up by participation in generic or universal humanity, though

3. Human nature recovered in Jesus Christ

By the hypostatic[5] union of the two natures in the Person of Jesus Christ, our fallen humanity in Adam was re-paired[6] to its original intended wholeness and imperishable divine life. In order to save the race as a whole and in its wholeness, it was necessary that the proper reparation or fix be applied to both the objectivity of the wholeness of humanity and to the subjectivity of the wholeness of each individual who constitutes it.

For this salvational fix to be effective for any individual, it needed to be first applied organically to the race or kind in its universal character. Before human beings could be remolded into the likeness of a better model, the better model had to become organically manifest in history. Because the original model, Adam, had fallen in its entirety, the new model, Christ, had to recover the full extent of the original fall.[7] The salvation of the wholeness of the race required that it be organically united with the divine nature, which is represented by the everlasting Word or Logos, the fountain of all created light and life. Such a union can only be established by the Holy Spirit through personal regeneration.

So, the Word became flesh; that is, He assumed humanity into union with Himself. This assumption by the Spirit is not limited to any particular individual, as if the intention is to apply to some predetermined part of humanity but not to some other part. Rather, the intention was to apply to the wholeness of humanity. However, such wholeness cannot apply to any individual part (person) that is not assumed into the whole. Indeed, to apply it to any part (person) not fully integrated into the wholeness of humanity would itself destroy the wholeness. Thus, wholeness is a spiritual reality or a quantum fractal, not a numerical quantity. Salvation is not about this or that person going to heaven. Nor is it a work of human accomplishment (i.e., the obedience of Christ) that can then be objectively applied or imputed to humanity as a class or kind. Rather, salvation is aimed simultaneously

---

there are various overlapping commonalities.

5   Hypostasis: The suppression of a gene by the effect of an unrelated gene.

6   Intentional hyphenation to suggest *pairing*—bringing two objects, ideas, or people together.

7   The importance of this insight cannot be overvalued. Salvation does not merely concern individuals, it is also the salvation of humanity as a biblical *kind*.

at individuals and at humanity as a whole. Christ's fix requires the unity of individuality and the corporate wholeness of humanity.

The purpose of the incarnation was to couple human nature in real union with the Logos, as a permanent source of life. Because sin preceded the incarnation of Christ, the Savior was called to suffer in order to repair the breach of sin. Because He was the bearer of a fallen humanity, He had to descend into the lowest depths of human sorrow and pain, in order to recover all sorrow and pain with the power of His own imperishable life. In all this, Jesus acted for Himself as an individual and simultaneously for the race He represents. For Christ to be the true seed of a new humanity, He, like Adam, had to contain in Himself the holistic wholeness of the race. Humanity dwelt in His person as the second Adam, but in a higher or more complete form because of the fullness of the Holy Spirit that also dwelt in Him.

4. The Value of Christ's Whole Life and Death, Based on the Generic Character of His Humanity

The value of Christ's suffering and death, as well as of His entire life, is derived from the understanding of the incarnation presented above. The repossession of humanity by God in Christ through unity with His people involved the necessity of Christ's suffering to demonstrate the reliability and integrity of the new model for humanity to emulate. The passion of the Son of God was the world's greatest spiritual crisis, in which the principle of health and healing defeated the principle of disease, and burst forth from the grave itself to reveal its immortality. This was the atonement, Christ's victory over sin and hell. As such it forms the only medium or way of salvation. There can only be one way of salvation because there is only one humanity. Thus, salvation itself has become the unifier of humanity in Christ.

Each individual to be saved must be assimilated into the value of Christ's atonement. Protestants explain this with the doctrine of imputation. But does imputation mean that God assumes something about us that is not true? Does He assume that we have something that we don't actually have? Does imputation rest upon a fiction in God's mind?[8]

Christ's atonement applies to Christians in the same way and to the same degree as the sin of Adam to all humanity. Adam's sin is not

---

8   Nevin answers "no" because we posses what Christ provides in a kind of seed form.

an alien evil or a mere abstraction arbitrarily imposed upon us. Rather, it is immanent to our human nature and condition. The atonement applies in the same way. The atonement is not an alien work, nor a mere abstraction because it must counteract the sin that actually dwells in us. Christ's atonement applies exactly as Adam's sin. If the sin is unreal, then so is the atonement. But if the sin is real, then the atone-ment is equally real. This is its true character. It is true for humanity because it is a work upon humanity by God in Christ. Thus, when Christ died and rose, humanity died and rose with Him in the same way Adam's sin involved humanity. The involvement is not figurative, but true, not imaginary, but actual.

5. Christian Salvation is New Life

Christian salvation, as comprehended in Christ, is new life in Christ in the same way that the old life was life in Adam. *It is not merely a doctrine for the mind to embrace. It is not simply an event to be remembered with faith, that provides the basis of exemplary piety or other volitional support.* While true, that kind of Christianity is shallow. Christianity is not merely the constitution of a new order of spiritual relations, nor is it a new system of divine helps for fallen, helpless men.

Rather, it is new life introduced into the very center of humanity itself. Though it is closely bound with the organic development of world history, Christianity cannot be understood in the same way that previous history is understood. Nor can it be built upon history, as if it were a product or fruit of history. Christianity is not simply the fulfill-ment or continuation of Judaism. Rather, Christianity claims the character of a new creation, by which the old history must pass away, and all things become new. Salvation is not simply the return to the state or condition of Adam in the Garden, but is the creation of a new kind of humanity. Christianity is to human history as a mature man is to his childhood.

This child/man analogy shows the relationship of Christianity to the old order. The old is not to be annihilated by it, but is taken up into it as a higher order of life. A man's childhood is not destroyed, denied, or ignored, yet it recedes in importance as maturity begins to flower.

Christ's incarnation is supernatural, not magical, not fantastic or visionary. It is not something to be meditated upon as a transient prodigy in world history. It is not an abstraction, but a reality that exists in the flesh of the saved individual. It is the supernatural link to the flow of the world's life. Life is a process, not a thing. Each saved individual becomes a reiteration of the ground and principle of the entire organism of humanity in its wholeness, which in Christ has found its true center and purpose. In this sense Christianity is indeed an objective fact, even as the first creation was an objective fact, a fact for all time, a world-fact.

6. New Life is in All Respects Human

The new life of which Christ is the source and organic principle is in all respects a real human life. It is in one sense a divine life because it springs from the Logos. But it is not the life of the Logos in and of itself. It is the life of the Word made flesh, the divinity of Christ in personal union with our humanity. It is not merely a theatrical show that Christ put on our nature, like many of the old Gnostics believed, and multitudes of Christians still appear to believe.

Christ has put on the lives of the regenerate truly and in the fullest sense. He is the archetypal model more perfectly than Adam was, even before the Fall. Humanity is more completely revealed in its most perfect form in Christ. However, this new humanity is not wholly different from that of Adam, but is the humanity of Adam itself filled with new meaning and power, and raised to a higher character because of its union with the divine nature of Christ. This new creation appeared originally in the form of regenerate union with Christ Jesus to the end of time, and exists in no other form.

7. The Extension of the New Life in the Church

Life in Christ, as here described, does not abide in Christ's individual person, but extends to and includes His people by the power of the Holy Spirit who is perfectly one with Christ. This extension of Christ's Person constitutes the church, "which is his body, the fullness of him who fills all in all" (Eph. 1:23). This is the new creation that involves His Person. The process by which the wholeness of this new creation is brought to life is organic not mechanical, dynamic not formulaic. It takes place in history, through the growth and development of ordinary human life in the light of Christ and through the exercise of Christ's teaching. The Lord does not manifest in His individuality to heal the world through some magical or unknown power that is external to humanity. Rather, He gathers regenerate humanity into His own Person by extending His own life into the lives of His people in order to share with them His light, His love, His strength and His wholeness. Indeed, this communion of Christ's characteristics with His people is the healing salve that binds up the wounds of the world.

As individuals, we are inserted into Christ by our regeneration, which provides the completion or capstone (1 Pet. 2:6) of our first birth that makes us fully ordinary and complete human beings. Christ provides the completion or fulfillment of all human character. However, we do not come into this new order of existence in Christ wholly at once.

The process is not magical or superstitious or imaginary. Rather, at some point in our lives we come to consciously realize that Christ has already apprehended us. By the time that we come to see that Christ lives in us, His presence is already a reality. With new eyes we look back at our individual history and conclude that our new regenerate eyes were given while we were completely unaware of the gift. And this point is central. Our new life in Christ comes to us from the overflowing of Christ's life. We are swept into it like an overwhelming flood. Yet, the flood of Christ's love does not force itself upon us.

Rather it sweeps away our fears and our resistance, as it floods our innermost desires with a subjective compulsion and attraction to the Person of Jesus Christ. In this way our regeneration becomes the principle or seed of our sanctification, our spiritual growth and maturity, which is simply the gradual transfusion of Christ's spiritual qualities and characteristics—His life—into us. His personal characteristics begin to grow in us, and that growth leads to the fulfillment of our wholeness as persons. The process then terminates with resurrection as Christ returns (John 14:3).

All analogies used to illustrate this great mystery are necessarily inadequate and always more or less perilous. Perhaps one of the better is found in the action of a magnet on iron.[9] The man in his natural

---

9   The formation of the modern theory of magnetism began with a series of revolutionary discoveries in 1820. Hans Christian Oersted discovered that an electric current generates a magnetic field encircling it. Later, André-Marie Ampère showed that parallel wires having currents in the same direction attract one another. Finally Jean-Baptiste Biot and Félix Savart discovered the Biot-Savart law which correctly predicts the magnetic field around any current-carrying wire.

   Between 1861 and 1865, James Clerk Maxwell developed and published a set of Maxwell's equations which explained and united all of classical electricity and magnetism. The mechanism that Maxwell proposed to underlie these equations in this

state centers upon himself, and is thus spiritually dead. In his regeneration, he is touched with a divine attraction, that draws him to Christ,
the true center of all life. In regeneration the tendency and action
don't come from himself, it doesn't grow out of what he was before.

Rather, his new divine attraction simply happens in obedience to
the magnetic attraction that has reached him from outside of himself.
His old nature continues to work. The iron is not at once made free
from its old tendencies and circumstances. But at every point the new
law of Christ produces an inward pull in the opposite direction. This
new attraction pulls in opposition to the temptation to sin. And
because the seed of Christ has been planted in his own innermost person, sin pulls him out of himself, where this new attraction to Christ
pulls him into himself. The attraction that first appeared to be from
outside of himself, outside of his sin nature, is suddenly found to be
pulling him into himself, into his new identity in Christ. Thus, what
was once a foreign attraction is now a native attraction, native to his
new birth. Says Christ, "when I am lifted up from the earth, (I) will
draw all people to myself" (John 12:32). Thus, God's objectivity in the
character of Christ becomes the subjective pattern or fractal of personal
identity in believers.[10]

8. Our Union with Christ Consists in Oneness of Life

As we are united with Christ, then, we are One with Him in the
fullness of His actual life, and not in an inferior way or to lesser degree
of it, but in a real, intimate union. This union ultimately results in our
being completely filled with the life of Christ, though our lives do not
completely fill Christ's life. He is the superior and we are the inferior,
though in union with Christ all of our inferiorities are thoroughly
washed in Christ's superiority.

The new birth involves a substantial and complete change in the
center of our being. It involves a shift of the center point from our
selves to Christ. Over time everything else in our lives finds and estab-

---

paper was fundamentally incorrect, which is not surprising since it predated the
modern understanding even of the atom. Yet, the equations were valid although
incomplete. The twentieth century saw a number of improvements and extensions
to the theory. Albert Einstein, in his great paper of 1905 that established relativity,
showed that both the electric and magnetic fields are part of the same phenomena
viewed from different reference frames.

10 This transfer or change provides the apex for Nevin's argument regarding regeneration and the Eucharist.

lishes a new orbit around this new center. It is not simply our understanding or our will that changes, though these things do change. It is
not that we are wrought upon in a natural or supernatural way. It is
not that something outside of us brings about a change in us—though
it does. It is not this or that particular power or ability or function that
we have that becomes the new center of our lives.

*Life is not thinking or feeling or acting. Rather, life is the organic unity
and interaction of all these things, which in Christ are inseparably joined
together with Him. Life is not piecemeal, but is always holistically whole in
all of its various parts and aspects.* In this sense, our union with Christ is
new[11] life. It is deeper than all thought, feeling, or exercise of will. It is
not a mere quality, nor a mere relationship of one thing to another.
Rather, it is a relationship in fact, a relationship of one thing to all others. It is like the relationship of the magnet to iron—all iron. And yet it
is a relationship that changes the center of the subject by giving it a
new gravity of being. Christ communicates the fullness of His own life
to the soul on which He acts, causing it to grow into the likeness of
Christ. This is the mystical union in Christ that we have been discussing. It is the basis of the holistic wholeness of our salvation, and is
the only medium through which we are able to have a genuine interest in Jesus Christ and the grace of salvation.

9. More Intimate and Deep than our Union with Adam

Our relationship with Christ is not simply parallel with our relationship to Adam, but goes far beyond it because it is immeasurably
more inclusive, intimate, and deep. Adam was the first man, the first
human archetype. Christ is the new and last or final man, the perfect,
whole and complete human archetype, in whom the perfection of
humanity has been brought into the world. In the presence of the perfect the imperfect fades into the background. Adam is related to the
human race as the first generic head, where Christ is the true center
and universal quantum fractal of human perfection. Human nature
began in Adam, but it finds its ultimate purpose and final manifestation
only in Christ. Life in Christ does not come to us through the exercise
of our free will, until we have been consciously joined to the person of
the divine Logos at the center of our being so that we are able to freely
will what God wants for us.

---

11 New: Original and of a kind not seen before.

In this deep sense, Christ is the universal human being in whom all human beings are bound in love and unity. Christ's Person is the root and/or seed that originates and defines the infinitude of all other personalities, whether in time or eternity. This new humanity not only springs from the life of Christ in the same way that we all spring from the life of Adam, but regenerate people continue to live in Christ's all-inclusive, eternally present, ubiquitous, and active personal Life.

Note

Personality is a function of self-consciousness. Our connection to Adam is mostly unconscious because consciousness emerges from unconsciousness. The archetype of Adam does not provide a center for life or the basis of our spirituality because the Holy Spirit is mostly dormant in Adam. In comparison, the archetype of Christ is itself our spirituality because Christ is the second Person of the Trinity, and includes the fullness of the Trinitarian Godhead, in whom the third Person of the Trinity is fully manifest. Human personality consists in the active sense of the fullness of this relationship as the truest, most full and proper life of its subject.

Individuals do not connect with Christ through the exercise of their own self-consciousness. Self-consciousness cannot know or connect with Christ at all, because the limits that define self-consciousness are inadequate for the contemplation of Christ. The ocean cannot be conceived, understood, or experienced by a glass of water. The full glass is unaware of the immense fullness of the ocean.

But the ocean can fill the glass with new water, and once full the glass can know the taste of the ocean. Such filling is called spiritual renewal. In spiritual renewal the glass is still a glass, but its content and character are completely different, though it looks the same. They now are more like the ocean. The glass is completely full of genuine ocean water, yet the ocean is not exhausted by the glass. Christ is the ocean in this analogy, as individuals are glasses. Christ then becomes the new center of the life of the glass. Or rather this relationship of glass to water are united in purpose, function, and being, though the water remains water and the glass remains a glass. In addition, every glass of ocean water has the same relationship to the ocean and the same relationship to every other glass of ocean water. These various relationships then maintain their individual uniqueness though they are in union with the ocean and with one another.

Schleiermacher speaks of the communication which Christ makes of Himself to believers, as molding the person. Christ in fact imparts a new consciousness that forms the basis of a common life that was not previously known, and which becomes the new center of our own personality in its most perfect form. Here, the Person of Christ is the ground and fountain of all Christian personality in the church. This does not mean that each Christian has the same personality. Rather, each glass retains its own unique size, shape, and characteristics. Nor does each glass contain the same ocean water. Each glass is filled with a unique and discreet body of water. It is only as individuals are in communication with Christ as the center of their own lives that self-consciousness becomes Christ-consciousness. As this dialog (or prayer) begins, believers are renewed in Christ Jesus.

Olshausen says, "*The personality of the Son, even as the comprehensive, takes all the personalities of his family into itself, and penetrates it with his life again, as if the lively central point of an organism from which emanates life and to which it returns.*" (Comm. John 14:20).

In this way, each Christian has a part in Christ's divinity, though the hypostatic union applies to Christians as it applies to Christ, though both the extent and degree are different.[12] The whole Christ lives and works in the church supernaturally, gloriously, mysteriously, and yet really and truly, "always, to the end of the world." Glory be to God!

10. Includes a Necessary Participation in the Entire Humanity of Christ

The mystical union necessarily includes individual participation in the entire humanity of Christ. Christians are joined in real life-unity with the everlasting Logos, with the Trinity of the eternal Godhead, including Christ's individuality and humanity—apart from which He cannot be human. This union involves immediate, direct, personal, mutual, though not equal likeness. Christians participate in the archetypal nature, divinity, and characteristics of Christ. This can only be doubted or denied by those who want no part in it.

---

12 Nevin is careful to say that Christians do not become God or divine in the same way, extent, or to the same degree that Jesus Christ is God. Rather, Christians participate in Christ's divine nature and are united in it, but are not identified with it. This is an important distinction in the light of the errors of German mysticism (Eckhart).

We must be careful not to exalt anyone to the same level, extent, or degree as Christ, who is the only begotten Son of God Himself (John 1:14, 18; 3:16, 18). All other sons are adopted. The mystical union in the image of Christ's hypostatic union itself is repeated as a fractal in the person of every believer. To doubt or deny this supposition is monstrous because it imposes a burden upon the archetype of Adam a weight that it cannot bear. To doubt or deny the reality of this requires the substitution of thought for reality, of idea for actuality. The hypostatic union denotes an actual, concrete existence, in contrast with abstract categories such as Platonic ideals. Because Christ's character is divine, any moral emulation of Christ requires the part to emulate the whole, the glass to emulate the ocean, what is finite to emulate infinity. All such emulation is necessarily false and imaginary at best because it cannot be accomplished.

The Word became flesh in Christ for the very purpose of reaching human beings in a real, fleshly way. The incarnation of Jesus Christ constitutes the only medium by which, and the only form under which human beings can be united with God. God enjoys incarnation in Christ, as Christ enjoys incarnation in Christians. Thus, the life of Christ is the only universal life that can ever find its way into our persons. Universal human life must be manifest as a single, whole person if it is to have any role as an archetype for single, whole people. And the wholeness of Christ's singularity as a person must necessarily be Trinitarian if it is to have any part in the Godhead.

We must beware of all Gnostic abstractions because abstraction is the essence of all Gnostic delusion. Gnostics always follow the model of the originator of Gnosticism—Plato. But neither, as a matter of our practical habits, let us not fall into the condemnation of Nestorius,[13] who taught the disunity of the human and divine natures of Christ.[14]

---

13 Nestorius (386-451) was Archbishop of Constantinople from 428 to 431. He rejected the long-used title of *Theotokos* (*Mother of God*) for the Virgin Mary, which brought him into conflict with Cyril of Alexandria, who accused him of heresy. The issue pertained to the incarnation of Christ, Nestorius could not hold Christ's divinity and humanity in one hypostasis. Nestorius defended himself at the First Council of Ephesus in 431, but was condemned for heresy. Despite his condemnation, many of his supporters split with the rest of the church, and relocated to Persia. Thereafter, Nestorianism became the official position of the Orthodox Church of the East.

14 Nevin called it "disunity." Belief in the Trinity is essential to Eastern Orthodoxy, Roman Catholicism, and orthodox Protestantism. Acceptance that God is Trinitarian is essential, understanding it isn't, though I don't know how the Trinity can

Nonetheless, because the reality of Christ, which includes His humanity, is the indispensable medium of our participation in the wholeness
of salvation, He is involved body and soul, just like we are. To ignore
or deny Christ's incarnate body in the process of our salvation turns
Him into an abstract phantom. The life of Christ is whole and His
wholeness is One.

For Christ to transform our personal identity into His own likeness, His totality or wholeness must interact with our totality or
wholeness. To divide the Person of Christ is to destroy the very thing
that His salvation provides—human wholeness. To divide His body
and soul destroys the reality of salvation. What God has joined
together, we have no right thus to put asunder. Christ's humanity is
not His soul apart from His body, just as His body cannot be separated
from His soul. Christ is, like us, neither soul nor body alone or apart.
Rather, Christ is the everlasting, indissoluble union of body and soul,
the fullness of which in Christ is salvation itself.[15]

11. Also Embraces the Whole Person of the Believer

As the mystical union embraces the whole Christ, so we too are
embraced by it, not in a partial, but in a whole way. Life always
appears as discrete wholes regarding quality, attribute, and distinction.
It is the whole-at-once of the nature in which life exists. In order for a
new life to become real, it must inhere in the totality of our nature. It
must fill the understanding, and rule the will, overflow the heart,
enthrone itself in the soul, and extend itself out over the entire body.

In fact, the life which is to be communicated to us is in all respects
a true human life before it reaches us, because He is the life of the
incarnate Son of God. How can Christ's life be communicated without
regard to His body or ours? It is a contradiction to imagine that real
union with Christ's humanity reaches only half of our nature. It cannot reach our soul without reaching our body. The person of Christ

---

  exist without unity. The believer does not need to know how God is Trinitarian.
  Orthodox churches tend to teach the Trinity by discussing what it is not, distinguishing the doctrine from the many alternatives.

15 To say that Christ's wholeness enters into human personality does not mean that
  individuals receive the totality of Christ's being. It only means that what they
  receive is their own wholeness, which includes both spirit and flesh. Van Til makes
  the distinction that our understanding of the world is completely reliable and true,
  even though we don't understand everything to the same degree that Jesus does.
  Thus, our knowledge is analogous to God's knowledge.

includes a true body as well as a reasoning soul, as the ancient church teaches.

Shall this same Christ, alive in His people, be converted into an incorporeal, Docetic,[16] Gnostic Christ, who has no real presence except in the abstract idea of the soul? Or may His bodily nature exist only in His soul alone? It cannot be! Christ's life is fully human, which means that it is like our own and requires the same things that we require—food, shelter, sleep, companionship, etc. In addition, Christ's fully human life, which cannot be separated from his fully divine life, is the very aspect of Christ that reaches our human life. We must necessarily meet Christ in material space because we live in material space. Some aspect of Christ's material body must reach us in order to become united to us because our bodies are not separated from our souls. This is how the mystical union is real. All other conceptions of the mysterious presence of Christ are abstractions, or they collapse into mere moral relationships that can only hope to influence people, as are imagined by Pelagians and Rationalists.

12. It is All the Result of a Single, Undivided Process

The mysterious presence is completed and manifest, not in two different ways, but by one and the same single, continuous and undivided process.[17] Much of the difficulty regarding Christ's mysterious presence arises from the inveterate prejudice that divides our experience in two. The subjective inner life of thought and feeling is habitually experienced through the predication of a being who is contained within our body.

From infancy the egoic "I" asserts itself as an other because it has needs that must be met—and those needs are focused in the body—food, attention, shelter, etc. The development of language then requires the assumption of "I" as a discrete entity in time and space and the predication of "I" as the subject of thought, the organizer and experiencer of thought. As soon as "I" thinks that its own body

---

16 Docetism (from the Greek δοκέω, "to seem") is the belief that Jesus' physical body was an illusion, as was his crucifixion. Jesus only *seemed* to have a physical body and to physically die, but in reality he was incorporeal, a pure spirit, and hence could not physically die.

17 The holistic wholeness of a living being must always hold particularity and universality (the one and the many) together. And such holding together can only be accomplished by the mystery of the Holy Spirit. To lose or deny the mystery is to lose or deny Christ's wholeness.

belongs to it, it has imagined itself to be an abstraction from the body, and established itself in dualistic philosophical categories.

This creates an intellectual time-bound duality in our nature which tends to dominate the absolute unity or wholeness which in fact comprises our identity. The Bible knows nothing of the abstract separation of soul and body, which has come to be so widely admitted into the religious thought of the world, ancient and modern. This bifurcation of our wholeness does not originate from wholeness, but from divisiveness, and is ultimately false to all true religion and philosophy, as it is pernicious to all Christianity. Soul and body comprise one life, identical in origin and completely bound together at every point, like the two sides of a coin. Body and soul exist as the presence and power of the self-same organic being.

It is not right to think of the body as the vehicle of the soul, as does Plato. Nor is the body merely a garment that can be put on or put off. It is not right to think of the soul in any way that separates it from the body. Just as one side of a coin has no existence apart from the whole coin, neither does the soul exist apart from the body. Both soul and body comprise one whole life. The body/soul exists in space/time in dynamic identity, such that its character becomes increasingly definite through the accumulation of various and diverse qualities.

Note

The unity of body and soul may seem to be contradicted by what the Scriptures teach regarding the existence of the soul between death and resurrection, and it must be admitted that it is a real difficulty. However, we must not obscure the truth because it is difficult to conceive. The difficulty is not to reconcile Scripture with psychology, but to bring Scripture into a fuller harmony with itself. Of course, Scripture teaches the difference between body and soul, especially regarding consciousness between death and the resurrection. But just because body and soul can be differentiated, does not mean that they can be separated, any more than distinguishing between the two sides of a coin means that one side exists independently from the other.

The doctrine of immortality in the Bible always includes resurrection. It is a *suspension from the dead* (ἀναρτήσεις ἐκ τῶν νεκρῶν). The whole argument in 1 Corinthians 15 and 1 Thess. 4:13-18 assumes that the life of the body/soul is indispensable to the perfect (holistic) state of our nature as human beings. Therefore, during the intermediate state the soul alone cannot possibly constitute a complete man. In addition, we should conceive of the body/soul as still existing, not absolutely destroyed but only suspended—perhaps like sleep.

The condition at that point is interimistic,[18] and must not be thought of as being complete or final. When the resurrection body appears, it will not be a completely new body created for the occasion and into which the soul can be transferred. Adam, the original man was made from dirt, and all other human beings issued from that original individual—Eve from Adam's rib, and children from Eve's womb. Paul speaks of the body as a seed that is planted into the ground to die, and while that seed is gone, it grows into a plant that produces many other seeds of the same kind.

Our problem is that we come to the idea of resurrection full of our own ideas of individualism, which are not in Scripture, and read them into the text. We must remember that Paul was speaking to the Corinthian church as a body, and not to any specific individuals. So, there is no biblical conflict with the idea that Paul was speaking about the resurrection of the church, the body of Christ, and not the kind of narrow-minded individualistic resurrection that we are in the habit of imagining. The resurrection of the church would necessarily involve the church in a different kind of body, different from anything that Paul and his cohorts had experienced or could imagine.

This resurrected body will have organic continuity with the body as it existed before death, just as the seed has organic unity with the stalk that grows from it. This implies that whatever body/mind that existed in the seed has not been annihilated, but only suspended in some sort of intermediate state, such as sleep. The continuation of the body/mind from seed to stalk suggests that the body/mind continues in the stalk, and the flower, and the fruit, and the new seeds that are produced.

From this perspective, however, the life of the body/soul must be regarded as resting in some way. Just as Adam was put to sleep during the creation of Eve, so perhaps the body/mind sleeps during the creative transition from seed to stalk, and waits in slumber for the proper time when Christ will call it to wakefulness with a shout. Then, upon awaking, it will find itself clothed in Christ's righteousness, yet with full awareness that its sinful past is dead and gone. So, it can assume its

---

18 Provisional, occurring in the interim.

rightful identity in Christ Jesus in order to engage its role in the body of Christ, the church—only now with a far higher order of existence.

Only then can salvation be complete. The new heaven and new earth will be the reality into which the resurrected church body will awaken. Ultimately, the soul includes the oneness of life through unity with Christ. The subject of salvation is the wholeness of the believer's person and identity, which includes both body and soul—but also includes unity with Christ and with the holistic whole of Christ's church, from the beginning of the process to its end.

It is all one process, one story—God's story—the action of one and the same living organic life—Christ's, dividing itself only so that its unity may become more free and fully complete. There is no room to dream of a bodily communication with Christ on the part of believers as being something different from the communication they have with Him right now. His flesh cannot enter our flesh in some kind of abstract form, dissevered from the fullness of His life, and having no union with our body/soul as the medium of such translation.

We are not called to a Capernaitic (cannibalistic) communion. Such a communion would not be mystical, but magical—incredible, useless, and unreal all at the same time. Thus, the process by which Christ is manifested in His people is not dualistic, but single and unitary. It lays hold of each subject, not in the periphery of his person, but in his innermost center, where the whole man, soul and body, is always one undivided life.

The mind, like the body/soul, includes the understanding and the will, which can be differentiated but not divided. The mind is composed of understanding and will, bound in union. One never appears apart from the other. In the same way, the person is neither the soul nor the body, separately considered, but is the totality which includes both body/soul and understanding/will. It is the whole person from the very center and ground of his personality who is saved.

The wholeness of Christ's life is borne into the wholeness of the believer. The communication of Christ to the believer moves from Christ's center to the believer's center. It happens through a single, non-material, self-identical, spiritual law that issues from the mouth of God. The power of Christ's life deposited in the soul immediately begins to manifest the new creation, bit by bit. It functions organically according to the law of Christ, which through regeneration is included in its own constitution. That is, it works as one human life manifest as a fractal of social unity in Christ, and as such becomes a law of regeneration in the body as truly as in the soul.

13. No Material Contact is Involved

In all of this there is no room for the supposition of any material, tactile incorporation of Christ's individual body into the persons of His people, as mandated by transubstantiation and consubstantiation. It is not necessary that Christ's flesh and blood, materially considered, should in any way pass over into our life, and become locally or physically present in us or in any form in order to make us partakers of His humanity.

Even in nature the continuity of organic existence, as it passes from one individual to another, is found to cohere in the end, not on the material medium through which the process is effected, but on the presence of the living force alone, immaterial altogether and impalpable. It is this that imparts both form and substance to the whole as it mounts upwards, for instance, from the buried seed and reveals itself at last through leaves and flowers, and in a thousand new seeds after its own kind.[19]

Properly speaking, the presence of the root in the branches of the oak is neither a local nor a material presence. It is simply the power of the oak life in which root and branch participate. So, why should it be impossible for Christ's life to reach into the persons of His people from His eternity into time, whole and entire.

The material medium is Christ's own individual body which appeared in history, and which connects to the individual bodies of believers, which also appear in history. The connection between Christ and believers is spiritual in that Christ both manifested the fullness of the Holy Spirit during His life, and then sent the Holy Spirit to abide eternally with His people (John 16:7).

Again, our habits of individualistic thinking in terms of Greek categories of thought impose upon the world, upon God, upon Christ and upon ourselves thoughts, ideas, and divisions that Scripture does not countenance. So, our efforts to analyze the work of the Holy Spirit in such terms and categories as are imagined by materialistic and ratio-

---

19   The life that resides in a seed cannot be found by dissection or any kind of physical examination. Even the DNA is not the life. Rather, the life of the seed germinates only when its context is properly suited to receive and nurture the influx of life that issues in germination.

nalistic philosophies fall short of the reality in which we live. We cannot use the categories of unbelief, whether we call it science,
philosophy, history, psychology, or any of a thousand pagan theologies to analyze or understand how Christ is able to be present to
believers. All we can say for sure is that Christ touches the souls of
believers by the power of the Holy Spirit, such that He plants a new
moral creation that exists in unbroken organic continuity with Himself, and goes on to take full possession of its subject, body and soul,
will and understanding. Praise be to God!

14. No Ubiquity of Christ's Body, nor Loss of His Proper Sepa-rate Personality

Such a relation of Christ to the church does not involve a doctrine
of Christ's ubiquity[20] or any idealistic abstraction of His body. Nor
does it require any kind of fusion or melding (complete identification)
of His personality with the personalities of His people. Yet, we can
distinguish between the individual man (his humanity) and the universal man (His divinity), joined in Christ in the same Person.

A similar distinction is found in Adam. However, Adam's universality is not of the same order as Christ's. But a comparison can be
made. Adam was simultaneously an individual and a whole race
because he was the first—the prototype and archetype. All of Adam's
posterity partake of his archetypal life, and grow from him as a root or
seed. And even with Adam, his individual person has not been lost in
the process. Why then should the life of Christ in the church conflict
with His humanity? Why do we dream of a fusion or merging of persons in regard to Christ but not in regard to Adam? We must abandon
such narrow-minded foolishness.

We not only spring from Christ, are born again in Christ into
new life, but stand in Christ perpetually as our ever-living and ever-
present root (John 15:6). His person is always the actual source and
bearer of our regenerated persons. And yet there is no mixture or confusion of our person not being distinct from His Person. Nor does the
One meld into into the other, as is imagined by the mystics.

Is not God the ultimate ground of all personality? Of course He is.
But this does not imply or suggest any pantheistic idea of God as consciousness itself. Neither does it imply any similar dispersion of Christ's

---

20 Ubiquity: the state of being or seeming to be everywhere at once.

personality into the general consciousness of the church. God is not like a giant puzzle of which human beings or any other species of life are the pieces. Rather, God is the Person Jesus Christ, who provides the foundation and power of the whole life and subsistence of the church eternally.[21]

In this view Christ is always personally present in the church as the result of the power of His divine nature. But His divine nature is also human in the fullest sense, and where His presence is revealed in the church in a real way, it necessarily includes His person in the one aspect as well as the other because they always appear together. With all this, however, we must not relinquish the thought of His separate, unique human individuality.

We distinguish between His universal humanity in the church and His individual humanity as a particular man, whom the heavens have received until the time of the restitution of all things. We do not doubt that His glorified body has qualities, attributes, and powers that immeasurably transcend everything we know or can know. And yet it is a body, a particular body with various parts and objective appearance. Of course, it must be defined and circumscribed by local limits, and cannot be supposed to be present in different places at the same time. We disavow all explanations that issue from or are related to anything magical.

---

21 It is not unusual to hear an objection to such an explanation of Christ's role in the life of the church leads to a sort of pantheism, in which no room is left for the sepa-rate individual consciousness of the believer. It is feared that the power of Christ will thwart the free will of the believer. But this objection must also hold against any kind of real union in Christ. If this is the case, then, as Professor Lewis has also remarked, all the best old English divines such as Howe, Baxter, Owen, etc., must fall under condemnation as teaching the Buddhist doctrine of spiritual annihilation. "Such a philosopher," Lewis adds, "as the author of the 'Blessedness of the Right-eous' would teach us that the soul's consciousness of being in Christ, and of having one life with him, might give a higher sense of a more glorious and blessed individ-uality, than could be derived from any other state of being. ... Paul was not afraid of saying, that 'in God we live, and move, and are,' or of speaking of the church as being 'the fullness of him that fills all in all,' or of declaring that 'our life is hid with Christ in God.' Neither whilst there remained in him the individual consciousness of so blessed a state, was he afraid of the declaration, 'I live, not I, but Christ lives in me.'"

15. This Union goes Beyond Every Other that is Known in the World

What we have described here as mystical union in Christ is more intimate and real than any union which is known by anything else in the world. The most simple kind of natural union may be described as marbles in a bag. In the bag the marbles share proximity and at times trajectory. But in no significant sense can be marbles be described as being in union. This is simple mechanical unity, one thing proximately joined to another in space. It is the lowest and most basic kind of unity.

Chemical combination provides another kind of unity, but it lacks the whole range of emotional reality, not to mention spirituality. In chemistry there appears to be an actual transfusion of one substance into another, but in reality it only involves the shifting of molecular structures that either absorb or radiate energy. The elements that are combined in atmospheric air share this kind of unity.

In nature, the closest kind of union is sexual union, where two bodies try to occupy the same space at the same time. Sexual union, however, is brief and often cluttered with motives and practices that fall far short of the purity and perfection of Christ's motives and practices. Nor is there anything in nature that keeps copulating couples together over time, other than love. Of course, God has provided marriage as a kind of living analogy of covenantal unity, which mimics the Trinitarianism of the Godhead, in that God is the third partner in Christian marriage.

Organic union, as it exists for instance between the roots and branches of a tree, appears to be more inward and close. Root and leaf touch each other like the two sides of a coin touch one another. Root and leaf are at the opposite ends of the flow of sap, and in this case the sap provides the unity of the union. This union is more true than the different parts of a crystal because the tree is alive and the crystal is not.

The union of head and members in the same human body is of vastly higher character because of the involvement of emotion and reason. But even this provides a poor analogy for the oneness of Christ with His people. There is nothing like Christian unity in the whole world, in any other form. It is bound by no local limitations. It goes beyond all nature, and transcends all emotion and thought.

Mystical union, like that of Hinduism and the host of other pagan spiritualities, goes too far by imagining a union of all things by way of identity. The union of spiritual identity does not allow for the more subtle textures of egoic personality and other hard boundaries found in the natural world. Nor does it account for the reality of time, temporal though it is.

16. Wrought Only by the Power of the Holy Spirit

The union of Christ with believers is accomplished by the power of the Holy Spirit. The new birth issues from the Spirit and plants the Spirit in the life of the believer. It is by the Spirit that the divine life is sustained and advanced in us at every point, from its commencement to its culmination. There is no other medium by which it is possible for anyone to be in Christ, or to have Christ in themselves. The new creation produced by regeneration exists in the power and presence of the Holy Spirit. "He who is joined to the Lord becomes one spirit with him." (1 Cor. 6:17), and the indwelling of Christ and His Spirit in believers is spoken of as the same thing.

And for this very reason we have no right to doubt this unity by thinking of the presence of the Spirit as a substitute for the presence of Christ Himself. Where the one is, there the other is also, truly and really at the same time. The Spirit, who proceeds from the Father and Son and subsists in everlasting union with both, constitutes the form in which and by which the new creation in Christ Jesus through regen‐ eration is upheld and revealed in its fullest extent. Such union is not natural, but spiritual.

Thus, the person of Christ Himself is the root of this creation. The Spirit was unleashed in New Testament times like before. And yet the manifestation of the Spirit through the incarnate Word of Scripture has extended the life and power of the Spirit. The Spirit dwelt in Christ without measure. Extant humanity itself will one day be com‐ pletely filled with the Spirit, and will ultimately appear translucent with the glory of heaven itself by the means of the Spirit. The Spirit springs forth first *as* and then *from* the person of Christ. Having been "made alive in the spirit" (1 Pet. 3:18), the flow of life pours itself onward (outward, forward) continually in the church, by the presence and power of the Holy Spirit because it exists in no other form.

However, when the Holy Spirit is abstracted or imagined to work apart from the actual presence of Christ himself, as though the Spirit is only the fountain and not the very life-stream of the new creation, it is falsely conceived.

Neither can the Spirit be supposed to be in a person or with a person by the mere intervention of a presence or power that does not involve at the same time and to the same extent the reality of the actual Person of Christ. "The Lord is the Spirit" (2 Cor. 3:17). He reveals Himself in His people, He dwells in them and makes them one with Himself in a real way, by His Spirit.

The new life of regeneration found in people is spiritual, not natural or physical, as if it simply belongs to the first creation. This, however, does not imply that this new life is limited to the soul as distinguished from the body. Body and spirit always manifest together and never exist apart from one another. Paul spoke extensively about a spiritual body as well as a natural body. The Spirit of Christ in His own Person fills each person—soul and body—giving them a new wholeness. Everything about the process is spiritual, glorious, and heavenly.

Christ has been taken up into the realm of the Spirit—the whole of His humanity and the whole of His divinity, and has been transfigured into the same life. Why, then, should the Spirit not ultimately extend itself in a kind of strict organic continuity to the wholeness of humanity by the active presence of Christ's Spirit manifest to the persons of His people? Spiritual life cannot exclude the body, neither ours nor Christ's.

17. Only Through the Instrumentality of Faith

Christ's life is received on the part of His people only by faith. Christ's life itself comes to us in its entirety from Christ Himself, by the power of His Spirit, though we apprehend it in stages over time, but never completely. A kind of magnetic attraction to Christ is poured upon us from outside of ourselves. If we have any part at all in the process, it is only in obedience to the divine magnetism thus brought to bear upon us. However, to be appropriated into the Spirit we must personally and intentionally surrender ourselves spontaneously to His power. The grace of such surrender comes only through faith, and it is the most comprehensive, fundamental act we are capable of because we must be entirely submissive to His dominion.

In obedience, we submit to a shift in the center of gravity in our being. The shift moves us completely away from the center of self, where our consciousness has been previously fixed, to Christ, who provides another center—Himself. This shift births a new life with a new center. Obviously, faith is not the cause of this life. It is only the medium (mode or vehicle) of its introduction into the soul, and is the condition of its growth and development when present. Nonetheless, personal faith is indispensable because the process of our sanctification is always spiritual, and not mechanical or magical. "Living faith in Christ," says Schleiermacher, "is nothing but the self-consciousness of our union with Christ."

18. The New Life is a Process which will Become Complete only in the Resurrection

The new life of the believer grows by stages and degrees, and will become complete only in the final resurrection. Only in this way can it issue out of human character rather than be imposed upon human character. The difference is the freedom of the will. All human life grows and matures through the process of gradual historical development. First there is the seed and then it springs up, "first the blade, then the ear, then the full grain in the ear." (Mark 4:28).

This new life struggles with the old, like Jacob and Esau in the same womb. The regenerate Christian deals with two forms of existence, a "law of sin and death" on the one hand, and "the law of the spirit of life in Christ Jesus" on the other (Rom. 8:2). And the power of the Spirit is constantly opposed and restrained by the power of sin and death. From its very start, however, the life of Christ in the believer is a whole life, and in all its subsequent progress it reveals its power continuously in the same character. From the beginning it includes in itself potentially everything that it will be found to finally become.

The life of a tree is always the same life it had originally in the seed from which it sprang. So it is with all life. Thus, everything that belongs to the new life of the Christian, everything that will be complete at the last day, must in fact be involved in its principle and process from the very beginning. In every stage of progress it is a true human life, responding to the nature of its organic root, and also to the nature of the person in which it is lodged—Christ. The new life in Christ always involves a new nature for the body as well as for the soul.

The full and final triumph of the process of sanctification is resurrection, which is reached by individuals only in connection with the consummation of the church as a whole. The bodies of the saints in glory will be the final continuity of the divine life of Christ organically implanted through regeneration. There is nothing discontinuous or contrary to the natural world in Christianity. Of course, it involves a supernatural constitution, but that constitution is clothed in a natural form as the believer puts on the robe of Christ's righteousness. In addition, it involves the process of historical development that is itself as regular and ordinary as the original creation itself. Though there are momentous and cataclysmic events, they always function naturally. What is supernatural and extraordinary is the new birth.

The resurrection body will simply be a result of the ultimate outworking of the new life that has been ripening unto immortality under the guise of the old Adamic nature. The winged psyche, like a butterfly, has its elemental organization in the worm and cocoon, and does not lose its central character in the tomb-like chrysalis. Let us not be told that this is to imagine that there are two bodies in the person of the believer. Nor does the new life involve two souls. Like the butterfly, the man is one being, a body/soul that undergoes significant change because a new organic law/life exists in the center of his personality, and is gradually extending its power over the entire constitution of his nature.

It does not lay hold of one part of his being first, and then proceed to another, like a military conquest of territory, as if a hand or foot could be renovated before the head, or the understanding apart from the will, or the soul without connection to the body. The whole individual is the subject of the new life all at once. The process of personal growth and maturity extends from the center to the extreme periphery of his person. The old body itself becomes the womb of a higher corporeality in a mysterious way. In the final analysis, the life/law of Christ's own glorious body—the church—is set entirely free from the first form of existence, through the process of death and resurrection, and made to supersede it forever in the immortality of heaven.

Section III

The Lord's Supper

19. Reality of the Sacrament

The Eucharist is not a sacrament of entry into the church, but is the celebration of membership in the body of Christ.

> "A sacrament is a holy ordinance instituted by Christ wherein, by sensible signs, Christ and the benefits of the new covenant are represented, sealed and applied to believers,"

says the *Westminster Shorter Catechism*, echoing the voice of the whole Reformed church as it sounded throughout Christendom for a century before. The signs, as such, do not make the whole of the sacrament. They are only one aspect of it.

The sign is simply the recognition and acknowledgment of the reality and presence of God's grace, and is not a thing in itself. The acknowledgment is the consequence of the faith of the communicant. God's grace, which is universal and ubiquitous, is concentrated with increased potency in the sacrament because the Lord commissioned it to be so. The mechanism of the increased concentration and potency of God's grace is the Word of the Lord, which brings light and order through its mystical fusion to the reality of the world. The veracity of God's Word binds His grace to the purpose and objects of its articulation.

In order to be whole, complete, and true, the sacramental ordinance must involve both aspects—the Word of God (sign) and the acknowledgment of the reality and immediate actuality of God's grace (seal). In other words, the grace is a necessary constituent element of the sacrament, and it must be acknowledged to be objectively inherent in the sacramental administration.

Whether God's grace becomes available to the use and benefit of the communicant depends on the acknowledgment of its inherent reality by and in the communicant. Everything depends on the exercise of faith by the communicant. Nonetheless, the objective presence of the grace itself, as an integral part of the sacrament is undeniable, certain and sure because of the veracity and reliability of God's Word. The grace belongs to the character of the ordinance by the power and authority of Christ's commission, which is not simply an idea, picture, or memory for the mind alone, but always conveys the power and authority of almighty God Himself, who created the world by speaking a Word.

The sign (word) and the thing signified (grace) by Christ's institution of the supper are intimately and mysteriously fused together through the sacramental transaction (the giving and receiving) in real but mystical union, one with the other in and through the presence of God's grace. The sacramental union is, then, a representative fractal of the wholeness of the cosmic unity of God in Christ in the world. It is not as though God's grace is in any way included in the administration of the sacrament as something materially transferable, like a rock that can be passed from one person to another, or a germ that is transferred by contact.

The reality of God's grace is spiritual and mystical, which is not a diminution but an elaboration of its reality. The conjunction of sacrament and grace does not make the sacrament causative. The exercise of the sacrament does not cause the grace to be real, rather the reality of the grace causes the sacrament to be effective through the acknowledgment of its reality, the faith of the communicant. The union inherent in the sacrament represents the union of sign and thing signified in the general use of language that reflects the veracity of God's Word, and provides the basis or foundation for Christian relationships. The sacrament represents and therefore provides human primunity,[1] which is always necessarily personal and can only be acknowledged, realized, and enjoyed by *people* in Christ. Note the use of the word *people* rather than *persons,* which highlights the corporate character of being in Christ.

---

1   Primunity is a compound word that joins *prime* and *unity*. Here, prime applies to unity rather than to integers. Primunity is the holistic wholeness that cannot be factored or divided. It is not a material or physical quality, but is the central and organizing quality of life, which is spiritual and ultimately mystical.

God's Word and language that reflects the veracity of God's Word always carries the power and authority of the grace it represents. The union of word and grace is ultimately mystical and always peculiar (unique) to sacrament, but it is not for this reason any less real. This union is, in fact, much more real in its mysteriousness than is the supposed clarity of any merely human language or relationships.

The grace that is acknowledged to be present in the Eucharist is "Christ and the benefits of the new covenant." It is not only the benefits of the new covenant that are presently available in the Eucharist, but Christ Himself—soul and body, who alone is the only medium of a real communication with real benefits in a real way. *Christ comes first, and then and only then all of His benefits* because the benefits inhere only in His person, and have no reality apart from Him and the holistic wholeness He alone provides.

20. Participation in the Body and blood of Christ, and in all of Christ's Benefits

> "The Lord's Supper is a sacrament wherein, by giving and receiving bread and wine according to Christ's appointment, his death is showed forth, and the worthy receivers are, not after a corporal and carnal manner, but by faith, made partakers of His Body And Blood, with all his benefits, to their spiritual nourishment and growth in grace"

says again the *Westminster Shorter Catechism*.

Here are sensible signs: bread and wine, genuinely given and genuinely received. Here also we can access God's present and eternal grace: Christ and His benefits, Christ's "body and blood, with all his benefits." The bread and wine are the sacramental elements that physically represent and mystically present God's grace for our acknowledgment. The elements and the grace are in primunity by the Word of God and Jesus' commission of the supper. They inhere together in the constitution of the primunity of the sacrament. Neither the elements nor the grace alone constitute the sacrament, but the sacrament is consecrated by the veracity of God's Word spoken by Jesus Christ and recorded in Scripture for the imitative benefit of the manifestation of the primunity of believers.

The ordinance coheres the elements and the grace through the sacramental transaction, which includes the actual presence of both, the one materially feeds the actual body, the other spiritually feeds the mystical primunity. Christ's body is not *in* or *under* the bread, locally or physically, nor does the bread *become* Christ's body. Nonetheless, the power of Christ's life in the sacramental institution is actually but mystically present through the institution of the Eucharist.

The one is as truly and really present in the institution as the other. The elements are not merely signs of what they represent, as if they serve simply to bring Christ to mind by the help of memory. The elements they pledge, the promise and manifestation of the sacrament's actual grace, is present and powerful. The elements are bound to the grace in mystical, sacramental primunion, far more intimately than any local or physical nexus imaginable. The Eucharist is much more than the mere commemoration of Christ's death, more than memory or imagination can conceive.

Worthy receivers are those who acknowledge that they have no worthiness of their own, but who acknowledge by participation in the worthiness of Jesus Christ as Lord and Savior, who is the only mediator of the holistic wholeness of Christ's primunity. Then and only then can those who are themselves worthless worthily partake of Christ's body and blood, with all His benefits, through the power and presence of the Triune Holy Spirit, for the nourishment of the body unto spiritual growth, and the spiritual nourishment of Christ's primunity.

21. The Lord's Supper and the Atonement Provided by Christ's Death

The sacrament of the Lord's Supper has direct and primary reference to the Atonement provided by Christ's death on the cross. In the words of institution, it is Christ's body broken and Christ's blood shed for the remission of sins that are symbolically lifted up as Moses' caduceus for the remedy and protection against the serpent (Num. 21:6-9). It is not simply *Christ*, but the *"body and blood"* of Christ that is at the center of the sacrament. It is Christ, who alone is worthy, and who was bodily sacrificed and bloodily slain for the sins of the world. Therefore, it is the restored life of the body of Christ, regenerated, and resurrected into the corporate wholeness of the body of Christ in which believers participate through the Eucharist.

The Eucharist itself is not a sacrifice, nor does it have any expiatory power in and of itself. It serves simply as the ratification and seal of the communicant in mystical primunity with Christ and His

church. The power of the Eucharist does not originate in the institution of the supper by the officiant, but in Christ's institution of it in the
Upper Room and His sealing of it on Golgotha. The resurrected
Christ then reiterated the centrality of the communal supping in Luke
24:30-31 and John 21:12, 15-17.

*Only through the liturgy of communal supping does the body and blood
of Christ feed the body of believers and seal what the sign has promised—
the salvation of God's people.* We are sinners by nature and habit, and as
such we need to practice the habits of redemption unto spiritual perfection. Only through the propitiation of Christ's suffering and death
can our sin be overcome, such that we become caught up in His glory.

Christ alone is our righteousness, whom we put on in order that
His life may be our life. Thus, Christ's righteousness constitutes our
justification, which first initiates our relationship in Christ as believers.
That "act of God's free grace, wherein he pardoneth all our sins, and
accepteth us as righteous in his sight, only for the righteousness of
Christ imputed to us, and received by faith alone" (*Westminster Shorter
Catechism*, Question 33). And so our whole subsequent Christian life,
as it grows from Christ's objective righteousness, may be said to
involve continual renewal of it, growth in it, and dependence upon it
to the end of our lives and beyond.

We need no additional atonement beyond Christ's original, but
we do need to perpetually repeat the story of Christ's atonement
because it is a kind of spiritual fractal that reshapes and enhances the
church increasingly into the likeness of Christ. The regular celebration
of the Eucharist keeps the story alive, but it also keeps it from becoming a mere abstract, intellectual activity. Thus, as we repeat Christ's
story and rely on His sacrifice on the cross, we appropriate the power
of His life through the accumulation of experience with it. The more
often we do it, the more real it becomes.

Accordingly, the Lord's Supper presents the story through the
words of institution, the symbol (or sign) through the presence of the
elements, and the bodily reality of Christ's life through our personal
feeding on Christ's body and blood. In this way the Eucharist provides
the central meaning of the holistic wholeness of Christian life through
the sacrament of Christ's death and the communion of his body and
blood.

22. A Real Interest in this Involves a Real Communication with the Life of Christ

As the means by which we are made partakers of the new covenant in Christ's death, the Lord's Supper involves a real communication with the Person of the Savior, who is now gloriously exalted in heaven. Our justification rests on the objective merit of Christ alone, by whose blood propitiation has been made for the sins of the world. But this justification must draw us into Christ's life in order that we become His in fact. It reaches us from outside of ourselves as an "act of God's free grace." God's grace is not natural to us, but is imposed upon us by the Holy Spirit as the means by which He can tolerate us in our sinful condition. This act of God is necessarily more than an abstract declaration or idea, more than words alone. All acts of God share and communicate the holistic wholeness of God's Triune Person. God's acts are ascribed with God's primunity, which provides the context for God's actions, and which makes us to be in fact what God has accounted us to be in Christ.

The ground of our justification is the righteousness of Christ, which was foreign to us prior to God's justification. That righteousness touches and transforms the central constitution (heart) of our being, restoring it to a wholeness greater than itself. A real life-union or covenant relationship in Christ, through the power and presence of the Holy Spirit, provides the means of true imputation of righteousness to us as a result of what Christ has done and suffered on our behalf. That imputation writes us into Christ's story by name.

From that point forward, our interest in Christ's merits can only be renewed and confirmed in the same way, by living out our role in Christ's story—actually and bodily, historically. In this way Christ Himself manifests bodily in us more and more in a real way, in order that He may be "made unto us of God, wisdom, and righteousness, and sanctification, and redemption" (1 Cor. 1:30).

The Eucharist, which serves to confirm our interest in the one sacrifice accomplished on the cross includes a real and true participation in the life of Jesus Christ by whom the sacrifice was made. No intelligible distinction can now be made between the crucified body of Christ and His resurrected and glorified body because both are in reality one and the same life/body.

To partake of the "broken body" and "shed blood" of the Lord in reality necessarily requires participation in Him as He is now exalted in His wholeness and fullness at the right hand of God Almighty. At the very moment that the words of institution call us to partake in Christ's death, symbolized by the brokenness of the bread, and the pouring out of the wine, we acknowledge our role in the holistic wholeness of Christ's exalted body, and the real presence of that Body in our lives—at the very center of our personal subjectivity.

We are not dealing with a dead contract or a dead sacrifice, available only to our memories of the dead. The "new covenant in Christ's blood" contains and communicates the dynamic power of the indissoluble and indivisible primunity of His actual life, by which Jesus was once, and once alone, put to bodily death, and now lives forever through the body of Christ, the church.

The virtue of this covenant is not only *represented*, but also *sealed* and *applied* to believers, which means not merely that they have in the sacrament a pledge that God will be faithful to His own promises, but that the grace which the sacrament exhibits is actually given over to them through the Eucharistic transaction itself. However, the grace or the merit of Christ's sufferings and death is transferred only through Christ's actual Person. So, it becomes actually ours only through actual contact with the actual Person of Jesus Christ.

"To eat the crucified body and drink the shed blood of Christ

" in the language of the Heidelberg Catechism, "is not only to embrace with a believing heart all the sufferings and death of Christ, and thereby to obtain the pardon of sin and life eternal; but also, besides that, it is to become more and more united to His sacred body by the Holy Ghost, who dwells both in Christ and in us, so that we, though Christ is in heaven and we on earth, are notwithstanding flesh of His flesh and bone of His bone. And that we live, and are governed forever by one Spirit, as members of the same body are by one soul."

23. This Extends to His Whole Person
The real communication that believers have with Christ in the Holy Supper extends to His whole person. For it to be real and not merely moral, it must be comprehensive. It must not merely inspire the will, it must also guarantee and assure the resulting eternal life in Christ. We may divide Christ in our thoughts by abstracting His divinity from His humanity, or His soul from His body, but no such

dualism exists in His actual person. To receive Christ at all is to receive His life, and His life is whole and comprehensive.

We do not partake of various rights and privileges, which have been secured for us by the breaking of His body and shedding of His blood, but we partake of the veritable and substantial life of Christ Himself, who alone is the fountain and channel through which His benefits are received. We partake not only of His divinity, nor only of His Spirit as if it can be separated from Himself, but we partake of His true and proper humanity. But neither can His humanity, His flesh and blood, be disjoined from His Spirit, but of the one life, which is the union of both, and in virtue of which the presence of the one must always involve the presence of the other in the same form and to the same extent.

24. The Eucharist as the Channel of His Grace

Christ communicates Himself to us, in a real way in the mysterious sacrament of the Eucharist. His communication is not merely a thought or recollection about Himself. Nor do we cause His communication by our faith. Rather, He is objectively present through the institution of the sacrament, and we receive Him sacramentally, and what we receive is His actual life. This implies no *opus operatum*, no mechanical or magical power in the use of the elements. Everything happens by the power of the Holy Spirit for the communicant, and reception of the benefits depends upon the faith of the communicant.

But still the grace and the action of the Holy Spirit as described here issues from the wholeness of Christ, in whom the sacrament derives its wholeness. And where faith in Christ alone is engaged by the communicant, the wholeness of the life of Christ is communicated.

This is the sound teaching of Dr. John Owen, the great Puritan divine, who tells us:

> "This is the greatest mystery of all the practicals of our Christian religion, a way of receiving Christ by eating and drinking, something peculiar, that is not in the hearing of the word nor in any other part of divine worship whatsoever; a peculiar participation of Christ, a peculiar acting of faith towards Christ."

The presence of Christ is not in, under, or around the bread and wine, but in the mysterious wholeness of Christ sacramentally received.

This mystery consists of two parts: one outward and visible, the other inward and invisible. The parts are not simply joined in time, like the sound of a bell, or the sight of a light that warns of something not directly connected to the bell or the light. Rather, they comprise a spiritual union that constitutes a spiritual wholeness. It is not spacial union, nor a temporal union, but as the old divines confessed, it is ultimately mystical and immediately sacramental. Union in Christ, demonstrated by participation in the Eucharist is peculiar (unique) to the hypostatic character of Christ and His role in the Trinity. Consequently, though we can have a degree of real knowledge and understanding about it, it is ultimately incomprehensible. But its ultimate incomprehensibility does not keep it from being intimately close. What we know is true, but we don't know everything. Indeed, much of the mystery of it issues from the fact that we experience its objectivity through our personal subjectivity—by faith.

25. The Communication is Always Through the Soul in a Central and Holistic Way

Christ communicates Himself to us in the sacrament in a spiritual, substantial, central, and holistic way. It is not that His body is communicated by one process, and His Spirit by another, but His whole life as a single undivided whole is communicated by one and the same agency. Nor is it by a mechanical transfer of some portion of His glorified body into our person, where it becomes a germ of physical immortality. Rather, it involves the wholeness of our lives becoming circumscribed within the wholeness of Christ's life. Such inclusion realigns our own subjectivity, our interests and desires, to be in alliance with the subjective interests and desires of Jesus Christ as recorded in Scripture.

This communication is independent of all material being, associations, contacts, or conjunctions, and is utterly dependent upon the reality, presence, and holistic wholeness of the Holy Spirit. It inheres in the dominion of the Spirit. Christ reveals His presence in us centrally and wholly, as the power of the new spiritual creation which is comprehended in His person, and in this way is made to extend itself out organically into and over the entire living man. Similarly, the life of the vine is reproduced with all its properties and qualities in every branch to which it extends.

26. Benefits Only for Believers

The Lord's Supper is the medium for the real benefits of Christ, but only in the case of genuine believers. The object of the institution is to confirm and advance the new life, where it has been already begun through baptism. The Eucharist has no power to convert those who are still in their sins, but because it actually conveys an objective reality it does have the power to exacerbate sin and sickness (1 Cor. 11:27, 30). However, the grace that it exhibits can only be apprehended by faith.

Concerning those who come to the Lord's table unworthily, Paul said, "For anyone who eats and drinks without discerning the body eats and drinks judgment on himself" (1 Cor. 11:29). This is because of the objectivity of the sacrament. If it conveys an objective reality, then its effects are universal, even though everyone is not effected in the same way. Thus, the sacrament also has an effect upon unbelievers. The sacrament communicates blessings to believers and curses to unbelievers, thus communicating universally.

The issue of faith manifests through the worthiness of the communicant. Those who are worthy receive Christ's benefits, and those who are not, receive God's judgment. So, what is the difference between believers and unbelievers in this case, since Paul confirmed the insight of the Psalmist (55:3) that no human being is worthy or righteous in God's sight, save Christ (Rev. 5:12)?

Because we have no worthiness or righteousness of our own, believers claim, assume, and put on Christ's worthiness (Isa. 6:10, 1 John 3:10). So, the worthiness that Paul spoke of is Christ's worthiness that is received by faith alone, but which must manifest as faith and works (James 2:14-26).[2]

Nor is it enough that the communicant think himself to be a regenerated person, but Christ must agree. In Matthew 7:21 Jesus rendered a judgment against people who thought themselves to be believers, and had even been prophesying, casting out demons, and doing mighty works and miracles in the name of the Lord. Yet, Jesus chastised them, and sent them away, presumably to hell. Why? Because they had not been called, but presumed themselves upon the Lord (Num. 15:30; Deut. 17:12, 18:20; Psalm 19:13; 2 Pet. 2:10). They

---

2   Nevin did not develop this issue like this, but he would certainly agree with it.

had determined *for themselves* that they were saved, and did not depend upon God for that determination.

Thus, receiving Christ's benefits through the sacramental transaction means actually receiving God's confirmation and seal. How do people know if they have actually received Christ, who alone is the gift of God's grace, and through who's wholeness Christ's benefits are distributed?

For those who enjoy that confirmation, no explanation is necessary. And for those who don't, none is possible. The communication comes solely and directly through the mediation of Jesus Christ to the believer. The seal of the sacramental transaction is the fact of its reality, and is the indispensable means for the actual reception of Christ's benefits.

And yet it is not our faith that gives the sacrament its power and efficacy, nor does it result from the actions of our faithfulness, or penitence, or love, or any other gracious affection that may be called into exercise in the sacrament. Our beliefs, actions, and/or behaviors do not constitute nor create the presence or acceptance of Christ. On the contrary, the impetus and power of salvation belongs to Christ alone, who is the ground from which all such affections draw their activity and strength. The power of the sacrament issues from Christ's faithfulness. It was Christ's faith alone that satisfied God, and in which we cohere. Thus, our own personal faith is the borrowing of Christ's objective faith. Our faith is not ours alone, but belongs to the holistic wholeness of the body of Christ because the body follows the lead of the Head.

"Your faith has made you well" (Mark 5:34), said the Lord to the woman who came behind him in the crowd, and touched the hem of His garment. But in fact the healing virtue went to her wholly from His own person. It was His power given to her through her faith, not because of it. Her faith, through which Christ's healing power was graciously communicated, provided the channel for Christ's healing power. Christ's healing power did not depend upon her request, though He did use it. The woman's faith simply provided an opportunity for her to receive the blessing, which was objectively present through the body of Christ.

So it is with us. The virtue of Christ's mystical presence is subsumed in the sacrament itself, and is not in any sense put into it by our faith. Our faith, which is simply Christ's faith borrowed and lent, serves only to bring us into right relationship with Christ, that relationship being in Him or in His covenantal body. Our faith does not make the sacrament real or effective, it simply receives what is objectively real. Faith can only access what is actually and objectively available.

27. Excludes Transubstantiation and Consubstantiation

As affirmed, Christ's mystical presence in the Eucharist excludes the ideas of transubstantiation and consubstantiation. According to the first of these errors, the bread and wine are changed into the actual substance of the Savior's body and blood. According to the Lutheran view the Savior's actual body and blood are contained and carried in or under the elements such that the reception of the elements, even on the part of the impenitent and unbelieving, is also supposed to involve the reception of Christ's actual body and blood.

Both of these views make the same error, but describe it differently. They presume an identification of Christ's presence in the Eucharist with the worldly elements of the bread and wine. According to the Roman theory, the transubstantiation is permanent, which means that the bread remains Christ's body even after the Eucharistic ceremony. According to the Lutheran doctrine, the relationship which binds them together only holds for the sacramental transaction itself. Nonetheless, while it holds, the elements bear in some way the divine life which they represent, such that Christ is received along with them in an oral, worldly manner.

In both cases, the communication of the bodily life of Christ is thought to be applied to the body of the believer in an immediate and direct way, not physically, of course, but supernaturally. However, on the one hand, this makes the sacramental reception of Christ to be something different from the oral reception of the elements, and on the other hand, the spiritual participation of Christ's body and blood becomes no more than empty words to which no meaning can be attached, except by magic, for the theory of elemental transmutation has long laid in the trash bin of history, along with alchemy.

In contrast to the Roman and Lutheran theories, Christ's presence in the Eucharist described here does not involve the identification of the body of Christ with the sacramental symbols of bread and wine in any way. Christ is not bound to the bread and wine, but to the holistic wholeness of the sacramental institution, which includes all of the various elements of the Eucharist—the context of the church, the story of Christ, the actuality of the atonement and the dispensation of the Holy Spirit, the words of institution, the participation of the communicant, etc. Through the Eucharistic liturgy the believer partakes of Christ's body and blood, as the Lord described in John 6:53. Where faith is present, the objective transaction involves the subjective reception, which is the vehicle or channel by which it is realized.

However, what is objectively outward, visible, and formal (the liturgy) is not itself the means for the subjectively inward, invisible, and informal connection or unity with Christ. The participation of Christ is wholly and holistically spiritual. He communicates Himself by the Holy Spirit into the soul of the believer cardinally, centrally, and wholly, according to the holistic character of the new creation to which this mystery belongs.

There is no mere material communication, as if the transference of Christ's life materially enters into the biological bodies of His people. All such ideas are merely superstitious. Ultimately, a corporeal communication amounts to a mechanical and formulaic union, and is at best the action of the power of the Holy Spirit in nature, which turns it into magic, as many ancient people believed. Such a characterization of the sacrament must necessarily be ascribed to the ordinance, as it was defined and celebrated in the ancient Church of Rome.

In addition, the superstitious, magical and alchemical understanding of the sacrament implies and imposes a pagan dualism upon human life by conceiving of life as being composed of two mutually exclusive Gnostic categories. Those categories have been described variously as self and other, one and many, flesh and spirit, etc. Such imaginary and mutually exclusive categories can only be bridged by magic, often historically associated with incantations and alchemical formulas. Such an idea contradicts reality as it is, and as we know it.

As every individual life enjoys wholeness and unity or oneness, so does Christ—only more so because of His role in the Trinity, which makes him a constituent element of humanity in both its particularity and its universality. Thus, the gospel of Jesus Christ, the story of His eternal life, is a single, holistic whole from creation to redemption, as well. The story of Jesus Christ reflects the holistic wholeness of His eternal life, and plays a central role in the constitution and story of humanity on earth. The new character and composition of regenerate humanity in Christ, in order to be real, must necessarily and perpetually spring from the centrality of Christ's own being, from the hypostatic union of Christ's humanity and divinity by the agency of the Holy Spirit. Accordingly, every fresh communication issues from the objective centrality of Christ and can be received only in the subjective centrality of the believer.

So the participation of Christ's life in the Eucharistic sacrament connects the objective reality of Christ to the subjective reality of the communicant. Thus, it always involves a real reception of either Christ's benefits or God's judgment. The believer is immediately nourished with the grace that is mystically conveyed to it in the holy ordinance, as the unbeliever is poisoned with God's judgment also mystically conveyed by the ordinance.

Thus, believers are united in Christ, and unbelievers are divided from Christ by the institution of the sacrament. And the blessings and fruition of Christ's benefits belong to the wholeness of the communicant, which includes the wholeness of his own individuality and the wholeness of the body of Christ by the agency of the wholeness of the Holy Spirit, the third Person of the Trinity.

The life pattern given to communicants in this central way is the prime spiritual fractal that grows and matures by imitation and repetition as it reaches into the wholeness of the communicants in the body of Christ. In this way, the character of humanity and the individual character(s) of believers are united in their journey into perfection in Christ. This life pattern eventually fills the undivided totality of communicants with its design and purpose. In whatever sense the Eucharistic communication is at all real, its reality is holistically whole for all involved because its central purpose is to bring, establish, and nurture human wholeness.

Section IV

False Theories Exposed

The way is now open for an appeal to Scripture, which must be regarded as the ultimate standard of truth regarding all of this. *Christianity is not a philosophical theory,[1] nor is it conveyed to us in the form of an infallible historic tradition.[2]* Indeed, the sacrament exists for the wholeness of Christ's body, as a permanent supernatural constitution of the church. However, in order to be understood correctly, it must be continually measured and interpreted by the written Word of God, which has been graciously committed to the keeping of the church for this very purpose.

The mere presumption here established in favor of this sacramental doctrine, though certainly of great weight in itself, is not itself enough to establish the doctrine. This can be done only by Christ's regeneration of humanity by establishing individuals in personal, covenantal relationship with Himself and with one another in the light of Scripture. For the Bible is the testimony of God's Word that sustains and confirms the testimony of God's church.

Other Views of the Sacrament are More or Less Rationalistic and Self-Destructive

Before we move on to this inquiry we need to notice the inextricable difficulties and contradictions that this subject of the believer's union with Christ has historically encumbered. These various encumbrances maintain that the Eucharistic union with Christ cannot seriously and consistently maintain the form and structure given to it

---

1 This simple observation provides a serious accusation against Protestantism.
2 This simple observation provides a serious accusation against Catholicism, Roman and Orthodox.

here. It is easy to raise objections to this doctrine of the church and its sacraments, where the objector shifts his own position at pleasure, without giving any properly scientific[3] account of his faith, in its ulterior connections and relations.

This is often done through the lack of serious theological cultivation, where all that is needed to satisfy or silence opposition to a new doctrine is to merely assert one's own difficulty holding together (or seeing the unity of) its complexity, or some historical problems that arise from some previous understanding of Christ or the church or science—or whatever. People commonly deceive themselves with easy solutions and faulty ideas. The currently reigning currency (doctrine or theory) lives by it own inflation until it expands beyond its useful value and collapses into a reevaluation. Those holding the bulk of the inflated currency desperately resist all efforts of reevaluation, but cannot in the long run stem the tide of history, the ongoing story of Christ in the world.

The Socinian Hypothesis

The Socinian (unitarian) view (Rationalism without disguise)[4] can never satisfy the faithful Christian heart or understanding. It makes Christianity to be like other religions, only in a more perfect form because Christianity provides a clearer revelation of divine truth, and a better system of ethical rules and precepts. It is thought to provide higher motives for virtue, particularly through the character and example of Christ. But ultimately, it cannot come to any sort of real union with God, which is the problem that all religions struggle with. In this regard, Socianianism is at best a version of Judaism, or rather an improvement on the philosophical schools of Paganism. It always throws man back upon himself, upon his own individual powers and resources, upon the abilities of the flesh (brain) to perfect his nature and make himself fit for heaven, upon works–righteousness.

But the holistic wholeness of life for the Christian rejects all humanistic works-righteousness. Christians know that a salvation of

---

3   Nevin's appeal to science is interesting, especially in the light that science and technology are the fruit of Christianity alone—not that only Christians can engage them, but that only Christianity can maintain them because they require genuine personal righteousness. Nevin desires a reasonable, biblically based account.

4   For more on Socianianism, see footnote 1, p. 65, and section "Socinianism of the Sixteenth Century," p. 176.

their own making or on the basis of their own power and/or decisions is not what they need. And with equal certainty, Christians know that it is not what they have found in Christ. Christians know that all Pelegian and/or Arminian theologies or their variants are in complete contradiction to the central teaching of the Bible, as well.

Christ is greater than Moses and all the prophets, and also infinitely more than Paul and the whole company of the apostles put together. He saves not merely by His doctrine and example, but by the actual spiritual redemption and real renovation that reaches the innermost life of His people. Christ does not merely save individuals, but He also saves the holistic wholeness of His church, which ultimately includes the wholeness of the world (John 1:29; 1 John 2:2, 4:14). If this is not the case, Christianity is shorn of its greatest glory, and the gospel is turned into a dream.

The Pelagian Hypothesis

The Pelagian tries to make more of our salvation by Christ than is given by Christ. The miracle of the incarnation and Christ's involvement in history are admitted and allowed to have their place in redemption. For Pelegians, Christ's power is ultimately nothing more than furnishing new motives and Pietistic aids that help us understand God's truth and adopt His way. Pelegians engage a method of salvation that is contrary to human nature, in that they think that they can do something that they cannot do—choose to follow Christ in their own power. In addition, they completely misunderstand the supernatural regarding salvation, in that they deny that salvation is a supernatural work of God. The reason that they think that they can do what only God can do is that they think that sin has only wounded them, and that their powers of judgment have not succumbed to sin.

In spite of what they think, the wholeness of humanity is external to the person being saved. No one can put himself into the wholeness of humanity. Pelegianism is an admirably contrived array of facilities by which sinners think that they have the power to escape the pollutions that are in the world through sin, and lay hold of glory, honor, and immortality by their decision to do so. But ultimately Pelegians are left to make use of their system precisely in the same way—on the Socinian hypothesis.

This hypothesis turns to Christ's precepts and example for salvation. Socianians and Pelegians (and indeed Arminians) are all thrown back upon the idea of salvation through morality that is effected by education in divinity (Bible and religious study). Their salvation must be self-constructed out of the material they suppose themselves to possess in their own nature.

These heretical theories have continued to develop over time. Many of these heretics believe that the force of truth itself directly influences the human mind to freely choose what is good. Thus, they think that they choose to become Christians because they sufficiently and rationally understand God's grace and goodness, that it is for their own personal benefit to become Christians. Thus, they justify or rationalize their choice to become Christians on the basis of their own understanding of God's goodness. Unaware of Jesus' caution in Matthew 7:21, they decide to become Christians by making a decision to do so that is justified and defended by their own understanding of God and Scripture. They understand in order to believe, rather than believe in order to understand. They decide and build a theology that justifies their decision.

They attribute salvation to the Spirit, but at the same time altogether reject the idea that God does anything more than try to influence their decisions. They assume that the whole of their salvation is accounted for by their own conscious decision for Christ. It seems that the central pillar of their concern is for their own autonomous freedom to "see the light" and freely ask for God's help as they extricate themselves from sin.

Thus, their central concern is for the establishment and maintenance of human freedom apart from Christ, in order that they may freely choose to be united to Christ. What they fail to understand is that apart from Christ, there can be no human freedom because humanity is enslaved to sin. Thus, freedom apart from Christ is likely the strongest of delusions in Satan's arsenal. Believing that their freedom is the ground of salvation, they are blinded to the fact that their salvation by Christ is actually the only ground of real human freedom.

The Theory of Divine Influence

But surely those who talk about spiritual influence, do not stop to consider the exact meaning of their own words. What do they mean when they speak of the Spirit infusing light and power into the truth? Can he do so (apart from a direct influence on the soul itself) in any other way than by ordering the presentation of the truth to the mind, so that it is placed in the most favorable position for exerting its influence? And what is this influence other than moral persuasion presented in a merely human way, by appeals addressed to the understanding and will?

In this way of thinking, in spite of all the high sounding terminology, the process of salvation always reverts to the process described above. It is salvation simply by the power of impersonal truth, presented in the form of objective doctrine and precept. This truth includes the supernatural facts of the gospel—the mission, sufferings, death, and resurrection of Christ, the outward apparatus of Christian redemption, etc. And along with this we have the "moral persuasion" of the Holy Spirit, which, according to this hypothesis, invests the whole process with something more than natural evidence and power, by imagining the addition of a certain spiritual something.

However, in the long run it all depends on the presentation of the information used to engage one's natural resources and capabilities. It is thought that nothing should be added to the person that would change or control one's "freewill," including anything that would effect one's judgment because that would make the judgment not one's own. It doesn't matter whether the facts contemplated are natural or supernatural, whether the truth which challenges my regard is brought to me by man or angel, or by God Himself. If the crucial decision depends upon *my* knowledge and/or insight, and nothing can be added to me that is not natural to me in my unsaved state, then Christ can only hope to effect my judgment, but cannot guarantee His effectiveness because any such guarantee would damage the freedom of my will.

Therefore, in this line of thinking I must remain under the dominion of my own fallen life and the illusion of the freedom of my will, in the realm of the flesh, and without any power to rise into the realm of the Spirit (John 3:6). Christ's mediation, which alone can break the power of sin, is dependent upon *my* sinful judgment to call it into action. But what I need as a sinner is beyond my own judgment and abilities because sin has co-opted those very things. And because Christ must await my bidding, He can never change what must be changed in order for me to abandon the sin that masquerades as my self-interest. Sin must abandon itself in my life; for if it doesn't, I must feed on what I cannot reach, for the morality I have that is controlled by my sin is the morality I must use to escape my sin. This is the result of a merely moral and rationalistic redemption that issues from "freewill."

At this point the moralistic rationalists bring a higher and more orthodox sounding idea to solve the problem. The Reformed doctrine of imputation or imputed righteousness[5] is introduced in order to provide what neither I in my sin, nor Christ because of His imagined respect for my freewill, can provide. In the light of this doctrine the work of Christ is no longer a mere display for moral effect, but is something to be appropriated and made available in the sinner himself, for the purposes of salvation.

Mere doctrine cannot suffice! The sin that binds me is more than words, so escaping its grip requires more than words. It calls for an actual personal participation in the reality and wholeness of what Christ has done and suffered in order for Christ's propitiation to actually be applied to sinners. How is this accomplished? By imputation, said both the Lutherans and Reformed confessions. In the same way that the sin and guilt of Adam were imputed to his posterity from birth, though they themselves had not personally sinned at birth, so the righteousness of Christ, and the benefits of His mediatorial work, are imputed to believers.

In this way Christ's righteousness counteracts Adam's sinfulness and restores the broken relationship between man and God. As the sacrifice of Christ's righteousness atones for Adam's sinfulness generally, in worship Christ's righteousness is credited to individual sinners on the basis of their confession of faith and repentance of sin. And because of this God treats believers as if the fullness of Christ's righteousness was their own, as if believers were no longer involved in sin.[6]

---

5   Imputed righteousness proposes that the righteousness of Christ is imputed to believers, that believers are treated as if Christ's righteousness is theirs because of their faith. It is on the basis of their alien (from outside of themselves) righteousness that God accepts people. This acceptance is also referred to as *justification*. Thus this doctrine is practically synonymous with justification by faith.

    The teaching of imputed righteousness is a signature doctrine of the Lutheran and Reformed traditions of Christianity, though there is some dispute as to the origin of the idea. Luther used the term in this sense as early as 1516. But Erasmus translated the Greek *logizomai* (reckon) as *imputat* in Romans chapter four. The Vulgate that Erasmus intended to correct usually translated it *reputat* (repute). Thus it may have originated with Erasmus.

6   Nevin was not questioning the integrity of the doctrine, but was pointing out that for the doctrine to be effective there has to be integrity between the sign and the thing signified, between the idea of the doctrine and the reality of the imputation.

The justification of sinners according to this doctrine is a forensic[7] act on the part of God. It is based entirely on the work of Christ, for He alone is righteous and He alone propitiated God by His sacrifice on the cross. How, then, does Christ's work apply to believers? Does it involve and require a requisite change of character? Or does it simply acknowledge a change of state? At what point does God attribute Christ's righteousness to believers? The problem is that the cessation of sin and the establishment of righteousness do not happen instantly. So, can God apply Christ's righteousness to a believer who confesses faith in Christ, but continues to sin?

The doctrine teaches that God regards His people as perfectly righteous, though they are not in fact yet perfectly righteous, and gives them full title to all the blessings comprehended in Christ's life. At the same time, He regenerates them by His Spirit, which brings them into a process of sanctification, at the end of which they become fully transformed in their own persons, into the image of their glorious Savior.

It is at this very point that the question rises: How can something be imputed or reckoned to anyone on the part of God, if it does not belong to the individual in reality? This is the old difficulty pressed against the orthodox doctrine by the Pelegians, Remonstrants, and Arminians of Holland (and previously by the Church of Rome), and constantly repeated by the Rationalists from that time to the present. And it must be admitted that the argument has both weight and teeth. Or rather we may say that there are conditions when this doctrine of imputation becomes no more than a philosophical abstraction that has no real connection to the real world. So, unless there is a real connection to the real world, the objections against the doctrine of imputation are insurmountable.

Imputation is often described as if God made an accounting entry to the credit column of the believer's account. Nevin's concern is that for the accounting entry to be valid, the "currency" exchange must be real. Otherwise, God is just fixing the books. In other words, believers who so confess Christ must actually become increasingly righteous, and that they can only do so, not by their own power, but only by the actual presence of Christ in their lives.

7   Forensics is a legal term concerned with causality and proof. Does the hair at the scene of the crime prove that the defendant was actually there? Does the evidence establish the guilt or innocence of the accused?

Abstract Legal Imputation

The judgment of God is always the truth. God cannot truthfully reckon to anyone an attribute or quality that does in fact not belong to the individual. He cannot declare an individual to be in a relation or state that is not actually his own, but belongs to another. A simple objective imputation, being the pleasure and purpose of God to account to one what has been done by another, cannot satisfactorily answer the question. Nor is the situation helped by the hypothesis of a legal, federal, or covenantal union between those involved. The idea is logically consistent, but is it necessarily real?

Such a thing is unreal if the logic only applies in the abstract world of thought, but has no necessary connection to concrete reality. In such a case the logic would itself only be an abstraction, internally consistent and coherent, but without an objective and necessary correlation to the actual world in which people live. God, who alone makes the imputation, is not subject to logic or law, but rather logic and law follow God's lead. So, there is no necessary connection between the logic of imputation and reality unless God actually makes such imputation. The necessity of the relationship does not depend upon the idea or doctrine of imputation, but upon God's action of imputation alone. Therefore, it is possible for people to imagine such a thing when it is in reality not the case, though the doctrine itself is logically valid.

Can we conceive of any situation where God could account to mankind the apostasy of the angels which did not keep their first estate (Jude 1:6)? Or where God would destroy the very people he once saved (Jude 1:5)? Or where ungodly men can actually turn the grace of our God into lasciviousness (Jude 1:4)? If everything regarding salvation depends on the actions of God alone, then the power of a mere intellectual connection between doctrine and reality cannot account for the transfer of sin and guilt from angels to men, or from Adam to his posterity, or from leaders to society.

The very fact that human reason and feeling revolt against God's sovereignty serves to show that His sovereignty in our salvation must rest upon some deeper ground than the mere idea or doctrine of justification by Christ, abstractly considered. For our unity with God to be nothing more than an idea or doctrine, or a law or principle, or even for it to naturally reside in our character as human beings, will always fall short of reality because if these things comprise the wholeness of God's reality, He cannot be sovereign.

In such a case, God can at best hope to influence us, but has no necessary command over us. All true Christians, whatever their understanding of this point know that their union in Christ rests on more than this, and that their possession of the benefits of Christ's death and resurrection rests upon a basis infinitely more sure and solid than ideas, doctrine, law, logic, principle, or moral influence. What more? Unity in Christ depends upon the reality of the holistic wholeness of Christ's life, in which they participate by the power and presence of regeneration by the Holy Spirit.

Do we then discard the doctrine of imputation in response to the opposition of the Pelegians and Rationalists? By no means! We seek only to establish the doctrine in the reality and wholeness of Christ, apart from whom it collapses. It is only when the reality of imputation is dissociated from the doctrine, when the thing signified by the sign is not present, that it becomes untenable. To relieve it from this objection, it must be stated and understood that it is true only as God makes it true, and not because we say that it is true. Indeed, imputation is an act of God, not an action or response of men. And if it is not God's doing, then it is not true regardless of what we may believe, say, or think about it.

The Bible knows nothing of the mere idea of imputation apart from the reality of God's action. The Bible does not teach that God imputes to someone what does not belong to the individual in fact. Of course, the fullness of Christ's righteousness does not come to humanity in an instant. Time is required because we live in time. So, the growth of that righteousness begins and matures in time. And because of God's sovereignty and His promise of redemption, God will complete what He has begun. The fullness of the flower is guaranteed to be in the seeds of Christ's righteousness, but the seed requires time to mature.[8]

The fall of Adam is similarly imputed to be the fall of his posterity, because it actually is the case. Adam was really the first man. The Garden was real,. The Serpent was real. The sin was real. And the Fall was real. Our union in Adam by God's law of federal or covenantal headship describes the method and means of our life union in Adam. The Fall undermined the wholeness of that life by a deceit introduced by the Serpent and assimilated by Eve and then Adam, and that deceit

---

8   In the one seed of Christ are the many seeds that become the forest of Christendom.

destroyed the veracity between the sign and the thing signified that God's Word had established.

Sin destroyed the necessary connection between words and reality, between the words of imputation and the reality of Christ's presence, which means that people can speak of imputation as an idea or doctrine where no such actual imputation exists. And we have inherited the broken morality of Adam, not only the idea of it, but its actuality in our own character and constitution. Our participation in the actual unrighteousness of Adam's life in history establishes the ground of our participation in his guilt and liability to punishment.

Note

"All mankind descending from Adam by ordinary generation," according to the Westminster Shorter Catechism, Question 19, "sinned in him, and fell with him, in his first transgression." This question and its response has produced much reproach and sarcasm at the expense of the great value of that document. It has been charged with teaching physical depravity by the transfer of sin to personal character.

Unfortunately, the defenders of the Catechism in their attempts to vindicate its doctrine at this point were not always planted on the proper ground for its defense. They have themselves conceived the idea that the reality of imputation depends upon the willingness of the receiver, which means that the receiver can destroy the necessary connection between the sign and the reality of the thing signified, between the idea of imputation and its reality. As such, it logically follows that God's moral influence can at best give its subjects only a quasi interest in the idea of imputation.

In addition, this idea of imputation as a mere moral interest cannot demand or cause the necessary connection between the doctrine and the reality. And the lack of this necessity undermines God's sovereignty, or the absolute freedom of God to do what He wants, with the sovereignty of human freewill.

So, the objection is effectively overcome by simply maintaining God's sovereignty and denying what contradicts it. So, imputation is not understood as any sort of transfer or deposit of something that simply belongs to another. The language of the Catechism is literally and strictly correct. We sinned in Adam, and fell with him in his first transgression. Adam's posterity was already but spiritually with him in seed form when he fell, which means that we were participants in his transgression and fall. So, it was ours from the perspective of Adam's wholeness as a person, his archetypal reality is our existential reality.

The person in which the Fall took place, Adam, contained within himself the actual complex whole of the entire human race. The individual existence of every particular sinner is but the historical outworking of the wholeness of Adam's life, which includes his sin and Fall. Accordingly, original sin is carefully described by the Catechism as consisting, not simply "in the guilt of Adam's first sin," but in his "lack of original righteousness" and in "the corruption of his whole nature." So it is in fact true. Adam's life had fallen, his relationship with God was actually tainted with sin, and because of this God imputed guilt and condemnation to him in his role as the federal head or archetype of humanity. His sin contaminated the design of his model.

So, the imputation by God was the result of the reality of his sin. The reality of the sin caused the imputation, the imputation did not cause the reality. And in the same way the idea of imputation is satisfactorily sustained in the case of the second Adam—Jesus Christ. In this respect Scripture considers the two cases to be parallel. We are justified freely by God on the basis of what Christ has done and suffered as our representative, on our behalf, which is his role and function as federal or covenantal head.

God imputed Christ's righteousness to our account to be regarded as our own because Christ actually accomplished our redemption. Again, God's imputation followed Christ's propitiation, His ascension and the dispensation of the Holy Spirit for regeneration. The reality of this produced the imputation, the imputation did not produce the reality. The idea, doctrine, principle of imputation does not depend upon us for its truth, it depends upon the reality of God operating in history to save humanity from extinction by uniting them in Christ. Thus, God's forensic declaration that pronounces sinners free from sin is like God's Word in the beginning when God said: Let there be light, and light was (Gen. 1:3). There is integrity between His words and reality, between the sign and the reality of the thing signified.

God's declaration not only proclaims sinners to be righteous for Christ's sake, but God also sets the righteousness of Christ in those sinners as a part of the holistic wholeness of Christ, which includes the holistic wholeness of those who actually are in Christ. And in doing this, God has set the very life of Christ in the redeemed in the same way. For righteousness, like guilt, is an attribute which requires a sub-

ject in which to inhere, and apart from its subject the quality of righteousness cannot be abstracted without ceasing to exist altogether.

In the case before us, this subject includes the mediatorial character and role in the life of the Savior Himself. Whatever merit there is—
virtue, efficacy, moral value, etc.—in the mediatorial work of Christ, it
is all included in the wholeness of His life by the power of God, and in
the presence of which alone it has reality and stability.

The imaginary idea that the merits of Christ's life may be
abstractly separated from His life, and conveyed to His people in an
abstract form, or on the basis of some mere constitutional idea, law or
principle is unscriptural and contrary to reason and logic. To any
power regarding the idea or doctrine of imputation, the legal union
between the words and the reality must be an actual life union. In the
very act of our justification, by which the righteousness of Christ is
accounted to be ours, it must of necessity have already become ours in
fact by our actual insertion into Christ Himself. The process of the
assimilation of Christ's righteousness may have barely begun, but it
must have necessarily and actually begun. Indeed, we are joined to
Christ mystically by the power of the Holy Spirit, and out of this reality we observe the law or principle of a new creation of which we are
a part. From its earliest beginning, even in the mind of God, everything that it will eventually become already belongs to its wholeness,
including all of its various parts.

In this way, the new life of the believer through regeneration and
by the creative fiat of God's justification is itself the bearer of all the
new relationships in which the new believer is brought to stand. In
addition, all of the other benefits received on Christ's account belong
to that new life. Every sort of imputation imaginable is false and unreal
if it is merely an abstraction and devoid of Christ's actual presence in
the lives of believers. Such a judgment is true even in the case of his
active obedience because in truth Christ's active and passive obedience
cannot be disjoined.[9]

---

9   John Murray, in *Redemption—Accomplished and Applied* (pp. 20-22), said that we
    cannot "allocate certain phases or acts of our Lord's life on earth to the active obedi-
    ence and certain other phases and acts to the passive obedience. The distinction
    between the active and passive obedience is not a distinction of periods. It is our
    Lord's whole work of obedience in every phase and period that is described as active
    and passive, and we must avoid the mistake of thinking that the active obedience
    applies to the obedience of his life and the passive obedience to the obedience of his
    final sufferings and death. ...

If we turn Christ's atonement into an abstract doctrine that requires only our belief in the idea that the transfer simply involves no more than moral influence, then we gut the effectiveness of the transfer of its ability to actually accomplishing what it promises. Ideas sometimes influence people, but they do not have the power of command. We need Christ's holiness as well as His legal pardon, and the gospel clearly presents Christ to be the fountain of holiness, no less than He is the author of pardon. The obedience by which we actually become righteous is ultimately found to be Christ's active obedience, and not ours, except as we receive and derive it from His person.

But if this righteousness produced by our new life in Christ is merely an abstract idea about the transfer of something that actually changes our commitment to sin, but does not actually have the power to do so, the whole idea is false. To actually have received a transfer that has initiated such a change is to know that it is not an abstraction. Imputation becomes unintelligible it does not actually involve the power of the wholeness of Christ's life in such a way as to actually accomplish what it describes. If the active obedience of Christ is not directly experienced, it can have no meaning because it remains an abstract and powerless idea. Where imputation does not directly belong to personal experience it becomes obscure and confused in the consciousness of the church, and the conception of Christ's obedience, both active and passive, is lost to the same extent.

Note

Both active and passive obedience in the end, as Ernesti and others have shown, are the same. They each pertain to different aspects of the vicarious work of Christ on behalf of His people. The value of Christ's sufferings depends on the perfect holiness of His character, and His

---

The real use and purpose of the formula is to emphasize the two distinct aspects of our Lord's vicarious obedience. The truth expressed rests upon the recognition that the law of God has both penal sanctions and positive demands. It demands not only the full discharge of its precepts but also the infliction of penalty for all infractions and shortcomings. It is this twofold demand of the law of God which is taken into account when we speak of the active and passive obedience of Christ. Christ as the vicar of his people came under the curse and condemnation due to sin and he also fulfilled the law of God in all its positive requirements. In other words, he took care of the guilt of sin and perfectly fulfilled the demands of righteousness. He perfectly met both the penal and the perceptive requirements of God's law. The passive obedience refers to the former and the active obedience to the latter."

character, in the circumstances of His life, could not be complete except by His sufferings.[10] However, His righteousness as a whole has two sides: one negative and the other positive. The first exhibits the way of victory over sin and death, the other was the free activity of His holiness in the form of His life. Both necessarily go together in the transfer of Christ's righteousness to the believer.

In the Roman Catholic Church the doctrine of participation in the active obedience of the Savior was obscured by their definition of good works. With the Reformation this doctrine came into full view. However, for the Rationalists it has no meaning. Knapp, and theologians like him, consider it unscriptural and absurd to speak of a vicarious obedience of Christ. They argue that it contradicts the principle in religion that every man's character is to be determined by his own works and not by the works of another.

This objection would be true if the reality of imputation has no subjective element or effect upon the will, but it only shows the necessity of a deeper and/or more holistic analysis. The works of Christ are not given to His people as something sundered from Christ's life, but rather they are given as the triumphant power of the holistic wholeness of His life, revealing itself in them and through them as active bearers of His righteousness. The virtue of Christians is actually their own, and yet at the same time the virtue of Christ works its proper fruits in them. It is not a case of the believer's works versus Christ's works, but of Christ's work working in and through the believer, empowering and motivating the believer to willingly accept the gift and take ownership of it by willingly engaging the work.

Of course, Christ is regarded as the source of new life for His people. This is what the scriptures teach. This is what the nature of Christian salvation plainly requires. This is what the orthodox faith of the church has always held. Christ is in the believer and the believer is in Christ (John 17:23), not simply in a moral relationship, and nor only through a legal connection, but by the actual bond of a common life. Ultimately, anything other than this is devolves into rationalism.

But it may be said that this common life is nothing more than the idea of the presence and influence of Christ's Spirit in the souls of His

---

10 There are at least two reason for this: 1) because God intended for Jesus Christ to provide propitiation for the sins of the world, and 2) because Jesus Christ actually suffered the cross for this reason. The first reveals the potential of Christ's character, and the second demonstrates the reality of His calling.

people that carries forward the work of grace, gradually transforming them into His image. In fact, this is often made as a claim for the highest character of orthodoxy. And in this way, people persuade themselves that it is possible to meet and satisfy all the demands for Christian salvation themselves, in their own strength. They profess to accept the doctrine of mystical union without qualification or reservation, and even speak of it with respect as being one of the most vital and precious truths of the gospel.

And yet this idea is understood to mean that the same Spirit which dwells in Christ, and which is called the "Spirit of Christ" on this account, also dwells in us, and eventually gives us the same mind! This is taken to be the scriptural view, for he that is joined to the Lord, it is said, "is one Spirit" (1 Cor. 6:17). All Christians are understood to be under the influence of Christ's Spirit, and to be filled and ruled by His presence.[11]

But here we are in great danger of being misled by mere words and phrases, to which no clear meaning exists in the minds of those who use them. When this happens it is necessary to insist on a more definite statement of precisely what is intended by those who think this way. If they simply mean that the presence of Christ is in the church and He is united with His people through the Holy Spirit, there would be no room for objection. This accords with Scripture and satisfies the demands of the heart and understanding.

From this perspective, Christ is said to dwell in His people personally, but only by His Spirit, which implies plainly that these two ideas —dwelling in His people, and only by His spirit—are completely identical. This perspective assumes that Christ's promise to dwell in His people means only that His Spirit dwells in them, abstracted from His holistic wholeness, forgetting or denying the Trinitarian character of the Godhead. Separating the Holy Spirit from the unity of the Godhead involves no contradiction regarding the idea of a spiritual mystery. And in this way the idea of mystical union with Christ is lifted above the natural world and is thought to be a higher order of existence, a "spiritual" existence.

Obviously, Christ does not dwell in His people physically, in the ordinary way that we understand our bodily existence. Nor does He

---

11   Nevin's central concern is turning Christianity into an abstract doctrine that requires mental assent and at the same time denying, disregarding or disallowing the reality of the wholeness and reality of Christ's actual person in the life of the church.

dwell in us as a part of the constitution of our present natural life. So, this perspective necessitates that Christ's dwelling in us refers to something supernatural, if the idea is to be associated with our faith at all. This idea of supernatural union with Christ is then said to be a new order of life that is comprehended in the Spirit. The idea of supernatural union is called our "spiritual life." This new life is understood to issue from Christ, and to reveal itself through the Spirit, as its medium, element or form. In this way Christ is thought to reveal Himself in the church to the end of time. From this perspective, Christ dwells in His people only in this way. His presence is in the Spirit, But not in the flesh.[12]

From this perspective, Christ dwells in His people by His Spirit, but only as a representation, an abstraction or idea in the mind of the believer, but not as an actual, integral element of their own individual, subjective person. But this sunders the Spirit of Christ from the reality and holistic wholeness or hypostatic union of Christ Himself, and suggests that believers are united with Christ's divinity, but not His humanity—as if the Spirit of Christ is only an idea (doctrine) and not a reality (life).

But the reality of union in Christ is mystical precisely because it does not divide the holistic wholeness of Christ. Only as the Spirit dwells in the holistic wholeness of the glorified Savior does He bond in unity with a living connection between Christ in heaven and His body, the church, on earth. Both head and body have been specifically created to possess the same holistic life. Christian union with God is intimate but not direct because it comes through Christ's mediation and reconciliation.

At this point several general difficulties come into view, which are not usually taken into consideration. First, we are not told explicitly whether the Spirit of Christ is identical with the idea of His divine nature or not. Does the actual presence of the Spirit involve an actual presence to the same extent as His divine nature? In the form in which the subject is often presented, it might seem that the wholeness of Christ, divine and human, is held to be in the church and in particular believers by or through His Spirit, as an entirely distinct form of existence, constituting the third person of the glorious Trinity.[13]

---

12 Obviously, the problem with this perspective is that it divides Christ's wholeness, his hypostatic union of humanity and divinity in one person.

13 Nevin is wrestling with the relationship of the one to the many. How is an individ-

Here is a point of some importance that requires careful consideration. Christ's divinity, which is joined hypostatically with His
humanity, cannot be present with regard to the relationship between
an individual Christian and the church.[14] If the Logos is at all present
in the church today, it is not an incarnate presence as it was in Christ,
but is present only in a mediated way through Christ, through which
we refract the light of His truth. The wholeness of Christ is not personally present in the church, but is present only by proxy or
substitution, by the agency of the Holy Spirit. How this is to be
counted a true and actual presence of the Savior Himself, answerable
to His own promise, and also to the strong terms in which the mystical
union is spoken of in the New Testament is not easy to perceive.[15]

But again. What is there that is peculiar or unique in the grace of
God in the New Testament from this perspective compared with the
grace enjoyed by the saints under the Old? Does it depend upon the
fuller revelation of God in Christ in the New Testament facts, the
greater privileges and opportunities for believers that are new in the
dispensation of the New Testament gospel? The scriptures plainly
teach that the difference includes these things, but is more than these
things. Christ, the angelic messenger of the New Covenant, was with
His people in the Old Covenant. And we know that there were communications of the Spirit then also, though in different forms.

But it is everywhere assumed in the New Testament that the presence of the one (new), and the communications of the other (old),
since the incarnation have taken on a wholly different character—yet
are of the same essence! The wholeness and/or completeness of God's
Trinitarian revelation through Scripture was provided with the incarnation and propitiation of Jesus and the dispensation of the Holy Spirit
upon all flesh (Luke 3:6; John 17:2; Acts 2:17). It falls to the theory
before us,[16] then, to clarify this difference. This theory certainly seems

---

ual related to humanity in general? How is Jesus' humanity related to His divinity?

14 The hypostatic union belongs to Christ uniquely as a member of the Trinity. We
are not in hypostatic union as Christ is. However, because humanity has been created in the image of God, Christians enjoy a similar kind of union, but it can only
been understood as "through a glass darkly," a likeness that comes short of being
identical. Our union might be called redundant or hyperstatic union, the difference
being that Christ's is original and ours is derived.

15 Amen! That's the mystery of it. Yet is is real, actually present in the present reality!

16 What theory? Nevin is talking about the Pelegian, Arminian and Rationalist theological abstractions that are devoid of any real presence.

to make no account of the difference whatever. This theory appears to reduce the difference described above to be nothing more than a difference of extent and degree, but the order or character of the grace is not distinguished. It is assumed that the incarnation of Christ was a matter of no actual and necessary effect on people, except regarding the individual manifestation of the Redeemer Himself. This theory teaches that Christ is now in heaven, in human and bodily form, where before His incarnation He was in heaven without this form/body.

And as He manifested Himself previously to the patriarchs and prophets in the Old Testament in His divine nature or by His Spirit, He now in the New Testament and beyond continues to manifest Himself to His church in the same way, except with greater grace that is now more free. The Spirit of Christ, by which He is said to dwell in His people, has not become different because of the fact of His incarnation from what the same Spirit was in relation to men before it, according to this perspective.[17]

He is not understood to be the medium of a new spiritual creation that was established or constituted by the miracle of His incarnation itself, nor as the divine life of God Himself flowing through the everlasting power of the incarnation upon the world in a new form or way. From this perspective, Christ's agency has nothing whatever to do with His incarnation, except in an outward mechanical way so that in the final analysis everything resolves itself into some kind of unified abstract relationship. Here the Spirit of God is understood to hold people in a unified sociological category, as if the incarnation makes no actual difference at all to the humanity of His followers. Is this what that theory means?

If so, let the thought be distinctly proclaimed and the difficulties which it necessarily draws in its train be honestly faced. Let the church know that she is no nearer to God after the fact of the incarnation of Jesus Christ, no nearer regarding their actual life and living, than she was under the Old Testament. Let the church know that the indwelling of Christ in believers is only abstractly or intellectually parallel with the divine presence that was enjoyed by the Jewish saints, who all died in faith "not having received the promises" (Heb. 11: 13).

---

17 The idea is that incarnation only effected the individual human body of Jesus the man, not His divinity.

Let the church know that the mystical union envisioned by Paul or John is nothing more intimate, vital, and real than the relationship to God enjoyed by Abraham or David or Isaiah, etc. And if this is not the intended meaning, let the true nature of the difference be explained as clearly as possible.

Again, taking the presence of the Holy Spirit for all it claims to be in relationship to Jesus Christ, what specific form of existence must the Spirit have? Under the Old Testament it was never more than an afflatus[18] or influence that was exerted on the soul of the person to whom it was given. Is this all that we are to understand it to be in the Christian church? This is exactly what that theory appears to mean. Christ dwells in us by His Spirit; and the Spirit dwells in us by His operations, influences, graces. And this, we are told, is the mystical union, a virtual[19] version of the life of Christ as distinguished from His benefits. But is not the actual life of Christ conveyed to believers? Let the process itself be examined for the answer.[20]

It is said that the same Spirit that works in Christ works also in us, fashioning us into an image of Himself.[21] And how does He accomplish this? By supernatural influence, according to this theory. But this answer from this perspective simply falls back on the idea that "influence" suggests a merely moral union with Christ, that it comes by the power of the truth abstractly conceived.[22] And we have already found this in its highest form and expression to be simple Pelagianism in disguise. Is Christ ultimately in us only or merely by the divine persuasion of His Spirit—through words and ideas alone?

It is difficult to agree with this idea because we intuitively know that there is more to it than this. But what, then, is that "more"? It is often said that the Spirit creates new life in the believer. Very well, that is true enough. But in saying this we are already beyond the realm of mere ideas and abstract moral persuasion. How so? We must under-

---

18 Afflatus: a creative impulse or divine inspiration.
19 Virtual: existing in essence or effect though not in actual fact.
20 Nevin struggles with translating certain German language into English. He also struggles with language to describe the mystery. The sense of this section is that the Pelegian, Arminian, etc. understanding of the mystical presence of Christ is virtual rather than real.
21 Remember that Christ's identity involves his role in the Trinity. So, in that image our identity will be similar, but not the same.
22 Such an idea of truth makes it moral, rational, logical, consistent, intelligent, intellectual, scholastic, etc., such that its influence is limited to the mind, to ideas.

stand what is meant by "new life." Being *new* it is obviously something that was not in existence before. So, whence then does this new creation come? Is it the divine life of the Spirit in the character as the renewed person that is new? Is it the life of God directly put into the human soul? If so, this would be a repetition of the hypostatic mystery of the incarnation, accomplished in the life of every new believer.[23]

Such a thought of course is not for a moment entertained by any who have personally experienced the difference between Christ's actual *life* and the mere idea of His *influence*. Whence then, we ask again, comes this "new life" in the Spirit? Is it a new creation out of nothing? Is it a higher order of existence with no organic, historical connection whatever with ordinary human life and living, and therefore abstractly spiritual? Is it originated in every individual Christian as something altogether new, superadded[24] to the regular constitution of the world?

If this is the case, instead of one great miracle centered and located the incarnation of the man Jesus Christ, we will have miracles of the same order without number or end created by the regeneration of believers. Every believer will be a discrete new creation equivalent to Jesus Christ, as imagined by Eckhart. Such creations would not be in Christ Jesus, but in the individual Christians themselves and would constitute a completely new life that has never been known in the world before. If this is true, where would we find the unity of the lives that were created *de novo* in each new instance? How would such creatures make the church whole or unified? And lastly, in what sense might such a thing be said to be the life of Christ, who is the head of the body known as the church?[25] A life created from nothing, acting in the name of Christ, without any regard whatsoever to Christ's mediatorial role, would be identical to Christ, but would not be in Christ. Such creatures would be equivalent to the Persons of the Trinity and

---

23 This was the error of Meister Eckhart, who understood Christian unity to bring each believer into hypostatic unity with the Godhead. But Eckhart overstated the biblical reality, which is *union* not *identity* with Christ. This can be analogously understood by set theory to be overlapping sets rather than identical sets.

24 Superadded: to add especially in a way that compounds an effect.

25 If each individual Christian is created to be divine in the same way and to the same degree as Christ is divine, God would be creating many heads and no body. The church would be a body composed exclusively of heads.

would expand the Trinity into a Panunity as competing Persons in the Godhead![26] Is this the mystical union that Scripture testifies to? No!

This theory simply destroys itself. In every way, it is found to be contradictory, unintelligible, inconsistent, and false. And yet this is the view that is is often provided as if it furnishes a clear and satisfactory account of union in Christ. And the suggestion of a real participation in the life of Christ generally and uniquely in the institution of the Eucharist is charged with mysticism and nonsense by Pelegians, Arminians, Socianians, Eckhartians, and Rationalists!

However, if the union in question is to be regarded as being any-thing more than merely moral or abstractly legal, such accusations must stop. We have already seen that the imputation of Christ's merits to His people requires that His actual life must be given to Christians along with their own spiritual regeneration, because the actual life of Christ is the only real bearer of His merits. His merits cannot be abstractly separated from the reality of the holistic wholeness of His life. We must come to understand that the mere action of the Spirit upon the soul, whether by persuasion or regeneration alone, does not include the holistic wholeness of Christ's life in any true sense what-ever.[27]

What is the conclusion then to which we are at last shut up?[28] Plainly this: *Christ dwells in us by His Spirit, but only because His Spirit constitutes the very form and power of His own presence as the incarnate and everlasting Word that cannot separate His divinity from His humanity and must include in some sense the wholeness of the Godhead.* The Holy Spirit, who is truly the Spirit of Christ, forms us—the church—into a new divine creation that is composed of "living stones" (Eph. 2:20-22, 1 Pet. 2:5) by conforming us to His glorious image.[29] However, the life thus wrought in our souls by His agency is not a creation out of noth-ing (*ex nihilo*). Rather, it is the very life of Jesus Himself, organically extended into the personhood of the believer. The reality of Christ's presence demands nothing less than this.[30]

---

26   If this were the case it would undermine the mediatorial role of Jesus Christ with regard to humanity, and destroy the uniqueness of the Trinity.

27   An act or action of the Spirit does not a whole life make. It is only one element or aspect of the life of the Spirit.

28   This is classic Nevin! Perhaps he is trying to appeal to mystics, whose books are full of statements and phrases that have more implication than substance.

29   εἰκών—likeness, representation, resemblance—but not identity.

30   The mystery of the incarnation does not make the incarnation illogical or unclear.

Everything less than this turns the salvation of the gospel into religious truths that cannot be ultimately or essentially distinguished from Judaizing and Paganizing heresies. Why is it considered to be incredible for God to raise the dead to new life in the way herein described? Those who are willing to suggest that regeneration creates a new creation out of nothing (*ex nihilo*) in the life of the believer surely ought not have any difficulty in allowing a new creation from the actual substance of Christ's life as it exists holistically, wholly, and historically, or that God actually extends the life of Christ into the believer's person by ingrafting the new onto the old (Rom. 11:17).

If the Spirit can create *de novo*, is it really so difficult to conceive of the actual formation and/or extension of Christ Himself in us through the same divine creative power? The idea of creation *ex nihilo* is much less real because it swims in absolute imaginary fantasy at a distance. Creation *ex nihilo* happened only once, and is completely beyond human understanding.[31] Can this be the reason[32] why it the gospel is understood to be more rational than mystical?

The Spirit as Influence Alone, or as a New Creation

Allowing that Christ does indeed dwell in His people by the real presence of His personal life through the Spirit, and not simply by the idea of the presence of His Spirit as a surrogate, it is necessary to include Christ's whole life in this mystical union. Because of its inherent unity, this issue can have but one unified resolution. The key to understanding the truth about this issue involves the reality and role of the mediatorial life of Christ in Christian salvation. In His mediatorial role, which is an aspect of His life, we find the holistic wholeness of the mystical union itself. Christ's mediation requires both the righteousness of Christ and all the benefits He has procured for His people. And the one cannot be separated from the other.

Rather, it is the logic and clarity of the biblical gospel that make the incarnation and Christ's presence a mystery. It can be clearly understood and explained, but not fully understood or explained.

31 Science still struggles with it, and likely always will.

32 Are people committed to Gnostic, Pelagian, and Arminian ideas because they are convinced that the mystery of the gospel is its abstract, other-worldly character that has been spiritualized by their own Pagan habits? Nevin argues that the real mystery issues out of its concrete, this-worldly reality, not some airy-fairy, other-worldly spirituality.

Christ's life is one and undivided, whole, and complete, and only in its wholeness and completeness is it able to actually communicate God's grace to men, and that communication comes through His mediatorial role. To be in real union with Christ the mediator, we must be in union with the whole of Christ. The consideration or presence of the idea of Christ's divinity is not enough. The wholeness of His life includes His humanity as a necessary part of its constitution and the actualizing element for His mediation. Christ can mediate salvation to us precisely because of His human nature. Apart from His human nature, He could not mediate salvation to human beings. We are not at liberty to exclude His humanity by supposing that only His soul is joined with His people, and not His body.[33]

Every abstraction of this sort will necessarily lead to error when pursued logically and consistently. Body and soul are both essential for a true human life. And if Christ's life is to be in us at all in a real way, it is impossible to avoid the conclusion that it must be in us in both His humanity and His divinity, in Spirit and in flesh, because they exist in hypostatic union. In fact, both forms of existence constitute the wholeness of the same living nature. And the extension of this nature by the power of the Spirit to the soul of the believer necessarily involves the reproduction of the holistic wholeness of Christ's life in the regenerate person.

---

33 Christ's soul cannot be extracted from his body any more than ours can be. Soul and body only exist in unity.

CHAPTER **IV**

The Biblical Argument

THE INCARNATION

The Key to All God's Works and Ways

"The Word became flesh!" (John 1:14). In this simple but sublime phrase, we have the whole gospel. From the glorious light of Christ which bursts into our view, everything that is dark and chaotic becomes radiant with the bright majesty and everlasting wholeness of truth itself. The incarnation is the key that unlocks the meaning of God's revelation in Christ.

It is the key that unlocks the meaning of all God's works, and brings to light the truth of the universe. The mystery of humanity, existing at the apex of the vast organic pyramid, is understood and solved by the wholeness of the fact of the incarnation. Nature and Revelation, the world and Christianity, spring from the same divine Mind. They are not two different life systems joined together in a mechanical or abstract way. They comprise a single whole, harmonious with itself in all its parts—a *uni*verse. Like soul and body they always exist together in unity. The sense of the one is necessarily included and comprehended in the sense of the other. The mystery of the new creation must involve the ultimate mystery of the old creation, and the key that serves to unlock the meaning of the new creation, must serve to unlock the innermost secret of the old creation.

Relation of Christ to Humanity

The incarnation of Jesus Christ as the second Person of the Trinity is the great central, objective fact of the world. It is this magnificent thought on which Heinrich Steffens[1] bases his system of Anthropology, that Man is to be viewed, "as the end of a boundless Past, the center of a boundless Present, and the beginning of a boundless Future." This is most certainly true of Him who is the center of humanity itself, the Son of Man, revealed in the Person of Jesus Christ. All nature and all previous history unite to form one grand, universal testimony of His presence. Everything has ultimate significance and wholeness only in His person. All facts must therefore be interpreted in the light of Christ.

Through all lower forms of existence, nature continuously looks up to the perfection of humanity. The inorganic struggles towards the organic, the plant towards the animal, and the animal nature, improving upon itself from one order of life to another, rests not till it is superseded finally by the human. Thus, everything converges towards the same end or purpose, each inferior nature foreshadowing that which is to follow, till the vast system becomes symmetrical and full, in a form of perfection which may be said to include at last and mirror the true sense of the whole.[2]

Note

It is hardly necessary to say, that the idea here presented implies no possibility whatever of the regular development on the part of any lower forms (creatures) of existence upwards to the sphere of that which stands above it. This thought has been justly repudiated by the Christian world as contrary to all revelation and religion, exhibited

---

1   Steffens was a "Philosophers of Nature," and a friend and adherent of Schelling and of Schleiermacher. More than either of these two thinkers he was acquainted with the discoveries of Modern science, and was thus able to correct the imaginative speculations of Schelling. He believed that Individualization is the main principle of nature and intellectual life. As organisms rise higher in the scale of development, the sharper and more distinct their features become, and the more unique their individualities. He worked to deduce this principle from his knowledge of geology, in contrast to Lorenz Oken, who developed the same theory on biological grounds. His influence was considerable, and both Schelling and Schleiermacher modified their theories in deference to his scientific deductions.

2   This is a statement of teleology: the belief that certain phenomena are best explained in terms of purpose rather than cause.

with extensive consideration by the author of the little volume entitled *Vestiges of Creation*.[3] It shows that evolution contradicts all sound philosophy.

The process of growth and historical development can never evolve from any form of existence more than was actually involved in it from the beginning.[4] But who can imagine that the life of the animal is ever potentially present in the life of the plant. To say that the law of existence in the one case is made to include at a certain point more than was comprehended in it before is only to play with words because a new life-form to appear must be a new creation. There is no intelligible sense whatever that it could be the product or birth of what existed previously. The difference between animals and man is just as broad as that between animals and plants. There is an impassable gulf between the two forms of existence, which nothing short of a new creation can ever bridge.

But all this has nothing to do with the view presented here. It is simply affirmed here that the lower forms of existence look prophetically towards those which are above them. They cannot be said in any sense to carry the higher forms of existence in their womb, though they foreshadow their presence. And in this way they always find their own meaning and wholeness in something beyond themselves. The evidence of this is so plain that the fact will not be called in question by anyone who has even the most general acquaintance with the actual constitution of the world and sufficient knowledge of Scripture.

Without man (humanity) the entire world would be shorn of its meaning. It is by the medium of human personality that the world becomes transparent with thought and finds significance. The world

---

3   V*estiges of the Natural History of Creation* is a unique work of speculative natural history published anonymously in England in 1844. It brought together various ideas of stellar evolution with the progressive transmutation of species in an accessible narrative which tied together numerous scientific theories of the age.

Vestiges was initially well received by Victorian society and became an international bestseller, but its unorthodox themes contradicted the natural theology fashionable at the time and were reviled by clergymen—as well as by scientists who readily found fault with it. Prince Albert read it aloud to Queen Victoria in 1845. Vestiges caused a shift in popular opinion which Charles Darwin believed prepared the public mind for the scientific theories of evolution by natural selection which followed from the publication of *On the Origin of Species* in 1859. In spite of its errors, it provided a popular repudiation of the theory of evolution.

4   Nevin anticipated the work of Werner Gitt, http://www.talkorigins.org/faqs/information/gitt.html

becomes self-conscious in man. Everything is dark until it becomes an object of human consciousness. Then shines the light of human reason. Man is the center of nature, who holds the key to all its mysteries. Man in his wholeness binds its manifold parts into one, and makes them complete as a single organic whole. And whence comes the wholeness of man?

As man is to nature in this way, Christ is to man. Humanity itself cannot be complete until subsumed in the wholeness of the Person of Christ. The world includes in its very constitution a struggle towards its wholeness, and cannot rest till this end is attained. Humanity longs for its true and real union with God as the necessary complement and consummation of its own life. The wholeness it seeks to embody can never be fully actualized in any other way.

The incarnation of Christ was the beginning of the completion and wholeness of humanity. Christ is the true ideal, the universal man, the archetype of human perfection. In Christ is the highest fulfillment of human life, which is at the same time the crowning significance of the world. In Christ, human consciousness, the medium through which light and order for growth and maturity in this world, finds its wholeness, from which new life pours forth to renew the world. Man finds himself in God, and awakens to the full capacity and maturity of his own being. Only then can he find rest in fullness and freedom, like God's eternal Sabbath, on the absolute ground of life itself.[5]

The one only medium of the holistic wholeness of life that can commune with God is the Person and mystery of the incarnation of the man Christ Jesus. The incarnation of humanity in Christ, or of Christ in humanity, or Christian union, completes the creation of God's world. The objectivity of the world anticipates the subjectivity of this realization, as the subjectivity of men yearns for union with the objectivity of the world for the wholeness and peace that alone can satisfy its central purpose of existence. Everything contributes to the one story of God's revelation in Christ.

History Always Looks to the Same Center

---

5   God's eternal Sabbath stands outside of time itself. See: Exodus 22:30; Leviticus 9:1; 12:3; 14:10,23; 15:14,29; 22:27; 23:36,39; Numbers 6:10; 7:54; 29:35; 1 Kings 8:66; 12:32,33; 2 Chronicles 7:9; 29:17; Nehemiah 8:18; Ezekiel 43:27; Luke 1:59; Acts 7:8; Philippians 3:5.

History is also drawn towards the same point of fulfillment. History, like nature, is one vast testimony of the revelation of God in Christ from beginning to end for those who have eyes to see it. How could it be otherwise? Unity in Christ has been the teleological goal of the world from creation. History, God's story, is the process by which this goal is brought forward in compliance to God's declarations through miraculous events and natural developments to its appointed end.

The introduction of sin—itself a world-fact, inseparably incorporated with this process almost from its start, and violently turning all humanity in a false direction—only served to add a deeper emphasis to the meaning of life. The necessity of a real union with Christ became a necessity at the same time that the Fall created a loud cry for atonement from humanity suffering for sin. The development of this need is the great burden of history, onward from the Fall.

Everything in Scripture before Christ had a prophetic reference to the coming of Christ. The whole creation groaned and travailed in pain together, reaching forward with earnest expectation to the hour of deliverance. Not only Judaism, but Paganism—and indeed, all humanity anticipated the great event of Christ's incarnation and the wholeness of humanity in Christ. Both Judaism and Paganism, directly or indirectly, anticipated Christ from different perspectives, hoping for the same end—union with God. Both found their inmost meaning of everything revealed and verified in Christ.[6]

Paganism is Negatively Prophetical of Christ

Paganism is, of course, essentially false in all its forms. But falsehood always involves some truth, which it caricatures, but from which at the same time it draws its life. In the past it has been quite popular for a superficial understanding of infidelity to attempt to bring the mysteries of Christianity into discredit by comparing them with the

---

6   "Unity coming through the whole disposition of our Lord Jesus Christ, and all things are recapitulated therein." —Ireneus. Dorner's comments are interesting on this point, in the Introduction to his *Christologie*, or *History of the Doctrine of Christ's Person*. Also, the *Introduction to the Doctrine of the Trinity in its Historical Development*, by G. A. Mem, 1844, is also a most able and excellent work which may be compared advantageously to the Introduction to the large, very learned, but less orthodox work of Baur on the same subject.

mythological dreams and traditions of the heathen world. But, it may be trusted, that time has come to an end.[7]

Christianity as the absolute universal religion must take up into itself and exhibit in a perfect (holistically whole) form, the various fragments and rudiments of truth that are contained in all Pagan religions. It is not a doctrine, but the unfolding divine fact of God's revelation in Christ, into which all previous religious tendencies and developments are ultimately understood and unified in their proper purpose.

All of life, however defective and seemingly monstrous, finds its truest meaning and value only as analogies and faulty approximations to the wholeness of unity in God. "But when that which is perfect is come, then that which is in part shall be done away" (1 Cor. 13:10). What is imperfect will serve to authenticate and magnify the perfection and wholeness of God in Christ. In the light of Christ the ancient religions will serve in this way, both Oriental and Western. They all conspire to bear testimony in favor of Christ, falling down as it were before Him, and presenting unto Him gifts, "gold and frankincense and myrrh" (Matt. 2:11).

Brahmanism, Buddhism, Parsism (Zoroastrianism), the religion of Egypt (Islam), and the religion of Greece (Greek philosophy and Mythology), each in its own way look ever in the same direction, and will be ultimately heard to utter the same story. They will one day all be understood to anticipate in one way or another human wholeness that is found only in Christ. For all of them proclaim the greatest desire of humanity: *to be in true union with God*. And the character of each of them is determined by the errors they make as they try to bring this great life problem to its proper resolution. These attempts toward such unity will ultimately simply fall away because the light of Christ will reveal their contradictions and inabilities.

The *Trimurti*,[8] or pantheistic triad of India, falls immeasurably short of the robust fullness of the Christian Trinity. The incarnation of

---

7   We can trust that the original revelation of God to Adam in the Garden was the revelation of true religion, which deteriorated into the various mythologies following the Fall. In addition, the fracturing of human unity following the Tower of Babel incident further contributed to the spread of Paganism around the world.

8   The *Trimūrti* is the triple deity of supreme divinity in Hinduism in which the cosmic functions of creation, maintenance, and destruction are personified as a triad of deities, typically Brahma the creator, Vishnu the preserver, and Shiva the destroyer. - https://en.wikipedia.org/wiki/Trimurti.

Vishnu cannot go beyond the character of a transient phantasm, an intellectual abstraction. Mithras, Osiris, the idea of a wrestling, suffering, redeeming god, Apollo among the Greeks, or Hercules, forcing his way to Olympus, all are found to be utterly helpless conceptions with regard to the purpose they are brought forward to serve. Their various solutions to the need for human wholeness always remain inadequate and disproportionate to the reality of the holistic wholeness of humanity in God that they struggle to reach.

They all begin and end in an impossible dualism. An impassable gulf continues to separate the nature of man (humanity) from the God of nature (divinity). Only in Christ and only by the Trinity are these two elements of human wholeness held in hypostatic unity. But only through the progressive revelation of God in Christ can the significance of all of this become more clear and full.[9] Under all its various manifestations, Paganism may be regarded as the unsuccessful effort of humanity apart from Christ to solve this problem. It's complete solution is being revealed in the Person of Christ as He establishes the unity of humanity with God. Christianity provides the key that interprets and correctly contextualizes this ancient mystery by establishing that very unity in Christ. All false religions simply prepare the way by anticipating the need for wholeness and demonstrating their inability to provide it. They foreshadow true union with God, and serve to authenticate it as it comes in fullness.

Judaism's Preparation for His Coming

From its beginning, Judaism has had respect to the coming of Messiah—Christ. The preparation of the heathen world, on the other hand, has only been only negative, in the sense that it seeks the unity *without* the only real Unifier. The religion of the Old Testament, from the time of Adam to the time of John the Baptist, was based on and issued out of a supernatural revelation that not only foreshadowed the anticipated fact of the incarnation, but was directly open to its manifestation and fulfillment. It is not simply the necessity of union with God found in its incessant cry for redemption and salvation revealed in both the Hebrew Scriptures and in the broader history of the world.

---

9   For more on this, see *Peter's Vision of Christ's Purpose in First Peter*, by Phillip A. Ross, Pilgrim Platform, Marietta, Ohio, 2011.

But the Hebrews took more seriously than others the effort to atone for their sin as a way to establish such union in their society.

Various heathen efforts have attempted to defy and/or deny their humanity or they sought for divinity, but have not, cannot, and will not find unity apart from the Trinitarian Godhead, of whom Jesus Christ is the second Person. In the religion of the Old Testament, God descended to man, and held out for his consideration the promise of the only real union of humanity with God, as the culmination of the final purpose of the gracious economy Scripture introduced. But the dispensation of the Old Testament did not culminate in this real union. But over time, God condescended to provide a series of increasingly rich and full covenants that provided an increasingly better vision of that unity, and at the same time revealed the human inability to accomplish what God has demanded.

But in the final analysis the Old Testament dispensation could only provide the outward trappings because the One in whom such unity must inhere had not yet manifested in the flesh to reveal the archetypal Son of Man, the second Person of the Trinity and the Holy Spirit, the third Person to be bound in unity with God the Father.

The wall of partition that separated the divine from the human could not be broken down apart from the incarnation of the Son and the dispensation of the Spirit. The tabernacle of the Most High was among men, but God in whom the holistic wholeness and holiness of humanity inheres required the manifestation of the Son and the Spirit in human history. Apart from this, God was, so to speak, between the cherubim and behind the veil. He spoke through dreams, and visions, in fits and starts, and in words of prophecy that grew increasingly full and distinct. But in the final analysis the Old Testament revelation of God was a revelation of God *to* man, and not a revelation of God *in* man, which provides the way for God in Christ to become truly and fully known.

The whole process of revelation constantly tends towards this ultimate end and purpose as its necessary consummation. The meaning of the entire world and existence itself is found only in reference to Christ. Not only did the Old Testament contain particular types and particular prophecies of the incarnation of Messiah Christ, the whole of the Old Testament itself is one vast and continuous prophecy of the fullness of this revelation. The Old Testament was itself the voice of one crying in the wilderness, "prepare ye the way of the Lord, make straight in the desert a highway for our God!"

The Gospel was in the womb of the Old Testament, growing and preparing for birth. All the great truths which have been brought to light by Christ were more or less foreshadowed in its pages, growing gradually and ripening for the birth towards which they labored, and to which they finally attained in the Person of Christ manifest in flesh. Without Christianity, Judaism would have no meaning or purpose. Judaism became real to the world only as it lost itself in Christ. Its loss became the world's gain, as the Seed became the Vine.

Similarly, Christianity will become real to the world only by losing itself in Christ. The outer trappings of religious paraphernalia and the barnacles of tradition must give way, must be lost for the world to find its holistic wholeness and holiness in Christ alone, who is Himself the new dispensation, and the Fruit of the Vine of the Seed. The law could make nothing perfect apart from Christ and the fullness of the manifest Godhead. Everything and all history has served only to harbinger the advent of the Messiah, and to proclaim His presence once He had come. Everything and all history has foreshadowed and foretoken the mystery of the incarnation of the textured God of grace and judgment, who alone provides the fusion of signs and the reality of their significance. Jesus Christ is the fusion of language and reality in the mind of man, the wholeness of humanity.

Here then, we reach the central fact of the constitution of the world, which is both ultimate and primal. All nature and all history are consciously flowing towards it, as the source of their principle and ground, and as their true and proper end/purpose. The incarnation, by which divinity and humanity are consciously united in Christ and made one in a real and abiding way, provides the reality of all communication, because Christ Himself is the integrity of language and reality, where meaning and reality are fused in the crucible of the holistic wholeness of life. The mystery of the universe is unveiled in the Person of Jesus Christ.

Section II

The New Creation

Relationship of Christianity to Previous Life

As we have now seen, Christianity has an important relationship with the order of the world as it existed before Christ, particularly to Judaism, but also to all religions. Some of the early heresies pretended to magnify Christianity by denying its historical connections. They suggested that the whole state of the world as it stood previously had been bad, and bad only, and that the world could contribute nothing to the glory of the Gospel. They denied any affinity whatever between the new creation in Christ and older orders of life.

Christianity must be understood as an entirely new order of life, come from heaven in broad, full antithesis, not only to nature, but also to the whole previous course of human history. Judaism must also fade, or rather in this special case, what is salvageable of Judaism by Christ, needs to be integrated into Christianity, and the rest put in museums for educational purposes. It is not that Judaism is an inferior revelation of God, but that it is the placenta of Jesus Christ. The Child has been born, and to continue to hold on to the placenta in the light of Christ is contraindicated. And to reject the Child in favor of the placenta is monstrous!

Yes, the history of Judaism is more significant than most histories, but it is still history—dead and gone. Yes, it was formative. Yes, it was foundational. Yes, it should not be forgotten, nor should any history be forgotten. But it is well past time to stop performing Cardiopulmonary Resuscitation (CPR) on the dead corpse of history, as if the world itself did not die with Christ. Indeed, Christ's salvation of the world requires the resurrection of the world, and the world cannot be resurrected by frightened, dispirited people pounding on the dead chest of history. We all must let bygones be bygones, and care for the Child before us. Raise the Child to know that he bears the name of his Father, and that he is to wear it with honor and respect.

To be real and true—"authentic" is the contemporary word—and to solve the great problem of life, the mystery must connect with the constitution and course of the world in its previous, historic condition. And it does! Christianity does not provide a violent rupture with nature or history, but fulfills and completes both nature and history. And in so doing, it provides the central and most intimate sense of both. Neither nature nor history could be complete without the presence and/or union of God in Christ—the Christian mystery. Both find their own true purpose, consummation and end in Christ.

The Gnostic error of abstract spirituality that denies or ignores either the humanity or the divinity of the hypostatic union, like all error, occludes some aspect of the truth, in this case a central aspect. The ancient Ebionites[1] denied the divinity of Christ. It especially appealed to the Jewish mind and began in the early church. It saw the Person of Jesus as a continuation of the old creation, in a particularly high form that made it necessary to continue the religion of the Old Testament. Without the new creation of regeneration the mystery was lost. The chasm between the divine and human was left unbridged. Christ was understood to be a mere man.

Against this Gnostic, Ebionitic heresy, the heresy of Gnostic Arianism was right to rebel, but it went too far by denying the humanity of Christ. Christ is not only the end of the old order of creation, and its necessary complement and completion, but He is also the principle of a new order of creation, in which the old simply cannot come. Again, "but when the perfect comes, the partial will pass away." (1 Cor. 13:10). What is partial cannot enter the realm of wholeness.

"And the Word became flesh and dwelt among us" (John 1:14). This is a greater truth than the continuation of the old order can contain. This is a fact that differs from all ordinary facts and events, not simply by transcending them in importance, but by being of another order altogether.[2]

---

1   The Ebionites regarded Jesus as the Messiah, but insisted on the necessity of following Jewish religious law and rites. They used only one of the Jewish Gospels, revered *James the Just* and rejected Paul of Tarsus as an apostate from the Law.
2   See footnote 40, p. 41.

Christianity, or the union of humanity in Christ, is the whole which is greater than its constitutive parts. As such, it is not the result or product of anything in the world, nor in the constitution of the world before its manifestation. Rather, the advent of Christ as the archetypal perfection of humanity is the introduction of a new power, a new quality of the world entirely. From that time forward Jesus Christ is the wholeness in whom all meaning and signification manifestly exist. When Jesus Christ unleashed the Holy Spirit, the revelation of God in Christ became central in the progress of the world's history. This cannot be over emphasized.

Compare Christ with any other fact of true world-historical importance, for instance the work of Plato or Aristotle and their respective philosophies, or the rise and fall of Rome, etc. In these cases, much depended on the minds of various men. Empires were born and fell, and for their duration they were exceedingly great. But there was no new creation in any of it. Plato, Aristotle, and the Caesars were all simply the products of previous history. The lives, ideas, and philosophies of these people were nothing more the natural development of the world.

Historical, and yet Supernatural and New

But Jesus Christ was not a product of the past. If anything, He is a product of the future realization of the holistic wholeness He embodies —and of God's decree. The ancient Jewish prophets foretold of His coming, and prepared the way for His approach. But the wholeness of humanity in Christ is not composed of any part of the world. The things of the world cannot add up to it. The incarnation was not powered by the world or by anything in the world, mineral, vegetable, animal, historical, or spiritual. The fact of Jesus Christ cannot be evolved from the world.

Here was a fact, which even the Old Testament could not generate. The ancients priests and prophets could only hope and pray that God would send Messiah. All of the theophanies and miracles of the Old Testament could furnish no parallel to the glory of Christ. For the revelation of the supernatural under the Old Testament was always imposed by God, it did not and could not arise from within the hearts of men. It could never enjoy the true unity of humanity and divinity because its purpose was to prepare not to fulfill. What is supernatural is by definition above and/or beyond nature. The only true and pure hypostatic union of God in Christ was not available until the Godhead had shown his face(s). Of course, God greatly influenced the process of history and the development of human culture through instruction, occasion, and even motive. But God's influence did not and could not do more than those who were influenced could do. Influence can change direction, but not create a new creation.

A Divine Creation in the World

But in the Person and wholeness of Christ the world becomes different. In Christ, the supernatural transforms the nature of the heart by completing it, by making it whole, by mending the brokenness of its parts. In Christ, the supernatural enters the heart, it subsumes the heart by providing it with a new center that includes humanity and touches God. The everlasting Word, wholly unknown apart from Christ, descended into the actual process of human history, giving history and the people who compose it a wholeness previously unknown. The wholeness of Christ incarnate then sent the Spirit of wholeness to be the principle and law of a new creation in Christ, as glorious and unique as God's creation in Genesis.

It is no mere figure of speech that Christ brings new life. Nor may we say of this new life that it is simply a moral improvement, a new way of thinking or an improved character. Christ provides no revolution of the old, no mere historical improvement of the past, not merely some rearrangement or new order of the world. Rather, He births something entirely new. He constitutes a measure of divinity into the very organism of the world itself.

From this perspective the incarnation parallels the creation of the world, when "the universe was created by the word of God, so that what is seen was not made out of things that are visible" (Heb. 11:3). As the creation of man on the sixth day brought a measure of perfection to what had come before, and while man was created from the dust of the earth, he was not a product or result of the earth. And in the fullness of time, God endowed the crown of creation—Man—with a greater perfection, a greater wholeness. The Word itself, by which the heavens and the earth were created, was made flesh, and dwelt among us. He came, not up from the earth, but down from heaven, not to judge humanity by earthly standards, but to raise humanity up to heavenly standards.

Judaism, the Shadow of What has Become Real in Christ

On the basis of the truths here affirmed, the unity of humanity in Christ—the fullness and fruit of Christian unity—attains the greatest reality and truth ever known to the world from any other perspective. Nature itself cannot compare because it is not eternal. Perfection arises only through God in Christ, who has now taken up residence in the wholeness of humanity, actualized in the mystery of the incarnation.

Yet, humanity is not God, nor does humanity become God or Christ. All flesh is grass, only the word of the Lord endures forever. The fashion of the world is always passing away. Only Jesus Christ is "the same, yesterday, today, and forever" (Heb. 13:8). There is no other principle of unity, reality or stability in God's creation. So, all history becomes true, full, complete and whole only in Christ.

This is most instructively exemplified in the religion of the Old Testament. It was altogether *of* God, *given* by God *for* God's purposes. It was for "the adoption, the glory, the covenants, the giving of the law, the worship, and the promises" (Rom. 9:4). The Old Testament provides the origin of humanity, and the history of the lineage of the flesh from whence Christ sprang. But still, we are expressly taught that it is related to the New Testament only as a shadow of the substance it represents. And this is to be understood, not simply of its types and ceremonies as such, but holds in full force of its whole constitution, moral as well as ceremonial.

Its truth was not in itself, but in a different order altogether and to which it could only point. The reality of the Old Testament was not absolute, but in all respects relative only. Its order was temporary. It made nothing perfect. It was merely a picture of good things to come. The Epistle to the Romans and the Epistle to the Hebrews, each in its own way, are full of this idea. Therefore, we cannot say that the New Testament is an extension or enlargement of the Old. "For the law was given through Moses; grace and truth came through Jesus Christ" (John 1:17).

Among all the prophets of the Old Testament, none was greater than John the Baptist. And yet we are assured in Luke 7:28 that the "least in the kingdom of God is greater than he." All previous revelations were only an approach to the truth manifested in Christ. "Long ago, at many times and in many ways, God spoke to our fathers by the prophets, but in these last days he has spoken to us by his Son, whom he appointed the heir of all things, through whom also he created the world. He is the radiance of the glory of God and the exact imprint of his nature, and he upholds the universe by the word of his power" (Heb. 1:1-3). Everything before Christ was only relative, but in Christ we have God absolutely "manifested in the flesh" (1 Tim. 3:16).

Christianity is the Absolute Truth

Christ is the only absolute Prophet, (Deut. 18:18, 19. Acts 3:22, 23) as He is the only absolute Priest (Heb. 8:4, 5). The relationship of God to the patriarchs and saints of the Old Testament generally wholly came short of the relationship in which He now stands to His people, as the God and Father of our Lord Jesus Christ. Their spiritual life, their union with God, their covenant privileges, all had an unreal, unsubstantial character compared with the parallel grace of the gospel. The Old Testament barely provided an approximation to the grace of the New Testament, or rather, the actual presence of grace.[3]

The full reality of religion, which is the union of divinity and humanity, the revelation of God *in* man and not simply *to* him, was only foreshadowed in the Old Testament. Its sacraments merely anticipated the presence of God, they were not sacraments that contained and revealed God's presence. Its salvation anticipated and promised more than it presented in fact. Old Testament salvation became real only in Christ. We are told that the patriarchs of the law could not be made perfect (Heb. 11:13, 39, 40) before His appearance. The dispensation of the Holy Spirit has its origin in the wholeness of the Person of Christ, (Luke 1:35, 3:22. John3:34,) and could not reveal itself in the world until He was glorified (John 7:39).

Christ's Person is the Great Miracle by which His Mission Authenticates Itself

The great argument for the truth of Christianity is the Person of Jesus Himself exhibited in the faith of the church in history. The incarnation is the fact of all facts that itself authenticates all truth in the world. Authentication requires authority, and Christ has it all. The miracle of Christianity is the new creation in which it starts. Everything else is simply the product and expression of the fullness of Christ's life.

---

3   "Christianity is nothing, if it be not the actualization and substantiation of a union, which was before, to a great extent, prophetical and ideal." F. D. Maurice.

Does this mean that all of the various miracles of Christ in Scripture are not miraculous? No. It simply means that they are explained by the character of Christ, the God-Man. The only inexplicable miracle is the fact of God's new creation in Christ, which is entirely the result of God's grace. Once we accept the fact of the gracious miracle of the new creation, everything else derives its logical explanation from the fact of Christ. And logic is a natural phenomenon of the world.

Nothing is so ordinary as the supernatural character of Christ's Person. Jesus Christ authenticates Himself through the testimony of the Father and the Spirit. All other credentials are of secondary value, for what on earth can testify to the reality of heaven? He is Himself the principle and ground, the alpha and omega of all truth.

Section III

The Second Adam

Christ is the principle of new life. To be so in truth He must be incorporated[1] into the innermost life or subjectivity of believers. As we have seen, the world centers in man, and everything else, out to the farthest reaches of the universe, takes its form and complexion from the character of man's living, spiritual heart. What does it mean that man is the center of the universe? It means that human consciousness is the means by which that center is defined and experienced. In order for human consciousness to be organically related to the world in a consistent, significant, and authentic way, the Word or Logos needed to consciously manifest in the flesh. That manifestation would then demonstrate the integrity between God's Word and the world. In this way, God guaranteed and Christ proved the correlation between the sign and the thing signified, between language and reality. The new creation in Christ reveals itself in the wholeness of humanity. And Christ becomes the second Adam or the head and archetype of the wholeness of humanity.

Christ a Real Man

The manhood of Christ is real. His incarnation was no mere theophany, no transient wonder, no illusion exhibited to the senses.

> "Christ, the Son of God, became man by taking to himself a true body and a reasonable soul, being conceived by the power of the Holy Spirit in the womb of the Virgin Mary, of her substance, and born of her, yet without sin" (*Westminster Larger Catechism*, Question 37).

---

1   Incorporate: formed or united into a whole.

John makes it the mark of Antichrist to call this in question (1 John 4:3, 2 John 7.) The character, position, and authority which Christ took upon Himself was truly and fully the character, position, and authority of Adam. And these things were not fastened onto Him externally like some kind of appendage. Rather, the bond was subjective, whole and complete. As the Early Church Fathers said: Christ has two natures, but is one whole and undivided Person.

Christ, however, was not simply a descendant of Adam, and a brother of the human family, like all other men who have been born since Adam. In order for Christ to have two natures, His lineage must include both human and divine DNA, so to speak. From His supernatural conception by the Holy Spirit came His natural birth from the womb of Mary. The story of the immaculate conception conveys this important and essential truth. He took human nature upon Himself in order to raise humanity into a higher degree of wholeness and perfection by uniting human nature with the character of God, not perfectly, but adequately. And in this way, Christ became the root or seed of new life for the whole human race.

His assumption of humanity was universal and not merely particular.[2] The Word became *flesh*. It did not merely become a single individual as one among many, but it became the flesh of humanity in its universal wholeness.[3] How else could Christ be the principle of universal life, the origin of a new order of existence for the human world? How else could the value of His mediatorial work be given to us in a real way, by a true imputation, and not merely as an imaginary legal or moral fiction?

The entire plan of Christian salvation requires and assumes this understanding of the incarnation and no other, beginning to end. To make Christ's incarnation merely an individual case is to turn Christianity into a mere theophany, where God would communicate with people like people communicate with each other, rather than fusing himself to the subjectivity of believers in order to change their consti-

---

2   "The justice of God requires that the same human nature which hath sinned, should likewise make satisfaction for sin." (*Heidelberg Catechism*, Question 16.) To be effective at all, the redemption must go as deep as the curse. So Christ united with human nature as such. Men are sinners, because the general life of humanity has become corrupt. Their nature then must be restored as the only ground on which it is possible for them to be saved. Thus, salvation is in Christ.

3   Not as one among many, but as the oneness or wholeness of the many.

tutional identities such that new lives are created. To conceive of salvation to be like the relationship between a king and his subject, or like the relationship of Adam as the federal head of his posterity, is to limit it to its historical character. As an historical fact, salvation is a cold, abstract piece of datum. which altogether overthrows the reality, centrality and veracity of this doctrine.[4]

His Humanity as Generic or Universal

Christ became man, not for Himself but for the human race, to circumvent the extinction of the human race. To do this, He took our sin upon Himself as His own to suffer God's just punishment for our sin—death and extinction. Extinction was necessary because Adam's sin applied to humanity as a kind or species. In this way Christ conquered death for humanity, not merely for individual people. Because Adam's sin issued, not from his actions but from his character, Christ needed to lift that fallen human character into everlasting union with God. The character of Adam as the human archetype needed to be changed—fixed, healed, made whole—in the same way that sin had damaged it. Thus, salvation in Christ provides a new wholeness for humanity in unity with God Himself. To do this, Christ became the new federal head and archetype of humanity as a whole and sum (ανακεφαλαιώσεις τών πάντων—*summarizing everything*) in a more full and comprehensive sense than this could ever be said of Adam.

---

4   "If Christ were only a man, as one along with and among many others, it would be indeed incomprehensible, how what he has suffered and done could be of any essential weight for mankind in general; he could only exert an influence by his doctrine and example. But he is to be viewed in fact, apart from his divine nature, as the man, that is, as realizing the absolute idea of humanity, and thus carrying it in himself potentially in the way of the spirit, as truly as Adam did in a corporeal way. This character of Christ's human nature is designated in divinity by the term *impersonalitas*; and we find even Philo, with an inward feeling of the deep truth, describing the Logos as τόν χατ' άλήζειαν άνζξωπον, that is *the idea of man*, the human ideal. In this general view, the Redeemer bears a twofold representative character; first, as he takes the place of sinful men, carrying their grief in his grief, as an offering for the sins of the world; and then again as fulfilling absolute righteousness and holiness in himself, so that the believer has not to produce them afterward anew, but receives them in germ along with the Spirit of Christ. The first is the *obedientia passiva* of theology, the last the *obedientia activa*." (Olshausen *Comm. in Rom.* v., 15.)

Parallel Between Christ and Adam

Paul in particular is very clear and very forthright in the representation of this federal or generic (universal) character on the part of Christ. He makes His relationship to the human race parallel to that of its natural head. Adam is τύπος τού μέλλοντος (*a type of the future*, Rom. 5:14), and Christ is ο έσχατος (*the ultimate,* 1 Cor. 15:45). In Rom. 5:12-19, they are compared together at length from this perspective.

Adam is exhibited, on the one hand, as the head of our human race in its fallen character. "Therefore, just as sin came into the world through one man, and death through sin, and so death spread to all men because all sinned" (Rom. 5:12). All were constituted sinners, included in Adam's sin by that first act of disobedience. All sinned in Adam and fell with him in his first transgression. He stood as their archetype and federal head because he was their true organic head. *In Adam*, according to the just affirmation of Augustine, *omnes tunc peccaverunt, quando in ejus natura adhuc omnes ille unus fuerunt (all who sinned were in their nature as that one man was).*

In all this, the apostle tells us, He was the "figure of him that was to come" (Rom. 5:14). Indeed, the gift of life in Christ more than overcomes the death and condemnation introduced by Adam. But the general structure of the relationship in the two heads is the same.

Christ is the new federal head and representative of humanity as a whole, or of the wholeness of humanity. "For if, because of one man's trespass, death reigned through that one man, much more will those who receive the abundance of grace and the free gift of righteousness reign in life through the one man Jesus Christ" (Rom 5:17). The imputation of Christ's obedience is not a mere imposition upon an unwilling or unconscious humanity, but includes a requisite change of character such that the individual becomes conscious, willing, eager. This subjective element distorts the parallel between them that grounds it in a real community of life. As the world fell in Adam organically, it is made to rise in Christ organically through the Person of Christ into a new spiritual (whole, holistic) life.

It is strange that those who hold the Augustinian view of Adam's organic union with his posterity as the only basis that can properly support the doctrine of original sin, should not feel the necessity of the same kind of organic union with Christ to be the indispensable condition regarding his salvation. Pelagianism, which sees only an outward,

abstract, moral connection between Adam and his posterity, recognizes in the race only an aggregation of single and separate units,
mechanically brought together.[5] Thus, Pelagianism consistently joins
hands with Rationalism to provide an abstract, theoretical understanding of the relationship of Christ to His church, which makes it into a
connection of mere moral influence. And in doing so, it shows itself as
superficial and as false as Socianism, Arminianism, Baptisticism,[6] Rationalism, etc.

The same parallel is found in First Corinthians. 1 Cor. 15:21, 22,
45–49: "For as in Adam all die, so also in Christ shall all be made alive."
The reference connects immediately to natural death and the resurrection of the body, but that is only one aspect of the death and life
contrasted in salvation in Christ. "The first man Adam became a living
being"; the last Adam became a life-giving spirit" (1 Cor. 15:45). By
our natural birth we are inserted into the life of Adam, and our spiritual birth provides a similar insertion into the life of Christ. In both
cases, the connection is inward and real because it is personally constitutional. The root of righteousness in Christ, corresponds to and
trumps the root of sin in Adam. The mystery of Adam, to quote an old
Rabbinic saying, is "the mystery of the Messiah."

---

5   More like marbles in a bag than the organic unity of parts in a biological entity.
6   Poetic license suggests that this indicates Baptistic theology.

Section IV

CHRISTIANITY A LIFE

Distinctive Nature of Christianity

Christ was not the founder of a mere religion or religious school, though it is of far greater eminence than those of Pythagoras, Plato, Moses, or anyone since. Yet, Christ was a teacher of truth—and more. Christianity is not a mere doctrine to be taught or learned like a system of philosophy or a rule of moral conduct. Rationalism always looks at the gospel in this way. As Moses made known more of the divine will than the world had understood before, so Christ is taken to be no more than a greater prophet of the same class or kind. But taking Christ this way fails to recognize the very thing that Christ provides, and wrongs His character.

The progressive revelation of God in Christ provides a true revelation of God throughout history. At Creation God truly revealed Himself in His Trinitarian fullness (Gen. 1:26-28). Moses' deliverance of the Law provided additional developmental texture for the revelation of God and the establishment of a godly culture on earth. So of course, Judaism provided continual advancement of the previous revelations such that it provided the vast expansion of truth, justice, and love that could be exhibited through the flawed and sinful character of humanity in Adam.[1]

The progressive order of revelation in the Old Testament and the New Testament was essentially the same. Each advance was not more than a kind of "report" that was received simply by the hearing of the ear.[2] This kind of revelation is always relative, never absolute. It never

---

1 These biblical advances provided for the development of natural science and technology over the long history of the world.
2 Both Judaism and science have a mechanical understanding of the world. Science

comes in any particular case to the full manifestation of the truth in its wholeness and completeness. Each advancing revelation simply adds to what had come before.

But with the advent of Christ we have a very different phenomenon. An entirely new kind of revelation bursts upon the world in the Person of Jesus Christ. He is the absolute truth itself, the wholeness of truth and revelation, who is personally present among men, and who incorporates Himself into their various lives. Christ Himself as the Person in whom hypostatic union dwells perfectly, provides the wholeness of humanity, which brings the whole of creation into the state of perfection. And wholeness is of a completely different order than the parts constituent thereof.[3] He is the substance, where all previous prophecy, even in its highest forms, had been only a shadow.

Unitarians (and Socinians generally) make much of Christ's holy example. He is understood as a great moral teacher who redeems us from our sins, they say, partly by His heavenly instructions, and partly by exhibiting Himself to us as a pattern of piety in His life and death. This, however, completely robs Him of His proper glory, significance, and function. At best it constitutes a return to Judaism, and the works-righteousness of the Jewish sacrificial system. Christianity is more than a mere model of goodness and virtue, though we concede that it is of the most perfect construction in this regard—even the very mirror of the divine will itself.

The Ebionetic Standpoint

It does not materially change the situation to make the gospel into an array of mere outward or moral power and influence. Many orthodox Christians come short of the truth in this regard altogether. They do not get beyond the old Ebionitic[4] perspective, but always understand Christianity to be nothing more than an improvement on the grace of the Jewish dispensation, and always see it as being in the same order or class, and not as an entirely new order of life.[5]

---

has its procedures and Judaism its sacrifices, which anyone can follow naturally.

3   See footnote 40, p. 41.

4   The Ebionites were a Jewish-Christian sect that insisted on the necessity of following Jewish religious law and rites, which they interpreted in light of Jesus' expounding of the Law. They regarded Jesus as the Messiah but not as divine.

5   Nevin used the word *grace* here, which is not wrong but he uses *life* in many other places to suggest the same idea. Christianity provides new life, not merely new grace.

It is commonly thought that Christianity provides greater light, enlarged opportunities, purer motives, a new supply of supernatural aids and provisions, and that these are the peculiar (unique) contributions of the New Covenant and constitute its commonly understood superiority over the Old. However, this perspective resolves Christian salvation into mere moral consideration, discipline, and/or influence. Indeed, all religion was understood in this way before Christ's incarnation. So, the error is understandable, though it is not acceptable.

If the whole Christian apparatus—including Christ's priestly work, the atonement, His intercession in heaven, and the gracious influences of His Spirit—is regarded as tools or helps to be assimilated by the natural man and nothing more, even though it is thought to work through a power that comes from beyond Himself, and even though the sinner enjoys a moral upgrade by this outward power, still at best the whole process remains parallel to the theory of Socianism by turning the actual work of redemption into a mere doctrine or example. At best, even this kind of understanding of Christianity makes it into no more than a mere exaltation of Judaism that continues to be bound by the limitations of Judaism. In such a case Christ is understood to be of the same class or order as Moses. Even if Christ is thought to be immeasurably greater than Moses, he would still be nothing more than a prophet in the same sense as Moses.[6]

In opposition to all this, we are arguing here that Christianity is a *life*. It is not a mechanical or logical rule or mode (way—ὁδός) of life simply, not something that can be reduced to mere practice—for that is the character of all morality.[7] Rather, life as it is defined by God in Christ is by its very nature and constitution the actual substance[8] and

---

6   This paragraph is critical to the understanding of Nevin's point. He is not opposed to the fact that Christ provides a moral upgrade to humanity. However, no moral upgrade can ever reach moral perfection because the order of perfection transcends the order of morality itself. Engaging Christ's moral upgrade is a good thing and it will help humanity immensely, but it misses the central point of Christ's incarnation. God could have sent another prophet with a sufficient message of moral upgrade. But that would have missed God's central purpose of the creation of Man (Adam, humanity)—to enjoy fellowship with God. Such fellowship requires, not merely the forgiveness of sin, but the restoration of human wholeness in Christ. This is the central point of the mystical presence of Christ.

7   Christianity is most certainly a kind of moral practice, but neither essentially nor merely so.

8   Not in the Greek philosophical sense of being the mere idea of a substratum abstractly conceived, but in a literal, organic sense of being the very life blood of a

wholeness of truth itself. This is the grand distinction made throughout this book. Thus, the reality of Christianity as life in Christ is
broadly separated from all other forms of religion that have or ever can
have claimed the attention of the world. "For the law was given
through Moses; grace and truth came through Jesus Christ" (John
1:17).

Testimony of John the Evangelist

Let us consider the view presented to us in the beginning of the
gospel of John. "The Word," that existed eternally with the Father,
that created the world, that had illuminated all the prophets—drawing
always nearer to men as the fullness of time approached for this last
revelation—now at length and in the Person of Jesus, "became flesh"
(John 1:1-18). He that had spoken to men in a mediated way in the
Old Testament, from a distance and through the prophets, has now
spoken immediately. Where God had spoken through the Mediator—
Christ—before, He has now sent the Mediator Himself to speak. Now
through regeneration "deep calls unto deep" (Psalm 42:7) as God the
Father speaks through God the Son to God the Holy Spirit, who
resides in the souls of believers.[9]

Life/Truth dwelt in Christ as an original and independent fountain, "For as the Father has life in himself, so he has granted the Son
also to have life in himself (John 5:26). As the Father created life, so the
Son creates new life. "And the life was the light of men" (John 1:4). In
this regard, God's light had revealed itself indirectly in human consciousness and by means of partial and relative representations of truth
from without, from outside of humanity, since the beginning of the
world. In this way the light shined into the darkness of sin and the
darkness, the sin, comprehended it not (John 1:5).

All of this was mere preparation for the great reality/mystery of
the incarnation. The preparation always and only points toward the
incarnation, and reveals its necessity. Here, in the incarnation, in
Christ, the self-subsisting wholeness of life itself entered into humanity
as a Person—Christ. The cry of ages, "Oh that you would rend the

---

living organism.

9   This is not a license to believe that every thought that occurs to you is from God.
     Great discernment must be acquired to keep us from confusing our own thoughts
     with God's communications. This has nothing to do with glossolalia or prediction,
     and everything to do with the correct understanding of God's Word.

heavens and come down, that the mountains might quake at your presence" (Is. 64:1), is met with a full, all-satisfying response—in Christ. The heavens themselves bow before Him. The everlasting doors fly open. The tabernacle of God is with man as never before. Humanity itself has become the *shekinah*[10] of glory in the Person of Immanuel, God with us.

The Truth in its absolute reality is revealed and accessible to the wholeness of humanity in the incarnate Word. "We have seen his glory," says the apostle, "the glory as of the only Son from the Father" (John 1:14). The revelation is real, commensurate with the nature of the wholeness of truth itself. "No one has ever seen God; the only God, who is at the Father's side, he has made him known" (John 1:18).

All previous revelations are merely relative and remote and at a distance, but here we are overwhelmed by the presence of the "true light" (John 1:9) itself. Previously, the light, the revelation of God came in parts, in installments, in upgrades and improvements, in broken and scattered rays. But now in Christ the light of God is revealed in its holistic wholeness.[11] Says Christ Himself, "Whoever has seen me has seen the Father" (John 14:9), who is both source and fulfillment.

What an infinite contrast this is with the idea of a mere moral teacher, or prophet of common sense! Such language as this from the lips of Moses is unthinkable! "That which was from the beginning," says John, "which we have heard, which we have seen with our eyes, which we looked upon and have touched with our hands, concerning the word of life—the life was made manifest, and we have seen it, and testify to it and proclaim to you the eternal life, which was with the Father and was made manifest to us" (1 John 1:1-2).

Declaration of the Savior Himself

Christ does not exhibit Himself simply as the mere medium by which the truth is brought nigh unto men. He always claims to be Himself the fullness of divinity and everything that the idea of salvation includes. He does not simply point people to heaven. He does not

---

10   Shekinah: Greek: δόξα, Hebrew: שכינה—the glory of the divine presence, conventionally represented as light.

11   This wholeness is revealed in an instant and as something entirely complete in itself. However, the initial experience of it does not constitute the fullness of it in its maturity. What is revealed as whole grows in its wholeness into a greater wholeness and completeness in time.

merely give right moral instruction. He does not present the mere promise of life that can be secured for them by God on the basis of them meeting certain conditions. Rather, he says, "I am the way, and the truth, and the life. No one comes to the Father except through me" (John 14:6).

People are brought to God, not by doctrine or example, but only by actually participating in the divine Himself—and this participation is gotten only through the Person of Christ, who is therefore the very substance of our salvation. This is the teaching herein propounded.

> "And this is the testimony, that God gave us eternal life, and this life is in his Son. 12 Whoever has the Son has life; whoever does not have the Son of God does not have life (1 John 5:11-12).

> "Truly, truly, I say to you, whoever hears my word and believes him who sent me has eternal life. He does not come into judgment, but has passed from death to life" (John 5:24).

Here again we have a present salvation, not a mere promise or hope, but an actual possession. The believer has everlasting life. Believers have already, "passed from death to life" (John 5:24).[12] It is somewhat controversial whether the whole passage,[13] from which this

---

12   He came to be a μεταβέβηκεν (*change of basis*) for life. Here Nevin waxes mystical. In Christ believers have already "passed from death unto life." The key word suggests a foundational change, a change of footing. The sentence verb is in the Third Person Perfect Active Indicative Singular. The perfect tense usually characterizes an action that was completed in the past but also has continuing results in the present; or, stated differently, it characterizes a state of completion that endures presently. Thus, Nevin seems to be saying that this μεταβέβηκεν (*change of basis*) has already happened, and will continue to happen to the end of time. In other words, it's a done deal, though people continue to experience it and grow in it in perpetuity.

13   "So Jesus said to them, 'Truly, truly, I say to you, the Son can do nothing of his own accord, but only what he sees the Father doing. For whatever the Father does, that the Son does likewise. For the Father loves the Son and shows him all that he himself is doing. And greater works than these will he show him, so that you may marvel. For as the Father raises the dead and gives them life, so also the Son gives life to whom he will. For the Father judges no one, but has given all judgment to the Son, that all may honor the Son, just as they honor the Father. Whoever does not honor the Son does not honor the Father who sent him. Truly, truly, I say to you, whoever hears my word and believes him who sent me has eternal life. He does not come into judgment, but has passed from death to life. Truly, truly, I say to you, an hour is coming, and is now here, when the dead will hear the voice of the Son of God, and those who hear will live. For as the Father has life in himself, so he has granted the Son also to have life in himself. And he has given him authority to execute judg-

declaration is taken (John 5:19-30), refers to the spiritual or to the bodily resurrection. We believe that it refers to both. And because of this double duty it shows how they are related to one another.

Ultimately, spiritual resurrection includes the resurrection of the body because body and spirit cannot be separated. Salvation is a single, lifelong process—and beyond—that begins at the point of new birth in this life and reaches into the full restoration of the wholeness of humanity itself at the day of judgment. As such, it is everlasting life, which is actually the constituent wholeness of the believer's person as the organic growth and development from embryo to chrysalis to maturity to the complete glory of heaven hereafter.

The foundation of eternal life is wholly in Christ, in the holistic wholeness of Christ. He came to earth not simply to tell people about it, but to reveal it in His own person and for their engagement and benefit. To "believe in Christ" (Acts 16:31), is to be substantially brought into communication with what He is in His wholeness. It is to pass from death to life (Rom. 5:10). Of such a person it is said, "he will never see death" (John 8:51). This new life of which he is the subject in his union with Christ and which now redefines his central being, cannot perish. It is everlasting and indestructible. When the individual dies, his true life, the wholeness of his life which is rooted in Christ, surmounts the catastrophe of bodily death. And in due time as the wholeness of humanity matures, all who are in Christ will display their triumph in the glories of the resurrection.

> "I am the resurrection and the life. Whoever believes in me, though he die, yet shall he live, and everyone who lives and believes in me shall never die." (John 11: 25-26).

The resurrection and life are simply different aspects of the same reality. The resurrection is simply the form in which the life reveals itself in its victorious struggle with death. Both are revealed together in Christ. It is in Him personally, in His life as the bearer of our fallen humanity, that death is swallowed up in victory by the power of the

---

ment, because he is the Son of Man. Do not marvel at this, for an hour is coming when all who are in the tombs will hear his voice and come out, those who have done good to the resurrection of life, and those who have done evil to the resurrection of judgment. "I can do nothing on my own. As I hear, I judge, and my judgment is just, because I seek not my own will but the will of him who sent me'" (John 5:19-30).

life of God Himself, of whom He is the incarnation. From Him, the same life, a life of infinite greatness and eternal existence, flows into His people as He communes with us.

Christ the Resurrection and the Life

Christ does not merely preach about the resurrection. It is appre-hended (acquired) in His Person. "…and which now has been manifested through the appearing of our Savior Christ Jesus, who abolished death and brought life and immortality to light through the gospel" (2 Tim. 1:10). The revelation *does not consist* in the fact that He has removed all doubt from the doctrine of a future state and made it certain that believers will live hereafter. *The revelation is not the doctrine, but the fact itself that is brought to light.* Immortality, in its true sense, has been introduced into the world by God in Christ.

Christ leads the way for His people in the triumph of the resurrec-tion. He is the "founder and perfecter of our faith" (Heb. 2:10, 12:2.) by whom God is "bringing many sons to glory." He is the first-fruits of the resurrection (1 Cor. 15:20, 23), the first-born among many brethren (Rom. 8:29), to whose image all must be conformed; the beginning, "firstborn from the dead, that in everything he might be preeminent" (Col. 1:18).

Superficially considered, this idea might seem to suggest the old Arian hypothesis that Christ is simply the first human being in history to undergo resurrection into eternal life, and as such is the model for humanity to follow. However, the Arians have lost sight of Jesus' humanity and mistakenly assume that identity with Christ in His divinity is the result of resurrection. The truth of the matter is actually quite different and more important because of the difference. Christ as captain is also the author and finisher of the Christian faith. The first-fruits are the life and power that follow Christ's resurrection, the life and power that constitute the harvest. The harvest is regenerated souls, the new life and power found in Christ.

In the first-born of the church, Christ is at the same time the fountain and the wholeness of new life—the new order of existence, the new way of life inaugurated by Christ, both the newness of per-sonal life and motivation and the newness of Christian social structures and morality. In the same way that all of Adam's progeny are "in" Adam, and are therefore "in" Adam's sin, so all of Christ's spiritual progeny are "in" Christ and "in" Christ's righteousness and salvation. It is not that in Christ Christians are super-human, but that in the light of Christ the Old Man (Rom. 6:6; Eph. 4:22; Col. 3:9;) is sub-human. Christ did not come to save a few people into a hermetically sealed heaven of pure joy and bliss. Christ came to upgrade the definition and constitution of humanity itself.[14]

This is very clear in the Colossians passage. In the first place the apostle refers to Christ as "head of the body, the church. He is the beginning, the firstborn from the dead" (Col. 1:18). But not in order to put Christ in the same order or category as creation (the world), not even as the eldest or best product of that creation. Rather, Paul refers to Christ this way so that "in everything he might be preeminent" (Col. 1:18), that Christ would be understood to be the first, the proto-type and fractal of the new humanity (Matt. 20:16). The wholeness of creation, which constitutes the newness of the new creation, sprang from Him as the everlasting Word, "and without him was not any thing made that was made" (John 1:3; Heb. 1:2), and by whom "all things consist" (Col. 1:17).[15]

And exactly parallel with this relationship to the natural or first creation, the apostle declares Christ's relationship to be the supernatu-ral constitution of the world revealed in the church, in a far higher order of life—an order that includes the holistic wholeness of human life in Christ, which dramatically changes everything. Creation itself becomes complete and whole only in Christ, in the church, which is the life of nature in the life of the Spirit. In the church, the New Man (life in the Spirit of Christ) trumps the Old Man (life without Christ). In the beginning, the Word or Logos was the principle of creation itself. But in the beginning, the fullness and wholeness of creation was not complete. It was there only in seed form. So, it was necessary that the Word or Logos also be the principle of the new creation in Christ —in whom the fullness and wholeness of creation is complete, and through which alone the first creation can have any real significance or

---

14 This is not an argument for Universalism in the sense that everyone ultimately gets saved. Rather, it is an argument that humanity itself will leave behind all who reject Christ for any reason. The wholeness of humanity does not require the inclusion of those who reject the reality of the maturity of human wholeness.

15 "Not for that reason only did the firstborn precede all his creatures, but because he is begotten from the Father, so that through him the 'hypostasis' is produced, which is the foundation of all" (Calvin *in loc.*) So he is the ἄρχων *(ruler)* of the second or new creation, as the resurrection commencing in his person is "*the repair of all things.*"

reality. Only in this way can the original creation be the shadow, prophecy and means of the new creation.

To the church Christ is head over all things (Eph. 1:22). As the church is the crown and complement of the whole world, so He from whom the world proceeds reveals Christ's spiritual life to be identical with "his body," which is "the fullness of him who fills all in all" (Eph. 1:23). And so He is "the beginning, the first-born from the dead" (Col. 1:18), not only the historical point from which the new creation begins, but also the principle out of which all is derived, so "that in everything he might be preeminent" (Col. 1:18). He is the first-born of the dead in the same way that He is the first-born of the creation, because the resurrection (which includes the entire life of the church) flows forth from Christ's Person, and has its reality only and eternally in Him.

However, Christ is not *in* the creation in the same way that He is *in* the church. The first creation provides a proportionate revelation of life, as Paul spoke of in Romans 1:19-20:

> "For what can be known about God is plain to them, because God has shown it to them. For his invisible attributes, namely, his eternal power and divine nature, have been clearly perceived, ever since the creation of the world, in the things that have been made. So they are without excuse."

Whereas in this new creation the absolute or holistic wholeness of life which Christ has in Himself (John 1:4) reaches into the world in a real way. The "eternal life, which was with the Father, ... was manifested unto us" (1 John 1:2). Thus, "it pleased the Father that in him should all fullness dwell; and having made peace through the blood of his cross, by him to reconcile all things unto himself" (Col. 1:19-20). The divine reconciliation has been accomplished "once for all" (Heb. 10:10) in His *Person* by the blood of *His* cross. It then becomes available to others only in the wholeness of the *life* and Person by whom that reconciliation on the cross actually took place in history. Only then can it include others through the power of new creation, of which the church is the result.

Christianity then is a *life*, not only as it is revealed in the story of the life of Jesus Christ, but also as the continuing actuality of His resurrected life which is being revealed through the church.[16] The life of

---

16 See footnote 9, page 281.

Christ is not over. He lives! And His life flows from Himself to His people—and always in this order. Christians do not simply bear His name like a badge, nor do they simply acknowledge His doctrine with a pledge. But rather, Christians are so united with Christ as to have part in the very substance and reality of his ongoing *life* itself. Their conversion is a new birth, "not of blood, nor of the will of the flesh, nor of the will of man, but of God" (John 1:12-13).

"That which is born of the flesh is flesh" (John 3:6). And as such, it can never rise above its own nature. No cultivation, no outward aid, no mere moral influence or appliances can ever lift the flesh into a higher order of life. Such a change requires help from outside of itself because we cannot lift ourselves up by pulling on our own proverbial bootstraps. "That which is born of the Spirit is spirit" (John 3:6), everything else necessarily falls short of the distinction between flesh and Spirit that John made. Accordingly, everything else is simply inferior to life in Christ. Living "in Christ" is also called *Christianity* (John 3:1-8). Those who live in Christ compose the church. The church is not a mere social or cultural institution. It is the life of Christ.

Testimony of the Apostle Paul

Paul agrees with John. Religion as it is understood as the gospel always involves the divinity of life in Christ and is not simply ordinary moral life regulated by divine rules. Paul understood the gospel to be the reality of new life in Christ that reshapes the soul by inclusion in the wholeness of the life of Christ by the power of the Holy Spirit.

> "If any man be in Christ, he is a new creature, old things are passed away; behold all things are become new" (2 Cor. 5:17).

The doctrine of free justification (Rom. 6-8) is vindicated from the objection of being accepting of sin on the ground that it involves an organic change in the subject—not the maturity of the change, but the reality of the birth of the change. It brings the new order of existence in Christ into the presence of the believer, which carries the guaranty of perfection and eventual holiness. And the reason that it must guarantee the perfection and wholeness of believers is because that perfection and wholeness are themselves not yet complete.

"How shall we that are *dead* to sin, *live* any longer therein" (Romans 6:2)? Baptism into Christ is baptism into His death, and at the same time into his resurrection. It is the translation of the subject (the

person) out of the realm of the flesh into the realm of the Spirit (Rom.
6:1-7), into the domain where Christ is dominant—the Kingdom of
God. Under the law, (Rom. 7) human righteousness is impossible. The
law shows us what righteousness looks like, but it cannot accomplish it
because law is nothing but moral rules. But, thanks be to God, "there
is now no condemnation to them which are in Christ Jesus" (Rom.
8:1). They are made "free from the law of sin and death" by the "law of
the Spirit of life" (Rom. 8:2) revealed in the Person of Christ.

Therefore, what was impossible for the law "in that it was weak
through the flesh" (Rom. 8:3) is accomplished by the grace that unites
us in the life of Christ. "That the righteousness of the law might be
fulfilled in us"—not merely forensically through imputation, but also
by the power of new life in our own nature. Christians "walk not after
the flesh, but after the Spirit" (Rom. 8:1-4), in the new life sphere of
Christ—the Kingdom of God.[17] The resurrection power of Jesus comes
as the sign and seal, as the promise and as the reality, of salvation. And
it will not subside until it has quickened the wholeness of humanity
into life and immortality in Christ (Rom. 8:9-11).

Christ is the substance and reality, and not merely the promise or
source of salvation. Indeed, this truth is so completely interwoven into
the New Testament that we often fail to notice the extent that it per-
meates the text. But compare it with similar language used regarding
Moses, the great apostle of the old dispensation. Can Moses himself be
called:
- "the wisdom of God and the power of God" (1 Cor. 1:24);
- "made of God unto us wisdom, righteousness, sanctification,
  and redemption" (1 Cor. 1:30);
- the substance of truth and life, in whom all God's promises are
  yea and amen (2 Cor. 1:20);
- the counterpart of the light that "shined out of darkness in the
  beginning," by which the true knowledge of the glory of God
  is now revealed in the souls of men (2 Cor. 5:4-6);
- the absolute principle of unity for the world, more deep and
  comprehensive than all forms of existence besides (Gal. 3:27-
  28, Eph. 2:13-22, 4:14-16; Col. 1:20; 3:10-11)?

---

17 Not by knowing about the *idea* of imputation, but by being the subject of the *reality*
of imputation.

Let these and other familiar representations of Christ be transferred to Moses, or any other ancient man of God, and the full weight
of the difference between Christ and all other prophets at once makes
itself clear.

> "I have been crucified with Christ. It is no longer I who live, but
> Christ who lives in me. And the life I now live in the flesh I live by
> faith in the Son of God, who loved me and gave himself for me. I
> do not nullify the grace of God, for if righteousness were through
> the law, then Christ died for no purpose" (Gal. 2:20).

The process of the new creation in the believer finds its proper analogy only in the all-victorious resurrection of the Savior Himself—of
which indeed the resurrection is nothing other than His organic continuation in the church (Eph. 1:18-23, 2:1-7).

We are God's workmanship "created in Christ Jesus for good
works" (Eph. 2:10). Christianity is the matter of living in Christ, in
"the power of his resurrection, and may share his sufferings" (Phil.
3:10), in comparison with this every moral advantage is of no account
(Phil. 3:7-11). The apostle says, "For you have died, and your life is
hidden with Christ in God. When Christ who is your life appears,
then you also will appear with him in glory" (Col. 3:3-4).

The Morality of the Gospel Always Based on This View

The wholeness of the morality of the gospel is rooted in the presence and power of new life that is derived in Christ. This is its most
important distinction in contrast with the virtue known in the world
apart from Christ. All Christian duties and responsibilities are engaged
on the basis of what the Christian has become by his heavenly birth, as
an individual who is subject to the Lordship of Christ. For Christians,
all relationships exist in Christ Jesus.

The motives of every virtue issue from the grace of the gospel,
which has already been established, though not completed, the actual
salvation of those who have been born again and have begun to live in
Christ. The virtues are all *fruits* of the Spirit, which serve only to
express that higher order of life (in contrast to the flesh—the wholeness
rather than the brokenness, the unity rather than the divisions) into
which believers are raised by their union in Christ.

All Christian morality is summed up in the principle, "walk by the
Spirit, and you will not gratify the desires of the flesh" (Gal. 5:16). It is

by living as the children of God, who have already been quickened by a new birth into life and sealed with the Holy Spirit of promise, that believers are urged to "put off the old self with its practices" (Col. 3:9). Why abandon old habits? Because the old man has been corrupted by "deceitful lusts" (Eph. 4:22).

God knows that we cannot simply stop doing a thing, that we must replace one habit with another, and not leave ourselves habitless (Matt. 12:43-45). So, we are to continually put on more and more the new man, which in the likeness of God is created in righteousness and true holiness (Eph. 1:13-14, 2:1-6, 4:1, 17-32; 5:1-33; 6:1-9; Col. 3-4; 1 Thess. 2:12, 4:1-12, 5:4-23; Tit. 2:9-14; 1 Pet. 1:13-23, 2:1-3, 2:9-12). Believers can exercise Christian morality because they have been filled with the Holy Spirit. It is *not* that we are called to Christian morality in order to be filled with the Spirit.

> "for at one time you were darkness, but now you are light in the Lord. Walk as children of lightht" (Eph. 5:8).

> "Put on as the elect of God, holy and beloved, bowels of mercies, kindness, humbleness of mind, meekness, long-suffering" (Col. 3:12).

> "If then you have been raised with Christ, seek the things that are above" (Col. 3:1).

> "And everyone who thus hopes in him purifies himself as he is pure" (1 John 3:3).

This is the tenor of Christian morality throughout the New Testament. Its superiority to other ethical systems does not come from the fact that it is a better statement of the duties that God requires than is found elsewhere. But rather, Christianity is superior to all other religions and moral systems because it 1) puts believers into active relationship with Christ and with other believers in Christ, which provides the power of Christ in a community that is intent on living in Christ; and 2) it reveals that all morality issues from Christ, which means that it is only clearly understood in Christ and can only be perfected in Christ in the fullness of time.

The fulfillment of every Christian duty requires the actual life of the Christian to actually be in the reality of Christ. The exercise of Christian duties cannot be accomplished in any other way because Christian behavior requires the reality of a new character that is altogether different than the old character. The whole structure of Christian life, individually and corporately, constitutes the new creation in Christ Jesus.

Section V

Distinctive Nature of Christianity

The actual Person of Christ, which necessarily includes His wholeness, is the principle and reality of Christian salvation. From Him the power of divine life flows into the persons of His people. This requires a close and intimate connection, which is established by Christ alone. However, union in Christ is more than its derivation, more than contact with the source, more than mental or intellectual assent. The order of the first Adam pertains to the wholeness of the individual, and the order of the second Adam pertains to the wholeness of humanity. The order of existence in Christ immeasurably transcends the order of existence regarding Adam.

The first man was made *a living soul* (1 Cor. 15:45. Gen. 2:7). Prior to the establishment of society, God had to establish individuals. Individuals are naturally created in the context of families, the first human institution and source of all other social organization. From the founding of the family forward, human history has been the struggle for higher levels of social organization. Mostly, church and state have been vying for top position, for control. With the advent of Christ, God has given us a Son, Jesus Christ, upon whom "the government shall be upon his shoulder" (Is. 9:6).

God's intention is to establish human society, not by the objective power of the state (brute enforcement), nor the objective power of the church (mere education), but by the subjective love of Christ. People cannot be controlled by any force outside of themselves. Thus, people must be changed at the level of subjective motivation, which is accomplished by the power and presence of the Holy Spirit through

311

regeneration, and is not dependent upon the whims or preferences of individuality.

Adam's life was relative to His own individual wholeness as a person. So, we see self-centeredness in Adam's progeny as the principle of organization. Such a principle is creaturely and limited by the constitution of individual personality. Therefore, life in Adam consists of the establishment and exercise of personal preference and the development of unique personality, and the various clashes and conflicts thereof.

> "The first man Adam became a living soul" (1 Cor. 15:45). And "however spiritual then might have been the meaning of these shadows, they were yet but shadows in themselves; and as they were made up of the elements of this world, they may justly be called earthly," said Calvin of Heb. 7:16 regarding the Old Man.

In contrast, "the last Adam became a life-giving spirit" (1 Cor. 15:45), a *life-giving Spirit*. In Christ, the first human nature is changed by this life-giving Spirit, which converts the original self-centered human nature into its own order of existence, a Christ-centered humanity nature. In Christ, the soul exchanges its natural self-centeredness for a divinely inspired Christ-centeredness, *an endless, indestructible, indissoluble life* (Heb. 7:16). Life was breathed into Adam, but in Christ life is perpetual. The life that was originally breathed into Adam, came from the community of the Trinitarian Godhead. Christ, who is life itself, breathed new life into His people, into the church (John 20:22).

Obviously, life cannot be separated from the wholeness or Trinitarian Person of Christ, unlike the life of Adam, which is carried forward by natural generation. Thus, the mystical presence of Christ is not genetic. It is a matter of grace, not race. The stream of living water from the spiritual Rock, which is Christ (1 Cor. 10:4) never stops. The new life of the believer in Christ participates in the eternality of Christ. This is the difference between the two Adams, between individual existence and the generic or universal life of Christ.

And for this reason the life of the individual Christian cannot be separated from life in Christ. "Because I live"—and only for this reason —"you also will live" (John 14:19). Christ lives in His people to the end of time, not simply as a natural organic root but as a quickening, life-giving spirit. He is mystically present with them, as believers are in His universal and eternal life. And what is more, all of this occurs without disrupting any aspect of the wholeness of the individual, personal consciousness of the believer. The human believer remains a human believer, and Christ remains Christ. Yet, each is enhanced by the presence of the other. Christ, then, is the absolute foundation of all true human personality for the entire body (church) of which he is the Head.

The Spirit in the New Testament

The union of Christ with His church is not natural but is spiritual —supernatural. We err grievously when we conceive of the Spirit as something separate from the presence of Christ Himself, as if Christ only provides an abstract medium of communication between His divinity and the soul of the believer. Father, Son, and Holy Spirit cannot be separated because they are one divine Person. Both of these suppositions stand in broad contradiction to the Scriptures, and in the final analysis equally reduce the doctrine of the mystical union to a mere abstract figment or moral idea and not something real.

The medium of communication is the Word of God, who is Christ Himself. It is not as if the medium of communication connects two disparate entities, but that the Word (the communication) united Christ and the believer into one expression. The union of Christ and believer is mystical precisely because it is real, not because it is some kind of "spiritual" idea.

We read of the Spirit of God as being present and active in the world before the incarnation of Christ. But we must not confuse the agency of Christ with the relationship that Christ has with the church. The language of "relationship" assumes the connection of two different persons, while the language of "agency" assumes unity and not mere connection. The result of Christ's agency is the union established between the divine nature and our human nature. It is by the incarnation itself that the way has been opened for the true descent of the Holy Spirit into the realm of human existence. John goes so far as to say there was at that time no Holy Spirit available, *"for as yet the Spirit had not been given, because Jesus was not yet glorified"* (John 7:39).[1]

This does not mean of course that the Holy Spirit did not exist, but rather it helps define the dispensation of the Spirit to the New Testament because the Old Testament did not know of such pouring out

---

1   The addition of the word in the text *given* is acknowledged by all to be added.

of the Spirit. It also teaches that the Person of Jesus Christ as the Word made flesh provides the only channel or medium by which this spiritual effusion can take place. Accordingly, the Holy Spirit as the Spirit of Christ is primarily active in the Savior Himself. We must remember, however, that the Spirit cannot be separated from the Person of Christ. Rather, He constitutes the form in which the higher nature of Christ reveals its power.

Ultimately, the whole Person of the Son of Man in His Trinitarian fullness is exalted into the same order of existence. Humanity itself, joined in real but mystical union with the everlasting Word, triumphs over the law of infirmity and mortality to which it was previously subject, and is caught up in the character of the Spirit, which is quite different from the character of the flesh. All this happens immediately, in an instant or twinkling of an eye, in the Person of Christ, the second Adam.

The full glorification of our new nature in Christ is established in fact as a new and higher order[2] of life in the world for humanity as a whole. With the final triumph of the Spirit in the glorified humanity of Christ, this higher order of life began to reveal itself with power on the day of Pentecost (Acts 2:1-4). Since that time, it has been continuously active in the world through the church,[3] which is itself the product and extension of the new creation. The whole process begins and ends in the Savior's person.

The Unity of Christ's Person is Two-fold

In accordance with the above analysis, while the Person of Christ is a unified whole, it is described from two perspectives—that of His body or flesh and that of His soul or spirit.[4] He is presented first as a

---

2   In mathematics and logic, a higher-order logic is a form of predicate logic that is distinguished from first-order logic by additional quantifiers and a stronger semantics. Higher-order logics with their standardized semantics are more expressive.

3   The definition of the church (εκκλησιαν) is essential here. Since Nevin argues that the theologies of the Roman Catholic Church, the Orthodox Church and the various churches of the Reformation each and all erred theologically with regard to the actual presence of Christ (evidenced in their various doctrines of the Lord's Supper), it can be argued that those same institutions have similar errors in their various doctrines regarding the church. So, our understanding of the church requires clarification in the light of the mystical presence of Christ.

4   This two-fold perspective is a function of Christ's hypostatic union of divinity and humanity.

mortal man, born of Mary, and later in His resurrected form. In taking on human nature Christ was an ordinary man, but without sin (Heb. 4:5, 5:2, 7). He appeared "in the likeness of sinful flesh" (Rom. 8:3), "born of woman, born under the law" (Gal. 4:4). The human nature which He assumed was fallen, subject to infirmity and liable to death. In the end, "he was crucified in weakness" (2 Cor. 13:4).

However, in spite of this low estate the greater reality of divinity was always present. Christ's divinity was not limited to the physical aspects of His mortal body, but pertained to the wholeness of His life as the Son of God. Following Paul's regeneration on the Damascus Road, the Spirit of Jesus Christ became present to Paul such that he spent the rest of his life proclaiming the reality and truth of Jesus Christ, which he had formerly denied.

The Spirit of Christ in Paul, as in all Christians, wrestled with the law of death in the Old Man (Rom. 7:5). The Spirit of Christ in Paul, as in all Christians, would eventually conquer the Old Man and take victory over death itself (1 Cor. 15:54). This victory was first displayed in Christ's resurrection. It was not possible that he should remain in the grave (Acts 2:24).

> "He was declared to be the Son of God in power according to the Spirit of holiness by his resurrection from the dead" (Rom. 1:4).

The "Spirit of holiness" (Rom. 1:4) is contrasted with the "flesh" (κατα σαρκα—*sarx*)[5] or common humanity, which is also described as of the "seed of David" (Rom. 1:3). That body or flesh, which Christ also had, is destined for death, in contrast to His holiness, which concerns His divinity. His divinity reveals the higher order of the holistic wholeness of Christ's Person that brought this triumph over death and demonstrated by His resurrection.

That same Spirit of Christ, also known as the Holy Spirit, animates regenerate Christians by raising them, both individually and corporately, into a new undying body. Clothed in that body (2 Cor. 5:2-4) provides regenerate Christians with the attributes and prerogatives of a kind of divine existence. Christians do not become Christ by melding their personal identities with His identity. Christians do not become

---

5   For a discussion of this issue, see the various *sarx/soma* contrasts in *Arsy Varsy— Reclaiming the Gospel in First Corinthians*, 2008, and *Varsy Arsy—Proclaiming the Gospel in Second Corinthians*, 2009, by Phillip A. Ross, Pilgrim Platform Books, Marietta, Ohio.

divine in the same way or to the same degree that Christ is divine. But Christians do participate in Christ's divinity in the church such that they fulfill their human character as Christ fulfilled His divine character. This is what it means to participate in Christ.

In Rom. 8:11, we see that the Spirit that raised Jesus Christ is the same Spirit that quickens or vitalizes believers. But how can the Holy Spirit, who is the third Person of the ever blessed and glorious Trinity be fused in unity with Christ, also animate believers, and yet still be not other than the life of Christ? Because the Trinity is one divine Person in three, there cannot be any actual separation between Christ and the Holy Spirit. And because the Holy Spirit is not limited to any particular body, nor to time, He can be wherever and whenever He chooses.

However, when Christ became a man He set aside His divinity. Neither as the Spirit of the Father nor as the Spirit of Christ Himself but proceeding from both, Christ's agency as the Holy Spirit constitutes the form in which the new creation in Christ Jesus is manifest and carried forward in history. And the Holy Spirit always proceeds from His own Person and subsequently into the church. The resurrection body of the Savior, restored to its Trinitarian wholeness at His ascension, is itself spirit (πνευμα) as distinct from the flesh (σαρξ—sarx) or common mortal body in which he had appeared before.

The two bodies are set in close contrast in 1 Pet. 3:18, where it is said: " For Christ also suffered[a] once for sins, the righteous for the unrighteous, that he might bring us to God, being put to death *in the flesh* but made alive in the spirit." "The flesh of the external man was seized," says Calvin, "by the Spirit of divine power, by which the death of Christ has emerged victorious."

This victory must be understood to extend to the holistic wholeness of the individual, objectively as well as subjectively, in order to redefine the very flesh itself as spirit. This redefinition does not make human flesh other than human flesh, but it endows it with the significance of the holistic wholeness of humanity as a single organic entity known as Jesus Christ. And the process of this redefinition is mysterious precisely because it produces a real bodily change, and is not merely mental, intellectual, or imaginary.

This change eventually provides the complete triumph of Christ's higher order of life over the limitations with which it had been called to struggle in its union with our fallen humanity. This triumph then raises humanity into the order of that very same life of Christ in which all reality inheres, and completely transfuses humanity with power, in unity with/as the everlasting glorification of the Son of Man.

1 Tim. 3:16 says that "God was manifest in the flesh," yet He

"but emptied himself, by taking the form of a servant, being born in the likeness of men. 8 And being found in human form, he humbled himself by becoming obedient to the point of death, even death on a cross" (Phil. 2:7-8).

But Paul added in a letter to Timothy:

"Great indeed, we confess, is the mystery of godliness: He was manifested in the flesh, vindicated by the Spirit, seen by angels, proclaimed among the nations, believed on in the world, taken up in glory" (1 Tim. 3:16).

And thus Christ finally came to full and proper victory in His resurrection.[6]

Christ's true character then has come fully into view, being vindicated or justified by this triumphant demonstration of resurrection

---

6   "By the word flesh Paul declares that Christ was true man, and that he was clothed with our nature; but, at the same time, by the word manifested, he shows that there were two natures. We must not imagine a Jesus Christ who is God, and another Jesus Christ who is man; but we must know that he alone is both God and man. Let us distinguish his two natures, so as to know that this is the Son of God who is our brother. Now I have said that God permits the ancient heresies, with which the church was troubled, to be revived in our time, in order to excite us to greater activity. But, on the other hand, let us observe, that the devil is constrained to do his utmost to overthrow this article of faith, because he sees clearly that it is the foundation of our salvation. For if we have not that mystery of which Paul speaks, what will become of us? We are all children of Adam, and therefore we are accursed; we are in the pit of death; in short, we are deadly enemies of God, and thus there is nothing in us but condemnation and death, till we know that God came to seek us, and that, because we could not rise to him, he came down to us. Till we have known this, are we not more than wretched? For this reason the Devil wished, as far as he could, to destroy that knowledge, or rather to mix it with his lies, so as to be perverted. On the other hand, when we see that there is such majesty in God, how shall we dare to approach unto Him, seeing that we are full of misery? We must therefore come to this union of the majesty of God with human nature. And thus, in every respect, till we have known the divine majesty that is in Jesus Christ, and our human weakness which he hath taken upon him, it is impossible for us to have any hope, or to be capable of having recourse to the goodness of God, or of having the boldness to call upon him, and return to him. In a word, we are entirely shut out from the heavenly kingdom, the gate is shut against us, and we cannot approach to it in any way whatever." — Fr. Ser. (*Calvin's Commentary*, 1 Tim. 3:16)

power itself. He was "taken up in glory" (1 Tim. 3:16) and set down at the right hand of God, "far above all rule and authority and power and dominion, and above every name that is named, not only in this age but also in the one to come" (Eph. 1:21; also Phil. 2:9-11, Heb. 12:2) as a result.

The difficulty of Heb. 9:14 also finds resolution in the same distinction regarding the transition of Christ's mortal body to His glorified body. The "eternal Spirit" through which He "offered himself without spot to God" must be understood as His divine order of existence, to which the holistic wholeness of His Person or body was exalted after his death. This resurrected body is contrasted with His dying body, in which He had previously appeared. His resurrected and glorious body was itself the complete triumph of the Spirit over all that was contrary to our fallen bodies. And in the power of this triumph He presented His Person (body/Spirit) before God once for all as an offering of everlasting value. It was by this triumph that He perfected forever all who are being sanctified (Heb. 9:11-14, 24-28, 10:10-14).[7]

His life in the Spirit flows into the Persons of his People
Thus made perfect in the Spirit, Christ's entire Person (including the wholeness therein contained) is raised above the power of death, and filled at every point with the immortality of heaven itself. The blessed Redeemer " became the source of eternal salvation to all who obey him" (Heb. 5:9). His glorification opened the way for the free outflowing of the Spirit, incorporated in the same divine life with which He Himself was filled, into the surrounding world (John 7:38-39). "Having received from the Father," said Peter on the day of Pentecost, "the promise of the Holy Spirit, he has poured out this that you yourselves are seeing and hearing" (Acts 2:33).

Christ became for others what He was shown to be within Himself, a quickening or life-giving spirit (1 Cor. 15:45) from whom the power of new life was carried forward into the world by the church,[8]

---

7   So the passage is interpreted by Bleek, in his *Commentary on the Epistle to the Hebrews*, 1840; which in point of learning and judgment, is the highest authority available.

8   This is the work of the people. But the idea of worship and liturgy is much more than the order of a worship service. It must include everything that the term *work* means regarding the calling, commissioning and conclusion of Christians.

even as the fallen life of the first Adam had been assumed in the course of nature by all his posterity.

Thus, in Rom. 8:9-11 the indwelling of the Spirit and the indwelling of Christ in believers are one and the same thing.[9] And so, in His last discourse with His disciples our Lord Himself explicitly identifies the promise of His own return with the promise of the Holy Spirit to dwell in His people. As we have already seen, the coming of this divine Paraclete required the removal of Christ from the earth, so far as His first form of existence (in the flesh—*sarx*) was concerned.

He must be glorified to make room for the effusion of the Spirit. "If I do not go away, the Helper will not come" (John 16:7). This was to make the way for His return in a higher form of existence.

> "And I will ask the Father, and he will give you another Helper, to be with you forever, even the Spirit of truth, whom the world cannot receive, because it neither sees him nor knows him. You know him, for he dwells with you and will be in you. *I Will Come To You*" (John 14:16-18, 22-23).

The best commentators of the present day (1850s), Olshausen, Tholuck, Luecke, etc., agree with Luther and Calvin that the coming to which the Savior here refers is to be understood neither of His resurrection nor of His second visible advent at the end of the world, but of His presence in the presence of the Holy Spirit, of whose mission He had just spoken. It is all the same promise of the same thing.

Of course, the Person(s) of the Trinity are distinct, but we must beware of separating them into abstract entities, any one without any other. They subsist through the most perfect mutual inbeing and intercommunication. The Spirit of Christ is not simply His representative or surrogate, but is Christ Himself in His Trinitarian existence. It is Christ triumphant over all the limitations of His mortal state and "received up in glory" (1 Tim. 3:16). Finally, He is fully invested and forever set in His proper order of being in the wholeness of the reality of the Holy Spirit.

In this form, He is present with the church more intimately and actually than He could be in any other. "For where two or three are

---

9   "To force apart the Spirit of Christ from the death of his body or any such similar thing makes him into an idol" (Calvin, on Rom. 8:9). By the *Spirit* here, he says, we are to understand, "the dwelling of Christ in us."

gathered in my name, there am I among them" (Matt. 18:20). "And
behold, I am with you always, to the end of the age" (Matt. 28:20).

Christ's Spirit Includes His Humanity and his Divinity

The higher order of Christ's existence in the Spirit involves His
humanity, including His individual body/soul, and His corporate
body/Spirit.[10] It was in view of Christ's humanity that any such exaltation was required. The fact that Christ took on human flesh required
that that same flesh, which had become constitutively related to Christ
through His incarnation, be exalted or raised in an order of magnitude. It needed to be exalted because Christ's humanity and His
divinity cannot be separated. They form one Person and the human
form is inadequate to God's reality. The denial of such exaltation is a
form of Ebionite Gnosticism.

The divine Logos had been in union with the Spirit from all eternity. But in becoming flesh this higher order of life was ignored and
constrained to the limitations of the fallen nature into which it was
incorporated. This was done, not for itself, but for the sake of Christ's
human nature, in order that it could later be raised by the triumphant
power of the Spirit into its original order of existence.

The glorification of Christ does not constitute the complete
advancement of human nature into a measure of divinity, but it does
mark the beginning of that process. Furthermore, the Spirit who came
into the world was not the spirit of humanity with a few extra dollops
of "spiritual stuff" added to it. The Holy Spirit sent by Christ into the
world was the full reality of the shadow of the Spirit known in the Old
Testament, the Spirit of sporadic, transient, and partial inspiration that
had been known previously.

Rather, the Holy Spirit of new life in Christ emerged in a new
way from the crucible of incubation of the Old Testament through
Jesus Christ in His human nature because of His incarnation, as well as
His divine nature. But remember, the two natures cannot be divided.
This spirit of new life was also in unity with the Word, which means

---

10 It is crucial to Nevin's argument that Christ's humanity is fully involved with the
    new life because of the holistic wholeness of the unity of the various persons of the
    Holy Trinity in the person of Christ. In addition, Christians enjoy a similar but not
    identical union in Christ. Our union is a kind of reflection through a glass darkly of
    a similar unity (*hypostatic—but to a lesser degree*) because we are created in God's
    image.

that it involves a form of creative, supernatural predication. As God had originally created the world by speaking it into existence, so Jesus as God incarnate speaks new life into His people (John 20:22).

"He will be with you forever" (John 14:16). The Spirit is constituted by Christ's presence and activity in the church. According to John 15:4 believers and Christ abide in one another by way of a mutual abidance. Believers become standardized in Christ through abidance, by becoming aware of Christ as the new human standard or archetype. Believers "put on Christ" (Gal. 3:27) by their baptism, by entering into union in Christ. That union in Christ is celebrated as Christ communicates Himself to His people, as He communes with them formally through the Eucharist and informally through table fellowship.[11]

The church manifests wherever two or three or more believers gather in order for fellowship in Christ. In the predication of such fellowship the Spirit abides as the church, as the Spirit comprehends, communicates, and reveals the blessed Redeemer. The life of the Spirit in such fellowship reveals the life of the entire (the holistic wholeness of the) glorified Person of Christ. In the process, believers are quickened by the glorification predicated unto God.[12]

The Spiritual or Pneumatic Body

"God is Spirit (πνεῦμαοr, *pneuma*): and they that worship Him must worship in spirit and in truth" (John 4:24).

When Paul says that Christ is a quickening or life-giving spirit, (1 Cor. 15:45) the reference is not simply to His divine or immaterial nature, but to His proper manhood in the flesh because body/spirit cannot be separated. He has in mind the previously referenced resurrection of the body of Christ. "For as in Adam all die, so also in Christ shall all be made alive" (1 Cor. 15:22). How?

By virtue of a new divine element that has been introduced into humanity by Christ's incarnation, and which has *already triumphed*

---

11 Table fellowship here is used analogously to suggest various forms of fellowship that are ordered, civilized and nourishing. In mind is not simply shared meals, but active Christian fellowship in the abiding light of Christ, where Christ is the subject of communication.

12 "Note the unity of the spiritual that we had with Christ. It is not of the soul only, but also of the body, such flesh of his flesh we also are, etc. At any rate, we are without the hope of the resurrection, except that His flesh is our flesh fully and really" (Calvin's Commentaries, 1 Cor. 6:15.

over mortality in the Person of the second Adam. Thus, Christ is now the *life-giving spirit* of the resurrection *for the body* as well as *for the soul*, to all who believe on Him unto salvation. What was new with Christ's incarnation was the fullness of time, which is a way of speaking about holistic wholeness. The fullness of time gives birth to holistic wholeness.

> "In him we have redemption through his blood, the forgiveness of our trespasses, according to the riches of his grace, which he lavished upon us, in all wisdom and insight making known[a] to us the mystery of his will, according to his purpose, which he set forth in Christ as a plan for the fullness of time, to unite all things in him, things in heaven and things on earth" (Eph 1:8-10).

"There is a natural body," says the apostle, "and there is a spiritual body" (1 Cor. 15:44). The first springs from Adam, the second from Christ. As we have borne the image of Adam in our fallen mortal state (flesh), we must also as Christians bear the image of Christ (spirit). This will be fully reached only in the final resurrection. Thus, what is sown at death will be raised into a spiritual body.

> "This corruptible shall put on incorruption; this mortal shall put on immortality; and so death shall be swallowed up in victory for ever" (1 Cor. 15:42-54, KJV).

> "He will transform our lowly body to be like his glorious body, by the power that enables him even to subject all things to himsel" (Phil. 3:21. John 3:2).

The spirit is not abstract from the body, though the Spirit of Christ is characteristically antithetic to the body driven by the morality of Adam. What is of Adam is incapable of sharing in Christ's life because what was of Adam was like a scaffold or placenta—to be discarded in the fullness of time, at the birth of Christ. Nonetheless, the last triumph of the Spirit consists precisely in the transfiguration of the body (what was of Adam) into the image of Christ (the birth of the holistic wholeness of humanity in Christ).

What is merely image this side of the final triumph (or trump, 1 Cor. 15:52), is becoming more real, more full and whole as history progresses. This present image will be transformed into the completed actuality of the final wholeness of the image following it. In other words, what is image in Adam becomes actual in Christ. It must also be noted that this change is not brought to humanity from something outside of humanity, but gestates in humanity until the fullness of time, when its actuality is realized in Christ, in His church. It is not as though a stone were suddenly transformed into a winged bird,[13] by some kind of transubstantiation, for such magic belongs to the imagination of blind, dark nature.

The glorification of the believer's body is the result of the same process that sanctifies his soul. The way that this change unfolds in both body and soul is the same. Both changes originate in the realm of the Spirit, not the body. The power of the change is spiritual and not natural or psychic.[14] Our life is now "hid with Christ in God; but when Christ, who is our life, shall appear, then shall we also appear with him in glory" (Col. 3:4). Our whole person will be quickened in the Spirit and made meet for heaven, like His.

As the "living stones" (1 Pet. 2:5) of this new creation, steadily advancing towards our appointed fullness, wholeness, and final purpose, Christians are described as being "are not in the flesh but in the Spirit, if in fact the Spirit of God dwells in you" (Rom 8:9). Thus, we become participants, but not in the power of our fallen nature that was derived from the first Adam, but in the spiritual order of existence where Jesus Christ is the principle and the Holy Spirit is the medium.

This kind of change cannot be the product of moral influence exercised by our sinful, mortal flesh. Our human flesh is not transubstantiated into something else. That's just not the way it works! Rather, we are changed spiritually by the actual presence of a higher form or order of life. The holistic wholeness of Christ draws out the holistic wholeness of our personality, which enjoys new life in Christ. Accordingly, our body becomes a temple of the Holy Spirit (1 Cor. 6:19) in Christ.

"He who is joined to the Lord becomes one spirit with him" (1 Cor. 6:17), not simply in his individual spiritual nature, but in the

---

13 Nevin's allusion to Islam: "He will say: 'I bring you a sign from your Lord. From clay I will make for you the likeness of a bird. I shall breath into it and, by God's leave, it shall become a living bird'" (*Koran*, Sura 3:49).
14 It must not go unnoticed that the Greek word translated as *physical* can also be translated as *psychic*. Thus, Nevin distinguishes between psychic and spiritual as not being of the same order.

totality (the holistic whole) of his regenerated person united with Christ, spiritually and bodily because the body/spirit is a whole.

> "You, however, are not in the flesh but in the Spirit, if in fact the Spirit of God dwells in you. Anyone who does not have the Spirit of Christ does not belong to him. But if Christ is in you, although the body is dead because of sin, the Spirit is life because of right-eousness. If the Spirit of him who raised Jesus from the dead dwells in you, he who raised Christ Jesus from the dead will also give life to your mortal bodies through his Spirit who dwells in you." (Rom. 8:9-11).

Note—Proper Conception of the Pesurrection

The whole spiritual life of the Christian is organically connected with the mediatorial life of the Lord Jesus Christ. This includes Christ's resurrection. While this idea is clearly taught in the New Testament, to admit of any doubt, many people are slow to acknowledge that this connection is both real, actual, and mysterious. We cannot completely explain how it works, but we know that it is true.

A very common explanation of the mystery is that the whole sal-vation of the gospel is accomplished in an objective and mechanical way by supernatural might and power, rather than by the Spirit of the Lord as the revelation of a new historical life in the person of the believer himself. This common explanation is that salvation "happens" to us by a working of the Spirit that is "outside" of or not a part of us personally, as if something outside of us (the Spirit) adds something to us.[15]

Salvation is incorrectly understood in the following way: An out-ward imputation of righteousness is "given" to us, as if we receive something objective to our person. Then a process of sanctification carries us forward though some sort of "spiritual machinery" that is brought to bear on the soul. This "spiritual" thing that happens includes the idea of an abrupt creation *de novo* by the power and will of the Holy Spirit, which creates something completely new and dif-ferent in us. And finally, a sudden extemporaneous reassembly of our

---

15 In opposition to this, Nevin teaches that the Spirit reveals something that already exists in us (as opposed to adding something completely new to us). And what is revealed is a new life or a new personal identity. And just like our old identity which concerns body and soul, so this new identity also concerns body and soul. Regeneration, which produces an objective change in believers, is experienced sub-jectively.

body occurs and produces an entirely, other-worldly and "spiritual" new person or identity, which gets superadded to the life that existed before.[16]

However, the Scriptures warrant no such idea. Of course, the new creation is supernatural,[17] but it is strictly conformable to the general order and constitution of organic life. It is a new creation *in* Christ Jesus, not *by* Him as an objective power in some other "dimension." The subjects of the new creation are saved only by being brought into the realm of Christ's life, as a regular, organic, historical, yet divine human process that results in the church, the corporate body of such saved people.

The new nature that is implanted in believers at regeneration is not a higher order of existence that is instantly created out of nothing by the fiat of God. Rather, it is truly and strictly a continuation or extension of Christ's life into the actual lives of believers. The growth of this life of Christ in believers provides for their sanctification. When they die their bodies sleep in Jesus in the same way that they are conscious or awake in Jesus. God then brings them with Him when the church is made complete or whole by His second coming (1 Thess. 4:14).

The resurrection of the head (Christ) and the ultimate resurrection of the members (His body) form one single, unified process, in the same way that the death of Adam and his posterity constitutes throughout human history as one and the same unfolding fact of life. In the same way, those who are in Christ shall all be made alive. Christ's resurrection is the pledge or promise (sign) of the resurrection of believers in the same way that the first fruits are a token of the coming harvest (1 Cor. 15:22-23). He is "the beginning, the first-horn from the dead" (Col. 1:18), which implies the consequence of a common law that applies to those who follow.

In due time the Spirit of Christ that dwells in believers quickens their mortal bodies in conformity with the power of His own resurrection. This quickening also brings to their awareness this extended life (wholeness) of Christ's universal nature/character within the individuality of their own separate, individual lives. It reveals what was previously hidden, and in the light of that revelation they are able to

---

16 This is the born-again testimony so often heard in relationship to revivals.
17 *Supernatural* literally means: a higher or greater degree of the natural, not something other than the natural. "Super" modifies "natural," it does not oppose it.

see themselves as sons of God through and/or in Christ. We are, however, not sons by blood, but sons by adoption, which includes the
redemption of the body (Rom. 8:23). Toward this adoption/redemp-
tion, the whole process of salvation struggles, and without which it
can never be regarded as complete (Rom. 8:11, 19, 23).

In the light of all of this argument, it is at best grossly inadequate
to speak of the resurrection of believers as being a miracle that creates
something discontinuous or completely new in the soul. The new life
of regeneration necessarily involves an inward (personal, subjective)
and historical (social, objective) connection with the resurrection life
of Christ because it is the very Life of Christ himself that is working in
them by the Spirit before their death.

True, it is ascribed to supernatural power (1 Thess. 4:16) and it
sometimes even seems like the change is instantaneous and without
preparation. The "moment" (ἄτομος) in 1 Cor. 15:52 literally refers to
something that cannot be cut in two, or divided, something indivisible
or *whole*. A "twinkling of an eye," or eye blink does happen rapidly,
but can also refer to the refocusing of one's vision. Thus, 1 Cor. 15:52
is as much about perception as about time.

That the final state of Christianity in glory will involve a miracle
(or mystery) that completely transcends the current order of the
church is most certainly to be expected. But it will be a real miracle,
not something that happens in some other "spiritual dimension" or
place. What makes miracles real is that they happen here and now to
these bodies. Anything else is imagination and speculation. It is possible, even probable, that what is mysterious to us now will be better
understood (though not completely understood) later, after the point
being described by Paul in these verses (the last trump and the twinkling of the eye) because hindsight is often better than foresight.

As to the instantaneousness of the change, (if it even applies to the
dead)[18] it applies only to the revelation that is to take place at that time,
to the *revelation* of God in Christ by the Spirit and the *realization* of
God in Christ by believers. As Olshausen justly remarks in his commentary on this verse, this by no means excludes the supposition of a
previous preparation in the life of the believer (or an historic develop-

---

18 Was Paul speaking literally or figuratively? Many people understand Paul to have
    spoken literally, as if believers will get "beamed up" into heaven like in Star Trek.
    Nevin doesn't think so, and finds Paul to be speaking figuratively, suggesting that it
    will be more of a realization that sweeps across the population like a popular craze.

ment) that facilitates this result. It implies that there has been no growth or development during death, or to those who are dead to Christ. But so far as the previous state is concerned, it suggests that the process of coming to new life that was previously hidden (unconscious), suddenly bursts into view in its completed form, its wholeness. For example, consider the birth of the butterfly as it mounts in the air on wings of light. Observe the process and you will see that the final stages of birth seem quite sudden in comparison to the stages of gestation. The existence of the larvae is long, boring, and uneventful in comparison to the efflorescent emergence of the butterfly.

Character of the Mystical Union

Here we see the character of the mystical union between Christ and His people. It does not in any sense occur in the realm of nature, nor is it physical. While it is true that the miracle of mystical union is not physical, it involves the physical bodies of believers. While it cannot be seen by the natural senses, it does effect the natural senses. We need to distinguish between the miracle or mystery itself and its effects. Nor are we at liberty to conceive of it as being merely moral, either. Its realm is that of the Spirit, which is a realm of wholeness, completeness, and perfection. In this realm, however, it is in the highest measure absolutely real, indeed, far more real, than it could possibly be under any other conceivable form.[19]

Christ is not sundered from the church by the intervention of His Spirit. On the contrary, in this way He is brought nearer to it, and made one with it more intimately and beyond measure than if we are still thinking of body and spirit as two separate things. This union applies to the personal holistic wholeness of the Savior on the one side, and simultaneously to the personal holistic wholeness of the individual believer on the other.

Nothing is more unbiblical than the idea that the spirit (πνεῦμα) is limited to the form of the mind in abstraction from body, whether we

---

19 Like the ancient Gnostics we are tempted to divide spirit from body in such a way that we see the body as physical and the spirit as ethereal. However, Nevin insists on holding body and spirit in unity. So when he speaks of spirit he doesn't mean "not of the body." Rather, he means that because the body as a whole is incorporated into the constitution of the spirit, he understands the body to be more real—and therefore more physical, more natural (*super* natural) than the body alone, when it is conceived to be a separate entity from the spirit.

think of mind as divine or human. The wholeness of the glorified Christ subsists and acts in the Spirit. Actually, Christ and His Spirit are one, indivisible. In this form Christ's character is communicated to His people, who are made to live and walk in the Spirit, both in soul and body. Christ lives in them, and they live in Christ. And yet, as their sanctification proceeds, this mutual indwelling becomes more intimate and complete, until, at last, in the final resurrection they are fully transformed into the same image, "as by the Spirit of the Lord" (2 Cor. 3:18; Phil. 3:21). The final transformation culminates in perfection, wholeness, and completeness in Christ.

Allegory of the Vine and its Branches

There is no more apt or beautiful illustration of this union between Christ and the church than the allegory of the vine and its branches (John 15:1-8):

> "I am the vine; you are the branches. Whoever abides in me and I in him, he it is that bears much fruit, for apart from me you can do nothing."

To understand this as nothing more than moral influence is to degrade it of it spiritual meaning.

> "It is not to be disputed," says Tholuck, "that a higher relation is here exhibited than that of master and disciple, nothing less in fact than a real oneness, (*eine wesentliche Einheit—an essential unity*) effected through the medium of faith."

It is also well remarked by Lücke[20] that the earthly, here as elsewhere, is exhibited by Christ as the image or copy of the heavenly.

Nature, which includes the race of Adam, ultimately finds its divine archetype only in the realm of the Spirit. So, when Adam's sin

---

20 Gottfried Christian Friedrich Lücke (1791-1855) received in 1814 the degree of doctor in philosophy from Halle; in 1816 he moved to the Friedrich Wilhelm University, Berlin, where he became licentiate in theology, and qualified as Privatdozent. He soon became friendly with Friedrich Schleiermacher and de Wette, and was associated with them in 1819 in the redaction of the Theologische Zeitschrift. Meanwhile his lectures and publications brought him into considerable repute, and he was appointed professor extraordinarius in the new University of Bonn in the spring of 1818. In the following autumn he became professor ordinarius. Lucke was one of the most learned and influential of the so-called "mediation" school of evangelical theologians (Vermittelungstheologie), and is now chiefly known by his Kommentar über die Schriften d. Evangelisten Johannes (4 vols., 1820-1832).

resulted in his separation from God, he was also separated from his created archetype, separated from his wholeness and fulfillment in it. Thus, the connection that holds between the vine and its branches is not so much an explanation of the life union between Christ and believers as it is a reflection of its mystery. Christ is accordingly the True Vine, in whom is revealed the holistic wholeness of reality, of which only a foreshadowing is present in all natural forms of life, or life apart from Christ.

The union of the vine and its branches is organic, which means that it is living, that it is animate—biological. The vine and its branches are not unified simply in an outward and or mechanical process. The vine reveals itself and actually lives in the branches, and the branches have no vitality apart from the vine. The vine is an entity that is composed of its branches. It has a relationship of whole to parts and parts to whole. Both vine and branches, whole and parts, exist as one and the same life entity. The qualities and characteristics of the vine, its nature or DNA, is continually reproduced in every branch that springs from it, no matter how far the branch is from the root. And all this serves to symbolize Christ's relationship to His people.

The popular idea of having a "personal relationship with Christ" is true, but woefully inadequate to the reality. All personal relationships with God are covenantal relationships. So, Christianity is like a marriage. We can speak of our personal relationship with our spouse, but that relationship says little about the reality of marriage, about the joys and sorrows that come with every marriage. My personal relationship with my spouse says nothing about my relationship with my children or in-laws, etc. No, marriage is much more than a personal relationship with one's spouse.

In the realm of the Spirit, distinguished from but not separated from the realm of nature, life in Christ is life in the very same life that exists in the root and in all its branches. The union between vine and branch is organic, biological. The parts do not exist separately from the whole, but grow out of it and continually exist in it, as their own true and proper life.

Similarly, Christ dwells in His people by the Holy Spirit, and is formed in them as the hope of their own personal glory. A form of Christ lives in the lives of His people. Christians grow up into Christ in all things, and in that process of growing up they themselves are transformed into Christ's image or form, from glory to glory by the

Spirit of the Lord. The life of Christ is reproduced in His people in the same true human character that belongs to Christ in His own Person. But Christ's context is not our context, the role He plays in history is not the role that we play. So, Christ remains Christ and we remain who we are, yet there is mutual sharing in Christ.

Allegory of the Body and its Members

The allegory of the body, used by Paul to illustrate the same idea, is also full of instruction. A common legal corporation may be represented by the same term (body) to indicate the idea of mutual submission to the will and/or mission of the corporation on the part of its members. For instance, the case of the *Apology of Menenius Agrippa*,[21] once used to promote civil discord at Rome and has been brought forward sometimes as a parallel to 1 Cor. 12:14-26. But Calvin says that the two cases are of a wholly different character because the ground of unity in the church is of a far deeper nature than can be found anywhere else. And of course, the unity of the church is the life of Christ Himself that mystically flows through its entire constitution.

> "For just as the body is one and has many members, and all the members of the body, though many, are one body, so it is with Christ. For in one Spirit we were all baptized into one body—Jews

---

21   Agrippa Menenius Lanatus was a consul of the Roman Republic in 503 B.C. According to Livy, Menenius was chosen by the patricians to persuade soldiers serving in the Roman army to re-enter the city and rejoin the community in 494 B.C. The soldiers had withdrawn from Rome in the first of secessions (*secessio plebis*), specifically to protest the oppressive debt laws, but more broadly to protest the severe inequity of power in the early Republic. Menenius told the soldiers a fable about the parts of the human body and how each has its own purpose in the greater function of the body. The rest of the body thought the stomach was getting a free ride so the body decided to stop nourishing the stomach. Soon, the other parts became fatigued and unable to function so they realized that the stomach served a purpose and they were nothing without it. In the story, the stomach represents the patrician class and the other body parts represent the plebs. Eventually, the patricians conceded to some of the plebs' demands, such as creating the tribunes of the people and establishing legal protection for all citizens against arbitrary intervention from an elected magistrate, and the soldiers returned to the city.

It is possible that St Paul, an educated Roman citizen, knew this story and used a similar parable when he admonished the Christians of Corinth that, for all their diversity of gifts, they were all members of one body (1 Cor. 12: 13 ff). However, the analogy also appears in *Memorabilia* (2.iii.18) by Xenophon (411-362 B.C.) and in *De Officiis* (III.v.22) by Cicero (106-43 BC).

or Greeks, slaves or free—and all were made to drink of one Spirit."
(1 Cor. 12:12, 13, 27; Rom. 12:4-5).

"And he put all things under his feet and gave him as head over all
things to the church, which is his body, the fullness of him who
fills all in all" (Eph. 1:22-23). "Rather, speaking the truth in love,
we are to grow up in every way into him who is the head, into
Christ,from whom the whole body, joined and held together by
every joint with which it is equipped, when each part is working
properly, makes the body grow so that it builds itself up in love"
(Eph. 4:15, 16, 5:23, 30; Col. 1:18, 24. 2:19).

The relationship of body and parts involves a real life union of the
most intimate character. The head is not in the members, nor in direct,
continuous contact with them. As such, the idea of local, contiguous
connection fails immeasurably to describe the bond between head and
body. Nor is this union simply that the members are ruled and controlled by the will of the head. It is the presence of a common life or
animating spirit that proceeds from the head into the limbs, and this
common life has no proper or specific existence in any single limb. But
does the spirit or organic unity remain in the body as some kind of
merely abstract power? Not at all. It rules the whole process of life
from assimilation to reproduction, and calls into action the material
reality of every limb. Therefore, the head is somehow mystically in the
members as the principle from which their existence is drawn.[22]

And so it is with the relationship of Christ to the church (to the
unity of the church), only in a far higher order of life. The head does
not provide a mechanical conjunction that brings about unity. In addition, that relationship, that union excludes every idea of a magical or
merely outward transfer of life from Christ to His people—especially as
is implied in the dogma of transubstantiation. But neither is the conjunction simply spiritual, for this would resolve it into a merely moral
character or inspiration.

In distinction from these ideas, we say that the relationship
between Christ and His church is organic in the fullest sense of this

---

22 This analogy would work better by talking about the whole and the parts of the
    body rather than the head and the parts. By using the word *head*, Nevin doesn't
    mean the physical thing that sits atop the shoulders. Rather, he means the "thing"
    (governing process) that directs the body. The head provides the coordination
    between the parts, and it therefore represents and functions as the whole of the
    body.

term. God does not simply inspire moral thinking or good behavior, He actually provides the subjective means and/or motivation for it to happen, and the objective content of moral principles. The new human life in Christ extends into the persons of Christ's people by the Spirit to form a central uncompounded person. Christ's body and Christ's Spirit cannot be separated but are in hypostatic union. And this is the Christ who dwells in believers, as believers also dwell in this Christ. In that mutual indwelling Christ is revealed with constant, regenerative energy, always repeated in the same form or fractal, and is always true to its own nature, until at last the whole man, spirit/soul/body, is transformed fully into Christ's image. The Person of Christ is the Person of the Holy Spirit.

Illustration from the Idea of Marriage

Another remarkable and significant illustration is employed in Eph. 5:22-33 regarding the same union. Even in the Old Testament, the marriage relationship was frequently made the type or symbol of the covenant established between God and His people. We see the same thing in Revelation, where the church is described as the bride, the Lamb's wife (Rev. 14:7, 21: 2, 9).

Yet, many people fail to understand what this doctrine of the mystical presence is about. De Wette and other rationalistic commentators resolve everything into morality and instruction. But such efforts do not do justice to the meaning of the texts or the reality of the Spirit of Christ.

Paul declares the relationship of believers to be like marriage, and calls them both a "great mystery" (Eph. 5:32) and it is clear that he struggles to express the idea because it is too vast for the reach and grasp of human understanding. Marriage, properly understood, is a mystery. And though it is not a New Testament sacrament because it belongs to the realm of Adam, it has some sacramental qualities that foreshadow union in Christ. Many of those qualities share significance and solemnity with the Christian sacraments, and provide true and valuable comparison with the mystical union between Christ and His church.

"In the same way husbands should love their wives as their own bodies. He who loves his wife loves himself." (Eph. 5:28). And in the same way, the Lord loves and cherishes the church "because we are members of his body" (Eph. 5:30). According to Pelagius, this means that "*his members ought to imitate him in all things,*" where the power of imitation is produced by moral influence.

How different is the commentary of Calvin:

> "The passage is classic on our mystical communication with Christ. It is not to be considered extravagant exaggeration, in this view, but simple truth; and it not only signifies that Christ partakes of our nature, but is intended to express something deeper and more emphatic. For the words of Moses, Gen. 2:24, are quoted. And what now is the sense? As Eve was formed out of the substance of her husband Adam, that she might be as it were a part of himself; so we, that we may be true members of Christ, by the communication of his substance, coalesce with him into one body" (*Calvin's Commentary, Eph. 5:30*).

The church may be described as a kind of organic union with Christ according to the beautiful allusion of Hooker, who said that Eve was "a true native extract out of Christ's body." Clearly, Paul has in mind here more than any merely figurative or moral incorporation with the Savior. The emphasis of Gen. 2:24 is on the last clause, "the two shall become *one flesh.*"

Paul applied this directly to the case of Christ and the church, and immediately added that it is a "great mystery" regarding the justification of his previous declaration (Eph. 5:30). The whole passage is written with the most thorough and comprehensive exegesis by Harless, whose commentary on the Epistle to the Ephesians is superb, and whose judgment here, especially when backed by the high authority of Calvin, commands respect by all.

Striking Phraseology of the New Testament

It is only on the ground of this real, inward life union between Christ and His people that we can properly appreciate or understand the common phraseology of the New Testament when it speaks of Christians and their peculiar character and state. In various ways, Christ is described as dwelling and working in His people. Nothing is more common than for Christians to be spoken of as being *in* Christ. All Christian relationships exist only *in the Lord.* All Christian graces are to be cultivated and all Christian works performed *in* the Lord. More examples are unnecessary.

The whole Christian life is represented in the same way. *In Christ* is only another way to say *Christian.* Indeed, this kind of language is so common and familiar that most people don't notice its peculiarity. But substitute *Moses* for *Christ,* and we immediately see how completely inappropriate such language is for a moral relationship. The whole New Testament assumes that the relationship of Christ to His people is more than moral, that it involves a real community of life through which He dwells in their hearts by faith. And that Christians may also be rooted and built up *in him* unto every good word and work (Eph. 3:16-19; Col. 2:6-10).

Those passages where Christians are represented as already having everything in Christ that is comprehended in the wholeness of Christian salvation are particularly striking. In the Savior Himself, His victory over death and hell was consummated in His resurrection and ascension. In the church, however, as a whole (corporately) and in every individual believer, the new life reveals itself as an ongoing process. In no sense can individual Christians be said to be whole and complete in themselves.

And yet as the Christian is spoken of as being in Christ, he is often spoken of as already possessing everything that salvation involves. This is because being in Christ means being in His wholeness as if it is already completed because Christ will in fact accomplish it.

Christians Complete in Christ

So, as we have already seen, the Christian is described as having eternal life *now*, though the full sense of his salvation remains to be completed. His life is hid with Christ in God right now. So, he is not only justified, but in this same sense he is already sanctified and glorified in Christ, as well. "You have been filled in him, who is the head of all rule and authority." (Col. 2:10). Paul seems at times almost to lose sight of the distinction between Christ and the Christian in the overwhelming sense he has of their unity. We are crucified, dead and buried with Christ, and have risen with Him again to a new and higher life (Rom. 6:3-11, 7:4, 8:11; Gal. 2:20 Phil. 3:9-12; Col. 2:12, 3:1-4).

This form of speaking is too strong, deliberate and consistent among the gospel writers to be considered as mere rhetorical flourish. Nor will it do to say that it is merely an analogy between Christ's outward history and the inward spiritual experience of the believer. The outward and inward (objective and subjective elements of experience) do indeed flow together, but only because the one is really and truly involved in the other.

Note

The acts of God for our redemption are all fulfilled and accomplished in Jesus Christ. The several steps of development in Christ's life, are for this very reason the various steps of the work of redemption, from His birth or incarnation on to His ascension. For He Himself is our redemption—not His doctrine, nor His work, nor His example. His work is not to be separated from His person, and His life and death are the very things by which our redemption has been accomplished. "It is sheer nonsense to give up the personal and historical Christ, and retain a firm hold upon Christianity" (Kliefoth. *Theorie des Kultus*, §188).[23] Kliefoth urges the true significance and importance of church festivals that are related to Christ. They are not simply a memorial of Christ, but the very bond to Christ—the actual, vital union that exists between Him and His people.

This new life in the Spirit extends to the whole man, first in Christ and then in His people. The organization of the whole is logically

---

23 Theodor Friedrich Dethlof Kliefoth (1810-1895) a German Neo-Lutheran. Kliefoth's peculiar conception of the church was due chiefly to his occupation with the old Lutheran church orders. With great energy he emphasizes the divine foundation of the church through the acts of salvation of the triune God; its divine basis in the Means of Grace, which mediate and vouchsafe the continuous effect of Christ and his spirit; the divine institution of the office of the means of grace; and the necessity of the organization and incorporation of the church in church order and church government. The church is for him the empirical congregation of the called, and not merely the congregation of true believers; and for him Lutheranism is not merely a doctrine or dogmatic tendency, but a distinctive church body whose peculiar historical development is to be perpetuated. He opposed the territorialism of state omnipotence, which denied the independence of the church, the collegialism of modern representative church government, which originated in the Reformed Church and seemed to him to endanger the privilege and authority of the office of the means of grace; unionism, which threatened to absorb the Lutheran Church as such, or at least its confession; and the amalgamation of church and politics, with its tendency toward the establishment of a national German Evangelical Church. On the other hand he aimed at the restoration of the Lutheran state churches and the strengthening of Lutheranism through a closer union. In this sense he represented the government of the Mecklenburg church at the Eisenach Conference after 1852; and in 1868 he founded with others the Allgemeine evangelisch-lutherische Konferenz.

prior to the organization of the parts. And being organically in both Christ and His people in the same way, the new life or regeneration effects both the inward, subjective experience of believers and the outward, objective reality of their historical lives and behavior for all of the members of the body of which Christ is the mystical head. Thus, every Christian is in Christ potentially[24] from the beginning, with everything that He is destined to actually become in Christ when His salvation is complete.

The power that is actively at work in the Christian is the same all-conquering life (Phil. 3:21) that functioned so mightily in Christ when He was raised from the dead and set at God's right hand in the heavenly places (Eph. 1:19-23). And because of this relationship the apostle adds that "And you were dead in the trespasses and sins ... even when we were dead in our trespasses, made us alive together with Christ—by grace you have been saved ... and raised us up with him and seated us with him in the heavenly places in Christ Jesus" (Eph. 2:1, 5, 6). All of these verses are in the past tense, not in the future tense.[25] Similarly, in Rom. 8:30 we see not only the calling of believers and their justification, but their glorification is also exhibited as something already complete.

> "or those whom he foreknew he also predestined to be conformed to the image of his Son, in order that he might be the firstborn among many brothers. And those whom he predestined he also called, and those whom he called he also justified, and those whom he justified he also glorified" (Rom. 8:29-30).

Olshausen on Romans

Olshausen's remarks are particularly striking, and so closely related to this topic. Allow me to quote them in full. "The essential point in

---

24 The potentiality here is not simply a possibility, as if it might happen. Rather, it is the potential of a seed to grow into a plant. In physics potential energy is the energy stored in a body or in a system due to its position in a force field or due to its configuration.

25 "And certainly, although, as respects ourselves, our salvation is still the object of hope, yet in Christ we already possess a blessed immortality and glory; and therefore, he adds, in Christ Jesus. Hitherto it does not appear in the members, but only in the head; yet, in consequence of the secret union, it belongs truly to the members" (Calvin, Comm. Eph. 2:6).

"Christ is the real type for every way of life for the saints to the end of time. Thus, what they are to become in the development of the seed has already been planted in them" (Ohhausen *in loc*).

the doctrine of Christ's active obedience is this, that His agency in our salvation is not negative in its form simply, but just as much positive. Christ does not simply take away sin in the case of men, and then leave them to work out holiness for themselves, but He has by His holy life wrought out this also, for Himself and for all His people; so that both, the destruction of the old and also the creation of the new, in the process of regeneration, are alike Christ's work, both completed by Him too in His earthly state; so as to be in the first place imputed to individual believers, and then communicated to them in a gradual way. This is here most distinctly expressed by the words δικαίωσε καί ἐδόξασε (*vindicated and glorified*). Even the first term implies a real communication of the δικαιοσυνη χζιστον" (*righteousness of Christ*, Comp. Rom. 3:21).

The other however, ἐδόξασε—*glorified*, represents it as a matter of actual possession even in its full form of holiness and perfection, though Paul had previously disclaimed this for himself and for Christians generally (Rom. 3:23). As then the whole human race in its natural state was originally in seed form in Adam, all history is simply the development of what his nature included. In the same way, Christ is also the real bearer of the entire church in the now planted Seed of Christ, the new creation, the sanctified humanity. He is this not only because the virtue of His atonement destroys the old Adamic sin nature, but to the same extent it also creates a new nature, which forms His own sacred image in every believing soul. Of course, the sacred image of Christ is necessarily Trinitarian. And this is why humanity is a reflection of God's image.

Only in this way does it become clear *how* faith is everything for Christian life. The Christian is not called to an independent holiness in-and-of or for himself, either before or after his conversion. Rather, Christians only receive the continuous stream of life that flows upon them from Christ. This flow from the eternal into the temporal, from the universal into the particular, from the ultimate into the proximate is the mystery of the presence of Christ. And the reception of this is faith itself.

Just as the seed begins to grow it needs to take in moisture, air, and light in order to grow into its potential. An unskillful gardener who tries to accelerate or augment its growth in whatever ways, only frustrates what he wants to advance. This is why passive reception produces the best result. Christ doesn't work from outside people like an influence or inspiration. Rather, He works from within the inmost depths of the Christian's being, infusing the will with the active force of His own (Christ's) life that changes people from the inside out. The will of the believer and the will of Christ are united so that the will of the believer becomes an image of the will of Christ, of the same kind but not to the same degree.

This is why the believer feels that the power that he possessed is not from himself, and why humility grows with sanctification. It is not he that is the source, will or origin of the work, but Christ lives and works in him. Gal. 2:20 is in the Greek aorist tense, and every attempt to ignore this tense must be rejected. The future is not yet in place. Just as God began creation with His Word, "Let there be light" (Gen. 1:3), so Christ finished God's new creation with His Word, "It is finished" (John 19:30).

With this Word, His whole church was completed as a κτίσις—*creation*, for all ages, negatively and positively. No mortal can add anything, however little, to Christ's finished work. All that unfolds in the individual members of His church through distant centuries is only the development of what was previously at hand in His person (Gal. 3:16). The church and every particular believer, along with the κτίσις—*creation,* which forms its necessary basis, are "God's workmanship created in Christ Jesus" (Eph. 2:10).

Redemption is a new, glorified creation, and the act of creation must remain forever the prerogative of God alone. The connection between creation and redemption requires this sense because it provides the certainty of salvation, and is superior to all earthly contingency. This is what Paul wishes to establish. There can be no true certainty, except as it issues from divine action. Salvation would be most uncertain if it rests upon the fluctuating subjectivity of fickle human beings, and not on the objective act of God in Christ alone. Only from this objective perspective does the gospel become a truly joyful message, which cannot be overthrown, and which at best infidelity itself can only reject.

Section VI

John 6:51-58

John 6 is of special interest and importance to the mystical presence of Christ. It has been variously interpreted in both ancient and modern times because it both shapes and informs one's understanding of Christ. Verses 51-58 guide the whole chapter to a startling climax that was particularly difficult for those who originally heard it, and for us. The issues are deeply entangled in the sacramental question.

A succinct history of the interpretation of the passage is provided by Lücke, in a footnote appended to the second volume of his *Coram*, on John, 2nd edition. In the Early Church, Origen and Basil the Great denied all reference to Christ's real presence in the sacrament of the Lord's Supper. Chrysostom, Cyril, and Theophylact held the opposite view, which subsequently became the position of the Roman Catholic Church.

The situation changed with the Reformation. Zwingli, Calvin, and Luther (though on different grounds) agreed that the passage refers only to the general reception of Christ by believers, and not to the Eucharist. Commentators are divided on the question of Christ's real presence, but the more important nineteenth century commentators generally agree that there is not sufficient ground to suggest any reference whatever in these verses to the Lord's Supper.

Regarding the actual, historical practice of the Eucharist, their position is undoubtedly technically correct when the scope is strictly limited to these verses alone. But it is equally clear that the idea of Christ's real presence embodied in Holy Communion finds an important parallel in these verses in the same way that the conversation with Nicodemus (John 3:5) finds a parallel in the sacrament of baptism. Yet, at that point in John's gospel Jesus' followers were not baptizing, nor is the word *baptism* mentioned to Nicodemus. But because we know that baptism and the new birth are related, we associate them, and rightly so.

Throughout John 6, Christ exhibits Himself to the Jews as the true source and support of all spiritual life.

> "Do not work for the food that perishes, but for the food that endures to eternal life, which the Son of Man will give to you. For on him God the Father has set his seal" (John 6:27).

> "I am the living bread that came down from heaven. If anyone eats of this bread, he will live forever. And the bread that I will give for the life of the world is my flesh" (John 6:51).

> "I am the bread of life; whoever comes to me shall not hunger, and whoever believes in me shall never thirst" (John 6:35).

> "For this is the will of my Father, that everyone who looks on the Son and believes in him should have eternal life, and I will raise him up on the last day" (John 6:40).

This study regarding the relationship of Christ to his church provides much light regarding the language of John 6. The language is figurative in one respect in the sense that all representations of the Christian mystery borrow from nature to allude to what belongs to the realm of the Spirit. But can we say that such representations refer only to doctrine? Is there no reality behind the doctrine? Is doctrine alone the proper food for the soul, the living essence?

Even De Wette says that such a suggestion is decidedly false. The references to Christ's actual Person—His body and flesh—are many and clear. Jesus refers to Himself as the bread of life. "Whoever comes to me shall not hunger, and whoever believes in me shall never thirst" (John 6:35). Of course we come by faith, but in doing so we necessarily engage our wholeness, body and spirit, and become joined to Christ's actual life as the center of a new consciousness within our own. Our actual individual persons and identities are expanded by the presence of Christ in our lives.

Those who infer from this passage that to eat Christ is faith, and nothing else, reason shallowly and inconclusively. Of course, there is no other way to eat Christ than by faith, but *the eating is the effect and fruit of faith rather than faith itself*. For faith looks at Christ holistically, not as a distant, "spiritual" reality, but an immediate, actual reality, that He may become ours and may dwell in us. By faith we are incorporated into Him, and He into us, to have life in common with him, and to become one with him.

CALVIN'S COMMENTARY, JOHN 6:35

"I am the bread of life. First, he shows that the bread, which they asked in mockery, is before their eyes; and, next, he reproves them. He begins with doctrine, to make it more evident that they were guilty of ingratitude. There are two parts of the doctrine; for he shows whence we ought to seek life, and how we may enjoy it. We know what gave occasion to Christ to use those metaphors; it was because manna and daily food had been mentioned. But still this figure is better adapted to teach ignorant persons than a simple style. When we eat bread for the nourishment of the body, we see more clearly not only our own weakness, but also the power of divine grace, than if, without, bread, God were to impart a secret power to nourish the body itself. Thus, the analogy which is traced between the body and the soul, enables us to perceive more clearly the grace of Christ. For when we learn that Christ is the bread by which our souls must be fed, this penetrates more deeply into our hearts than if Christ simply said that he is our life.

It ought to be observed, however, that the word bread does not express the quickening power of Christ so fully as we feel it; for bread does not commence life, but nourishes and upholds that life which we already possess. But, through the kindness of Christ, we not only continue to possess life, but have the beginning of life, and therefore the comparison is partly inappropriate; but there is no inconsistency in this, for Christ adapts his style to the circumstances of the discourse which he formerly delivered. Now the question had been raised, Which of the two was more eminent in feeding men, Moses or Christ himself? This is also the reason why he calls it bread only, for it was only the manna that they objected to him, and, therefore, he reckoned it enough to contrast with it a different kind of bread. The simple doctrine is, "Our souls do not live by an intrinsic power, so to speak, that is, by a power which they have naturally in themselves, (145) but borrow life from Christ."

He who cometh to me. He now defines the way of taking this food; it is when we receive Christ by faith. For it is of no avail to unbelievers that Christ is the bread of life, because they remain always empty; but then does Christ become our bread, when we come to him as hungry persons, that he may fill us. To come to Christ and to believe mean, in this passage, the same thing; but the former word is intended to express the effect of faith, namely, that it is in consequence of being driven by the feeling of our hunger that we fly to Christ to seek life.

Those who infer from this passage that to eat Christ is faith, and nothing else, reason inconclusively. I readily acknowledge that there is no other way in which we eat Christ than by believing; but the eating is the effect and fruit of faith rather than faith itself. For faith does not look at Christ only as at a distance, but embraces him, that he may become ours and may dwell in us. It causes us to be incorporated with him, to have life in common with him, and, in short, to become one with him (John 17:21.) It is therefore true that by faith alone we eat Christ, provided we also understand in what manner faith unites us to him.

Shall never thirst. This appears to be added without any good reason; for the office of bread is not to quench thirst, but to allay hunger. Christ therefore attributes to bread more than its nature allows. I have already said, that he employs the word bread alone because it was required by the comparison between the manna and the heavenly power of Christ, by which our souls are sustained in life. At the same time, by the word bread, he means in general all that nourishes us, and that according to the ordinary custom of his nation. For the Hebrews, by the figure of speech called synecdoche, use the word bread for dinner or supper; and when we ask from God our daily bread, (Mat. 6:11,) we include drink and all the other parts of life. The meaning therefore is, "Whoever shall betake himself to Christ, to have life from him, will want nothing, but will have in abundance all that contributes to sustain life."

(145) "Qu'elles ayent en elles naturellement."

This union involves everlasting life, not simply as a promise but as an actual possession. Yet, we are more possessed by it than it by us, for no temporal entity can completely obtain, contain, or explain what is eternal. Even the resurrection is included in both the promise and the possession as the necessary consummation of our new form of existence through regeneration. The subject of this life may die but, says the Savior, "I will raise him up at the last day" (John 6:40). Here is something far deeper and infinitely more real than doctrine alone, or mere moral influence of any kind. Christ actually gives us actual life by uniting Himself to us in a real though mystical way.

It is commonly thought that John 6:51 advances this idea by referring to Christ's death as the point at which his mediatorial character finds completion. At the point of union, the mediation is complete. It cannot be doubted that this is its meaning.

"For the bread of God is he who comes down from heaven and gives life to the world" (John 6:33).

The idea of Christ's flesh being given for the life of the world cannot point to anything other than His sacrifice for sin on the cross. The Jews bristled at such an idea, saying,

> "The Jews then disputed among themselves, saying, 'How can this man give us his flesh to eat?' So Jesus said to them, 'Truly, truly, I say to you, unless you eat the flesh of the Son of Man and drink his blood, you have no life in you. Whoever feeds on my flesh and drinks my blood has eternal life, and I will raise him up on the last day'" (John 6:52-54).

The correspondence between these words of Jesus and the words used in the institution of the Lord's Supper are undeniable. In both cases the participation of the believer in Christ is expressed by eating His flesh and drinking His blood. Whatever the sense of the representation is in the one case, is necessarily the sense in the other. The words of institution in the Eucharist refer directly to Christ's death. We are called to partake in His *body* broken and His *blood* shed for sin.

The reference is the same in John 6:51-58. The Savior had previously spoken of His person as the bread of life (John 6:35). Here He brings attention to His death. It is by His death that He is constituted the author of eternal life to all who turn to Him for this purpose (John 5:24). "Truly, truly, I say to you, unless you eat the flesh of the Son of Man and drink his blood, you have no life in you" (John 6:53). In conclusion,

> "This is the bread that came down from heaven, not like the bread[a] the fathers ate, and died. Whoever feeds on this bread will live forever" (John 6:58).

The passage then looks directly to the redemption wrought by Christ on the cross, but not as something abstracted from His life, nor as some idea that had been presented earlier. Rather, it simply represents the form[1] by which the individual life of Jesus Christ was sacrificed for the benefit of a dying world, and how it actually accom-

---

1   Careful attention must be paid here in that Nevin's use of the word *form* refers to Christ's universal or divine nature and alludes to liturgy—not simply in the sense of an order of worship, but in its root meaning as *the work of the people*. Liturgy is what people do in response to their salvation.

plished this end. It required a deadly conflict with Him who had the power of death (Heb. 2:14, 15). In order to establish Christ's divine immortality, He must first triumph over death through resurrection. There can be no immortality apart from conquering death. Christian salvation is essentially atonement, by which the power of sin and hell was broken by Christ's death upon the cross.

> "It will be counted to us who believe in him who raised from the dead Jesus our Lord, who was delivered up for our trespasses and raised for our justification." (Rom. 4:24-25).

In the final analysis salvation by the atonement of Jesus Christ is a matter of His actual life actually connecting with our actual lives. To say that Christ has satisfied our needs, or that He accomplished for us what we cannot accomplish for ourselves simply points to the reality that His life and our lives are actually, really, personally, historically, mystically, and eternally intertwined. He is actually and personally "the bread of life" (John 6:48). For this to be true, Christ must be understood and assimilated as is presented in the text. We must eat (feed on) His flesh (body) and drink His blood (Spirit), actually and truly participate *in* His life, which was made an offering for sin. It is precisely *this* that emphatically constitutes Christ's "breadness," that which actually sustains life, and which came down from heaven, and which, if any man eat (feed upon), he shall live forever. Glory, halleluiah!

We are not given salvation and life by the atonement through something separate from Christ's actual and whole Person, but only by faith in the reality of His actual Person itself. And remember, Christ's Person necessarily includes both His humanity and His divinity. To eat the flesh and drink the blood of the Son of Man does not acquire the merits of His death in any kind of abstract way. Actual blessing and merits can only be actually acquired through the actual body of Christ Himself. Christ is constituted in the same way that God is, for they share one hypostatic human/divine nature. And the actual nature of Christ's actual life provides the actual righteousness and life that we need.

Clearly, this is the sense of the passage before us, considered in the context of the whole discourse of which it is a part. The hunger that the world is suffering spiritually, does not consist merely in religious instruction or new impulses, motives or inspiration for the human will.

The nourishment that is referred to must come in the form of actual[2] life.

Accordingly, in this form it is exhibited by Jesus Christ as it is found nowhere else because He alone is the Head, the Seed, and the Source of it, because He alone is the second Person of the Trinity. Here is the new birth of the Spirit (John 3:3, 5, 6) that is secured by a living reception of Christ Himself (John 1:12-13). Here is the water that quenches forever the deep inward thirst of the human soul, that never can be more than momentarily allayed from any other quarter, "a well of water springing up into everlasting life" (John 4:10-14). "If anyone thirsts, let him come to me and drink" (John 7:37-38).

Here again is the true bread of life in the same form. "Whoever drinks of the water that I will give him will never be thirsty again. The water that I will give him will become in him a spring of water welling up to eternal life." (John 4:14). Christ is Himself personally this bread because it is only in His person that the life of the everlasting Word, which is the true Light of men, that is revealed in the realm of our common human existence (John 1;4, 14). Only in this form does Christ quiet the gnawing hunger of humanity by supplying the very substance of actual life itself. Apart from this actuality our human hunger, our lack of human wholeness, like the grave, cannot be satisfied. Death can only be met (matched) by eternal life because apart from eternal life all life ends in death.

"Whoever believes has eternal life" (John 6:47). But how? What becomes of his sins? What becomes of the curse of the broken law? The sentence of death that is lodged in the inmost constitution of his nature? The life that is in Christ includes all that is necessary to completely satisfy the demands of the entire case. The life that is in Christ has triumphed over death and the power of death. By his self-sacrifice Jesus has put away sin and forever perfected all who are sanctified by His blood (Heb. 8:26; 9:10, 14). The power of this sacrifice imparts to

---

2   Actual: 1) existing in act or reality, not just potentially; 2) factual, real, not just apparent or false; 3) in action at the present time; now existing; 4) active, not passive. The meaning here points to this sense of *actual* and involves the Christian idea of *liturgy* as the work of worship—and *worship* is understood to involve the work of worthiness and the worthiness of work. Holy Communion is not just a ceremony that happens at church. The ceremony is a formal reminder of the actual truth that is involved in actually living in the worthiness (righteousness) of Christ in our work (our calling, our passion, our profession) as an act of worship.

Christ's life its saving, renovating value, in the circumstances in which it is offered for our use.[3]

Christ's self-sacrifice engages the holistic wholeness of human life itself as it struggles against sin and death. It is not merely the doctrine about Christ that brings salvation, but the fact of it. And this fact can never be separated from Christ's Person, however it may be considered. It is from this perspective that the bread of life is Christ Himself, slain for the sins of the world, received into the life of the believer and made one with Him by the power of the Holy Spirit.

We must eat His flesh and drink His blood. We must feed on Christ! Otherwise we can have no life in Him. His flesh is meat indeed, His blood drink in fact. It is αἷμα—*blood* in reality, not in a shadowy sense, or merely in some relative sense, but absolutely and truly in the realm of the Spirit. Our participation involves us in His everlasting life. It is not simply a form of hope and promise, but is an actual present possession. It is not simply present as a mode of existence for the soul in some other-worldly "spiritual" sense, but it embraces human wholeness in the absolute totality of our nature, subjectively and objectively, and reaches out to the resurrection of the body itself as its legitimate and necessary end.

Christ once crucified and now in glory is the Person, principle, and engine of immortality in every true believer. This is not just the sense of *true versus false*, but of *real versus unreal*—true vs. abstract, true vs. mental assent apart from bodily reality. As the resurrection and the life, Christ will raise up believers at the last day.

> "Whoever feeds on my flesh and drinks my blood abides in me, and I in him." (John 6:56).

Stronger still:

> "As the living Father sent me, and I live because of the Father, so whoever feeds on me, he also will live because of me" (John 6:57).

Language cannot more clearly teach that the salvation which we have by Christ, including His mediatorial grace, comes to us only by the actual communication of His own life.

---

3   This is not merely an allusion to Holy Communion during worship, but also alludes to the wholeness of the circumstance (history) of humanity and to all that humanity does and is as a race, a biblical kind created by God; or in a word: *culture.*

All this at the same time is accomplished in a purely spiritual way, through the activity of faith. But it is not any less real because it is spiritual. Rather, it is more real because it is spiritual. This is no mere oral communication with Christ's flesh and blood. The communication is real. It is not the mere thought or image of Christ that is apprehended, but the very substance of His life itself, as it was once offered for sin and now reigns gloriously exalted in heaven. This is the mystery of the new creation in the Spirit.

The common understanding may object and evade this sense of this completed or perfection of Christ's presence in a Romans 7 kind of struggle between the New Man and the Old Man, who both still inhabit one's body. Like the Jews we ask, "How can this man give us his flesh to eat?" (John 6:52). Nonetheless, the testimony of God is clear and sure: "God gave us eternal life, and this life is in his Son" (1 John 5:11), and it becomes ours only as we have the Son Himself in us by the power of the Holy Spirit.

This then is the very nature of faith as it is concerned with our salvation. It brings its subject truly and really within the power and control of Christ's life, and subjects the believer's whole being to Christ's organic life, which includes all of His actions, especially His atonement of sin by His death on the cross. That atoning death causes the believer to become a new person, or as the apostle said it, a καινή κτίσις[4]—*new creature.* This new creature becomes increasingly what it was created to be over time, though growth and maturity, on to the final resurrection in Christ Jesus our Lord.

> "It is the Spirit who gives life; the flesh is no help at all. The words that I have spoken to you are spirit and life" (John 6:63).

This observation of the Savior occurs in close connection with this verse, and refers directly to the offense of those who reacted to this teaching as "a hard saying" (John 6:63). Jesus had been speaking metonymically.[5] Those who reacted this way thought that Jesus intended to bewilder and confound unbelieving Jews. But Jesus was not trying to bewilder unbelievers, though unbelievers are indeed

---

4 Strong's G2937 (from G2936). It literally means an original formation, properly *the act of creation* and by implication *the thing that is created.* It can be translated as: building, creation, creature, *ordinance.*

5 Metonymy: using the name of one thing for that of another with which it is closely associated.

bewildered (Matt. 13:13). Rather, Jesus was simply teaching that believers must be actually joined to the Savior through their belief and reliance upon this doctrine. Such belief may begin with a simple mental agreement regarding the power of His suffering and death, but it cannot remain in the abstract realm of thought.

Any Bible study that remains abstract and/or intellectual remains devoid of all reality. The idea that faith is mere mental assent belongs to that very carnalism[6] that thinks itself vastly superior because of its mental and/or "spiritual abilities." Such abstract spiritualism always remains in the same kind of abstraction that made it so difficult for the Jews of Capernaum to understand Jesus (John 6). Indeed, the things of the Spirit appear foolish to the paucity of human understanding unaided by Christ. The idea that the words "the flesh profits nothing" (John 6:63) pertained to Christ's flesh or body is patent nonsense.

The true reference is to the unredeemed flesh of the unbeliever. To think that these words suggest purely moral communication or influence by the Author of life that might influence that same unredeemed flesh of unbelievers must be pronounced as crass and as supercilious as the idea of an actual oral manducation of Christ's material flesh itself.[7]

Spirit and flesh here are opposed in a quite different and far deeper sense. The flesh represents the realm of physical[8] nature as embodied in the fallen life of Adam—soul, body, etc. The Spirit designates a higher order of existence, of which Christ Himself is the principle (πνεύμα ζωοποιούν—life-giving spirit) that produces a new divine creation with regard to the holistic wholeness of our being. It is this that quickens or gives life to both soul and body. The flesh on the other hand, whether considered to be soul or body, profits nothing. The flesh can't do what only Christ can do.

The bearing all this has on the question of the Eucharist should be immediately evident to every thoughtful person. Of course, these verses have no direct reference to communion because it was instituted later. They simply refer to Christian life in general. But clearly the idea is essentially the same, except in a different form. If this perspective regarding the extra-sacramental life of believers, or the life of believers

---

6   Gnosticism really, in the sense of the super apostles (υπερ λιαν αποστολων) of 2 Cor 11:5.

7   Another swing by Nevin at transubstantiation.

8   The physical also includes the psychic.

generally, is accurate, then it also has application to the sacrament itself. What is true regarding the general life of Christians cannot be less true of the sacrament. If anything, it would be more true of the sacrament because the sacrament represents or concentrates what is true in the general life of the believer.

Those who deny the real or actual communication with Christ's Person in the Eucharist must also deny the real or actual extra-sacramental union to the same extent. They must deny ordinary Christian unity through union with Christ. This does not imply that the communion of the sacrament and the general Christian life are simply the same thing. It only means that the order of life in the two cases is the same.

We require food in the same sense that life requires life, and not in some different sense. So, if the new life of the Christian is only a moral relationship with the Savior, the power of the sacrament must also be moral. But if the new life involves a real incorporation with the Person of the Redeemer, then the power of the sacrament cannot simply involve good thoughts and feelings, nor mere inspiration or influence. It must also involve a real participation of one's own life in Christ's life.

This teaching of the mystical union must necessarily constitute the right understanding of the Holy Supper because the communion of Christ's body and blood, concentrating in itself the central truth of Christianity, involves nothing less than it was understood to be involved in Calvin's theory, originally and universally held by the Reformed Church.[9]

"In the Supper," to use the language of Ursinus,

> "we are made partakers not only of the Spirit of Christ, and of his satisfaction, justice, virtue and operation; but also of the very substance and essence of his true body and blood, which was given for us to death on the cross, and which was shed for us, and are truly fed with the self-same unto eternal life."

And yet this implies no local presence of the Savior's body in the elements, no oral or corporeal contact with the elements in any way.

The mystery holds not merely in the realm of the flesh, but in the realm of the Spirit because of Christ's hypostatic union of body and spirit. To concentrate the mystery of the actual miracle of the creation

---

9   Nevin is saying that Calvin was right, not that the doctrinal variations of every
      Reformed church was right.

of new life in Christ in the body or in the spirit is to miss the beauty and elegance of the wholeness of genuine spiritual body life in Christ. We feed upon the broken body and shed blood of Christ by faith. The body and blood of the Lord must be manducated by the actual mouth of faith. Real faith involves actual eating. All pretense in this regard must be abandoned in Christ.

In the final analysis, that which is imparted to us through faith by the power of the Holy Spirit is the true divine/human life of the Son of Man Himself, objectively present in the sacramental transaction and actually received into our persons in this form.

Section VII

The Sacrament Of The Lord's Supper

It must ever betray a most poor and narrow conception of the nature of Christianity as a whole to suppose that the question of Christ's presence in the Eucharist may be settled by a few texts of scripture, taken in an isolated way, and without regard to the general revelation of God in Christ that they provide. The scriptural evidence for any great truth cannot be reached by proof-texting. The doctrine of the Trinity for instance cannot be found directly in Scripture by any such formal, categorical statements like those we use in our catechisms and confessions. We may say the same thing of the doctrine of Original Sin.

Unitarians and Pelagians have taken advantage of this situation to create distrust with regard to both the Trinity and sin. So important and fundamental as these doctrines are, they have questioned their absence in plain and direct terms. Why did God leave these things open to skepticism and cavil?

But the objection is specious. We need only examine the truth regarding Christian revelation to see the worthlessness of the objection. Christianity is life, not mere doctrine. The Holy Spirit inhabits the people He regenerates, and not the mere words of Scripture. Biblical revelation is not theorem, but fact—history. However, we are not talking about traditional facts, but actually existing, living, and eternally enduring facts—God and His people. These facts are not disjointed or fragmentary, but are a glorious body of living facts, organically bound together and growing into and out of each other. They constitute a single, unified supernatural organism.

A theology that builds all its doctrines upon mere abstract texts may claim to represent biblical character in a most eminent sense, but it can be only an abstraction and not a reality, much less a living being. That kind of theology belongs to the genius of sectarianism, which magnifies various elements of Scripture to the exclusion of others by focusing on distinction and partiality rather than union and wholeness. Sects always pretend—and even believe themselves—to be "biblical" in the highest degree. They claim—and rightly so—to stand upon the Bible alone, upon *Sola Scriptura*. In the end however, their biblical character invariably resolves itself into a limited, partial, circumscribed, and abstract conception of revealed truth that is devoid of life.

Isolated texts, viewed through the medium of some particular sectarian perspective, are conceived in such a way as to exhaust the whole proof, whether for or against some particular position. But no limited, partial, sectarian, abstract use of the Scripture can be more unbiblical.

Christianity is not a skeleton nor a corpse to be dissected. The Bible cannot be understood by examining various fragments of Scripture. Such fragmentation is the essence of sectarianism. Sectarians think that Scripture can be boiled down to a few basic principles and as long as people give lip service to these core doctrines, they will be okay. But nothing could be less true. When Christianity is boiled down, what is left is bones and soup. Boiling Christianity down to its bare essentials kills it.

From a sectarian perspective, everything is based on the position of the beholder himself, and his power of observing and comprehending the revelation. Rather than seeing the whole of biblical revelation, sectarianism makes the wholeness of Christianity in the image of the sect. This should not be!

Christians must stand in the whole truth, have sympathy with it, submit to the authority that belongs to its wholeness. Only in this way can they have the power to do justice to the whole of Scripture. Can Voltaire[1] be expected to understand the apostle Paul? Hardly! Can we

---

1   François-Marie Arouet (1694-1778), better known by the pen name Voltaire, was a French Enlightenment writer, historian and philosopher famous for his wit and for his advocacy of civil liberties, including freedom of religion and free trade. Voltaire did not believe that any single religious text or tradition of revelation was needed to believe in God. Voltaire's focus was rather on the idea of universal laws underlying every religious system, along with respect for nature reflecting the contemporary pantheism. Like other key thinkers during the European Enlightenment, Voltaire considered himself a deist. Voltaire's opinion of the Bible was mixed. Although influenced by Socinian works such as the *Bibliotheca Fratrum Polonorum*, Voltaire's skeptical attitude to the Bible separated him from Unitarian theologians like Fausto

trust the rationalism of Priestley,[2] or the spiritualism of the Quaker to understand Christ's divinity? Or the true character of the church? No! Everything depends on the perspective of the interpreter, upon his comprehension and catholicity.[3]

Biblical interpreters must be faithful and regenerate in order to be organically connected to the biblical reality they are interpreting. And then each part of Scripture must be studied and expounded in relation-ship to every other part, and to the glorious structure of its wholeness.[4] This perspective of part-to-part, part-to-whole, and whole-to-part reveals the Trinitarian character of catholic, biblical, Christian theol-ogy. Only in this way can the Bible prove any doctrine and be entitled to universal respect.

Consequently, the issue of Christ's bodily presence in Commu-nion can never be settled by the words of institution: *This is my body, This is my blood.* This or that particular verse or section of Scripture alone does not address the "this" to which the formula points. "This" points to the reality of the holistic wholeness of Christ's body in the world. Sure, the bread represents it, but it does not exhaust that repre-sentation.

The theological position of the interpreter inevitably determines the meaning of every particular text or section. Consequently, the Roman Catholic sees it one way, the Lutheran another, and the ratio-

---

Sozzini or even Biblical-political writers like John Locke.

2 Joseph Priestley (1733-1804) was an English theologian, Dissenting clergyman, nat-ural philosopher, educator, and political theorist who published over 150 works. Priestley's science was integral to his theology, and he consistently tried to fuse Enlightenment rationalism with Christian theism. In his metaphysical texts, he attempted to combine theism, materialism, and determinism, a project that has been called "audacious and original." He believed that a proper understanding of the nat-ural world would promote human progress and eventually bring about the Christian Millennium.

3 Nevin has been arguing for Christian catholicity, but not for the Catholic church. Catholicity is the quality of being universal or existing everywhere. Care must be taken here because he is not arguing for one super denomination, nor for Universal-ism, but for spiritual unity grounded in the actual, but mystical, presence of Christ.

4 This is not a small or insignificant calling, and is not for everyone. Those who don't do the diligence need to trust those who do. Those who do get involved must first be teachable, and then be able to teach. However, the task is not primarily academic, but is spiritual.

   One of Nevin's students, Emanuel V. Gerhart, who became President of Mer-cersburg Theological Seminary, after Nevin, wrote as Nevin here describes. See *Institutes of the Christian Religion,* 2 volumes, 1894, Funk & Wagnalls, New York.

nalistic Socinian or Unitarian yet another. The idea of settling the sense of the Eucharist by the words of institution is absolutely quixotic. It cannot be done like that.

The ambiguity itself produces suspicion in order to guard the Eucharist from being too narrowly misunderstood. Indeed, every determination begins with a wrong understanding of Christian revelation, as we have attempted to demonstrate. Many ask why the doctrine of the Trinity is not clearly stated, or why Christ's humanity and divinity are not clearly defined, as they are in, for instance, in the Westminster Catechism? Or why is it not clearly stated that infants are to be baptized? Or why do Christians celebrate the Sabbath on Sunday rather than Saturday? Etc. Why are these and other similar questions not clearly answered in the Bible?

The reason is at once simple, but it does not conform to the expectations of those who ask. Because the Bible is the Word of God, and God is Christ, the Son of God, and the Holy Spirit at the same time and to the same extent, the answer must issue out of the Trinity, and exhibit to some extent the character of the Trinity. The simple answer is that the subject of the inquiry is a Trinitarian, supernatural Being, in whom we inhere. Our own being emanates from the Being we know as the Trinity. This Being is alive. He lives! He/They each live!

The implications of this fact involve us in a diversity of overlapping perspectives issuing out of the Person(s) of the Godhead. The answer is a unified complex of perspectives that serve a common purpose or end. It is not a "one answer or one perspective fits all" kind of answer.

And because we live in Christ, our lives are caught up in His life. In this regard, Christ is not going to answer these questions *for* us, but rather he answers them *through* us. The "us" here is both plural and regenerate. He doesn't answer them *for* the church but through the *church*. His answer to such questions is not *mere* doctrine, but transcends all doctrine—even thought itself. Of course, doctrine is involved in His answer(s), but not a single doctrine, rather a holistic set of integrated doctrines. The doctrinal answer, if there is one single answer, must capture and express the holistic wholeness of Scripture in the light of Christ. But, again, the answer is not *merely* doctrine or words!

His answer to our questions is to shape us into His church, which is the actual body of Christ. It is not that the church is merely *like* the body of Christ, but that it actually *is* the body of Christ. Nor is the church a lesser body than Christ, but is the very same body in its resurrected form. This is both the mystery of the presence of Christ, and the answer to our most convoluted questions.[5]

The Lord's Supper can only be understood when it is seen in its relationship to the whole body of truth, which has been brought to light by the Bible because of the incarnation of the Son of God through the Holy Spirit in the Person of Jesus Christ. This perspective of the new creation in Christ Jesus, and His actual but mystical relation to the church, places the Eucharist[6] in its true and proper light.

The great difficulty here is coming to a complete and abiding sense of the truth and reality of Christianity itself as a supernatural constitution permanently established by Christ as the birth of a new humanity in the world.[7] We are victims of our own history in that we want to hold on to the old, historic definitions and ideas of "spiritual" and "supernatural" that derive from the Old World, the Old Creation before the incarnation of the Son of God as Jesus Christ (in humanity). It is an error that throws an individualistic, abstract, magical, Docetic[8] character over the incarnation, and makes Christianity into a mere abstract spiritualism regarding the flesh, the body of Christ.

It creates a hard and fast division between spirit and body, between an abstract, other worldly spiritualism and the divine reality of the Spirit/body of Christ—the church. We must not sunder the

---

5   We call ourselves "individuals," which means not dividable. We usually think that "individual" means that our identity or person cannot be divided into smaller parts or units, which is true. However, our true identity and person is only fully defined when it is integrated into God, the ultimate unity, through Christ, His only Son, by the Holy Spirit.

6   *Eucharist*, from Greek εὐχαριστία (*eucharistia*), means "thanksgiving." The verb εὐχαριστῶ (to thank) is found in the major texts concerning the Lord's Supper, including the earliest: 1 Cor. 11:23-24. The Lord's Supper (Κυριακὸν δεῖπνον) derives from 1 Corinthians 11:20-21. *Communion* is a translation of the Greek κοινωνία (koinōnía); other translations are *participation, sharing, fellowship* in 1 Cor. 10:16.

7   What is created is a new humanity, not merely Christian doctrine—though doctrine is part of it. What is created is the living Truth of Christ's eternal character in which Christians are "caught up" in the fullness of His body/Spirit, the church.

8   Docetism (δοκέω, "to seem") is the belief that Jesus' physical body and crucifixion were illusions. It teaches that Jesus only *seemed* to have a physical body and to physically die, but in reality he was incorporeal, a pure spirit, so could not physically die. This belief treats the sentence "the Word was made flesh" (John 1:14) as figurative. Docetism has historically been regarded as heretical by most Christian traditions.

supernatural in Christ from the life of His body, which is the church. Christianity is actually and truly a new creation in Christ Jesus, a supernatural order of life, a social being, revealed and made constant and abiding in the midst of the course of nature and history.[9]

As such, it includes resources—powers and divine realities that are not only peculiar to itself, but completely transcend the Adamic or natural constitution of human life. At the same time, this new creation exists as a true historical reality or kind, *homoChristos*. The supernatural has been grafted to the natural, not in the sense of being different than what previously existed, but in the sense of being the fulfillment and completion of something previously, if only partially, existent, so as to become to the end of time its central character.

To question the actuality of such supernatural resources and powers regarding Christianity, when properly seen and understood, is to question the fact of the revelation of God in Christ. At best we must either fall back to the old Ebionitic idea of Christian Judaism, or we must agree that the power of a truly divine life (the holistic wholeness and unity of the human/divine body/Spirit) manifest as the church actually constitutes the character of the church—not transiently and sporadically like it was under the old Testament, but with real imma- nent sustainability and power.

The supernatural, as it appeared originally in Christ himself, cor- responds with the form of the supernatural that has been made permanent and historical in the church. For it is all one and the same life or constitution. The church must have a true theanthropic[10] char- acter throughout. The union of the divine and human in her constitution must be both subjective and objective, in order to provide a continuing, historic revelation of God in Christ (the church), such that the life of the church exists as the life of the Spirit.

As believers are assimilated into this reality, this social being known as the church, the process of assimilation cannot fail to provide eyes to see, ears to hear, and understanding to discern the body of Christ regarding the Lord's Supper that Paul mentioned in 1 Cor. 11:32. It doesn't happen all at once, but it does happen sufficiently, in fits and starts.

---

9   It is not merely a grafting of the Gentiles into the vine of Israel, but is the grafting of
     Israel into the greater Vine of the eternally existent God in Christ. The graft
     changes the character of both strains as they are united into one.
10   Theanthropic: both divine and human in nature or quality.

The Eucharist holds the central and primary place in Christian worship. The circumstances in which it was originally instituted (the light in which it has always been regarded in the church, and our spiritual nature itself, which no rationalism can explain or suppress) all conspire to demonstrate the actuality or presence of Jesus Christ in and through the Eucharist. The actual body of Christ celebrated in the Eucharist remains mysterious, not because it is other worldly but precisely because it also belongs to *this* world.

The mystery of Christianity, focused in the Eucharist, is a single visible transaction.[11] Though transparent to the senses, it actually brings additional clarity to all of our senses,[12] and brings to our attention the symbols (bread and wine) of this new life (body and blood) in Christ through spiritual—but real—sustenance. And the sustenance seals the sacrament. No matter how poorly this is understood, even for the lowest rationalistic idea of the Spirit, the Lord's Supper constitutes the most significant and impressive exhibition of the grace of God in the New Testament, the most graphic picture of the salvation which has been procured for us by the Savior's sufferings and death.

The Eucharist is not mere bread and wine, but is the human response to God in Christ invoked and represented by the words of institution. The Eucharist is the liturgy[13] of our response to God in Christ. It is not merely the bread, but the holistic wholeness of our response to God in Christ that is the "this" of the institutional words symbolized by the bread and made real in the body of Christ, the church. The Eucharist concerns the holistic wholeness and holiness of the church, which is the result of our response to God in Christ and constitutes our gratitude and thanksgiving.[14]

All that is lacking at this point is the sealing of the sacrament or the sacramental seal. And the Eucharist provides the seal as well as the sign of God's transparent grace that it represents.[15] The seal is our own

---

11 A variant definition of *transaction*: (in computing) a data modification or other procedure on a database that is guaranteed to perform completely or not at all. The Eucharistic transaction modifies the identity of the individual with the comprehensive identity of Jesus Christ, the new archetype.

12 See Appendix III, *The Eight Senses of Man*.

13 Refer to *liturgy* in footnote 8, page 318, footnote 1, page 343 and footnote 2, page 345.

14 Refer to the definition of *Eucharist* in footnote 6, page 355.

15 The historic language of sacramental sign and seal points to the reality of the linguistic coherence between the subject of the sign and the object of the seal. The

true and full persuasion of the supernatural character of Christianity[16] itself as a permanent (eternal) and not simply a transient fact in the history of the world. Low views of the sacrament invariably betray a low view of the mystery of the incarnation and a low view of the church, as well, because the new and higher order of life in Christ is the power of the mystery that continues to reveal itself through all ages.[17]

Those who entertain the lower views usually teach the necessity of a higher personal spirituality to compensate. The rationalization for this is to expand the exaltation of the character of Christ, but it is done by making what is objective, bodily, and material into something "lower" in order to make Christ into something "higher." The effort always introduces a false dichotomy or bifurcation of the very thing that the doctrine of the Trinity holds together in unity—body and soul.

This has always been the case. Those who hold low views of the sacraments have always affected to be more spiritual than others.[18] And who were those sticklers for the highest order of spirituality in the early church? The Gnostics, who at the same time turned the incarnation itself into a Docetic abstraction. This low view of the Spirit is anchored in the flesh side of this false dichotomy and can never get beyond it because it begins with the false assumption of a false dichotomy.

The correction of this false dichotomy between body and soul is not to emphasize one side or the other. But to manifest new life in Christ by the power and presence of the Holy Spirit through regeneration one's self. Because the actual fact of Christ's incarnation is faithfully and fully apprehended in the life of the individual as an objective, bodily fact, it is seen to be at the center of history and to be

---

thing signified is identified with the actuality of the seal. The transparent action of God through the Eucharist binds the reality of God's promise or covenant to the life of the communicants, which unites the lives of believers, body and soul, to the Life of Christ, body and soul, and eliminates the problem of "the one and the many" by bridging the gap between them in the life of the communicant/believer and Christ, the Son of God.

16 The doctrine of the Trinity is absolutely unique to Christianity.

17 The low church/high church dichotomy is historically related to different wings of the Reformation. Both terms and their histories are clouded with political and ecclesiastical subterfuge. It might be better to refer to them as inadequate views and more complete or whole views.

18 Paul was very critical about such super apostles (2 Cor. 11:5, 12:11).

the very fountain of a present and living new creation of believers (regeneration), bodily in the church. Personal regeneration allows people to understand that the church is, in truth and in deed, the single and unified repository and extension of Christ's theanthropic, hypostatic life itself.

The church, having a truly supernatural constitution, contains powers and resources that are continuously and increasingly available, that wholly transcend the Adamic order of the world. Such powers and resources involve a real communion and interpenetration of the human by the divine. Comprehend the holistic wholeness of life in Christ, and you will be comprehended yourself by the mystery of Christ's presence, and see that the Eucharist is the very epitome of the mystery of Christian salvation itself.

Only the bridging of the divine and human in one's self personally by the Holy Spirit through regeneration constitutes the only true and right position regarding the presence of Christ in the Eucharist. Christianity alone provides such a supernatural constitution in the actual history of the world. And only those who comprehend this, and who are also mysteriously comprehended by It, can be trusted to interpret Scripture and teach in the church.

Shall we go to the spiritual Gnostic, or narrow sectarian to learn the truth of Christ's presence in the church? Shall we ask a rationalist,[19] empiricist, unitarian, or universalist to explain the words of institution in the sacrament of Christ's body and blood? It would be just as helpful to study Paul at the feet of Voltaire. The very first and most indispensable condition of a safe and sound judgment about Christianity is to personally stand in the fullest sense of Christianity itself—that Christianity alone provides a true and real revelation of the supernatural in the flesh.

This is of more importance than all exegetical helps or biblical commentaries combined. Most emphatically, this was the position of the most primitive church.[20] This alone constitutes the most correct standpoint available to humanity regarding divine truth in terms of both the doctrines and institutions of Christianity for the intellectual as

---

19   Rationalism is any view that appeals to reason as the primary source of knowledge or justification, and is Nevin's term. He then added specific names, which I have deleted. I have provided additional categories to help explicate Nevin's insight.

20   Nevin probably traces its history back to Melchizedek (Genesis 14:18).

well as the most simple and uneducated believer. This alone satisfies both head and heart.

The most ancient church saw in Christ a new order of life, fully divine and yet fully human at the same time. The most ancient church understood that Christ was really active in the flesh in the church, and who was destined to triumph in the form of a true earthly millennium, sooner or later, over the entire world as it existed before Christ's incarnation. They believed and taught that in the realm of this new creation, they were actually and mystically united with the Savior Himself, by the power of the Holy Spirit in order to participate in His very nature and life, His super-nature and eternal life.

It was not possible for them to understand the communion of Christ's body and blood in the Lord's Supper as a mere sign or token. And their opposition to the Gnostics shows that they did not understand it abstractly. Only as the intellectualism of Greek philosophy and Gnosticism penetrated and eventually captured the ancient church, did the abstraction of the false dichotomy regarding body and soul begin to reshape the ancient church into its own abstract, false image. Ancient Christians and all who are unfeigned in their own regeneration see nothing less than the real communication of the Savior's life, divine and human, in the lives of Christ's people in and through the church. They understood and interpreted the words of institution accordingly, as conveying the assurance of this supernatural grace, to be perpetuated in the ordinance to the end of time.

As Christianity finds precursors and foreshadows in the religion of the Old Testament, so are the sacraments of baptism and communion specifically prefigured in circumcision and the Passover. Those sacred feasts which were also customarily held in all ages in connection with Pagan sacrifices were also shadows or remnants of the Lord's Supper.[21] In all systems of worship, religion has always been made to center in the altar and the offering of sacrifice. By partaking of what was thus offered, the worshiper was supposed to come into intimate communion with the object of worship.[22]

---

21 The religions of the world developed out of the broken remains of the wholeness of the God's original Trinitarian revelation in the original revelations of God, to which the story of biblical creation points.

22 Scheibel. *Das Abendmahl des Herrn (The Lord's Supper)*, chap. 1. See: *The New Schaff-Herzog Encyclopedia Of Religious Thought: Liutprand-Moralities* V7, Samuel Macauley Jackson (Editor), Charles Colebrook Sherman (Editor), George William

From the most ancient of times the religious sacrifice must be eaten to fully serve its purpose, and thus it is united in the most intimate and living way with those who sought to propitiate the favor of heaven by its means. Whatever value or merit it might provide became available through the actual participation in the sacrifice itself, in direct communication with the institution of the Eucharist. The same idea, variously modified, may be said to run through the entire sacrificial system of the Old Testament. However, it is most strikingly exhibited in the institution of the Passover.

The Passover was instituted (Ex. 12:1-27) in connection with the deliverance of Israel, and to perpetuate the memory of the children of Israel, on the night when the Lord smote the first-born of the land of Egypt, but spared the Israelites who sacrificially slaughtered a lamb, put the blood of the lamb on their doorposts and ate the sacrificial lamb. The Passover liturgy was later ordained to be observed perpetually in commemoration of this event. The offering was required to be a lamb without blemish. The lamb must be slain as an offering for sin, and its blood sprinkled on the door posts. This liturgical rite became an atonement or satisfaction such that God's curse was not permitted to enter the dwelling thus protected.

> "The blood shall be a sign for you, on the houses where you are. And when I see the blood, I will pass over you, and no plague will befall you to destroy you, when I strike the land of Egypt" (Ex. 12:13).

But it was not enough that this outward exhibition of the blood should take place. The ordinance also required that the sacrifice *be eaten by the people.*

More was intended by the eating of the sacrifice than a mere representation of generic communion with God. The eating represented the necessity of a true, living, bodily connection with the sacrifice itself. The lamb whose life was poured out as an offering for sin must itself be incorporated individually and bodily, as well as spiritually, in the life of the worshiper in order to provide a fair and full claim on the value of its vicarious death. It became a personal atonement by actually and physically entering into the lives of the participants.

It lay in the very nature of the Israelite economy itself that all this should take place in a merely subjective, personal and sectarian way,

Gilmore (Editor), Kessinger Publishing, 2006.

effecting only Jews in good standing.[23] The Jewish atonement itself was only a type or shadow of the greater Christian atonement. And the union of the individual with the sacrifice was a relative and imperfect shadow of union with Christ, as well. It was all a mere foreshadowing of the glorious mystery of redemption that was later revealed in Christ.

Scholars agree that the continuing institution of Passover was more than a mere commemoration of the deliverance from Egypt. The Egyptian deliverance event was itself a type or model of spiritual deliverance, which has been accomplished for the wholeness of the world by the death of Christ. The Passover celebration continuously reminded Israel of the prophecy of the promised deliverance through Christ, the long awaited Messiah of the Old Testament. The Passover involved an acknowledgment of spiritual need for the removal of sin, with a profession of faith in God's covenanted grace, as it would one day come through Christ. For the true Israelite (Rom. 9:6), it carried a sure pledge that the atoning grace of Messiah would preserve him personally from the power of the destroying angel. However, all of this could only happen through actual union with the sacrifice itself, as previously discussed.

In the final analysis, the shadows of the Old Testament found their fullest meaning in the actual presence of Jesus Christ, the God/man. The death of Jesus fulfilled the purpose of all the sacrifices, particularly the Passover offering. "Behold," said John the Baptist, when he pointed him out to his disciples, "Behold, the Lamb of God, who takes away the sin of the world!" (John 1:29). Consequently, Paul expressly called him "our Passover," (1 Cor. 5:7) who has been sacrificed for us.

However, this sense of it is even more expressively given by the Savior Himself through the institution of the Eucharist. By His own appointment, the sacrament of the Lord's Supper was formally substituted for the Passover. In this way it was concluded that the Passover had looked forward from its beginning to the sacrifice of Christ as the true atonement for sin. And accordingly, the Old Testament Passover was fulfilled by the self-sacrifice of Jesus Christ, the Paschal Lamb of God. The sacrament of the Passover came to an end with its fulfillment in the greater sacrament of Christ's body and blood.

---

23 The Old Testament economy or religion eventually became the epitome of sectarianism by its neglect to bring the gospel to the Gentiles.

The two institutions then are parallel, having similar significance and weight. Both look directly to the broken body[24] and shed blood of the Redeemer, as the great and only true propitiation for the sins of the world. Their relationship, however, is like that of the two Testaments: the Old Testament was a relative anticipation of Messiah, the New Testament is the absolute fulfillment and reality of Messiah, come in the flesh for the people of God. The sacraments of the Old Testament are not a proper measure of the sacraments of the New.

The Old Testament made nothing perfect—complete, whole. Its ordinances and ministrations were shadowy and incomplete—anticipatory. Their real meaning is revealed only in Christ, because Christ is their fulfillment. To make baptism equivalent to circumcision or the Lord's Supper equivalent to Passover is to misunderstand the new life in Christ. It would be like attributing to the Levitical priesthood what can only be attributed to him who is a priest forever after the order of Melchizedek.

At best, the Passover was an anticipation or dream of the grace that is actually exhibited only in the Eucharist. It was only a picture or sign and not the actual thing pictured or signified. It was not a sacrament at all in the full New Testament sense. Rather, it was an abstract anticipation of what was to come, a mere symbol of the anticipated real sacrament. Nonetheless, it served its purpose as a place holder until the true sacrament came into being. It served as a model for the Eucharist until the conditions of the Eucharist could be historically fulfilled, at which time whatever meaning it had was transferred to the real thing—the Christian Eucharist.

The Lord's Supper was instituted under circumstances that clearly show that it was intended to take up into itself the wholeness of the typological significance of the Old Testament, which had its central representation in the Passover. Thus, the central symbol of the Old

---

24 It is a concern and curiosity that the body of Christ was not actually broken (John 19:33). Yet, in the institution of the central symbol of Christianity, we celebrate (or remember) Christ's "broken body." We can resolve this difficulty by understanding the Lord's brokenness symbolically, but not without encouraging the very kinds of abstractions that Nevin is arguing against. Another solution might be to understand Paul's words of institution in 1 Cor. 11:24 differently; "Grasp and speak of this breaking and eating of bread (this [Passover] meal) in remembrance of me as my corporate body (σῶμα, sōma)." The broken body of Christ in the Eucharist is the wholeness of his body, the church. We might understand "broken" to be "distributed."

Testament—the Passover liturgy—was assimilated into the central symbol of the New Testament, the Eucharistic liturgy. Through the Eucharist the actual corporate body of Christ as the church the Old Testament shadows became real.[25]

On the night in which he was betrayed—at the close of the Passover celebration, with His sufferings in public view, and with the full awareness that the Old Dispensation would pass away as the New Dispensation was reborn in Him—our Savior simply took bread, blessed it, broke it, and gave it to His disciples, saying,

> "'Take, eat; this is my body.' And he took a cup, and when he had given thanks he gave it to them, saying, 'Drink of it, all of you, for this is my blood of the covenant, which is poured out for many for the forgiveness of sins'" (Matt. 26:26-29).

This instituted the sacrament of the Lord's Supper in the place of the Jewish Passover, for the use of the church for all subsequent time.

Now it is necessary to appreciate the immeasurable glory of that occasion for history and eternity on the one hand, and to discern the frigidity of rationalism and every perspective that can find nothing more in the words of institution than a memorable occasion to reflect on the Redeemer's sufferings and death, on the other. We may not take the words in their mere, plain, literal sense, as is done by the Church of Rome, but neither have we any right to pretend that what we imagine as abstract philosophical speculation or romantic stimulation has any power to change or save humanity, on the other hand. The occasion is too important to miss its true significance.

Note

To understand the importance of our Savior's words of institution, we must know the context of the situation in which they were given. That most wretched rationalist, Paulus of Heidelberg,[26] resolves the

---

25 It is important to note that the institution of the Supper in the Upper Room, was vastly different in form and liturgy than the Roman Catholic Mass. Because of the seriousness of the Roman Catholic error of transubstantiation, which caused them to mis-deify the bread and wine, they handled the elements and developed liturgies that built upon this error. Therefore, we must be suspect of simply reclaiming old liturgies, thinking that "old" means "faithful."

26 Heinrich Eberhard Gottlob Paulus (1761-1851) was a German theologian and critic of the Christian Bible. He was known as a rationalist who offered natural explanations for the biblical miracles of Jesus.

whole transaction to be nothing more than Jesus thinking about His upcoming violent sacrifice on the cross to suggest that the broken bread was a symbol that intended to illicit sympathy for His suffering. *Think of this as my body*, he suggested that Jesus said. The affecting words made an indelible impression on the minds of all present because it was all "very psychologically" powerful, Paulus argues. As long as they lived, when they broke bread together, the sacrament was a simple association that served to recall Him to their thoughts (Comm. in Matt. 26:26).

And yet Paulus paints a psychologically powerful scene in order to show that the symbolic and hyperbolic was no more than subjective, common human passion. We may well shudder at such exegesis. This sentiment and its rationalistic perspective are all too common, and are equally suspect though sometimes spoken of in more respectful terms because it makes the sacrament to be nothing more than common or merely human relations. However, in reality no occasion could have more spiritual or historic importance than the Holy Eucharist.

We must feel its weight and glory, and allow its truth to over-whelm our interest. We must allow the words and their context to be present to our soul. Let the calm, divine self-possession of the Son of Man, who has a clear vision of the past and the future, be clearly understood. Feel the weight of the historical and spiritual significance that a new creation, on the order of the first creation, was in fact inau-gurated in the Person of Jesus Christ, and that the shadows of all past world history yield to the reality they foreshadowed.

Realize the importance of the fact that Christ's atonement, the central truth of Christianity, had never yet been clearly spoken by the Lord until it was first proclaimed here as a prelude to the sacrifice that was about to take place. The Lord put it into a form that lodged the fact of His atonement in the heart of Christian worship forever. Let the fullness of the glory of Christ's atonement for the whole world be considered and felt. Only then can we see the emptiness and vapidity of the interpretation that finds nothing but cold logic in the actions and words of Christ, as presented in this sacrament of His body and blood.

What the Passover only prophetically symbolized, what was in the Old Testament only a shadow, is exhibited here as the real and actually present salvation of the world. Christ solemnly substituted Himself for the paschal lamb. The Old Testament ceremony gave way to the power and glory of the actual grace it foreshadowed. Participation in the Old Testament promise becomes, in Christ, participation in the reality (both historical and spiritual) itself. "It is the Lord's Passover" (Ex. 12:11), said Moses to the Jews at the time of its institution. And so every subsequent year this word was repeated,

> "It is the sacrifice of the Lord's Passover, for he passed over the houses of the people of Israel in Egypt, when he struck the Egyptians but spared our houses." (Ex. 12:27).

This did not mean that the paschal elements were themselves this ancient deliverance.[27] But it did mean that they were more than a mere Fourth of July commemoration. They were the pledge and seal of the ratification of the covenant itself. It was the fulfillment of the ancient Messianic promise. In contrast with all this, Christ referred to His own expiatory death that was immediately at hand, and actually gave Himself to His disciples in the sacrament of the Supper, and for the hope of even more blessings yet to come.

> "This is my body, which is for you" … This cup that is poured out for you is the new covenant in my blood." (1 Cor. 11:24; Luke 22:20).

Did He mean that the elements themselves were His body and His blood, taken literally? Of course not. Did He merely mean that they were symbolic of His sufferings and death, to be contemplated by the mind? Surely He meant more than this. Obviously, the elements were symbols, but they were also seals that confirmed the presence of the reality that they symbolized. Present in the Eucharist[28] is the substance itself of which the Passover was only a type. The new covenant in Christ's death fulfilled what had been previously promised in the Old.

This truly is the Lord's Passover in its complete and most true sense—not the simple sacrifice of a typical lamb, but Christ's body, Christ's blood. Not the pledge and seal of blessings to come, but the inauguration of the New Covenant itself, the pledge and seal of blessings already here, and ordained in this sacramental transaction for the use of the church to the end of time.

---

27 Another reference to the error of transubstantiation.

28 Not in the bread and wine but in the holistic wholeness of the Eucharist as the central institution of ongoing, eternal Christian worship.

All of this, however, now serves as an actual living connection to (and communication with) the reality of the sacrifice itself through the extended reality of Christ's actual body.[29] The bread and wine are not Christ's bodily flesh or blood. They are the Lord's actual bodily signature on the New Covenant that was ratified by His death. Think of a last will and testament that takes effect only on the death of the testator. The reality of the covenant, now signed, is made actual by pledge (promise) and seal (signature) through the outward form of your own actual bodily/spiritual participation in the Eucharist.

Christ's participation is no less real than your own, or is as real as your own. Participation in the covenant requires and implies participation in the actual life because it is through Christ's actual life that the expiatory value of the covenant derives its reality and historical power. The paschal lamb must not be merely symbolically eaten, but actually fed upon and incorporated body and spirit into the actual life of the worshiper in order to give the worshiper an actual part in the covenant of which it is the seal. We can have an actual part in Christ's covenant only as we ourselves actually, bodily and spiritually partake in the actual covenant of Christ's actual body—blood and spirit.

Communion with the covenant necessarily involves and requires communion with the sacrifice. To think that Christ's sacrifice was primarily focused on His fleshly body reduces His spirit to fictional, abstract nonsense. Similarly, to think that Christ's sacrifice was only or merely a supernatural function of His spirit elevates it into the realm of the abstract imagination. Both of these errors flatten the textured reality of the holistic wholeness of the Holy Spirit. One error makes it all physical, the other makes it all spiritual. The reality requires more than Roman Catholic *ex cathedra* transubstantiation, more than Lutheran *ex cathedra* consubstantiation, and more than *ex cathedra* rationalistic dismissal.

"It is the spirit who gives life; the flesh is no help at all" (John 6:63). But the idea of actual participation in Christ's actual life as the necessary condition for genuine interest in His sufferings and death

---

29 We sometimes say, "You are what you eat." In the case of the Eucharist, this is spiritually true, which makes it much more true than if it were merely literally true. The spiritual dimension is an extension of the actual body, like a limb. The limb only functions within the holistic wholeness of the body, and it functions to extend the reach or bounds of human being.

runs through the whole Eucharistic transaction. The bread is given *to be eaten*, the wine *must be drunk*. To quote the words of Ebrard:

> "The breaking of the bread serves to bring into view Christ's death; the eating of the broken bread is a symbol that this death is appropriated in the way of a living union with the Savior himself. As Christ, in giving the bread to eat and the wine to drink, declares them to be the pledge of the New Covenant itself in his blood, it follows that the bread and wine are not simply symbols, but that they serve to place him who eats and drinks in real communion with the atonement through his death. And since such communion with Christ's death can have no place without a life-communion (*Lebensgemeinschaft*) with Christ himself or, in other words, since the New Covenant only holds in the form of a real inward and living fellowship, it follows again that the Lord's Supper involves for the worthy participant a true, personal, central communication and union with Christ's actual life."

We have Christ's actual life in the same way that the Lord presented it to the disciples:

> "Truly, truly, I say to you, unless you eat the flesh of the Son of Man and drink his blood, you have no life in you" (John 6:63). "The cup of blessing that we bless, is it not a participation in the blood of Christ? The bread that we break, is it not a participation in the body of Christ?" (1 Cor. 10:16).

These words are not intended to explain the nature of the Lord's Supper, they simply appeal to the actual, bodily participation by both the communicants and the Lord. The representation is simply suggested, and is not about the mode or method of our communication with the body and blood of Christ in the sacrament.

The only trustworthy implication is that the communion is real, that it is more than figurative or moral language.[30] It is the communion of Christ's actual body and blood, a real participation in His true human life, as the one only and all-sufficient sacrifice for the sins of the world. It is

---

30 If communion is merely symbolic or moral, the transaction depends upon us to "get it" and run with it. But in fact, the power of the Eucharist does not depend upon us mere humans, but only upon the actual power of Jesus Christ, body and spirit. What is perfect cannot depend upon what is not perfect.

"figurative language, I confess," says Calvin, "only let not the truth of the figure be put out of the way—that is, let the thing itself also be present, to be apprehended by the soul as really as the outward elements are by the mouth."

Ephesians 5:22-32 has been already discussed in connection with the general subject of mystical union. We must add here, however, that while it includes a distinct reference to the sacrament of Baptism (verses 26-27), it points to the actuality of communion where believers become "members of his body, of his flesh, and of his bones" (verses 30-32). This is the result of Christ's communion with His people in the sacrament of the Holy Supper.

This is the view of Theodoret, Calvin, Beza, Calovius, and Grotius, and is approved and endorsed in our own time (1850s) by such men as Holzhausen, Harless, Olshausen, etc. Calvin remarked:

"Paul describes here that the union we have with Christ, of which the symbol and pledge is given us in the Holy Supper. Some indeed complain that the application of the passage to the Supper is forced, since there is no mention here of the Supper, but only of marriage; in this however they are altogether mistaken. For whereas they allow only a commemoration of Christ's death in the Supper, and will not admit an actual communication, such as we assert from his own words, we urge against them this testimony: Paul declares that we are members of Christ's body, of his flesh and of his bones. Need we wonder then that he gives us his body to partake of in the Supper, that it may be to us the nutrition of eternal life? Thus we show, that we teach no other representation in the Supper, than that whose truth and power are proclaimed by Paul."[31]

---

31 Ebrard. *Das Dogma von heil.* Abendmahl. vol. i., p. 119. It may pertain to The Consensus of Zurich, 1549. "In the sacramental controversy—the most violent, distracting, and unprofitable in the history of the Reformation—Calvin stood midway between Luther and Zwingli, and endeavored to unite the elements of truth on both sides, in his theory of a spiritual real presence and fruition of Christ by faith. See § 57, pp. 455 sqq. This satisfied neither the rigid Lutherans nor the rigid Zwinglians. The former could see no material difference between Calvin and Zwingli, since both denied the literal interpretation of 'this is my body,' and a corporeal presence and manducation. The latter suspected Calvin of leaning towards Lutheran consubstantiation and working into the hands of Bucer, who had made himself obnoxious by his facile compromises and ill-concealed concessions to the Lutheran view in the Wittenberg Concordia (1536).

The wound was reopened by Luther's fierce attack on the Zwinglians (1545), and their sharp reply. Calvin was displeased with both parties, and counseled modera-

Harless, one of the most even-handed and circumspect commentators, agrees that it is beyond doubt that the reference points to the Lord's supper, not so much on the basis of any particular expressions taken separately, but because the whole thought from verse 23 to 32 is in complete harmony with its various details. The general idea is about the close, constant, real, and actual communion between Christ and His church His body. Reference is first made to Baptism as the pledge and promise of the seal of this intimate relationship. Apart from the reality of the seal, the promise would be broken, therefore, the verse moves to the Eucharist, in which the same mystery becomes real and is confirmed or sealed.

> "If we have come to understand the nature of the Lord's Supper," says Harless, "as unfolded in the Scriptures and held by the Protestant Church, we shall be forced to allow that the image itself, which is employed by the apostles, carries us irresistibly to this institution as its proper object."

Paul calls this whole subject "a great mystery" (Eph. 5:32). This is itself sufficient to overthrow the rationalistic view that attempts to resolve the whole representation by appealing to nature alone. Clearly, the rationalists employ faulty exegesis. The union of the believer with Christ is a great mystery, according to Paul. The two different beings are one flesh (denominated one Spirit in 1 Cor. 6:17). This union, whether flesh or spirit, must be real. It must involve an actual community of life with the glorified Son of Man in His whole Person, or language is meaningless.

> "They are preposterous," says Calvin, "who allow in this matter nothing more, than what they have been able to reach with the measure of their understanding. When they deny that the flesh and

---

tion. It was very desirable to harmonize the teaching of the Swiss Churches. Bullinger, who first advanced beyond the original Zwinglian ground, and appreciated the deeper theology of Calvin, sent him his book on the Sacraments, in manuscript (1546), with the request to express his opinion. Calvin, did this with great frankness, and a degree of censure which at first irritated Bullinger. Then followed a correspondence and personal conference at Zurich, which resulted in a complete union of the Calvinistic and Zwinglian sections of the Swiss Churches on this vexed subject. The negotiations reflect great credit on both parties, and reveal an admirable spirit of frankness, moderation, forbearance, and patience, which triumphed over all personal sensibilities and irritations." (Philip Schaff. *Creeds of Christendom, with a History and Critical notes. Volume I. The History of Creeds*, p. 472.)

blood of Christ are exhibited to us in the Holy Supper, *Define the mode*, they say, *or you will not convince us*. But as for myself, I am filled with amazement at the greatness of the mystery. Nor am I ashamed, with Paul, to confess in admiration my own ignorance. For how much better is that, than to extenuate with my carnal sense what the apostle pronounces a high mystery!"

Appendix I

The Contemplative Shape of Calvin's Eucharistic Thought
by Michael J. Pahls (Copyright © 2003) Used by permission.

> "Indeed, the believer, when he sees sacraments with his own eyes, does not halt at the physical sight of them, but by those steps (which I have indicated by analogy) rises up in devout contemplation to those lofty mysteries which lie hidden in sacraments."[1]

One might profitably approach Calvin's work on the Eucharist as contemplation rather than simple exposition. I use this distinction because, although one does find a good deal of theological and scriptural exposition in his treatments of the doctrine (a hallmark of Renaissance humanist and Reformation theological approaches), Calvin's approach to the Eucharist also reveals a number of structural and tonal qualities which link him to the contemplative and mystical spiritual traditions of the church. Even in instances where Calvin

---

1   John Calvin, *Institutes of the Christian Religion* John T. McNeill, ed.; Ford Lewis Battles, trans. (from the 1559 Latin Text edited by Peter Barth and Wilhelm Niesel [Ioannis Calvini, Opera Selecta Vol. III, IV, V. Munich: Chr. Kaiser, 1926-1952] including collations from the earlier editions of that text and versions of the Institutes). *The Library of Christian Classics*, Vols. 20 and 21 (Philadelphia: Westminster, 1960) 4. 14. 5, 1280. Priority will be given to the 1559 edition of the *Institutes* in this paper because it represents Calvin's most mature reflections on the Eucharist and because it was completed after his polemic engagements with his Lutheran critics. Other sources will be treated as they prove illuminating on the conclusions in the Institutes. Other sources of Calvin's Eucharistic thought include, "A Short Treatise on the Lord's Supper" (1541), "A Confession of Faith Concerning the Eucharist" (1537), "Summary of Doctrine Concerning the Ministry of the Word and the Sacraments" (1537), "The Clear Explanation of Sound Doctrine Concerning the True Partaking of the Flesh and Blood of Christ in the Holy Supper" (1561). All of these appear in English in Calvin: Theological Treatises John T. McNeill, ed., J.K.S. Reid, trans. *The Library of Christian Classics*, Vol. 22 (Philadelphia: Westminster, 1954.)

engages in harsh polemic and pastoral "contextualization" regarding the *modus* of Christ's presence, his spiritual disposition is never without a certain worshipful "gaze" and prayerful register. For Calvin, the Eucharistic celebration is a "visible word" (Augustine) that shows forth and really accomplishes the believer's salvific union with Christ. In his view, such a profound mystery cannot be simply captured by a sterile explanation. Indeed, the very reason for the institution of the Sacraments is that our limited capacities cannot fully apprehend nor appropriate this rich promise of the Gospel apart from their right use.[2] Calvin's concern is always to facilitate a proper apprehension of the Eucharist as communion (union) with God in the flesh and blood of Christ the Son by the worshiping Christian. Considered in this light, it appears that the opening quote may be taken as something of an auto-biographical comment whereby Calvin bids us to join him in a contemplative participation in the Eucharistic mystery. It will be argued here that in his Eucharistic exposition, Calvin the biblical and systematic theologian, is inseparable from Calvin the contemplative and mystical theologian.[3]

I. Calvin's Contemplative Theological Strategy

In contemplation of the Christian mysteries, there is first a revelatory word or symbol that invites imaginative awe and prayerful meditation. This revelatory word or symbol is followed by what one may profitably call a "critical moment" in which meditation encounters "vain imagination" or a "false mysticism" through conflict with the rule of faith. Resulting from this critical moment, a theological definition or a dogmatic conclusion is made which serves to both govern meditation and sanctify the imagination in order to facilitate contemplation. Understood this way, theological definitions mark off cognitive and affective boundaries to inhibit vain imaginings and false mysticism, but they leave a certain openness that is then apprehended through communion and not analysis. To borrow a metaphor from

---

2   So Calvin, "Since, however this mystery of Christ's secret union with the devout is by nature incomprehensible, he shows it figure and image in visible signs best adapted to our small capacity." *Institutes* (1559) 4.17.1 (1361).

3   On the subject of Calvin's theology of Pietas see Sou-Young Lee, "Calvin's Understanding of Pietas" in *Calvinus Sincerioris Religionis Vindex: Calvin as Protector of the Purer Religion*, Wilhelm Neuser and Brian Armstrong, eds. *Sixteenth Century Essays and Studies*, Vol. 36. (Kirksville, MO: Sixteenth Century Journal, 1997) 225-40.

common experience, theological definitions "fence" the back yard of a divine mystery and mark its limits, but they do not thereby render an account of each blade of grass.

In Calvin's meditations on the Sacrament of the Lord's Supper, the words of institution introduce the Eucharist as a revelatory symbol of the true salvific presence of Christ. He then encounters a "critical moment" in which the Eucharistic theologies proffered by Roman Catholicism, Lutheranism, and Zwinglianism are found to be vain imaginings when considered in light of Chalcedonian Christology. For Calvin, the theological definitions of these representative schools inhibited contemplative communion and authentic participation in the mystery of the Eucharist because they did injustice to the Person of Christ. Calvin then employs Christology as a constructive tool to theologically define and expound the Eucharist in order to circumscribe and correct the vain imaginings of his opponents. By this he opens again the *via contemplativa* which facilitates a renewed and "reformed" participation in the Mystery. This outline of Calvin's Eucharistic project will now be traced out in detail.

II. CALVIN'S "CHRISTOLOGY" OF THE EUCHARISTIC SYMBOL

The "words of institution" as presented in 1 Corinthians 11 and the accounts of the Last Supper in the synoptic gospels (Matthew 26, Mark 14, and Luke 22) constitute the stepping off point for every theological presentation of the doctrine of the Eucharist and, while Calvin's presentation of the Supper in the 1559 edition of the Institutes does not prioritize their consideration, they are clearly assumed to be central to the debate.

A. The True Presence of Flesh and Blood

In his consideration of the words of institution, Calvin clearly aligns himself against Zwingli and with the majority of the church in arguing for a true presence of Christ in the Eucharist. This was simply to take Christ at his word.[4] In his *Short Treatise on the Lord's Supper*, Calvin states,

> "We will confess, without doubt, that to deny that the true communication of Jesus Christ is presented to us in the Supper, is to render this holy sacrament frivolous and useless—an execrable blasphemy unfit to be listened to".[5]

Calvin goes so far as to use the pregnant theological term "substance" in his assertion of the true presence:

> "I confess that our souls are truly fed by the substance of Christ's flesh."[6]

In describing the authenticity of presence of Christ in the Eucharist, Calvin does prefer the term "true" to "real" because the latter was often associated with Lutheran and Roman Catholic arguments for a localized presence.[7] Indeed, Calvin did reject the notion of localized presence for reasons that will follow, but even in his strong rejection of Lutheran and Catholic views, Calvin readily asserted that his disagreement was not over the actuality of Christ's flesh and blood, "but only the mode of reception."[8] The Eucharist, therefore, carries an objective force and communicates a peculiar and specific grace.[9] Although the Eucharist must be apprehended by faith in the believer, it is that presence and not faith that clothes the Sacrament with its power.[10]

B. The Person Who is Present: A Chalcedonian Critique

---

4   "All these things are so perfectly promised in the sacrament, that we must certainly consider him truly shown to us, just as if Christ himself present were set before our gaze and touched by our hands. For this word cannot fool us or lie to us: 'Take, eat, drink; this is my body which is given for you; this is blood which is shed for the forgiveness of sins [italics mine]." *Institutes of the Christian Religion*: 1536 Edition, trans. Ford Lewis Battles (Grand Rapids: Eerdmans, 1975) 103.

5   "Short Treatise on the Lord's Supper", 170.

6   Quoted in Ronald Wallace, *Calvin's Doctrine of Word and Sacrament* (Eugene, OR: Wipf and Stock, 1982) 199.

7   See Joseph Tylenda, "Calvin and Christ's Presence in the Supper—True or Real?" SJT 27 (1974) 65-75.

8   Quoted in Wallace, *Calvin's Doctrine of Word and Sacrament*, p. 199.

9   John Williamson Nevin, "The Doctrine of the Reformed Church on the Lord's Supper" The Mercersburg Review 2(5) (September 1850), 432. Idem., *The Mystical Presence* (Philadelphia, J.B. Lippincott, 1846) 117-26.

10 Ibid., 431.

Calvin employs Christology as the "critical fulcrum" upon which the distinctive features of his theology turn. As Allister McGrath has argued,

> "Calvin's thought is thoroughly Christocentric, not merely in that it centers upon God's revelation in Jesus Christ, but also in that this revelation discloses a paradigm which governs other key areas of Christian thought. Wherever God and humanity come into conjunction, the incarnational paradigm illuminates their relation. If there is a center of Calvin's religious thought, that center may reasonably be identified as Jesus Christ himself."[11]

Similarly, Wilhelm Niesel has stated that,

> "More decisive is the appreciation of the fact that the form of Calvin's theology was shaped by the axis on which it revolves. Jesus Christ controls not only the content but also the form of Calvinistic thought."[12]

With the revelatory symbol under consideration and the scope of the controversy defined, Calvin evaluated the various theologies of the representative Christian communions and found them to be deficient in their ability to sufficiently account for the very presence they desired to defend. For Calvin, contemplation of and authentic participation in the true presence of Christ required one to satisfy the protective Christological definitions of Chalcedon.[13] Any explanation of the presence of Christ in the Eucharist must carefully avoid the vain imaginations of Christological heresy and protect the veracity not only of the presence but of the person who is present. Calvin therefore offers the following guidelines in the believers contemplation of the Eucharist:

> Let us never (I say) allow these two limitations to be taken away from us: (1) Let nothing be withdrawn from Christ's heavenly glory —as happens when he is brought under corruptible elements of this world, or bound to any earthly creatures. (2) Let nothing inappropriate to human nature be ascribed to his body, as happens when it is said either to be infinite or to be put in a number of places at once. *But when these absurdities have been set aside, I freely accept whatever can*

---

11 *A Life of John Calvin* (Oxford: Blackwell, 1990) 149.
12 Wilhelm Niesel, *The Theology of Calvin*, trans. Harold Knight (Philadelphia: Westminster, 1956) 247.
13 Ibid.

*be made to express the true and substantial partaking of the body and
blood of the Lord, which is shown to believers under the sacred symbols of
the Supper—and so to express it that they may be understood not to
receive it solely by imagination or understanding of mind, but enjoy the
thing itself as nourishment of eternal life* [15].[14]

C. Distinctio Sed Non Seperatio — Distinct but Inseparable

Calvin's first application of Christology to his Eucharistic theology
is in his understanding of the Sacraments in general as signs of the
realities they represent. According to Augustine, the sacraments are
visible words whereby the truth of God's promises is tangibly shown
and instrumentally applied to the believer. Calvin therefore introduces
the Chalcedonian definition of the two natures in Christ into the theological apprehension of theological symbols themselves by arguing
that in the Sacraments the sign and the thing signified are "distinct but
inseparable." In Book 4 of the 1559 *Institutes*, Calvin says,

> *"For the distinction (between the sacrament and the matter of the sacra-
> ment) signifies not only that the figure and the truth are contained in the
> sacrament, but that they are not so linked that they cannot be separated;
> and that even in the union itself the matter must always be distinguished
> from the sign, that we may not transfer to the one what belongs to the
> other."*[15]

And yet he also states,

> "Now we ought to guard against two faults. First we should not by
> too little regard for the signs, divorce them from their mysteries, to
> which they are, so to speak, attached. Secondly, we should not, by
> extolling them immoderately, seem to obscure somewhat the mys-
> teries themselves."[16]

In other words, just as we must not divide the singular Person of
Christ when we distinguish between his human and divine natures, so
we must not posit a division between the physical signs of bread and
wine and the spiritual realities which they convey when we distinguish between the sacrament and the matter of the sacrament.

This being the case, whence enters the applicability of the "*communio idiomatum*" (communion of the properties) which was such a

---

14   *Institutes* (1559), 4. 17. 19, 1381-2.
15   Ibid., 4. 14. 15, 1290.
16   Ibid., 4. 17. 5, 1364-5.

feature of Chalcedon? Calvin describes the communion of the properties in the following manner:

> "... they [the Scriptures] sometimes attribute to him what must be
> referred solely to his humanity, sometimes what belongs uniquely
> to his divinity; and sometimes embraces both natures but fits nei-
> ther alone. And they so earnestly express this union of the two
> natures that is in Christ as sometimes to interchange them."

Interestingly Calvin describes a "sacramental phraseology" (*sacramen-
tali modo*) that unites the elements of bread and wine with their
spiritual realities in similar to the *communio idiomatum*:

> "There is no reason for anyone to object that this [the words of in-
> stitution] is a figurative expression by which the name of the thing
> signified is given to the sign."[17]

Elsewhere he states,

> "...those things ordained by God borrow the names of those things
> of which they always bear a definite and not misleading significa-
> tion, and have the reality joined with them. So great, therefore, is
> their similarity and closeness that transition from one to the other is
> easy.[18]

Calvin employs this strategy of exposition for the express purposes
of affirming the instrumentality of the Eucharistic symbol.[19] In the
same manner in which the full humanity and full divinity of Christ
qualify him to be the perfect mediator between God and man, so does
the Eucharist become the instrumental means whereby the believer's
union with Christ through the Holy Spirit by faith is presented, confirmed, and effected. Calvin states:

> "Therefore, if the Lord truly represents the participation in his
> body through the breaking of bread, there ought not to be the least
> doubt that he truly presents and shows his body. And the godly
> ought by all means to keep this rule: whenever they see symbols

---

17 Ibid., 2.14.1, 483
18 Ibid., 4. 17. 10, 1371.
19 Brian Gerrish has rightly described Calvin's Eucharistic theology as "symbolic
    instrumentalism" distinguishing it from the pure "symbolic parallelism" of Bullinger.
    See his *Grace and Gratitude: The Eucharistic Theology of John Calvin* (Minneapolis:
    Fortress, 1993) 167 and id., "John Calvin and the Reformed Doctrine of the Lord's
    Supper" McCQ 22 (1969) 85-98.

appointed by the Lord, to think and be persuaded that the truth of the thing signified is surely present there. For why should the Lord put in your hand the symbol of his body, except to assure you of a true participation in it. But if it is true that a visible sign is given us to seal the gift of a thing invisible, when we have received the symbol of the body, let us no less surely trust that the body itself is also given to us."[20]

In employing the conclusions of Chalcedonian Christology to illuminate the nature of the Eucharistic symbol, Calvin was introducing a new understanding of the nature of the sacraments as symbols. As Peter Leithart affirms in his comparison of the Eucharistic theologies of St. Thomas, Martin Luther and Calvin that,

"Calvin was rejecting the centuries-old separation of figure and reality; he attempted to get out of the dead end and ambiguities of Medieval and early Reformation Eucharistic debates by affirming that the Eucharist was both symbolic and real, or perhaps better, by offering a new understanding of the nature of religious symbols."[21]

In other words, Calvin's employment of Christology and specifically the doctrine of the Incarnation allowed him to overcome the dualism inherent in both Roman Catholic, Lutheran, and especially Zwinglian Eucharistic theologies.

D. *Finitum Non Capax Infinitii* — The Finite Cannot Contain the Infinite

The second application of Christology in Calvin's Eucharistic theology represents his desire to withdraw nothing from Christ's heavenly glory. To Calvin's mind, authentic contemplation of and participation in the Eucharistic mystery requires that the believer do justice to the full divinity of Jesus Christ. In addition to being absurd to the physical senses (the bread and wine clearly remaining bread and wine to the senses), both the Roman Catholic and Lutheran assertions of a "local presence" of Christ represented to Calvin an idolatrous attempt to confine the Second Person of the Trinity to the physical dimensions of the bread and wine—a notion he labels a "gross form of

---

20 Ibid., 4. 17. 10, 1371
21 Peter Leithart, "What's Wrong With Transubstantiation? An Evaluation of Theological Models" WTJ 53 (1991) 317.

enclosing."[22] In response Calvin asserts his famous "extra Calvinisticum"—that when we are contemplating God's revelation of himself
in Jesus Christ, we must not think, "that the Godhead left the heavens
in order to confine itself to the chambers of Christ's body, but that
although it filled all things, yet it dwelt corporeally precisely in the
humanity of Christ, i.e., dwelt therein both naturally and ineffably.[23]
This belief that finitude, even the finitude of Jesus of Nazareth's
human body, cannot contain the infinite being of the Triune God, is
then directly applied to the Eucharist. Calvin rejects the notion that we
feed only on the divine and spiritual nature of Christ, but he also
rejects that we feed (commune) with his humanity to the exclusion of
his divinity. Calvin is concerned that we partake of the whole Christ—
God and man. Against those whom he labels "literalists," Calvin
argues:

> "If it is objected that bread is therefore Christ and consequently
> God, they will indeed deny it, for this is not expressly stated in
> Christ's words. But denial will gain them nothing, since all men
> agree that the whole Christ is offered us in the Supper. But it is an
> intolerable blasphemy to declare literally of an ephemeral and cor-
> ruptible element that it is Christ."[24]

Elsewhere Calvin states,

> "He is both God and man for us, for in the first place, he makes us
> alive by the power of his Holy Spirit: then he is man within us, for
> he makes us participate in the sacrifice he offered for our salvation,
> and declares to us that it is not without cause that he has appointed
> his flesh to be our food indeed, and his blood our drink indeed."[25]

Calvin takes a similar tack when offering critique of the Roman
Catholic practice of adoring the consecrated host. Far from being a
sanctioned practice to facilitate Eucharistic contemplation, Calvin says
this practice is an idol which evokes a vain imagination:

> "For what is idolatry if not this: to worship the gifts in place of the
> Giver himself? In this there is a double transgression: for both the
> honor taken from God has been transferred to the creature, and he

---

22 Institutes (1559), 4. 17. 16, 1379.
23 Ibid., 4. 17. 30 , 1402-3.
24 Ibid., 4. 17. 20, 1383-4.
25 Quoted in Wallace, *Calvin's Doctrine of the Word and Sacrament*, 200.

himself is also dishonored in the defilement and profanation of his gift, when the holy Sacrament is made a hateful idol." [26]

E. *Vere Homo* — Truly Human

Closely related to his Eucharistic application of the "extra Calvinisticum" is Calvin's assertion that any contemplation of the Sacrament must equally account for the true humanity of Christ and must maintain a particular fidelity to the doctrine of the bodily Ascension of Christ into heaven. In their attempts to explain the mystery, Calvin's Lutheran opponents argued that by virtue of the *communicatio idiomatum*, the human nature of Christ partakes of the divine attribute of omnipresence and can thus be present on many altars at once. In a related manner, Calvin's Roman Catholic opponents argued that the bread and wine were transubstantiated so that they are locally transformed and become literal flesh and blood. Calvin condemns both of these positions on the basis that they do grave injustice to the true humanity of Christ. After all, when one asserts that humanity has become omnipresent (ubiquitous) does this not reintroduce a Eutychian confusion of Christ's divinity and humanity? Calvin responds,

> "But as we have proved by firm and clear testimonies of Scripture, Christ's body was circumscribed by the measure of a human body. Again, by his ascension into heaven he made it plain that it is not in all places, but when it passes into one, it leaves the previous one." [27]

In another place he states that this error has actually frustrated the true contemplation of the Eucharist:

> "For here Satan has deported himself with wonderful subtlety in order to draw men's minds from heaven and imbue them with a perverse error—imagining that Christ is attached to the element of bread." [28]

Calvin responds with a full affirmation of the true humanity of Christ:

> "Christ's body is limited by the general characteristics of all human bodies, and is contained in heaven until Christ returns in judg-

---

26 *Institutes* (1559), 4. 17. 36, 1413.
27 Ibid., 4. 17. 30, 1401.
28 Ibid., 4. 17.12, 1372.

ment, so we deem it unlawful to draw it back under these corruptible elements or to imagine it present everywhere.[29]

Calvin is often criticized as having a primitive understanding of
heaven as a place having extension in space,[30] but one must keep in
mind first that Calvin is simply taking seriously the Scriptural testimonies that Jesus was taken bodily into heaven (Acts 1) and that his
physical departure was necessary in order that the Holy Spirit would
be given (John 16:7) and giving them their full redemptive-historical
weight. Calvin is no slave to Medieval metaphysics. He does recognize
that in the glorious mysteries of the Ascension and Glorification of
Christ, the prophetic hope has been realized and God has come to
dwell in and with his people by the Holy Spirit. It is in this union with
Christ, in the power of the Holy Spirit that the post-Pentecost church
communes with her Lord. Thus it is the Spirit that Calvin designates as
the "bond of connection" uniting the Eucharistic symbol and the Spiritual reality allowing God's people to truly partake of the body and
blood of Christ.[31] In this vein Calvin refers his readers to the Apostle:

> "For Paul, in the eighth chapter of Romans, states that Christ
> dwells in us only through his Spirit. Yet he does not take away that
> communion of his flesh and blood which we are now discussing,
> but teaches that the Spirit alone causes us to possess Christ com-
> pletely and have him dwelling in us."[32]

F. Incarnation and Sacrament: A Veiling and A Revealing
God has accommodated himself to the limited and sinful capacities
of human beings and has savingly revealed himself. As Wallace argues,
however,

---

29 Ibid., 4. 17.12, 1373.
30 A notable example is G.R. Evans: "The distinction between holiness brought to
    earthly things by God himself for our benefit and therefore actually present in them,
    and a holiness 'really' in heaven but seen 'through' earthly things would seem to
    suppose a spatial separation between the created and divine, the world and the spirit.
    Calvin does seem to take something of a physicist's view of heaven ... that the body
    of Christ now ascended is his natural body, that it is finite and is physically and spa-
    tially present in heaven "Calvin on Signs: An Augustinian Dilemma." *Renaissance
    Studies* 3 (1989) 40.
31 *Institutes* (1559), 4. 17. 12, 1373
32 Ibid.

"whenever we read of God as appearing to men in the Old Testament, we always find that it is really something other than God that appears, as a sign that God is there. This sign or symbol of God's presence holds the attention of the worshiper and obscures the glory of the One who is revealing himself by means of it."[33]

In every act of revelation, therefore, there is simultaneously a veiling and an unveiling so that the revealed truth of the sign or symbol must be apprehended by faith. For Calvin, this was not only true of the Old Testament signs and symbols, but of God's most perfect self-revelation in the Incarnation as well. Calvin thus says of the humanity of Christ, "The abasement of the flesh was like a veil by which His divine majesty was concealed [36]."[34] The glory of God's self-revelation in Christ is apprehended only by the faith of his disciples. Wallace summarizes Calvin thusly:

"Whatever signs of his divinity Jesus gave during his earthly life, and whatever rays of divine glory shone through the veil of his flesh, His divine nature could be discerned only by those who had faith. Those who were offended in Him 'wanted eyes to see his conspicuous glory.'"[35]

As in previous cases this Christological principle has direct application to Calvin's Eucharistic theology. The Sacraments are simple signs that both reveal and conceal the mysteries they exhibit. The Apostle Paul declares that the Eucharist is not discernible to those who partake of them unworthily (1 Cor. 11:29). Commenting on this passage Calvin states,

"What he [Paul] means is that they handle the sacred body of Christ with unclean hands, and, worse, they treat it as if it were worthless, giving not a thought to its great value."[36]

Calvin leaves no ambiguity in his writings concerning his belief that we may not be united to Christ nor may we receive any of his saving benefits except by faith. Because of this he rejects the notion that a non-Christian can truly feed on the body and blood of Christ. In the Eucharist, he argues that Christ is really presented to the believer and

---

33 *Calvin's Doctrine of Word and Sacrament*, 5.
34 *Commentary on Philippians* 2:7. Quoted in Wallace, 13.
35 Ibid., 19-20.
36 *The First Epistle of Paul to the Corinthians*, trans. John W. Fraser, *Calvin's Commentaries*, ed. D.W. Torrance and T.F. Torrance (Grand Rapids, Eerdmans, 1960) 253.

unbeliever alike, and that both may partake of the sacrament (Calvin calls this a mere "sacramental eating"),[37] but only those who have faith participate in his body and blood. Calvin states (with Augustine),

> "I hold that men bear away from this Sacrament no more than they gather with the vessel of faith."[38]

III. A "Reformed" *Via Contemplativa*: Calvin's Mystical Turn

Having demonstrated the manner in which Calvin utilized the dogmatic formulations of Chalcedon to critique those approaches to the Eucharistic Mystery that he considered deficient, it now remains to see how the guidance and governance of Calvin's "Christological Eucharist" opens to the believer a renewed and "reformed" *via contemplativa* whereby the believer may mystically apprehend and thereby authentically participate in the spiritual reality that the Sacrament holds forth.

A. Knowing and Unknowing

There is a transcendent openness in Calvin's Eucharistic theology that invites a "contemplation" of the mystery it symbolizes and sets fourth. Calvin specifically invites this deeper and experiential apprehension of the mystery:

> "I freely admit that no man should measure its sublimity the little measure of my childishness. Rather I urge my readers not to confine their mental interest within these too narrow limits, but to strive to rise much higher than I can lead them. For whenever this matter is discussed, when I have tried to say all, I feel that I have as yet said little in proportion to its worth. And although my mind can think beyond what my tongue can utter, yet even my mind is conquered and overwhelmed by the greatness of the thing. Therefore, nothing remains but to break forth in wonder at this mystery, which plainly neither the mind is able to conceive not the tongue to express."[39]

Contemplation, as Christian spirituality understands it, is an action of the believer but more importantly it is a gift of God. In Calvin's Eucharistic thought, there is an emphasis on the right understanding

---

37 *Institutes* (1559), 4. 17. 34, 1408-9.
38 Ibid., 4. 17. 33, 1407
39 Ibid., 4. 17. 6, 1367.

and proper preparation for the celebration of the Sacred Meal, but far more important is his emphasis on the Eucharist as God's gift.[40] Additionally, the gift is apprehended and participation accomplished by faith—itself a gracious gift. For the believer, then, to apprehend and participate in the Eucharist requires a prior action of divine grace, not only in the gift presented, but in the grace by which the gift is received.

Contemplation also has a transcendent feature where the divine object in which the believer turns from a *kataphatic* "knowing" through the affirmation of theological formulation to an *apophatic* "knowing by unknowing." The revelatory symbol points to an incomprehensible mystery that is incapable of being fully captured or articulated.[41] As Calvin states, "What then, our mind does not comprehend, let faith conceive: that the Spirit truly unites things separated in space."[42] While Calvin does acknowledge that the Eucharistic symbol suggests the mystery, he also recognizes that it does not exhaust the mystery. The mystery is commended to the experience of the believer without being completely codified either verbally or symbolically. Herein lies the practical payoff of the *finitum non capax infinitii* (*the finite is not capable of eternity*) as well as the *distinctio sed non seperatio* (*distinction without separation*) in Calvin's Eucharistic imagination. Knowing focuses the "apophatic light" of unknowing and protects it from becoming the "false light" of vain speculation, but one comes to the limits of knowing and the believer is left to apprehend by faith what the mind cannot conceive.

There are, then, at least some superficial affinities in Calvin's Eucharistic thought with mystical contemplation. The superficialities become actualities, however, when we consider Calvin's treatment of the mystery which the Eucharist symbolizes and accomplishes—the union of the devout with Christ.

B. A Mystical Union with Christ

---

40 See Gerrish, "John Calvin and the Reformed Doctrine of the Lord's Supper", 93. Id., *Grace and Gratitude* 19-20.

41 Herein lies both the necessity and the limitations of the Sacramental symbol in Calvin: "Since, however this mystery of Christ's secret union with the devout is by nature incomprehensible, he shows its figure and image in visible signs best adapted to our small capacity." *Institutes* (1559), 4.17.1, 1361.

42 *Institutes*, 4. 17. 10, 1370.

For Calvin, "Union with Christ is the special fruit of the Lord's Supper."[43] This union or communion is defined by Calvin as,

> "...that joining together of Head and members, that indwelling of Christ in our hearts—in short, that mystical union—are accorded by us the highest degree of importance, so that Christ, having been made ours, makes us sharers with him in the gifts with which he has been endowed. We do not, therefore, contemplate him outside ourselves from afar in order that his righteousness may be imputed to us but because we put on Christ and are engrafted into his body —in short, because he deigns to make us one with him."[44]

Two features of this quote are immediately significant. First it is telling that Calvin describes the union itself as "mystical," a term closely related to "contemplation." Secondly, Calvin expressly adopts the unitive posture which is a feature of contemplative spirituality. In other words, Calvin reckons that the nature of the believers saving union with Christ is such that there is no longer a subject/object relationship between the believer and the Savior. Christ has, rather engrafted the believer into his body and experiences a genuine oneness. The mystical union of the believer with Christ is "real, substantial, and essential."[45] Keeping with his apophatic approach to Gospel mysteries, Calvin clarifies his understanding of the "secret communion" with Christ in a letter to Peter Vermegli:

> "...we become truly members of his Body, and life flows into us from him as from the Head. For in no other way does he reconcile us to God by the sacrifice of his death than because he is ours and we are one with him. ... How this happens, I confess is something far above the measure of my intelligence. Hence I adore this mystery rather than labor to understand it. ... He dwells in us, sustains us, gives us life and fulfills all the functions of the Head."[46]

Calvin argues that union with Christ is the redemptive function of the Holy Spirit[47] and here Christology again intersects with the Sacraments. As we have argued, Calvin's position is that believers truly partake of the human flesh and blood of Jesus Christ:

43   Ibid., 4. 17. 2, 1361.
44   Ibid., 3. 11. 10, 737.
45   *The Mystical Presence,* 58.
46   Quoted in Gerrish, "John Calvin and the Reformed Doctrine of the Lord's Supper" 88.
47   *Institutes* (1559), 3. 1. 1, 538.

"It is not merely a question of being made partakers of his Spirit: we must also participate in his humanity, in which he rendered all obedience to the Father. ... When he gives himself to us in order that we may possess him entirely ... our souls must feed on his body and blood as their proper food."[48]

It is in the feeding that Calvin understands the believer to possess the blessing of this union—a union that in connection with the Eucharist is labeled "mystical":

"We now understand the purpose of this mystical blessing (mystica haec benedictio), namely, to confirm for us the fact that the Lord's body was once also sacrificed for us that we may now feed upon it, and by feeding feel in ourselves the working of that unique sacrifice; and that his blood was once so shed for us in order to be our perpetual drink."[49]

This "Spiritual" feeding on the body and blood of Christ are symbolized for the believer, whose faith is nourished, sustained, and increased. This is, of course, the point of the symbol. Calvin does not halt at a mere parallelism, however. As has been seen, the Eucharistic symbols have an instrumental function. The Holy Spirit, then is active in the Supper, feeding the believer by nourishing, sustaining, and increasing the mystical union "just as" the believer partakes of the bread and wine.[50] The elements thus retain their substance, but the spiritual reality cannot be separated from them. Calvin, however, has maintained that the body and blood of Jesus Christ are locally present at the right hand of the Father in Heaven. How, then can there be a true feeding?

C. The Eucharistic Ascent

The high-water point of Calvin's mystical turn is in his theology of the "Eucharistic Ascent." Rather than dragging Christ down to earth under the form of corruptible elements, Calvin argues that believers must be "raised up" to heaven in order to feed upon him there. In the 1539 edition of the Institutes, he argues,

---

48 Quoted in Gerrish, "John Calvin and the Reformed Doctrine of the Lord's Supper", 93.
49 *Institutes* (1559), 4.17.1, 1361.
50 Ibid., 4. 17. 3, 1363.

"But if we are lifted up to heaven with our eyes and minds to seek Christ there in the glory of his Kingdom, so under the symbol of bread we shall be fed by his body, [and] under the symbol of wine we shall separately drink his blood to enjoy him at last in his wholeness. For though he has taken his flesh away from us, and in the body has ascended into heaven, yet he sits at the right hand of the Father."[51]

Calvin was deeply concerned to maintain an actual rather than a purely notional communion with Christ.[52] We must, therefore, understand Calvin to be advocating a quite literal, if mystical, understanding of this "ascent."[53] Thus, the believer is truly and locally present in heaven with the glorified Christ as he or she communes with the Lord. The ascent is not something that we accomplish in our own strength but something God does in the descent of his Spirit. Arguing against the Lutheran notion of ubiquity, Calvin argues,

"For they think they only communicate with it if it descends into bread; but they do not understand the manner of descent by which he lifts us to himself."[54]

In addition to his belief that it is literal, Calvin's also believes that the Eucharistic assent to God is liturgical. In Calvin's conception of the Eucharistic mystery the stress is on the action of God as it is dramatically portrayed in the Divine Liturgy of the assembled church.[55] For this reason, he joins the preaching of the Word to the Eucharist to the degree that there can be no Sacrament apart from the Word. The liturgical aspect of the Eucharistic ascent is also consistent with the notion of the divine liturgy as a participation in the eternal and heavenly liturgy which takes place among the assembled saints gathered in

---

51 Quoted in Christopher Kaiser, "John Calvin Climbing Jacob's Ladder" Perspectives 13(4) (1998), 10.

52 "... no one should think that the life that we receive from him is received by mere knowledge." *Institutes* (1559), 4. 17. 5, 1365.

53 In favor of a literal understanding of Calvin, Kaiser sites the words of the Mutual Consent between the Churches of Zurich and Geneva: "Christ, then, is absent from us in respect of his body, but dwelling in us by his Spirit he raises us to heaven to himself, transfusing into us the vivifying vigor of his flesh, just as the rays of the sun invigorate us by this vital warmth." Scottish Journal of Theology, Vol. 56, Issue 03, "John Calvin Climbing Jacob's Ladder," 11.

54 *Institutes* (1559), 4. 17. 16, 1379.

55 Nicholas Wolsterstorff, "Not Presence but Action: Calvin on Sacraments" Perspectives 9 (2) (1994) 21.

the heavenly sanctuary around the throne of Christ.[56] In the progression of the liturgy, Christ gathers his people into his presence from their worldly vocations, proclaims his Word to them and declares the forgiveness of their sins, pledges and consummates his union with them in the Sacrament and, then dismisses them with his blessing to again be salt and light in the world. By joining the contemplation of the Eucharistic mystery with the liturgical action of the church, Calvin joins the traditionally star-crossed spiritual dispositions of contemplation and action, of individual piety and corporate spirituality. The contemplation of the Eucharist is inseparable from the active participation in the mystery in the eating and drinking with the assembled ecclesiastic community. Applying this understanding against the adoration of the consecrated host, Calvin argues,

> "They consecrate the host, as they call it, to carry it about in procession, to display it in solemn spectacle that it may be seen, worshiped, and called upon. I ask by what power they think it duly consecrated. To be sure, they will bring forward these words: 'This is my body.' But I will object, to the contrary, that at the same time this was said: 'Take and eat.' And I shall do this with good reason. For when a promise is joined to a command, I say that the latter is included in the former, so that, separated from it, it becomes no promise at all."[57]

IV. Conclusion

Calvin has traditionally been considered a harsh and somewhat sterile dogmatician who was more concerned with fine points of deductive logic than the existential experience of the spiritual riches he spoke of. Hopefully this examination of the contemplative features of his Eucharistic theology will contribute yet another blow in the destruction of this caricature. Calvin offers a critique to each of the Sacramental positions of his day, but those points of critique proceed from a heart that is deeply touched with concern that both the individ-

---

56 Kaiser makes this point and ties it directly to Calvin's interactions with St. John Chrysostom. "John Calvin Climbing Jacob's Ladder", 12. Cf. the thought of Vatican II, "In the earthly liturgy we take part in a foretaste of that heavenly liturgy which is celebrated in the Holy City of Jerusalem toward which we journey as pilgrims, where Christ is sitting at the right hand of God, Minister of the holies and of the true tabernacle." Constitution on the Sacred Liturgy, 1.8 in *Vatican Council II Volume 1: The Concilliar and Post-Concilliar Documents*, Austin Flannery ed. (Northport, NY: Costello, 1996) 5.

57 *Institutes* (1559), 4. 17, 37, 1413.

ual Christian and the assembled church enjoy an authentic communion with Christ through an authentic participation by faith in the
Eucharist. Finally, we see that Calvin is concerned to positively
account for the Apostolic witness of Scripture as well as the Ecumenical assent of the church. Calvin's hope, therefore, was to render an
account of the Eucharist which was Evangelically rooted, critically
Reformed, faithfully catholic, and spiritually satisfying.

In the tiny chapter, "What is Contemplation?", Thomas Merton
closes his thoughts with the following, pregnant observation:

> "Contemplation is more than a consideration of abstract truths
> about God, more even than affective meditation on the things we
> believe. It is awakening, enlightenment and the amazing intuitive
> grasp by which love gains certitude of God's creative and dynamic
> intervention in our daily life. Hence contemplation does not sim-
> ply 'find' a clear idea of God and confine Him within the limits of
> that idea, and hold him there as a prisoner to Whom it can always
> return. On the contrary, contemplation is carried away by Him
> into His own realm, His own mystery and his own freedom. It is a
> pure virginal knowledge, poor in concepts, poorer still in reason-
> ing, but able, by its very poverty and purity, to follow the Word
> 'wherever He may go.'"[58]

At the far side of a consideration of the contemplative shape of his
Eucharistic theology, Calvin, I suspect would have found great satisfaction in this definition.

---

58 *New Seeds of Contemplation* (New York: New Directions, 1961) 5.

APPENDIX II

JOHN CALVIN TRACTS & LETTERS— THE SUPPER OF OUR LORD

In which is shown its true institution, benefit, and utility.
1540 A.D.

SHORT TREATISE ON THE HOLY SUPPER OF OUR LORD JESUS CHRIST

Reason Why Many Weak Consciences Remain In Suspense As To The True Doctrine Of The Supper.

As the holy sacrament of the Supper of our Lord Jesus Christ has long been the subject of several important errors, and in these past years been anew enveloped in diverse opinions and contentious disputes, it is no wonder if many weak consciences cannot fairly resolve what view they ought to take of it, but remain in doubt and perplexity, waiting till all contention being laid aside, the servants of God come to some agreement upon it. However, as it is a very perilous thing to have no certainty on an ordinance, the understanding of which is so requisite for our salvation, I have thought it might be a very useful labor to treat briefly and, nevertheless, clearly deduce a summary of what is necessary to be known of it. I may add that I have been requested to do so by some worthy persons, whom I could not refuse without neglecting my duty. In order to rid ourselves of all difficulty, it is expedient to attend to the order which I have determined to follow.

The Order To Be Observed In This Treatise.

First, then, we will explain to what end and for what reason our Lord instituted this holy sacrament.

Secondly, what fruit and utility we receive from it, when it will likewise be shown how the body of Jesus Christ is given to us.

Thirdly, what is the legitimate use of it.

Fourthly, we will detail the errors and superstitions with which it has been contaminated, when it will be shown how the servants of God ought to differ from the Papists.

Lastly, we will mention what has been the source of the discussion which has been so keenly carried on, even among those who have, in our time, brought back the light of the gospel, and employed themselves in rightly edifying the church in sound doctrine.

At Baptism God Receives Us Into His Church As Members Of His Family.

In regard to the first article: Since it has pleased our good God to receive us by baptism into his church, which is his house, which he desires to maintain and govern, and since he has received us to keep us not merely as domestics, but as his own children, it remains that, in order to do the office of a good father, he nourish and provide us with every thing necessary for our life. In regard to corporal nourishment, as it is common to all, and the bad share in it as well as the good, it is not peculiar to his family. It is very true that we have an evidence of his paternal goodness in maintaining our bodies, seeing that we partake in all the good things which he gives us with his blessing. But as the life into which he has begotten us again is spiritual, so must the food, in order to preserve and strengthen us, be spiritual also.

For we should understand, that not only has he called us one day to possess his heavenly inheritance, but that by hope he has already in some measure installed us in possession; that not only has he promised us life, but already transported us into it, delivering us from death, when by adopting us as his children, he begot us again by immortal seed, namely, his word imprinted on our hearts by the Holy Spirit.

The Virtue And Office Of The Word Of God In Regard To Our Souls.

To maintain us in this spiritual life, the thing requisite is not to feed our bodies with fading and corruptible food, but to nourish our souls on the best and most precious diet. Now all Scripture tells us what the spiritual food by which our souls are maintained is: that same word by which the Lord has regenerated us; but it frequently adds the reason, viz., that in it Jesus Christ, our only life, is given and administered to us. For we must not imagine that there is life anywhere else than in God. But just as God has placed all fullness of life in Jesus, in order to communicate it to us by his means, so he ordained his word as the instrument by which Jesus Christ, with all his graces, is dispensed to us. Still it always remains true, that our souls have no other pasture than Jesus Christ. Our heavenly Father, therefore, in his care to nourish us, gives us no other, but rather recommends us to take our fill there, as a refreshment amply sufficient, with which we cannot dispense, and beyond which no other can be found.

Jesus Christ The, Only Spiritual Nourishment Of Our Souls.

We have already seen that Jesus Christ is the only food by which our souls are nourished; but as it is distributed to us by the word of the Lord, which he has appointed an instrument for that purpose, that word is also called bread and water. Now what is said of the word applies as well to the sacrament of the Supper, by means of which the Lord leads us to communion with Jesus Christ. For seeing we are so weak that we cannot receive him with true heartfelt trust, when he is presented to us by simple doctrine and preaching, the Father of mercy, disdaining not to condescend in this matter to our infirmity, has been pleased to add to his word a visible sign, by which he might represent the substance of his promises, to confirm and fortify us by delivering us from all doubt and uncertainty.

Since, then, there is something so mysterious and incomprehensible in saying that we have communion with the body and the blood of Jesus Christ, and we on our part are so rude and gross that we cannot understand the least things of God, it was of importance that we should be given to understand it as far as our capacity could admit.

The Cause Why Our Lord Instituted The Supper.

Our Lord, therefore, instituted the Supper, first, in order to sign and seal in our consciences the promises contained in his gospel concerning our being made partakers of his body and blood, and to give us certainty and assurance that therein lies our true spiritual nourishment, and that having such an earnest, we may entertain a right reliance on salvation. Secondly, in order to exercise us in recognizing his great goodness toward us, and thus lead us to laud and magnify him more fully. Thirdly, in order to exhort us to all holiness and inno-cence, inasmuch as we are members of Jesus Christ; and specially to exhort us to union and brotherly charity, as we are expressly com-manded. When we shall have well considered these three reasons, to which the Lord had respect in ordaining his Supper, we shall be able to understand, both what benefit accrues to us from it, and what is our duty in order to use it properly.

The Means Of Knowing The Great Benefit Of The Supper.

It is now time to come to the second point, viz., to show how the Lord's Supper is profitable to us, provided we use it profitably. Now we shall know its utility by reflecting on the indigence which it is meant to succor.

We must necessarily be under great trouble and torment of con-science, when we consider who we are, and examine what is in us. For not one of us can find one particle of righteousness in himself, but on the contrary we are all full of sins and iniquities, so much so that no other party is required to accuse us than our own conscience, no other judge to condemn us. It follows that the wrath of God is kindled against us, and that none can escape eternal death. If we are not asleep and stupified, this horrible thought must be a kind of perpetual hell to vex and torment us. For the judgment of God cannot come into our remembrance without letting us see that our condemnation follows as a consequence.

The Misery Of Man.

We are then already in the gulf, if God does not in mercy draw us out of it.

Moreover, what hope of resurrection can we have while consider-ing our flesh, which is only rottenness and corruption? Thus in regard to the soul, as well as the body, we are more than miserable if we remain within ourselves, and this misery cannot but produce great sadness and anguish of soul. Now our heavenly Father, to succor us in this, gives us the Supper as a mirror, in which we may contemplate our Lord Jesus Christ, crucified to take away our faults and offenses, and raised again to deliver us from corruption and death, restoring us to a celestial immortality.

The Supper Invites Us To The Promises Of Salvation.

Here, then, is the singular consolation which we derive from the
Supper. It directs and leads us to the cross of Jesus Christ and to his resurrection, to certify us that whatever iniquity there may be in us, the
Lord nevertheless recognizes and accepts us as righteous—whatever
materials of death may be in us, he nevertheless gives us life—whatever
misery may be in us, he nevertheless fills us with all felicity. Or to
explain the matter more simply—as in ourselves we are devoid of all
good, and have not one particle of what might help to procure salvation, the Supper is an attestation that, having been made partakers of
the death and passion of Jesus Christ, we have every thing that is useful
and salutary to us.

All The Treasuries Of Spiritual Grace Presented In The Supper.

We can therefore say that in it the Lord displays to us all the trea-
sures of his spiritual grace, inasmuch as he associates us in all the
blessings and riches of our Lord Jesus. Let us recollect, then, that the
Supper is given to us as a mirror in which we may contemplate Jesus
Christ crucified in order to deliver us from condemnation, and raised
again in order to procure for us righteousness and eternal life. It is
indeed true that this same grace is offered us by the gospel, yet as in
the Supper we have more, ample certainty, and fuller enjoyment of it,
with good cause do we recognize this fruit as coming from it.

Jesus Christ Is The Substance Of The Sacraments.

But as the blessings of Jesus Christ do not belong to us at all,
unless he be previously ours, it is necessary, first of all, that he be given
us in the Supper, in order that the things which we have mentioned
may be truly accomplished in us. For this reason I am wont to say that
the substance of the sacraments is the Lord Jesus, and the efficacy of
them the graces and blessings which we have by his means. Now the
efficacy of the Supper is to confirm to us the reconciliation which we
have with God through our Savior's death and passion; the washing of
our souls which we have in the shedding of his blood; the righteousness which we have in his obedience; in short, the hope of salvation
which we have in all that he has done for us. It is necessary, then, that
the substance should be conjoined with these, otherwise nothing
would be firm or certain. Hence we conclude that two things are presented to us in the Supper, viz., Jesus Christ as the source and

substance of all good; and, secondly, the fruit and efficacy of his death and passion. This is implied in the words which were used. For after commanding us to eat his body and drink his blood, he adds that his body was delivered for us, and his blood shed for the remission of our sins. Hereby he intimates, first, that we ought not simply to communicate in his body and blood, without any other consideration, but in order to receive the fruit derived to us from his death and passion; secondly, that we can attain the enjoyment of such fruit only by participating in his body and blood, from which it is derived.

How The Bread Is Called The Body, And The Wine The Blood Of Christ.

We begin now to enter on the question so much debated, both anciently and at the present time—how we are to understand the words in which the bread is called the body of Christ, and the wine his blood. This may be disposed of without much difficulty; if we carefully observe the principle which I lately laid down, viz., that all the benefit which we should seek in the Supper is annihilated if Jesus Christ be not there given to us as the substance and foundation of all. That being fixed, we will confess, without doubt, that to deny that a true communication of Jesus Christ is presented to us in the Supper, is to render this holy sacrament frivolous and useless—an execrable blasphemy unfit to be listened to.

What Is Requisite In Order To Live In Jesus Christ.

Moreover, if the reason for communicating with Jesus Christ is to have part and portion in all the graces which he purchased for us by his death, the thing requisite must be not only to be partakers of his Spirit, but also to participate in his humanity, in which he rendered all obedience to God his Father, in order to satisfy our debts, although, properly speaking, the one cannot be without the other; for when he gives himself to us, it is in order that we may possess him entirely. Hence, as it is said that his Spirit is our life, so he himself, with his own lips, declares that his flesh is meat indeed, and his blood drink indeed (John 6:55). If these words are not to go for nothing, it follows that in order to have our life in Christ our souls must feed on his body and blood as their proper food. This, then, is expressly attested in the Supper, when of the bread it is said to us that we are to take it and eat it, and that it is his body, and of the cup that we are to drink it, and that it is his blood. This is expressly spoken of the body and blood, in order that we may learn to seek there the substance of our spiritual life.

How The Bread And Wine Are The Body Of Jesus Christ.

Now, if it be asked whether the bread is the body of Christ and the wine his blood, we answer, that the bread and the wine are visible signs, which represent to us the body and blood, but that this name and title of *body* and *blood* is given to them because they are as it were instruments by which the Lord distributes them to us. This form and manner of speaking is very appropriate. For as the communion which we have with the body of Christ is a thing incomprehensible, not only to the eye but to our natural sense, it is there visibly demonstrated to us. Of this we have a striking example in an analog case. Our Lord, wishing to give a visible appearance to his Spirit at the baptism of Christ, presented him under the form of a dove. St. John the Baptist, narrating the fact, says, that he saw the Spirit of God descending. If we look more closely, we shall find that he saw nothing but the dove, in respect that the Holy Spirit is in his essence invisible. Still, knowing that this vision was not an empty phantom, but a sure sign of the presence of the Holy Spirit, he doubts not to say that he saw it (John 1:32) because it was represented to him according to his capacity.

The Sacrament Is Represented By Visible Signs.

Thus it is with the communion which we have in the body and blood of the Lord Jesus. It is a spiritual mystery which can neither be seen by the eye nor comprehended by the human understanding. It is therefore figured to us by visible signs, according as our weakness requires, in such manner, nevertheless, that it is not a bare figure but is combined with the reality and substance. It is with good reason then that the bread is called the body, since it not only represents but also presents it to us. Hence we indeed infer that the name of the body of Jesus Christ is transferred to the bread, inasmuch as it is the sacrament and figure of it. But we likewise add, that the sacraments of the Lord should not and cannot be at all separated from their reality and substance. To distinguish, in order to guard against confounding them, is not only good and reasonable, but altogether necessary; but to divide them, so as to make the one exist without the other, is absurd.

The Proper Body And Blood Of Jesus Christ Received Only By Faith.

Hence when we see the visible sign we must consider what it represents, and by whom it has been given us. The bread is given to us in the figure the body of Jesus Christ, with the command to eat it, and it is given to us by God, who is certain and immutable truth. If God cannot deceive or lie, it follows that it accomplishes all that it signifies. We must then truly receive in the Supper the body and blood of Jesus Christ, since the Lord there represents to us the communion of both. Were it otherwise, what could be meant by saying that we eat the bread and drink the wine as a sign that his body is our meat and his blood our drink? If he gave us only bread and wine, leaving the spiritual reality behind, would it not be under false colors that this ordinance had been instituted?

The Internal Substance Is Conjoined With The Visible Signs.

We must confess, then, that if the representation which God gives us in the Supper is true, the internal substance of the sacrament is conjoined with the visible signs; and as the bread is distributed to us by the hand, so the body of Christ is communicated to us in order that we may be made partakers of it. Though there should be nothing more, we have good cause to be satisfied when we understand that Jesus Christ gives us in the Supper the proper substance of his body and blood, in order that we may possess it fully, and possessing it have part in all his blessings. For seeing we have him, all the riches of God which are comprehended in him are exhibited to us, in order that they may be ours. Thus, as a brief definition of this utility of the Supper, we may say, that Jesus Christ is there offered to us in order that we may possess him, and in him all the fullness of grace which we can desire, and that herein we have a good aid to confirm our consciences in the faith which we ought to have in him.

In The Supper We Are Reminded Of Our Duty Towards God.

The second benefit of the Supper is, that it admonishes and incites us more strongly to recognize the blessings which we have received, and receive daily from the Lord Jesus, in order that we may ascribe to him the praise which is due. For in ourselves we are so negligent that we rarely think of the goodness of God, if he does not arouse us from our indolence, and urge us to our duty. Now there cannot be a spur which can pierce us more to the quick than when he makes us, so to speak, see with the eye, touch with the hand, and distinctly perceive this inestimable blessing of feeding on his own substance. This he means to intimate when he commands us to show forth his death till he come (1 Corinthians 11:26). If it is then so essential to salvation not to overlook the gifts which God has given us, but diligently to keep them in mind, and extol them to others for mutual edification; we see another singular advantage of the Supper in this, that it draws us off from ingratitude, and allows us not to forget the benefit which our Lord Jesus bestowed upon us in dying for us, but induces us to render him thanks, and, as it were, to publicly profess how much we are indebted to him.

The Sacrament A Strong Inducement To Holy Living And Brotherly Love.

The third advantage of the Sacrament consists in furnishing a most powerful incitement to live in holiness, and especially observe charity and brotherly love toward all. For seeing we have been made members of Jesus Christ, being incorporated into him, and united with him as our head, it is most reasonable that we should become conformable to him in purity and innocence, and especially that we should cultivate charity and concord together as becomes members of the same body. But to understand this advantage properly, we must not suppose that our Lord warns, incites, and inflames our hearts by the external sign merely; for the principal point is that he operates in us inwardly by his Holy Spirit in order to give efficacy to his ordinance, which he has destined for that purpose, as an instrument by which he wishes to do his work in us. Wherefore, inasmuch as the virtue of the Holy Spirit is conjoined with the sacraments when we duly receive them, we have reason to hope they will prove a good mean and aid to make us grow and advance in holiness of life, and specially in charity.

What It Is To Pollute The Holy Supper And The Great Guilt Of So Doing.

Let us come to the third point which we proposed at the commencement of this treatise, viz., the legitimate use, which consists in reverently observing our Lord's institution. Whoever approaches the sacrament with contempt or indifference, not caring much about following when the Lord calls him, perversely abuses, and in abusing pollutes it. Now to pollute and contaminate what God has so highly sanctified, is intolerable blasphemy. Not without cause then does St. Paul denounce such heavy condemnation on all who take it unworthily (1 Corinthians 11:29).

For if there is nothing in heaven nor on earth of greater price and dignity than the body and blood of the Lord, it is no slight fault to take it inconsiderately and without being well prepared. Hence he exhorts us to examine ourselves carefully, in order to make the proper use of it. When we understand what this examination should be, we shall know the use after which we are inquiring.

The Manner Of Examining Ourselves.

Here it is necessary to be well on our guard. For as we cannot be too diligent in examining ourselves as the Lord enjoins, so, on the other hand, sophistical doctors have brought poor consciences into perilous perplexity, or rather into a horrible Gehenna, requiring I know not what examination, which it is not possible for any man to make. To rid ourselves of all these perplexities, we must reduce the whole, as I have already said, to the ordinance of the Lord, as the rule which, if we follow it, will not allow us to err. In following it, we have to examine whether we have true repentance in ourselves, and true faith in our Lord Jesus Christ.

These two things are so conjoined, that the one cannot subsist without the other.

To Participate In The Blessings Of Christ, We Must Renounce All That Is Our Own.

If we consider our life to be placed in Christ, we must acknowledge that we are dead in ourselves. If we seek our strength in him, we must understand that in ourselves we are weak. If we think that all our felicity is in his grace, we must understand how miserable we are without it. If we have our rest in him, we must feel within ourselves only disquietude and torment. Now such feelings cannot exist without producing, first, dissatisfaction with our whole life; secondly, anxiety and fear; lastly, a desire and love of righteousness. For he who knows the turpitude of his sin and the wretchedness of his state and condition while alienated from God, is so ashamed that he is constrained to be dissatisfied with himself, to condemn himself, to sigh and groan in great sadness. Moreover, the justice of God immediately presents itself and oppresses the wretched conscience with keen anguish, from not seeing any means of escape, or having any thing to answer in defense. When under such a conviction of our misery we get a taste of the goodness of God, it is then we would wish to regulate our conduct by his will, and renounce all our bygone, life, in order to be made new creatures in him.

The Requisites Of Worthy Communion.

Hence if we would worthily communicate in the Lord's Supper, we must with firm heart-felt reliance regard the Lord Jesus as our only righteousness, life, and salvation, receiving and accepting the promises which are given us by him as sure and certain, and renouncing all other confidence, so that distrusting ourselves and all creatures, we may rest fully in him, and be contented with his grace alone. Now as that cannot be until we know how necessary it is that he come to our aid, it is of importance to have a deep-seated conviction of our own misery, which will make us hunger and thirst after him. And, in fact, what mockery would it be to go in search of food when we have no appetite? Now to have a good appetite it is not enough that the stomach be empty, it must also be in good order and capable of receiving its food. Hence it follows that our souls must be pressed with famine and have a desire and ardent longing to be fed, in order to find their proper nourishment in the Lord's Supper.

Self-Denial Necessary.

Moreover, it is to be observed that we cannot desire Jesus Christ without aspiring to the righteousness of God, which consists in renouncing ourselves and obeying his will. For it is preposterous to pretend that we are of the body of Christ, while abandoning ourselves to all licentiousness, and leading a dissolute life. Since in Christ is naught but chastity, benignity, sobriety, truth, humility, and such like virtues, if we would be his members, all uncleanness, intemperance, falsehood, pride, and similar vices must be put from us. For we cannot intermingle these things with him without offering him great dishonor and insult. We ought always to remember that there is no more agreement between him and iniquity than between light and darkness. If we would come then to true repentance, we must endeavor to make our whole life conformable to the example of Jesus Christ.

Charity Especially Necessary.

And while this must be general in every part of our life, it must be specially so in respect of charity, which is, above all other virtues, recommended to us in this sacrament for which reason it is called the bond of charity. For as the bread which is there sanctified for the common use of all is composed of several grains so mixed together that they cannot be distinguished from each other, so ought we to be united together in indissoluble friendship. Moreover, we all receive the one body of Christ.

If then we have strife and discord among ourselves, it is not owing to us that Christ Jesus is not rent in pieces, and we are therefore guilty of sacrilege, as if we had done it. We must not, then, on any account, presume to approach if we bear hatred or rancor against any man living, and especially any Christian who is in the unity of the church. In order fully to comply with our Lord's injunction, there is another disposition which we must bring. It is to confess with the mouth and testify how much we are indebted to our Savior, and return him thanks, not only that his name may be glorified in us, but also to edify others, and instruct them, by our example, what they ought to do.

All Men Imperfect And Blameworthy.

But as not a man will be found upon the earth who has made such progress in faith and holiness, as not to be still very defective in both, there might be a danger that several good consciences might be troubled by what has been said, did we not obviate it by tempering the injunctions which we have given in regard both to faith and repentance. It is a perilous mode of teaching which some adopt, when they require perfect reliance of heart and perfect penitence, and exclude all who have them hot. For in so doing they exclude all without excepting one. Where is the man who can boast that he is not stained by some spot of distrust? That he is not subject to some vice or infirmity? Assuredly the faith which the children of God have is such that they have ever occasion to pray: Lord, help our unbelief. For it is a malady so rooted in our nature, that we are never completely cured until we are delivered from the prison of the body.

Moreover, the purity of life in which they walk is only such that they have occasion daily to pray, as well for remission of sins as for grace to make greater progress. Although some are more and others less imperfect, still there is none who does not fail in many respects. Hence the Supper would be not only useless, but pernicious to all, if it were necessary to bring a faith or integrity, as to which there would be nothing to gainsay.

This would be contrary to the intention of our Lord, as there is nothing which he has given to his church that is more salutary.

Imperfection Must Not Make Us Cease To Hope For Salvation.

Therefore, although we feel our faith to be imperfect, and our conscience not so pure that it does not accuse us of many vices, that ought not to hinder us from presenting ourselves at the Lord's holy table, provided that amid this infirmity we feel in our heart that with- out hypocrisy and dissimulation we hope for salvation in Christ, and desire to live according to the rule of the gospel. I say expressly, pro- vided there be no hypocrisy.

For there are many who deceive themselves by vain flattery, mak- ing themselves believe that it is enough if they condemn their vices, though they continue to persist in them, or rather, if they give them up for a time, to return to them immediately after. True repentance is firm and constant, and makes us war with the evil that is in us, not for a day or a week, but without end and without intermission.

The Imperfections Of Believers Should Rather Incline Them To Use The Supper.

When we feel within ourselves a strong dislike and hatred of all sin, proceeding from the fear of God, and a desire to live well in order to please our Lord, we are fit to partake of the Supper, notwithstand- ing of the remains of infirmity which we carry in our flesh. Nay, if we were not weak, subject to distrust and an imperfect life, the sacrament would be of no use to us, and it would have been superfluous to insti- tute it. Seeing, then, it is a remedy which God has given us to help our weakness, to strengthen our faith, increase our charity, and advance us in all holiness of life, the use becomes the more necessary the more we feel pressed by the disease; so far ought that to be from making us abstain. For if we allege as an excuse for not coming to the Supper, that we are still weak in faith or integrity of life, it is as if a man were to excuse himself from taking medicine because he was sick. See then how the weakness of faith which we feel in our heart, and the imper-

fections which are in our life, should admonish us to come to the Supper, as a special remedy to correct them.

Only let us not come devoid of faith and repentance. The former
is hidden in the heart, and therefore conscience must be its witness
before God. The latter is manifested by works, and must therefore be
apparent in our life.

Times Of Using The Supper, Propriety Of Frequent Commu-nion.

As to the time of using it, no certain rule can be prescribed for all.
For there are sometimes special circumstances which excuse a man for
abstaining; and, moreover, we have no express command to constrain
all Christians to use a specified day. However, if we duly consider the
end which our Lord has in view, we shall perceive that the use should
be more frequent than many make it for the more infirmity presses,
the more necessary is it frequently to have recourse to what may and
will serve to confirm our faith, and advance us in purity of life; and,
therefore, the practice of all well ordered churches should be to celebrate the Supper frequently, so far as the capacity of the people will
admit. And each individual in his own place should prepare himself to
receive whenever it is administered in the holy assembly, provided
there is not some great impediment which constrains him to abstain.
Although we have no express commandment specifying the time and
the day, it should suffice us to know the intention of our Lord to be
that we should use it often, if we would fully experience the benefit
which accrues from it.

Impropriety Of Abstaining On Frivolous Grounds, Pretended Unworthiness In Ourselves.

The excuses alleged are very frivolous. Some say that they do not
feel themselves to be worthy, and under this pretext, abstain for a
whole year.

Others, not contented with looking to their own unworthiness,
pretend that they cannot communicate with persons whom they see
coming without being duly prepared. Some also think that it is superfluous to use it frequently, because if we have once received Jesus
Christ, there is no occasion to return so often after to receive him. I
ask the first who make a cloak of their unworthiness, how their conscience can allow them to remain more than a year in so poor a state,

that they dare not invoke God directly? They will acknowledge that it is presumption to invoke God as our Father, if we are not members of Jesus Christ. This we cannot be without having the reality and substance of the Supper accomplished in us.

Now, if we have the reality, we are by stronger reason capable of receiving the sign. We see then that he who would exempt himself from receiving the Supper on account of unworthiness, must hold himself unfit to pray to God. I mean not to force consciences which are tormented with certain scruples which suggest themselves, they scarcely know how, but counsel them to wait till the Lord deliver them. Likewise, if there is a legitimate cause of hindrance, I deny not that it is lawful to delay. Only I wish to show that no one ought long to rest satisfied with abstaining on the ground of unworthiness, seeing that in so doing he deprives himself of the communion of the church, in which all our well-being consists. Let him rather contend against all the impediments which the devil throws in his way, and not be excluded from so great a benefit, and from all the graces consequent thereupon.

Abstaining Because Of Pretended Unworthiness In Others.

The second class have some plausibility. The argument they use is, that it is not lawful to eat common bread with those who call themselves brethren, and lead a dissolute life—*a fortiori*, we must abstain from communicating with them in the Lord's bread, which is sanctified in order to represent and dispense to us the body of Christ. But the answer is not very difficult. It is not the office of each individual to judge and discern, to admit or debar whom he pleases; seeing that this prerogative belongs to all the church in general, or rather to the pastor, with the elders, whom he ought to have to assist him in the government of the church. St. Paul does not command us to examine others, but each to examine *himself*. It is very true that it is our duty to admonish those whom we see walking disorderly, and if they will not listen to us, to give notice to the pastor, in order that he may proceed by ecclesiastical authority. But the proper method of withdrawing from the company of the wicked, is not to quit the communion of the church. Moreover, it will most frequently happen that sins are not so notorious as to justify proceeding to excommunication; for though the pastor may in his heart judge some man to be unworthy, he has not the power of pronouncing him such, and interdicting him from the

Supper, if he cannot prove the unworthiness by an ecclesiastical judgment.

In such case we have no other remedy than to pray to God that he would more and more deliver his church from all scandals, and wait for the last day, when the chaff will be completely separated from the good grain.

Excuse, That Having Already Received Christ, It Is Unnecessary To Return Often To Receive Him.

The third class have no semblance of plausibility. The spiritual bread is not given us to eat our fill of it all at once, but rather, that having had some taste of its sweetness, we may long for it all the more, and use it when it is offered to us. This we explained above. So long as we remain in this mortal life, Jesus Christ is never communicated in such a way as to satiate our souls, but wills to be our constant nourishment. ...

Fraternal Concord Among The Churches.

Meanwhile it should satisfy us that there is fraternity and communion among the churches, and that all agree in so far as is necessary for meeting together, according to the commandment of God. We all then confess with one mouth, that on receiving the sacrament in faith, according to the ordinance of the Lord, we are truly made partakers of the proper substance of the body and blood of Jesus Christ. How that is done some may deduce better, and explain more clearly than others. Be this as it may, on the one hand, in order to exclude all carnal fancies, we must raise our hearts upwards to heaven, not thinking that our Lord Jesus is so debased as to be enclosed under some corruptible elements; and, on the other hand, not to impair the efficacy of this holy ordinance, we must hold that it is made effectual by the secret and miraculous power of God, and that the Spirit of God is the bond of participation, this being the reason why it is called spiritual.

Source: http://www.godrules.net/library/calvin/142calvin_b7.htm

APPENDIX III

The Eight Senses of Man
Dichotomous Human Sensory Inputs
by Phillip A. Ross

"seeing they do not see, and hearing they do not hear"
—Matthew 13:13

For millennia it has been thought that human beings have five senses—smell, hearing, sight, touch, and taste. Each of these senses provides a portal through which information about the world is gained. Each sense provides information about the world to the brain or mind. As such, the senses are absolutely foundational with regard to our understanding of the world in which we live.

To lack any one of these senses is to be handicapped. A deficient sense, one either not working at all or working poorly, provides deficient information about the world. This is not to say that those who are blind or deaf, etc., are not fully human—they are! However, their experience and knowledge of the world is not as full and complete as it could be. Often those who are sense deprived in one area find that their other senses compensate by becoming more robust, delicate, and sensitive. Nonetheless, the absence or loss of one of the our senses is like the misfiring of a cylinder in an automobile engine.

Each sense provides a certain kind of information about the world in which we live. And when all the senses work together they provide a robust understanding of ourselves and our environment. And conversely, the failure or degradation of any of our senses results in an impoverished understanding of ourselves and our world.

But why do we limit ourselves to five senses? Many people have suggested that we also have a sixth sense, which is akin to intuition. Because sensory inputs provide information about the world, and sometimes people know something, but don't know why or how they know it, they propose that there is another human sense that provides such information. The sixth sense has long been a mystery to humanity, dismissed by some and embraced by others. The sixth sense is often spiritualized in that it is attributed to communication from another dimension. But whether one accepts it or denies it, it has never attained the canonized status of the other five senses. Most of the time, most people simply pay no attention to it. Or perhaps they engage it half consciously without recognizing its contribution to life and understanding.

In an effort to understand ourselves and the world in which we live more fully and completely, I am standing on the shoulders of Walter Lowen, who has posited a model of the human brain or mind structure that has eight sensory inputs.[1] Lowen, an engineer by profession, found himself intrigued by the Meyers-Briggs Typological Interpretation (MBTI) of Jungian psychology, and developed a brain/mind schematic diagram in which the sixteen Meyers-Briggs types are explained from a logical/electrical perspective.

I will not reproduce Lowen's work, but will attempt to provide a layman's description and analysis of the eight sensory inputs posited by Lowen. In order to do so I have renamed some of the inputs or senses in order to make them more accessible to the layman.

Each of the senses I will define here are understood to provide input to the human mind or brain. They are always found in pairs that are dichotomously related. That is, they are envisioned as poles on a continuum of sensory input or experience. Each of the four types of senses manifest as two dichotomous but related sensory mechanisms.

In general Lowen's work provides an interesting operative model of how the brain/mind/body perceives or receives sensory input. We must remember when dealing with such modeling that modeling itself is primarily a logical construct that tries to make sense of information. Such modeling regarding brain functioning puts a lot of stock in the idea that logic actually correlates to biological function

---

1   *Dichotomies of the Mind: A Systematic Explanation of Human Behavior*, by Walter Lowen, John Wiley & Sons Inc., 1982.

and/or visa versa. However, in this case there is a good argument that such correlation should actually be the case, in that logic itself is a mental construct that provides accurate descriptions for many processes in the world at large. So, there may be sufficient basis to assume that logic itself is a linguistic projection of biological brain structure that adequately reveals significant mental or mind structure. To repeat, logic and language may provide a sufficient reflection and/or projection of the structures and/or functions of the brain. It makes sense that logic, language, and brain structure or function will correlate.

I have taken the basic organization of Lowen's insights about the eight senses and expanded and augmented them to fit more consistently into a dichotomous model. Why a dichotomous model? Because of the polar nature of Jungian psychology and MBTI typology, i.e., introversion vs. extroversion, thinking vs. feeling, sensate vs. intuitive and judging vs. perceiving. These basic type descriptions are not the eight senses, but they provide the logical structure for the senses. I have renamed and redefined some of the sensory categories of the various modes to establish a more functional labeling of them, and to maintain consistency, balance, and harmony.

Each of the eight senses receives a flow of information and/or stimuli as information/data enters into the mind. As Lowen correctly observes, the direction of the information flow or sensory data is significant. It can be said that the direction of the flow is either introverted or extroverted depending on whether the flow is centripetal or centrifugal. Nonetheless, each of these four sense categories has an extroverted and an introverted pole. The nature and function of these poles will come to light in the discussion of each sensory input.

The eight sensory inputs, arranged in their dichotomous pairs, are:
- touch/taste,
- smell/intuition,
- vision/imagination, and
- hearing/resonance.

Note that the traditional five senses are included and that three other brain/mind functions or sensing nodes are accounted for. This essential grouping is based upon the polarity of perception, where the poles may be described as extroverted and introverted. Perception and its attendant data flow faces either outward (extroverted) or inward (introverted). We perceive information about the objective world around us, and we perceive information about our own subjective bodies, which can in turn be understood to be objective to the brain or mind. Nonetheless, our perceptions of our own bodies are as real as our perceptions of our environment.

Touch is extroverted because it faces the exterior world, whereas taste is introverted because it faces the interior or subjective world of the body. Similarly, smell is extroverted because it faces the exterior or objective world. Intuition is introverted because it faces inward and provides essential subjective data. Vision or eyesight is extroverted and faces outward, whereas imagination is introverted and faces inward. Hearing listens outward to the world of sounds, where resonance listens inward to the world of thought harmonics.

To be a fully developed human being requires the development and maturity of each of our eight senses. Perhaps the lack of maturity and development of so many people is related to the fact that human growth and development of the fundamental interior sensory inputs are for the most part misunderstood and ignored.

IMMEDIATE SENSES: SENSING POLES

Touch is on the objective side of the continuum in that it conveys information about the outermost body edges: the skin. The sense of touch provides objective information about the interface between the body and it's immediate environment. On the other side of this immediate sense continuum we find the sense of taste. Taste is a subjective function of the tongue, an inner, subjective organ of the body. Taste is related to touch because in order to taste something it must touch the tongue. Taste senses certain environmental elements as they are in the process of assimilation, becoming part of the subjectivity of the body. Taste supplies information and/or stimuli that is a more internal, subjective experience of the environment. The differences between the objective and the subjective aspects of touch and taste are determined by the direction of the information flow. Touch faces outward and is objective, where taste faces inward and is subjective.

The immediate senses are intimately related to our most basic understanding of self. They help to distinguish the difference between self and other. These senses are at the boundary between the body and its environment. It is through the sense of touch that we are aware of the difference between ourselves, our bodies, and that which is other, the external world. It is through these immediate senses of touch and taste that we as babies (and adults) first come into contact and relationship with that which is other, whether that otherness is rocks and dirt, food and drink, or other people.

ACOUSTIC SENSES: FEELING POLES

Audition is what we usually refer to as our sense of hearing. Auditory information and/or stimuli first stimulates the objective pole (audition) of the acoustic senses, in that the source of hearing normally comes from outside of the body. On the subjective side of the acoustic sense continuum is the sense of resonance, a kind of inner hearing that we usually refer to simply as thinking. Resonance is a subjective hearing of inner thought harmonics, the source of which is audition and, consequently, facilitates the human ability to communicate with language by providing deeper (broader, more complex) meanings through various resonating associations with other thoughts (words, ideas, etc.). Language, which is first heard by a child, then, becomes a kind of mental harmonic manipulation, akin to music. The harmonics generate an inner, subjective mental linguistic flow, a flow that runs in the same circuits as Lowen's information transactions. We might say that resonance provides the data for the common experience of hearing or thinking, an inner dialog or running commentary on one's experience as one thing resonates with another.

VISUAL SENSES: THINKING POLES

The objective pole of vision is similar to that of audition: it contacts and processes information from outside the body. The sense of eyesight is well established. But there is also an inner seeing which I call imagination. Unlike resonance, which is related to the feeling (F) poles, imagination is related to the thinking (T) poles. It could be commonly described as insight, inner vision, or simply imagination—the kind that children develop as they learn to play. Imagination, then, is the experience of the comprehension and association of ideas and images. Imagination is engaged as a person who learns something exclaims, "Now I see!" The thing learned is imagined or grasped in its wholeness.

REMOTE SENSES: JUDGING POLES

The remote senses, related to judgment, or what Lowen calls the intuition (N) poles, and involve the transmission and/or manipulation of diffuse information through remembrance. Smell, the objective remote sense, is the easiest to understand. An odor is diffuse and our sense of smell receives and compares that received data with our memory of similar data (similar smells). The experience of smell can be activated from quite a distance if the sense is significantly developed. The sense of smell conjures up a memory of the smell, or if it is a new smell it catalogs the smell for later use.

The subjective remote sense, intuition, works in a similar way. Unlike resonance, which is primarily word oriented, or imagination, which primarily associates mental images or pictures, intuition compares data received with memory. It perceives information from the comparison of experience and memory, thereby producing essential meaning. Intuition is the sense that experiences meaning as essence and feature derived from the association of ideas, images and language.

CIRCUITS

Earlier I said that each of the senses has an extroverted or introverted information flow. I mean that all of the objective (touch, audition, vision, and smell) and subjective (taste, resonance, imagination and intuition) senses can be either acute or obtuse. That is, they have input connections in both of Lowen's C and D circuits. The circuit is a function of the focus of the information transaction: obtuse (C) or acute (D).

In order to understand Lowen's circuits we might think of them as water passing through a nozzle. The C circuit is obtuse in the same way that a nozzle on a hose sprays water obtusely, where the pattern of the spray is wider than the circumference of the nozzle. Attention in the C circuit is on the outside or extroverted side of the nozzle and is experienced obtusely.

The D circuit is acute. Here we must imagine that the direction of the water flow is reversed, where the water of the spray is now being sucked into the hose, something like what a vacuum cleaner does to air. Attention in the D circuit is on the inside or introverted side of the hose and is experienced acutely.

The C circuit experiences information generally. We could even say that the C circuit senses impose general order upon experience. It sprays, imposes, or broadcasts various presuppositions upon its experience of the world in the sense of providing a context for understanding. Nothing is experienced or understood as a brute fact. Rather, all experience and understanding require a context in order to be meaningful. In the C circuit, that context precedes experience.

In the D circuit the context is derived from the experience in that experience precedes context. It must be understood that every person has and uses both circuits of each sensory input, and that the circuits provide a kind of tension between opposing ways of understanding and experiencing the world.

There is a tension between experiencing the world in order to know it, and knowing the world in order to experience it. For instance, sometimes people see what they expect to see rather than seeing what is actually in front of them. Similarly, people hear what they expect to hear rather than hearing what is actually said. To touch or taste something with an expectation provides a different experience than touching or tasting without an expectation. Human knowledge and/or experience requires both context and analysis or categorization.

Working from Lowen's sixteen pole model let's specify poles, transactions, and circuits, and try to unpack some of what it all means.

TOUCH

The sense of touch is experienced in both the C and D circuits; that is, it's information can be either acute or obtuse. Each circuit will, of course, yield a different experience (information transaction) related to touch. The information transaction of sense in the C circuit results in a general body awareness. The experience is unfocused, obtuse, unpointed. When someone asks, "How are you feeling?" they are generally inquiring about your experience of the sense of obtuse touch. The early signs of illnesses like a cold or the flu usually affect this sense, and it is here that we experience a contextual body malaise or dis-ease.

The experience of touch in the D circuit is quite different. Touch in the D circuit is primarily a tactile awareness of environmental edges. This is usually the experience that people identify as physically touching something. We usually think of the experience as touching something particular—soft, hard, wet, dry, etc. The information transaction is acute, and is experienced as a particular feeling associated with a particular body part, i.e., a hand or finger through the skin. When we identify a particular touch experience we utilize the D circuit, which is experienced as focused, acute, particular. To feel the edge of a knife as sharp or a feather as soft is a function of acute touch.

TASTE

The sense of taste is also experienced in both the C and D circuits. In general, taste is a more subtle experience than touch. However, the experience of C circuit taste generates information about the overall effect of taste combinations. Taste experienced obtusely results in an unfocused lack of appreciation for the experience of eating. There is no identification of the particular elements of taste, i.e., sweet, sour, bitter, etc. Rather, taste is processed generically as appealing or unappealing. People who are C types eat only to live. They generally don't care as much about food or how it tastes as does a D type.

The experience of taste in the D circuit provides an acute appreciation of the subtleties of taste. To have a developed D circuit taste is to be a connoisseur, to have great taste appreciation and sensitivity, even to the point of being finicky. In other words, the sense of taste can be either focused or unfocused.

AUDITION

Hearing also can be focused (D) or unfocused (C). When we are reading a book we often hear noise without listening to it, which is an experience of audition in the obtuse C circuit. Conversely, in a crowed room at a party we are able to focus on one voice and listen to one conversation in the midst of many, which is an experience of the acute D circuit audition. Without the ability to focus our hearing we couldn't do this. Most people have experienced both types of hearing.

RESONANCE

I have defined resonance as an introverted, subjective experience that develops with language and is experienced as thinking, or an inner voice or dialog. Resonance is not commonly understood as a sense, but I believe it is. Most people will know it as "common sense," a voice or inner dialog that provides life direction. Christians know it as a personal relationship with Christ. Paul recommended that we "pray without ceasing" (1 Thessalonians 5:17). One definition of resonance involves a relationship of mutual understanding or trust and agreement between people.

When a single string on a stringed instrument is plucked it vibrates using the physical ends of the string as poles and produces a tone. What we don't hear unless we listen very carefully is that the other strings on the instrument are also vibrating and producing various related tones. The other strings are vibrating at various tones known as thirds, fifths, octaves, etc. The wave lengths of these tones are shorter than the dominant tone and are called harmonics. The other strings resonate harmonically with the dominate tone. I am suggesting that the fact of our subjective thinking process results from similar harmonic processes within the resonance sense (thinking). While we are thinking a dominant thought there are other harmonic thoughts resonating harmonically to the dominate thought.

The development of language provides a kind of sense experience for the mind. We usually call it thinking. When we think a thought it is like plucking a single string on a stringed instrument, which sets in motion harmonic vibrations in the other strings. Intuition, then, is a perception of the harmonics of thinking.

SENSORY OVERVIEW:

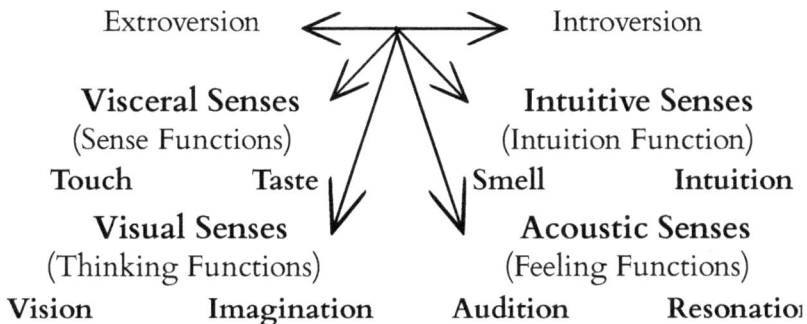

Extroversion ←————————→ Introversion

Visceral Senses
(Sense Functions)
Touch   **Taste**

Intuitive Senses
(Intuition Function)
Smell   **Intuition**

Visual Senses
(Thinking Functions)
Vision   **Imagination**

Acoustic Senses
(Feeling Functions)
Audition   **Resonatio**

A map of the sense inputs that provide **sense experience** to the mind:

VISCERAL SENSES: Sensing (S) poles

Extroverted Objective $\longleftrightarrow$ Introverted Subjective

Touch $\longleftrightarrow$ **Taste**

acute (D) $\longleftrightarrow$ obtuse (C)
discerning   less discerning

acute (D) $\longleftrightarrow$ obtuse (C)
discerning   less discerning

A map of the acoustic inputs that provide **auditory experience** to the mind:

ACOUSTIC SENSES: Feeling (F) poles

Extroverted Objective $\longleftrightarrow$ Introverted Subjective

Audition $\longleftrightarrow$ **Resonation**

acute (D) $\longleftrightarrow$ obtuse (C)
discerning   less discerning

acute (D) $\longleftrightarrow$ obtuse (C)
discerning   less discerning

A map of visual inputs that provide **visual experience** to the mind:

VISUAL SENSES: Thinking (T) poles

Extroverted Objective $\longleftrightarrow$ Introverted Subjective

Vision $\longleftrightarrow$ **Imagination**

acute (D) $\longleftrightarrow$ obtuse (C)
discerning   less discerning

acute (D) $\longleftrightarrow$ obtuse (C)
discerning   less discerning

A map of the intuitive inputs that provide **intuitive experience** to the mind:

INTUITIVE SENSES: Intuition (N) poles

Extroverted Objective	⟷	Introverted Subjective

Smell ↓	⟷	**Intuition** ↓

acute (D) ⟷ obtuse (C)
discerning   less discerning

acute (D) ⟷ obtuse (C)
discerning   less discerning

www.ingramcontent.com/pod-product-compliance
Lightning Source LLC
Chambersburg PA
CBHW062145080426
42734CB00010B/1570